AFRICA'S GLOBAL I

/ AFRICAN
/ ARGUMENTS

African Arguments is a series of short books about contemporary Africa and the critical issues and debates surrounding the continent. The books are scholarly and engaged, substantive and topical. They focus on questions of justice, rights and citizenship; politics, protests and revolutions; the environment, land, oil and other resources; health and disease; economy: growth, aid, taxation, debt and capital flight; and both Africa's international relations and country case studies.

Managing Editor, Stephanie Kitchen

Series editors

Adam Branch
Alex de Waal
Alcinda Honwana
Ebenezer Obadare
Carlos Oya
Nicholas Westcott

Additional longer monographs and edited volumes are published in association with the series, under the auspices of the International African Institute.

Associate editors

Eyob Gebremariam
Elliott D. Green
Jon Schubert

JANA HÖNKE, ERIC CEZNE and
YIFAN YANG (Editors)

Africa's Global Infrastructures

*South-South Transformations
in Practice*

HURST & COMPANY, LONDON

IAI   International African Institute

Published in collaboration with the International African Institute.
First published in the United Kingdom in 2024 by
C. Hurst & Co. (Publishers) Ltd.,
New Wing, Somerset House, Strand, London WC2R 1LA

A Cataloguing-in-Publication data record for this book
is available from the British Library.

ISBN: 9781805260226

www.hurstpublishers.com

CONTENTS

v

CONTENTS

ABOUT THE AUTHORS

Jana Hönke is professor and holds the Chair for Sociology in Africa at the University of Bayreuth, Germany. She is the PI of the ERC Africa's Infrastructure Globalities (INFRAGLOB) project (2018–25).

Eric Cezne is a postdoctoral researcher at the Department of Human Geography and Spatial Planning at Utrecht University, the Netherlands.

Yifan Yang is an INFRAGLOB project researcher and a PhD candidate at the University of Bayreuth, Germany.

Raoul Bunskoek is a researcher with the ERC INFRAGLOB project, University of Bayreuth, Germany, and senior research fellow and coordinator of the Clingendael Institute's China Centre.

Barnaby Joseph Dye is Lecturer in the Politics of Development, Department of Politics and the Interdisciplinary Global Development Centre (IGDC), University of York, UK.

Mathias Alencastro is a fellow at the Brazilian Center for Analysis and Planning in São Paulo.

Ricardo Soares de Oliveira is professor of the International Politics of Africa at the Department of Politics and International Relations, University of Oxford, UK.

ABOUT THE AUTHORS

Laura Trajber Waisbich is a departmental lecturer in Latin American Studies and Director of the Brazilian Studies Programme at the Latin American Centre, Oxford School of Global and Area Studies, University of Oxford.

Jan Sändig is a senior research fellow with the INFRAGLOB project and in Peace and Conflict Studies at the University of Bayreuth, Germany.

Benard Musembi Kilaka is a lecturer at Maseno University, Kenya, and a researcher at the School of Global Studies (SGS), University of Gothenburg, Sweden.

Elisa Gambino is a lecturer in Global Development, with a focus on Global Political Economy at the University of Manchester, UK.

Mandira Bagwandeen is a senior fellow at the Nelson Mandela School of Public Governance and a lecturer in the Department of Political Studies at the University of Cape Town, South Africa.

Michael Godet Sambo is a research associate at Instituto de Estudos Sociais e Económicos (IESE) and a lecturer at the Faculty of Economics at the Universidade Eduardo Mondlane (UEM), Mozambique.

Phyllis Bußler is a research associate and PhD candidate at the Department of Economic and Social Geography at the University of Cologne, Germany.

Vineet Thakur is a lecturer in International Relations at the Institute for History at Leiden University, the Netherlands.

LIST OF ABBREVIATIONS

ABC	Agência Brasileira de Cooperação (Brazilian Cooperation Agency)
ACIDH	Action contre l'Impunité pour les Droits Humains
AFREWATCH	African Resources Watch
AIIB	Asian Infrastructure Investment Bank
ASM	Artisanal and Small-scale Mining
AV	Atingidos pela Vale (Vale Affected)
BNDES	Brazilian Development Bank (Banco Nacional de Desenvolvimento Econômico e Social)
BRI	Belt and Road Initiative
BRIC	Brazil, Russia, India, China
BRICS	Brazil, Russia, India, China, South Africa
Camex	Council of Ministers of the Chamber of External Commerce
CCCC	China Communications Construction Company
CCP	Chinese Communist Party
CDB	China Development Bank
CDM	Congo Dongfang Mining
COFIG	Comitê de Financiamento e Garantia das Exportações
COMMUS	Compagnie Minière de Musonoi

LIST OF ABBREVIATIONS

CRBC	China Road and Bridge Corporation
CSO	Civil Society Organisation
CSR	Corporate Social Responsibility
DRC	Democratic Republic of the Congo
ESG	Environmental, Social, and Corporate Governance
FDI	Foreign Direct Investment
FGD	Focus Group Discussion
FIDC	Indian Forum for International Development Cooperation
FOCAC	Forum on China–Africa Cooperation
FoE	Friends of the Earth
Gécamines	Générale des Carrières et des Mines
HLMC	Hubei Lianfeng Mozambique Co. Lda
HR	Human Resource
HRW	Human Rights Watch
IDEAS	India Development Economic Assistance Scheme
INGO	International Non-governmental Organisation
IR	International Relations
JICA	Japan International Cooperation Agency
JIRCAS	Japan International Research Center for Agricultural Sciences
KES	Kenyan Shilling
KPA	Kenya Port Authority
LAPSSET	Lamu Port South Sudan Ethiopia Transport Corridor
LoC	Line of Credit
MASA	Ministério da Agricultura e Segurança Alimentar
MCSC	Mecanismo de Coordenação da Sociedade Civil para o Desenvolvimento do Corredor de Nacala
MDIC	Ministério do Desenvolvimento, Indústria, e Comércio Exterior

LIST OF ABBREVIATIONS

MEA	Ministry of External Affairs, India
MOFCOM	Ministry of Commerce, People's Republic of China
MPLA	Movimento Popular de Libertação de Angola
NDB	New Development Bank
NGO	Non-governmental Organisation
OECD	Organisation for Economic Co-operation and Development
OIA	Overseas Infrastructure Alliance
OMR	Observatorio do Meio Rural
ORAM	Rural Association of Mutual Aid
OVL	ONGC Videsh Limited
PEM	Plano de Extensão e Modelos
PPP	Public-Private Partnership
PRC	People's Republic of China
ProSAVANA	Projeto de Desenvolvimento Agrícola da Savana Africana (African Savannah Agricultural Development Project, Japan–Brazil–Mozambique)
PT	Workers' Party (Partido dos Trabalhadores, Brazil)
RAID	Rights and Accountability in Development
RBL	Regadio do Baixo Limpopo
RIS	Research Information System for Developing Countries
SARW	South African Resource Watch
SGR	Standard Gauge Railway
SICOMINES	Sino-Congolaise des Mines
SOE	State-owned Enterprise
SOMIDEZ	Société Minière de Deziwa
SSC	South-South Cooperation
TFM	Tenke Fungurume Mining
UK	United Kingdom

LIST OF ABBREVIATIONS

UNAC   National Peasants Union (União Nacional de Camponeses), Mozambique

WANBAO   WANBAO Africa Agriculture Development Limited

LIST OF FIGURES AND TABLES

ACKNOWLEDGEMENTS

This book has been made possible through the collective efforts and invaluable contributions of numerous individuals who have dedicated their time, insights, and expertise. We extend our heartfelt gratitude to each and every person who has played a role in shaping this work. We would also like to acknowledge the exceptional support we received from the European Research Council through the 'Africa's Infrastructure Globalities' project (INFRAGLOB, grant #759798), in the context of which the idea for this volume emerged and took shape. It also enabled the research for the framework and conclusion chapters as well as Chapters 2 and 5. Our sincere thanks go to the participants of the two online workshops, 'South-South Infrastructure Globalities', held at the University of Bayreuth between 2020 and 2021 amid the challenges of the Covid-19 pandemic. We would like to acknowledge the invaluable contributions of our authors to this volume, and extend special thanks to Barnaby Dye for his particular contributions on India to the Introduction. We equally thank Ohene Opoku Agyemang (Shangdong University), Chris Alden (London School of Economics and Political Science), Asamaniwa Asa (Peking University), David Styan (Birkbeck, University of London), Jo-Ansie van Wyk (University of South Africa), Yuan Wang (University of Oxford), Ulrikke Bryn Wethal (University of Oslo), and Hang Zhou (SOAS University of London). Their participation in thought-provoking discussions has enriched our understanding and contributed to the depth of this work.

We express our gratitude to Frank Gadinger (University of Duisburg-Essen) for his insightful contributions as discussant during

ACKNOWLEDGEMENTS

the presentation of the book at the Athens Pan-European Conference organised by the European International Studies Association in 2022. His expertise was invaluable for further linking debates on international practice with South-South relations literature and research. We also thank two anonymous reviewers for their detailed and constructive engagement and feedback.

Furthermore, we extend our thanks to Dominik Kopiński (University of Wroclaw), Pádraig Carmody (Trinity College Dublin), Diego Amaral (Universidade Federal de Sergipe), Sigrid Quack (University of Duisburg-Essen), Weiwei Chen (Open University), and others who engaged with the book during the European Conference of African Studies (ECAS) in Cologne, and the workshop 'Global Infrastructures and the Environment: Rethinking Legitimation, Socio-spatial Dynamics, and Resistance' at the Centre for Global Cooperation Research at the University of Duisburg-Essen in 2023. Their insightful comments and interest have contributed to the refinement of our ideas.

Certainly, the book would not be the same without the fruitful discussions we have had with our colleagues Jan Sändig, Adam Sandor, Sarah Katz-Lavigne, Bretton McEvoy, Patricia Ndlovu, and Joschka Philipps in the 'Global Political Sociology from the Global South' research colloquium at the University of Bayreuth. Finally, we acknowledge the remarkable efforts of our INFRAGLOB student assistants Jiaxiu Zhao, Zhiying Mao, Zhengxu Li, Noah Rottler-Gurley, Galina Akhunzhanova, and, with special mention, Katja Sugg, whose support during the workshops and manuscript editing has been instrumental in the successful completion of this project.

Lastly, we extend our deepest appreciation to our dedicated editors, Stephanie Kitchen and Alice Clarke, for their unwavering support, guidance, and companionship throughout this journey.

In conclusion, this book stands as a testament to the collaborative spirit and collective endeavour of everyone involved in its making. Your contributions have helped to create a meaningful contribution to the field. Thank you for having been a part of the journey.

Jana Hönke, Eric Cezne and Yifan Yang
August 2023

INFRASTRUCTURE GLOBALITIES

EMERGING PRACTICES AT THE AFRICAN FRONTIER

Jana Hönke, Eric Cezne and Yifan Yang[1]

The 19th century was Europe's, the 20th century of the United States, and the 21st century must be ours.

(Brazilian President Lula da Silva—on the
promises of South-South relations
during a trip to Nigeria in 2006)

The past two decades have been pivotal for South-South relations: materially in terms of increasing resources, investments, and institutions, ideationally in terms of alternative development narratives and models, and ontologically in terms of new geographies of cooperation but also struggle (Fiddian-Qasmiyeh and Patrick Daley, 2018; Mawdsley, 2019). Such trends have markedly come to the fore in Africa. For most of the 2000s and early 2010s, a supercycle of sustained high commodity prices nurtured growth, a widening middle class, and a thriving consumer market across the continent (Bowman et al., 2021). Infrastructure development intensified as Africa saw post-conflict stabilisation and a shift away from Western finances and resources. This was accompanied by the arrival of a flurry of Southern partners and investors on the wings of an 'Africa rising' sentiment and the optimistic prospects of 'South-South cooperation' (*The Economist*, 2011; Frankema and van Waijenburg, 2018).

This is now a familiar story, and South-South relations' boom in the post-2000s has generated a concomitant research boom. The involvement of resource-hungry, geopolitically ambitious rising powers such as China, Brazil, and India in Africa was particularly eye-catching and merited significant attention from academic, policy, and business establishments. Works have unpacked, for instance, the range of discourses and practices that accompanied their diplomatic (see Carmody, 2013) and economic engagement (see, for example, Mawdsley and McCann, 2011; Abegunrin and Manyeruke, 2020; Alencastro and Seabra, 2021). Moreover, the extent to which these relations spur growth and development has been debated alongside concerns over the risks of them reproducing structural dependencies (Taylor, 2014; Carmody, 2017). A core question—usually asked at the macro-level of states and their international relations—has been whether these newly emerging configurations challenge Western-centred global governance and associated development models (Mawdsley, 2012b; Horner, 2016; Stuenkel, 2016). The problem with this line of inquiry is, however, that it constructs a binary of either competition and replacement of one order with another, or convergence towards a liberal world order.

This book argues, instead, that it is more helpful to conceive the 'global' in smaller, more pluralistic, and procedural terms. To do so, we put forward the notion of 'globalities'. Globalities refer to the many ways in which actors use diverse ideas of the global, as well as practices and technologies that travel, to construct and sustain connections to other localities (Law, 2004; Blok, 2010). Little is still known about these bottom-up processes of assembling and (re)making of practices in Africa's South-South relations. The contributions therefore ask, which ideas and practices of governance travel to African localities, what ways of managing business–society relations are in use around Global South projects, and how are they adapted, transformed, and contested?

These questions allow for a better understanding of increasingly multiple international relations that foreclose the idea of binaries between supposedly clear-cut models or ordering categories such as the South, East or West. They do so in Africa and beyond; we hence confirm Africa's importance for understanding inter-/transnational relations today (Cornelissen, Cheru and Shaw, 2012; Death, 2015; Tickner and Smith, 2020). This also takes up the challenge for African (and other Area) Studies and International Relations to more 'fully, but critically, engage with each other' (Harman and Brown, 2013: 70). Finally, the book contributes to account more adequately for different forms of African agencies to examine Africa's South-South relations (Mohan and Lampert 2014). Achille Mbembe has repeatedly called for bringing Africa's multiple belongings to the fore to overcome Eurocentric knowledge about the continent, and the world at large. The book takes up this spirit, and inspiration from connected sociologies (Bhambra, 2014) and other work that has transformed and extended our knowledge beyond the 'colonial library' and its 'othering gaze' (Mudimbe, 1988; see also Wai, 2020: 65) to examine Africa's South-South relations.

Methodologically, the book zooms in on large-scale Chinese, Brazilian, and Indian economic projects in Africa as frontier zones of such emerging practices. It analyses how state strategies, business–society relations, and development practices meet, and elites, practitioners, non-governmental organisations (NGOs), and communities mimic, transform, and make transnational practices, embodying and constantly negotiating various rationales and technologies of governance. The chapters examine projects such as dams, ports, roads, agro-industries, and mines that are invested, built, and/or operated by Chinese, Brazilian and Indian actors. These sites integrate expanding circuits of capital and (transnational) relations of exchange of various forms and destinations with Africa's long and multiple entanglements with various parts of the world. Through these manifold relations, in a range of contexts of possibility and making, ideas of the 'global' and of the 'South-South' (see also Hönke et al., 2022) are continuously transformed. We hold that zooming in on these dynamics offers unique entry points to better understand emerging globalities in Africa and our contemporary world more broadly.

To shed light on such processes, we focus on the entanglements and interactions of African actors—at the diplomatic and strategic, commercial and project, and grassroots levels—with public entities, businesses, and/or civil society from China, Brazil, and India. We look at projects and actors from these three countries for two reasons. One has to do with their marked prominence in Africa. Many have posited the Southern B(R)ICs as the best representatives of a set of up-and-coming rising powers destined to transform global governance and disrupt North-South hierarchies (see Thakur, 2014; Nayyar, 2016; Stuenkel, 2020). Due to their size, economic power, and geopolitical dispositions, China, Brazil, and India were thus often deemed the 'big players of the South', with attributes and capacities (e.g. development financing, capital investment, and political determination) to act as 'catalysts' and 'locomotives' of South-South relations (see Robinson, 2015; Gosovic, 2016). The other reason is, relatedly, that the enthusiasm and interest in their presence in Africa has generated an abundant and fruitful strand of literature seeking to describe, unpack, and scrutinise their various undertakings (Brautigam, 2011; Mawdsley and McCann, 2011; Carmody, 2013; Taylor, 2014; Stolte, 2015). However, this has often been done in a context of expansion and proliferation. Certainly, the heavy focus on the B(R)ICs has obscured the roles of a range of other actors engaged in what Soulé (2020) aptly describes as a variety of 'Africa+1' arrangements. Such a focus has also been criticised for generating problematic and inaccurate perceptions of South-South relations, as these are often seen through the eyes and interests of a few selected emerging powers (Bergamaschi, Moore and Tickner, 2017). Yet, without losing sight of such caveats and biases, this focus provides the book with a unique opportunity to enhance the above literature in the face of emerging trends and new temporalities spurred by more volatile commodity markets, pandemic disruptions, and faltering euphoria for 'South-South cooperation'. We do so while critically reflecting on the longer-term intricacies, and instabilities, of Africa's polycentric infrastructure globalities.

In the following we first review the emergence of Southern actors in Africa, particularly China, Brazil, and India, and discuss recent developments, turns, and ruptures in these countries' engagement in large-scale infrastructure and economic projects on the continent. We then critically review the literature on what is often interpreted as 'South-South cooperation'. We note that conventional studies often fall short of sufficiently conceptualising and addressing the amplitude and trans-scalarity of South-South encounters, as we propose to move beyond idealised, state-centric interpretations and to understand South-South relations as a contingent assemblage of actors, processes and practices. Thereafter, we put forward the core concepts used throughout the book: globalities, practices, and frontier zones, and argue for the analytical relevance of scaling down to Chinese-, Brazilian-, and Indian-planned, built or run ports, roads, agribusinesses, and mining projects as sites in which 'global' practices are (re)made. Finally, we introduce three empirical angles—beyond models, contestations, everyday entanglements— and how the individual chapters in each contribute to the research agenda set out.

China, Brazil, and India (and their large-scale economic projects) in Africa

For much of the previous two decades, an outlook of economic growth in many parts of the Global South has led to a more polycentric development landscape (Mawdsley, 2019). Correspondingly, this has bestowed a variety of Southern countries—as well as their sub-national, private, and civil society actors—with capacities for greater, more attractive, and sustained ties with other developing nations, ranging from development finance to trade and investments, to technical transfers (see de Renzio and Seifert, 2014). Between 1980 and 2010 developing countries 'have increased their share of world merchandise trade from 25% to 47% and their share of world output from 33% to 45%' (Kaul, 2013: 2). By 2010, South-to-South aid flows accounted for 10% of the total volume of aid, approximately USD 20 billion—a twofold increase from the early 2000s (Chaturvedi, Fues and Sidiropoulos, 2012: 255).

This momentum has been emblematically captured through analyses of China, Brazil, and India—as emerging donors and investors—in Africa (Brautigam, 2011; Carmody, 2013; Mawdsley, 2014b; Taylor, 2014; Gray and Gills, 2016; Gu et al., 2016; Scoones et al., 2016; Bergamaschi, Moore and Tickner, 2017; Kragelund,

2019; Seibert and Visentini, 2019; Alencastro and Seabra, 2021; Dye, 2022b). Due to the magnitude of its presence in terms of trade, investment, and geopolitical alliances, China's role in Africa has undeniably drawn the most attention, with the other Southern B(R)ICs topping the list of most popular topics (see Carmody, 2013; Taylor, 2014). While China, Brazil, and India's relations with both colonial and postcolonial Africa have been forged over a *longue durée* (Brautigam, 1998; Dávila, 2010; Shinn and Eisenman, 2012), there was an unprecedented change of scale and intensity in the 2000s. Due to their increasing ability to boost and sustain ties with other developing countries, China, Brazil, and India have often been interpreted as 'locomotives' or 'catalysts' of South-South relations (Gosovic, 2016; Nayyar, 2016).

In Africa, studies have analysed such dynamics in several ways: through the role of presidential or summit diplomacy mechanisms (i.e. the Forum on China–Africa Cooperation (FOCAC) and the Africa–South America Summit), the engagement of multilateral groupings such as the BRICS and the India-Brazil-South Africa (IBSA) Forum, as big business in a 'new scramble' for the continent, or by making sense of discursive and operational aspects of projects (Burges, 2012; Scoones et al., 2016; Carmody, 2017; van Noort, 2019; Dye and Alencastro, 2020; Soulé, 2020). Another common analytical tendency has been to compare Chinese, Brazilian, and Indian approaches to Western-led frameworks, for instance the development regime of the Organisation for Economic Co-operation and Development (OECD) Development Assistance Committee (DAC) and World Bank/International Monetary Fund lending mechanisms (see, for instance, Brautigam, 2011; Chaturvedi, Fues and Sidiropoulos, 2012; Kragelund, 2019). In this vein, stressing a qualitative difference away from Western patterns of relations, many have observed how Chinese, Brazilian, and Indian development projects have recurrently resorted to affective discursive framings of non-interference, solidarity, and win-win partnerships. This was furthermore aided by self-representations of these countries as 'champions of the South' contesting the inequalities of (neo) liberal orders (Gray and Gills, 2016). Others have proposed a more measured reading: while bringing their own distinctive ways to the governance of large-scale projects in Africa and elsewhere, China, Brazil, and India also adopt existing global norms and partly align with existing practices, especially regarding macro-economic standards and policies (Kennedy, 2017: 4; Hameiri and Jones, 2018)—entanglements that this book seeks to shed further light on.

Projects with Chinese, Brazilian, and Indian involvement are the empirical focus of this volume, as they have been—with varying degrees of success—the most important new investors in many parts of Africa since the 2000s. China's trajectory on the African continent is nothing short of remarkable. China's relationship with Africa has been on the rise since the turn of the century, long before the Belt and Road Initiative (BRI) emerged as a prominent framework. In 2021, although hindered by the fallout of the Covid-19 pandemic, trade between China and Africa reached USD 254.2 billion, Chinese foreign direct investment to Africa amounted to USD 3.74 billion, and newly signed contracts for contracted work in Africa totalled USD 77.9 billion (MOFCOM, 2022). Yet, these figures do not reflect the diverse patterns of Chinese engagement on the continent. Among other things, scholars have highlighted instances of intra-Chinese competition for finance and projects, as well as the heterogeneity of and hierarchical divisions among Chinese actors (Lam, 2017; Lee, 2017). The Chinese state has, for instance, selectively endorsed certain actors for the sake of resource security, soft power, and commercial prospects for national firms (Brautigam and Tang, 2012). Indeed, the development of numerous large-scale investment projects across the continent is run by large state-led conglomerates and their subsidiaries, such as China Communications Construction Company (CCCC), China Petroleum & Chemical Corporation, or Sinohydro Corporation, and China Ocean Shipping Company. Meanwhile, alongside central state-owned enterprises (SOEs), provincial SOEs and private sector companies of various sizes form a substantive part of Chinese investment in Africa with various degrees of autonomy (Gu et al., 2016).

In terms of how to engage in Africa, ideological factions have long existed in defining China's relation with the Global South. China has traditionally favoured a more state-centric, hands-off approach to politics in host countries (Inoue and Vaz, 2012; see also Hirono,

2013), aided by ideas of 'solidarity, mutual benefit, and shared identities' (Mawdsley, 2011: 266; see also Shih et al., 2019; Nordin, 2016). Yet, in recent years, scholars have also observed the adoption of a more interventionist stance. This is in terms of adopting certain environmental and social regulations, but also at times regarding what development to strive for. As Cheng and Liu (2021: 6) quote a Chinese official: 'Before however these countries were governed was none of our business, but now is different as their unhelpful development models directly affect our interests, forcing China to shape their paths in ways that suit our needs'.

Marked by a pronounced retreat in recent years (Alencastro and Seabra, 2021), Brazil's trajectory in Africa has been less impressive and dwarfs comparatively to China's. Importantly, however, Brazilian trade with the continent peaked at USD 28.5 billion in 2013—a sevenfold increase since the early 2000s (Stolte, 2015: 2)—and significant development, business, and civil society ties were forged with Lusophone Africa in particular (Alden et al., 2017; Cezne, 2019). In what Dye and Alencastro (2020) have termed the 'corporate turn' in contemporary Brazil–Africa relations, the intensification of political and diplomatic ties coupled with African countries' infrastructure needs amid a global drive for commodities presented appealing opportunities for Brazilian resource and engineering firms on the continent, specifically during the Workers' Party administrations of Lula da Silva and Dilma Rousseff (2003–16). Central to these dynamics were construction contractors such as Odebrecht, OAS, Camargo Corrêa, and Andrade Gutierrez, the state-owned oil enterprise Petrobras, the mining multinational Vale, and agribusiness companies. Besides diplomatic backing, many of these corporate actors have benefitted from public finance lending by the Brazilian Development Bank (BNDES) as well as from synergies and complementarities with state-funded development cooperation programmes. The qualitative dimension of Brazil–Africa relations has also merited some attention, with scholars observing how supposedly common historical-cultural ties and geographical similarities have been harnessed to further the appeal of interactions across the South Atlantic (Seibert and Visentini, 2019). From the mid-2010s, however, Brazil's struggling economy and political turmoil, the revelation of the Lava Jato (Car Wash) corruption scandals, and the leadership of President Jair Bolsonaro (2019–22)—privileging anti-globalist postures and connections with politically conservative governments in the West—have halted many of the country's foreign initiatives in and with Africa (Casarões and Barros Leal Farias, 2021). However, Lula's re-election in 2022 for a third term in office has sparked renewed interest in deepening foreign policy and economic ties. Such developments present, nonetheless, a timely opportunity to reflect on the multiple implications linked to the role of Brazilian actors in Africa after the surge of the 2000s and early 2010s (see Alencastro and Seabra, 2021), what has emerged from those encounters, and what is to remain and change as Brazil sets its eyes on Africa again.

India's rapid increase in investment, trade and political presence in Africa sits between China and Brazil.[2] As with China and Brazil, Indian relations with the continent have a longer twentieth-century history (Mawdsley, 2011; Harris and Vittorini, 2015), but the contemporary landscape of ties, and infrastructure construction, started in the 1990s. Economic deregulation unlocked international investment and corporate expansion, which was led by India's large, family-owned conglomerates (Taylor, 2016). Their growth was supported by India's major trade bodies, the Federation of Indian Chambers of Commerce & Industry and Confederation of Indian Industry, who set up research desks on Africa and led business delegations to support deals (Dye and Soares de Oliveira, 2022). As with subsequent periods, India's diaspora in Africa, an inheritance of British colonial history, was a key agent facilitating ties with India, embedding Indian companies in African political and commercial networks and creating demand for Indian goods (Modi, 2010; Dubey and Biswas, 2016). Following a near-exclusively private-sector exploratory phase, the state started to support ties with Africa, chiefly through a standardised, subsidised infrastructure-financing scheme, called the India Development Economic Assistance Scheme (IDEAS), granted by the Ministry of External Affairs and managed by Exim Bank (Dye, 2022b, 2022a). This support, amidst wider governmental interest and the global commodity boom, transformed trade and investment. From 2002 to 2005 India led greenfield foreign direct investment

(FDI) into Africa and trade rose from USD 7.2 billion in 2001 and to $29.5 billion by 2007/08.[3]

High-level political engagement began with the 2008 first India–Africa Forum Summit, a meeting of leaders from the country and continent. This event, and its follow-up in 2011, demonstrated the Indian state's political commitment. With this support, by 2015, IDEAS loans reached $6.7 billion provided to projects involving infrastructure specifically (Dye, 2022b). Trade peaked in 2015–16, at $78 billion, whilst total FDI to Africa reached $8.3 billion in 2014. However, 2016 then marked the start of a period of divergence. After the 2014 commodity bust, investment decreased to $1.7 billion and trade, post-2016, trailed to $49.6 billion by 2017. Additionally, a change in the IDEAS scheme, described by Dye et al. in this volume (see Chapter 3), caused IDEAS infrastructure finance to fall. This mixed picture stands in contrast to a boom in political ties. The 2016 summit, as with future planned summits delayed by Ebola and Covid-19, hosted senior leaders from every country on the continent. Meanwhile Indian prime minister Narendra Modi has declared Africa a strategic priority, and his administration has boosted diplomatic efforts by opening embassies and organising numerous high-level trips (involving the prime minister, vice-presidents, or president). The Covid pandemic certainly stalled the economic and political dimensions of India's relations in Africa, but, with the support of the diaspora, political support and an established corporate base, India is set to continue its growing presence on the continent.

While we speak of Africa at a level of generalisation in this introduction, it is worth noting that 'Africa' naturally includes an extraordinary diversity of countries, societies, and realities, all of which can never be adequately captured through simplistic, catch-all references, and stereotypes (see Mudimbe, 1988). In this regard, by zooming in on case studies across the continent, the different chapters seek to bring contextually nuanced portrayals of the workings of South-South relations and how they (re)make Africa's contemporary infrastructure globalities. At the same time, there is only so much that a snapshot of China, Brazil, and India, plus actors from these countries within specific empirical settings, can achieve and reveal. Thus, across the chapters we guard against vacuous generalisations, but pursue core theoretical concerns through a selected number of pertinent case studies. The conclusion draws out the main findings and discernible key trends (and absences) in Africa's infrastructure globalities. It also outlines emerging themes and future research directions that emerge from decentring the empirical and conceptual gaze.

Researching South-South encounters: State of the Art

In disciplines such as International Relations, Development Studies, and Global Political Economy, the literature has commonly conceptualised and described contemporary South-South relations—such as those of China, Brazil, and India in Africa—through the framework of 'South-South cooperation' (SSC) (Kaul, 2013; Prashad, 2014; Bergamaschi, Moore and Tickner, 2017; Kragelund, 2019; Mawdsley, 2019). SSC roots are often traced to the 1955 Bandung Conference but its 'boom', as discussed, is prominently linked to trends in the 2000s. This has led to the formation of a dedicated body of research, as scholars, policymakers, bureaucrats, civil society organisations, and think tanks have sought to unpack SSC's role, meanings, and potentials. This epistemic community, broadly speaking, understands SSC as the transfer and exchange of resources, expertise, and technology among actors in the Global South. Scholars broadly converge, though the literature nuances this picture, that SSC is anchored by a somehow affective discursive framing: one that evokes mutual benefits, horizontality, as well as experience-based and demand-driven transfers set within claims to postcolonial solidarities and empathy (see Chacko, 2011; Liu, 2013; Mazimhaka, 2013).

Notwithstanding, two major critiques have been levelled: (1) that understandings of SSC are heavily value-laden and (2) state-centric. On the first critique, as Bergamaschi and Tickner (2017: 4–10) suggest, the expansion of SSC has led to a great deal of generalisation and myth, either excessively positive or negative. On the one hand, through vocabularies of mutual solidarities, affinities, and benefits, SSC has inspired unwarranted idealisations, with its desirability and appropriateness often assumed *a priori*. On the other hand, SSC has

11

been dismissed by many as means for new forms of dependency, exploitation, and indebtedness, a perspective that has centrally informed studies of China in Africa in particular (Lumumba-Kasongo, 2011; French, 2014; Garcia and Bond, 2015; Amanor and Chichava, 2016).

The second critique concerns the usual state-centric focus in SSC research agendas. In this regard, literature has frequently treated state actors, particularly central governments (mostly from the emerging powers themselves), as key drivers and references in these arrangements. While the involvement of the private sector has not been ignored, analyses often intertwine corporate engagements with the state interests and foreign policy priorities of their home governments (Tan-Mullins, Mohan and Power, 2010; Stolte, 2015). Concomitantly, greater attention has been dedicated to civil society and people-to-people contacts. While this has contributed to further important critical readings of SSC processes, studies have continued to centrally engage with state-led discourses and framings, contrasting these with ground-level practices at project sites. On this account, analysts reinforced suspicions that the benevolent, affinity-nurtured South-South narratives furthered by public entities are inherently contradictory and do not manage to live up to ideals, particularly when commercial interests are at stake (Gonzalez-Vicente, 2011; see Rowden, 2011; Amanor and Chichava, 2016).

These constraints, far from reflecting a selective research bias alone, are just as much the outcome of methodological obstacles: data from Southern countries is scarce and often incomplete or not accessible (Development Impact Group, 2016; Besharati, Rawhani and Rios, 2017; Waisbich, Silva and Suyama, 2017). Where data exists, it is often fragmented across and within multiple governments and entities. In this sense, scholars frequently over-rely on information extracted from the discourses and policy documents of governments themselves. This has in turn contributed to the predominance of overly idealised and descriptive accounts of official strategies and policies. Such difficulties are further compounded when dealing with non-state actors, for instance Southern-based businesses—which have been notoriously more restrictive systems for scholars to access (see Tan-Mullins, 2014).

Mawdsley (2019: 261) contends, however, that many of these challenges indicate a field in maturation and 'the effect of increasing visibility'. In this vein, particularly from the mid-2010s, a growing number of country-specific and field-based research studies have made great strides in enriching the field with more information and data, bringing depth, context, and a bottom-up perspective to SSC studies. Scholars have gradually moved beyond state-centric frames of reference, extending the usual focus on the policies and interests of emerging donor governments to include sub-national, private, and civil society entities (Garcia and Bond, 2015; Gu et al., 2016; Driessen, 2019), as well as the agency of host governments in Africa, particularly ruling elites, in shaping relations (Mohan and Lampert, 2013; Phillips, 2019; Gadzala, 2015).

The debate is also increasingly multi-layered and identifies a wide spectrum of South-South ties: besides classical government-to-government bilateral interactions, there are instances of triangular cooperation (McEwan and Mawdsley, 2012), decentralised SSC (conducted by subnational governments or other state entities (see Sørensen, 2018)), commercial exchanges and foreign direct investments (see Horner, 2016), and people-to-people contact ('SSC from below', see Garcia and Bond 2015). Many of these perspectives have nuanced conventional, parochial readings of SSC by stressing, for example, how corporate interests can actively influence and direct state policies—rather than the other way around. Moreover, it has been acknowledged that state–business articulations may not only stand at odds with the needs of Southern populations, but that these populations may also transnationally act 'from below' to produce alternative, contestation-oriented types of South-South links and discourses to challenge perceived hegemonies (see Shankland and Gonçalves, 2016; Cezne, 2019).

Against this backdrop, in recent years, SSC research agendas have been underpinned by greater reflexivity as well as conceptual and methodological pluralism, in what Waisbich and Mawdsley (2022) call the 'critical turn in SSC' (see also Mawdsley, Fourie, and Nauta 2019). As such, across academic (as well as policy and practitioner) circles, the affective and horizontal framings of 'cooperation' are more resolutely scrutinised and underpinned by a greater relational, practice-oriented focus, steering analyses towards the *how* of processes in practice and in action. This has also been followed by a more polyvalent, multifaceted understanding of what configures the 'South': beyond the state, agencies in 'South-South' entanglements can englobe private entities, civil society movements, and academia, to name only a few. These are viewed as actors in their own right— and not necessarily subordinated or subsumed to statist frameworks. They may form multiple relational configurations, signifying, forging, and performing South-South relations, and indeed 'the global', in distinct ways.

Practices of making infrastructure globalities

It is on the heels of these emergent research trends that this book places itself. It approaches South-South relations as the outcome of varied relational interfaces entangling foreign policy strategies, private interests, cultural signifiers, technical apparatuses, project praxis, bureaucracies, quotidian dynamics, and interpersonal contacts. Importantly, therefore, 'China', 'Brazil', 'India', and 'Africa' need to be unpacked to include the broader range of actors and their relations, including how they make global practices on multiple scales and through entanglements that cross-cut public-private, local-global, and formal-informal dichotomies. These processes are also embedded in the historically thick, postcolonial hierarchies of North-South relations, and the institutions and practices of the old, Western-dominated global order.

Consequentially, first, we do not use the 'cooperation' qualifier (which has been widely used to denominate and characterise, as highlighted, processes of South-South relations), and second, we introduce the notion of *globalities* to think in more pluralistic and procedural terms. The 'global' is often perceived as a single political and social space at the planetary scale (Bartelson, 2010: 219). By contrast, the concept of 'globalities' shifts the focus from the idea of 'the global' as one overarching structure, to 'the global' as many heterogeneous projects that embody various ideas and practices of what 'the global' means (see Law, 2004; Blok, 2010). We hold that such a globalities-based understanding reflects more adequately the capaciousness of Africa's South-South, infrastructure-mediated transnationalism. 'Cooperation' is something that may arise (or not) through these South-South entanglements, but it is not a defining trait. Rather, these dynamics are approached as instances of co-functioning, predicated on practices that aggregate heterogeneous elements.

Such an approach embraces polyvalent and multifaceted global *practices* more adequately, while avoiding ascribing practices as models to a singular origin or intention. As some have started to describe (Carrai, 2021; Tang, 2020; Carrozza and Benabdallah, 2022), distinct sets of knowledge and practice travel from China, Brazil and India to Africa and inform how actors from these countries approach the governance of their projects, and by extension, their relations with African societies. At the same time, we have shown elsewhere how Chinese and Brazilian actors play with different, liminal identities and related narratives and practices (Hönke et al., 2023). Hence there is no single or coherent 'Southern' or 'Chinese/Brazilian/Indian' practice. Furthermore, multiple (re)interpretations of any such practices are in use, as what 'South-South' signifies is also defined by African modes of relating and contesting (Cezne and Hönke, 2022; Soulé, 2022). While often focused on governments and elites, the debate around African agency offers useful insight in this regard (Gadzala, 2015; Hodzi, 2020; more broadly Mohan and Lampert, 2013). Finally, South-South relations do not take place in a vacuum but are embedded in the narratives and unequal material structures of North–South relations and (remnants of) the liberal global order. These dynamics are thus co-produced and re-assembled through a multiplicity of technologies, discourses, and practices.

To examine what emerges from South-South relations when concrete deals are struck, and projects are put to work and contested on the ground, contributes to better understanding emergent global practices. Practices we understand as fairly coherent, routine ways of going about things (Hönke, 2013: 30), 'organized around shared practical understandings' (Schatzki, Knorr-Cetina and Savigny, 2001: 2). Thus, practices are historically and socially situated, meaningful actions recognised within a frame of reference (Best, 2014: 22; Nicolini, 2016). The officer in charge of community relations

15

for a business operation, for instance, operates in the context of the possibilities and limitations set by a dominant understanding of problems and how they are normally addressed. At the same time, this engineer reproduces, but also subverts or changes, that very structure of possibility. Starting from the idea that all social phenomena, small and large, are constituted by and experienced in terms of 'micro' situations (Emirbayer, 1997; as in Nicolini, 2016: 99), so-called 'large-scale phenomena' are understood here as emerging through the aggregation of interconnected practices and their reproduction regimes. At the same time, practices eventually make up 'macro' social phenomena and are hence part of long-term, complex, and far-reaching social processes.

While such processes and structures are replicated in and through social practices, they are made by social actors. At the same time, they are beyond individuals' control and shape their behaviours and practices (Nicolini, 2016: 100). The structures that shape Global South corporate engagement in Africa are multiple of course, and often contradictory: norms of liberal global governance and diverse types of transnational and national legislation to regulate business behaviour operate alongside learned ways of going about things in transnational companies. Yet Southern corporations' practices, be it China's CCCC, Brazil's Vale or India's Tata Steel, similarly to those of OECD constituencies, are marred with practical constraints and influenced by capitalist markets and local circumstances. However, distinct ideas and embodied practices are also at play that have grown from domestic historical experiences and practices, the history and practice of South-South relations, as well as the deeply embedded postcolonial hierarchies of 'West' and 'the rest' of the world in the post-1945 international order. Hence practices are also sites of struggle (Law, 1992: 386), and in these, 'the global' is imagined and (re)made in multiple ways.

In the following, practices hence serve as one of the core methodological entry points. By shifting attention away from grand strategy and programmes, the chapters zoom in on those building relations for making large-scale investments happen. While implementing large-scale projects, they adapt, refine, and make new practices—in building elite relations and forging relational development (see Chapter 2 by Bunskoek and Chapter 3 by Dye et al.), in contestation (Chapter 4 by Waisbich, Chapter 5 by Sändig and Hönke, and Chapter 6 by Kilaka), and in business–society encounters (Chapter 7 by Gambino and Bagwandeen and Chapter 8 by Sambo and Bußler).

The making of these multiple practices is best approached, we argue further, in the context of locally situated yet globally connected *frontier zones*, our second methodological entry point. Frontier zones are large-scale infrastructure sites such as Lamu Port in Kenya or the Nacala port and railway in Mozambique with significant Global South investment. In them, expanding circuits of capital from different sources are manifest and visions and practices of political ordering (and development) meet and are renegotiated.

The lens of infrastructure has generated significant theoretical innovations in a variety of domains of the social sciences over the last two decades, as have contributions on economic hubs as global zones. Infrastructure has historically been crucial to state-building, serving as vehicles for the material regime of logistical power that assisted in the formation of territories and indirectly ruled nation states (Mukerji, 2010). Debates about the political economy of the African state have long stressed how much control over the sites that connect '*l'Afrique utile*' with the outside world has been a major source of revenue for colonial and postcolonial states (Boone, 1997; Cooper, 2002, 2014). Yet while much of the literature focuses on domestic elites and patronage-based politics within African states (e.g. Gray, 2015; Kelsall, 2013; Beresford, 2015), other studies usefully stress the reconfiguration (not decline) of the state through the internationalisation, privatisation and indirect discharge of state functions to commercial actors (Hibou, 1999; Schlichte, 2008; Hönke, 2010, 2018a; Schubert, Engel and Macamo, 2018).

At the same time, infrastructures are frequently described in linear temporalities consistent with modernisation theory, progressivist historiography and colonial endeavours (Bowker, 2015): hence in the tense of development—the future perfect (Hetherington, 2016). Postcolonial governments, together with a plethora of international and transnational actors, have continued to reproduce such temporalities and structures. Not only companies but the governments of China, Brazil, and India, as well as other Global South countries, have supported building roads, telecommunications, and other (economic) infrastructure for such purposes. The rapid construction of economic infrastructures in the Global South that has followed also shifts the geography of infrastructure expertise. The upshot is that companies from the Global South are found throughout Africa, Asia, and Latin America (and increasingly across Western contexts), exporting labour, capital, and construction equipment beyond their national borders (Anand, Gupta and Appel, 2018). Meanwhile, states in Africa are among those gaining access to a new variety of financial and engineering arrangements.

These political-economic, political-strategic, political-legal, and political-technical relationships create new zones of 'extrastatecraft' (Easterling, 2014)—a portmanteau for activities conducted in addition to, and in collaboration with, statecraft—that unfold in several ways. This is particularly important as infrastructure projects are not merely a collection of relationships in and of themselves; they also connect to a plethora of other interactions that they facilitate, modify, or sever (Ferguson, 2005; Appel, 2012; Campbell, 2012; Joniak-Lüthi, 2019). And they are always also political projects that transport and embody dominant rationales of governance (Larkin, 2013). Economic projects are embedded in different social and temporal relationships and allow investigating occasions of changes and continuities as well as learning and adaptations (Joniak-Lüthi, 2019). Hence, they are ideal focal points through which to explore multiple emerging global practices and their transformations.

From this vantage point, we conceptualise Africa's economic hubs with Global South investment as frontier zones—areas where social relations intersect and accumulate and remake transnational practices—to capture the multiple topologies of Africa's global relations.[4] They serve as ideal focal points through which to explore multiple emerging global practices and their transformations, and hence for the situated theorising from Africa that Mbembe and Nuttall (2004) and the Comaroffs (2012) have called for.

Mostly, frontier zones have been described as where projects of denationalisation are pushed forward, as neoliberal economic and political governmentalities are inserted gradually in localities, advanced both from outside and from inside states (Sassen, 2006: 381; see also Ong, 2006: 20). Brenda Chalfin (2010) lucidly elaborates on the workings of such neoliberal frontiers in the Ghanaian port of Tema. More generally, transnational zones, gateways and corridors have been identified as a core feature of neoliberal capitalism (Opitz and Tellmann, 2012), yet they have done so as standardised sets of technologies and practices. While Deborah Cowen's *Deadly Life of Logistics* (2014) shifts important emphasis to lines of tension in global logistical spaces and how different governmental logics clash, here the main tension remains between a global 'space of logistics' on the one hand, and nation state territoriality on the other.

We argue, however, that 'global zones' are differently made and characterised by a larger variety of situated practices made and shaped in the manifold transnational relations of Africa's economic hubs, ports, and infrastructure zones. Today more than ever, these zones are frontier zones of multiple globalities, which are significantly made in South-South relations. Practices of governance are characterised by a proliferation of diverse transnational technologies, professionals, and practices. It is even more striking that to date, much of the existing work on global zones concentrates empirically on Western actors, and the diffusion of discourses and technical standards of liberal global governance, at least implicitly. This book, therefore, traces how frontier zones are constantly evolving and subject to change, characterised by the rapid transformation of transnational practices in and through them. In contrast to claims about a homogenised Western or neoliberal global governance, *Africa's Global Infrastructures* demonstrates new ways to understand the multiplicity of globally circulating technologies and practices in the making.

Finally, the lens of infrastructure globalities allows us to address other uneasy questions that the SSC scholarship has paid less attention to: who benefits from the presence of infrastructure projects? Who has their resources for social and physical reproduction taken away? Which communities will have to fight for their rights, and how will they do so? How do communities and NGOs adapt their practice to projects from Global South contexts themselves (see Chapter 6 by Kilaka, and Chapter 5 by Sändig and Hönke in this volume)? While

19

infrastructure connects and facilitates interactions between socio-spatially diverse 'communities of practice' (Bowker and Star 2000), allowing for the remaking of national and transnational political collectives (see Chapter 4 by Waisbich), it also generates various forms of violence and exclusion (Rodgers and O'Neill, 2012; see also Chapter 6 by Kilaka).

Contributions

The chapters in this book question the tangibility and distinctiveness of 'models' exported to Africa, whether 'Northern', 'Southern', or 'Chinese'. In the frontier zones of Global South capitalist expansion, knowledge, skills, and agency are creatively assembled, beyond and across bound categories such as 'Chinese', 'Brazilian' or 'Western' policies and practices. And they are appropriated, contested and remade including through the engagement of marginalised and counter-hegemonic voices. To show this, individual chapters turn to African frontier zones of various sorts and reach: mining and construction sites, transnational non-governmental organisations (NGO) forums, elite bargains and political institutions that enable projects and shape practices at national and transnational scales. They analyse how multiple ideas and practices of transnational governance emerge, operate, and transform, and they do that on the basis of situated observations from multi-sited but in-depth cases studies from across Africa; from individual country contexts as well as transnational entanglements including sites in Brazil, China, the Democratic Republic of the Congo, India, Kenya, and Mozambique. Taken together, the contributions offer 'privileged insight into the workings of the world at large' (Comaroff and Comaroff 2012: 1) and their future, drawing on qualitative methods, including discourse, document, ethnographical analyses, and a range of original materials. The volume brings together scholars from four continents; junior scholars fresh from the field with refreshed perspectives and established scholars with ample and variegated expertise, from various fields such as African Studies, International Relations, Development Studies, Anthropology, China Studies, and Sociology.

The chapters are grouped around three thematic sections: (1) *Beyond Models*, (2) *Contestations*, and (3) *Everyday Entanglements*. The first section *Beyond Models* offers a discussion of whether and how Global South actors bring along models and practices of their own. Further, they consider the imprint elite politics and political institutions in China, Brazil and India have on corporate practices in Africa. The idea of 'counter-models' to emerge from South-South relations is inherent in arguments around how they, especially China, might challenge Western global governance or ways of doing development.

Chapter 2 by Raoul Bunskoek critiques that in such depictions of China, only great powers matter. China is seen as such a great power, whereas in Africa none (yet) could be found. As a result, within China–Africa relations, Chinese agency is seen to matter, whereas African agency does not. Moreover, in its interactions with African actors, China is seen to be motivated by concerns of mainstream IR theories, namely self-interest and increasing its own 'hard power' through an accumulation of natural resources. By contrast, taking both Chinese and African foreign policy discourses and practices seriously, the chapter reconceptualises the 'Chinese' model of development by arguing that in fact little is 'Chinese' about it, nor does it constitute a 'model'. Rather, what constitutes Chinese development practices is highly dependent upon the locality in which it is implemented and, hence, on African agency/ies. Instead of new models, the chapter argues, development(s) negotiated in place-specific, situated relations are more likely to constitute the future.

In Chapter 3, Barnaby Joseph Dye, Ricardo Soares de Oliveira, and Mathias de Alencastro offer an intricate analysis of the practices of Indian and Brazilian infrastructure builders in Africa. Africa's twenty-first-century international relations have transformed, with ties growing to other countries across the Global South. However, the study of this transformation persistently overlooks the true diversity of 'new' actors on the continent by focusing foremost on China. This chapter therefore addresses two alternative, prominent countries that have become major financiers and builders of infrastructure in Africa: India and Brazil. They provide an overview of the main financial mechanisms, companies and regulations involved in India and Brazil's infrastructure engagements, tracing how these translated into practices on specific projects. This focus on infrastructure practice also demonstrates key similarities and differences between Brazil and India's African relations. For instance, companies from both countries have deployed similar political strategies to win contracts and governmental support both domestically and in recipient nations. In contrast, India's private-sector independence differs from state-leadership in Brazil's push towards Lusophone Africa, despite Indian infrastructure firms being generally smaller and less experienced than their Brazilian counterparts. The chapter thus reveals how Brazilian and Indian models, policies, and practices are forged through Africa's infrastructure globalities.

The section *Contestations* analyses how South-South investments are contested in Africa and whether they are contested differently. The chapters treat transnational movements and transcalar advocacy as well as the unfolding of local controversies and 'weapons of the weak'-type practices (Scott, 1986). They analyse shifting power dynamics in African contexts and across the Indian Ocean and the South Atlantic. All of them interrogate African agency in shaping Chinese, Brazilian, and Indian companies' practices.

In Chapter 4, Laura Trajber Waisbich examines the emergence, from below, of South-South cooperation monitoring movements. Approaching both domestic and transnational levels, she discusses how social mobilisation and civil society groups in China, Brazil, and India (sometimes in articulation with African partners) have attempted to participate, influence—and finally—contest and resist cooperation projects implemented by the three countries in Africa. Drawing on multi-sited fieldwork, project documents, and interviews with grassroots movements, the chapter offers a comparative analysis of the framings and repertoires used by Chinese, Brazilian, and Indian civil society actors, and the issues citizen-led action brings to the forefront. In doing so, it highlights the centrality of Africa's infrastructure globalities to social mobilisation in China, Brazil, and India in the context of South-South contacts and exchanges.

Chapter 5 by Jan Sändig and Jana Hönke discusses advocacy practices against Chinese mining companies against the background of the authoritarian, closed political context in China. China has become the largest investor in Africa. In the Democratic Republic of the Congo (DRC), Chinese mining companies now control most of the copper and cobalt mines. While these mining operations create ample local grievances, advocacy groups face many obstacles to assisting mining-affected people in both the DRC and China. Using the case of the DRC, the chapter examines how NGOs have responded to the growing Chinese presence and whether NGO advocacy impacts Chinese business practices. Far from a shortage of advocacy, it shows that NGOs from the DRC and INGOs from the Global North have targeted the mining companies and relevant state actors through domestic, transnational, and transcalar pathways. Advocacy practices against Chinese mining companies have many similarities with those against Western and other Southern mining investment in the domestic context of the DRC. Some opportunities for contention, however, remain notably closed in the Chinese case, due to the non-involvement of NGOs from China and the limited opportunity to reach the Chinese government and a Chinese public. Nevertheless, the chapter shows that indirect effects of advocacy, alongside requirements put in place by the Chinese state, have contributed to changing the business practices of Chinese corporations. This chapter hence further specifies the practices that emerge from the frontier zones of South-South relations and remake existing practices.

Bernard Musembi Kilaka, in Chapter 6, then zooms in on situated controversies in the realm of project implementation. By exploring one of the most prominent controversies, around the construction of the Lamu Port in Kenya, he analyses how Chinese companies have become key players in Kenya's infrastructure boom in recent years, capitalising on a unique set of competitive practices. Some of these practices have been mired in controversies with host communities. In some instances, local agencies impacted the trajectory of construction activities. The chapter discusses what enables and constrains the exercise of local agency, examining practices of political mediation, environmental activism, and disputes over local content. Drawing from work by Behrends, Park and Rottenburg (2014) on travelling models, the chapter illustrates how corporate practices travel. But also local actors in Lamu drew inspiration from other contexts in which communities and civil society groups successfully challenged mega-projects to adapt their practices.

The *Everyday Entanglements* section turns to the making of Africa's infrastructure globalities in lifeworlds on the ground, such as those forged around the global workplace of Global South companies, and in community development.

Chapter 7 by Elisa Gambino and Mandira Bagwandeen offers an analysis of a global sense of workplace in Sino-African projects. The proliferation of Sino-African construction sites has prompted reflections on whether and how Chinese domestic practices of labour governance are 'transported' to African infrastructure projects. While the practice of 'living at work' is widespread in the infrastructure sector, labour relations unfolding in Sino-African construction sites speak to wider debates on the intersection of diverse governance practices. Drawing from critical geographer Doreen Massey's (2005) conceptualisation of place, this chapter posits that the specificity of place as a 'spatio-temporal event' emerges from its relations to broader (transnational) trajectories, such as narratives of labour control, job insecurity, infrastructure-led development, labour agency, and aspirations of social mobility, which unfold at a specific 'moment' of the ever-evolving global economy. Thus, the chapter argues that workplace dynamics, situated at the intersection of narratives 'within' and 'without' Sino-African construction sites, have differentiated implications for the politics of production in Sino-African labour relations.

This is complemented by Chapter 8, in which Michael Godet Sambo and Phyllis Bußler zoom in on Brazilian and Chinese agro-infrastructural projects in Mozambique: the now cancelled tripartite Nippo-Brazilian-Mozambican ProSAVANA rural development programme and the Chinese-funded rice farm WANBAO. They ask how these projects—sitting at the interstices of development cooperation and commercial interests—fared in relation to initial prospects and expectations, particularly in terms of social and economic improvement for local communities. In this vein, and without losing sight of site-specific and regional contextual nuances, the chapter discusses the ways in which supposed beneficiaries encounter their Southern donors and partners. In doing so, local communities act to shape and reshape ground-level interactions and practices, transforming pre-conceived models and even contributing to the demise of projects.

The *concluding section* starts with Chapter 9 by Vineet Thakur that reflects key contributions of the book to the understanding of South-South relations and how they affect broader changes in international relations. It critically assesses the potential of thinking through globalities and from economic frontiers. Drawing from the author's extensive work on India and non-Western IR, the chapter also reflects on how the book speaks to debates around agency, non-Western international relations and the decolonising of knowledge production, and racism in Africa's multiple international relations.

The final chapter by the editors draws out core findings across chapters and offers a concise summary of the multiplicity of distinct and converging practices that have emerged at the African frontier. It discusses the effects of these emerging patterns on African societies, and for evolving globalities beyond the continent. Finally, the chapter reflects on the infrastructure globalities in the context of recent crises and transformations of our time: the ruptures of the Covid-19 pandemic, the Russian invasion of Ukraine, the climate crisis and energy transitions, and proposes future avenues for research.

PART ONE

BEYOND MODELS

2

BEYOND THE 'CHINA MODEL'

TOWARDS A RELATIONAL UNDERSTANDING OF DEVELOPMENT PRACTICES IN CHINA–AFRICA RELATIONS

Raoul Bunskoek[1]

Introduction

Specific wording says a lot about how actors perceive the world and, by extension, their resulting practices. The Ministry of Commerce of the People's Republic of China (PRC) (2021: 54) stated in a recent *Foreign Investment Cooperation Country (Region) Guide Kenya*, that Kenya already treats Mombasa, Lamu, and Kisumu as 'Special Economic Zone Pilot Areas' (经济特区试点区域). Whereas the concept of special economic zones most likely sounds familiar to anyone vaguely familiar with post-1978 domestic economic developments in China, the two characters that follow it, *shidian* (试点), generally translated as 'pilot' but more literally meaning 'experimental point', actually say a lot more about Chinese-styled development and, hence, a particular Chinese 'globality'.

As this chapter argues, this globality is characterised by a tendency by Chinese actors on the ground in African countries not to adhere to top-down 'commandments' or a blueprint coming from Beijing, as is usually expected by observers looking at 'authoritarian'

China through mainstream International Relations (IR) theory. Rather, Chinese actors on the African continent, just as they did in China domestically, tend to dynamically adapt to local contexts, shaping development from the ground up relationally. In doing so, 'experimental points' are the departure points from which successful trials then travel more broadly, in a process which official Chinese sources call 'proceeding from point to surface' (*youdian daomian*, 由点到面) (Heilmann and Perry, 2011: 62).

The chapter illustrates such Chinese-styled development, drawing loosely from Nicolini's concept of 'zooming in and out'. In his own words, '[t]heorizing practice … requires a double movement of zooming in on and zooming out of practice obtained by switching theoretical lenses and following, or trailing, the connections between practices' (Nicolini, 2009: 1392). Rather than switching theoretical lenses, however, his methodology is employed here to zoom in on practices by Chinese actors in both China domestically as well as in several African countries, and then to zoom out to show a set of more macro knowledges and practices that travel from China to African localities and vice versa.

The chapter proceeds as follows. First, it provides a historical view to embed Chinese-styled development in its domestic historical and socio-cultural context. Second, it shows how it was 'exported' to African localities and, third, how it was then and is still being shaped by an intermingling of African and Chinese agency/ies in the process. The fourth section provides a preliminary relational (re)making of Chinese-styled development in Africa. It also suggests that such a relational (re)making of development might constitute the future of 'Western' development rather than vice versa. The final section answers the main question, concludes, and points to fruitful areas of future research.

Governing China's gargantuan territory

The governing of the gargantuan 'Chinese' territory over centuries by whoever represented 'China' at the time—e.g. dynasties, warlords, nationalists, communists—has always been a huge challenge. In practice, this challenge was mostly dealt with through an extreme amount of decentralisation (Ge, 2018). This made localities highly autonomous, responsible for taking care of their own affairs, and in fact quite 'free'. In Heilmann and Perry's (2011: 14) words, '[i]n effect, localities are generally left to fend for themselves, receiving only erratic and episodic central support'. Only when things really got out of hand, which usually was when entities rose up that threatened the legitimacy of the centre (e.g. rural uprisings, invasions by nomads or other outside forces, etc.), would the centre step in to restore 'order' (*zhi*) (Wang, 1968; Kwan, 2016). When the centre became unable to fend off foreign invaders or re-establish order, as happened during the period from 1839 to 1949 in China, now known as the 'century of humiliation', it lost its legitimacy (or, 'mandate of heaven') (Wang, 2013). It is in this light that one should see the following remarks by Sun Yat-sen[2] on why China had to 'revolt' (*geming*) at the beginning of the twentieth century:

> Bluntly speaking, it is for the exact opposite goal of the revolution in Europe. Europe revolted because it previously did not have enough freedom, so it came to strive for freedom. For us, it is because we have too much freedom, we have no group and hence no resistance. We are just 'like a sheet of loose sand' [unable to cooperate]. Because we are like a sheet of loose sand, we were subjected to the invasion of foreign imperialism, we had to bear the economic trade war oppression of the Great Powers, and we are now simply unable to resist. (Sun, 1924, translation by author)

Sun's remarks are about a century old now. Although the establishment of the PRC in 1949 and its further developments assured the protection of China's national sovereignty against foreign invaders, a feat that was achieved by the ideological bringing together of the 'group' through Marxism-Leninism-Mao Zedong Thought (now Xi Jinping Thought), China's political system is still highly decentralised (Wang, 2014). In fact, as Mao Zedong himself said already in 1956, '[W]e must *not* follow the example of the Soviet Union in concentrating everything in the hands of the central authorities, shackling the local authorities and denying them the right to independent action' (emphasis by author).[3] Therefore, after an initial streak of centralising policies after the establishment of the

PRC in 1949, the Chinese Communist Party (CCP) announced the general policy of 'centralised leadership and divided responsibility' (*tongyi lingdao, fenji fuze*) as early as 1951 (Lardy, 1975: 45). It is in this light that Gungwu Wang (2014) perceives the oscillation between centralising and decentralising forces as the main influencers of Chinese politics. Similarly, Yifu Lin et al. (2013) refer to the 'centralisation-decentralisation cycle' and see reform in China after the 1970s as largely an exercise in decentralisation.

Western[4] observers, however, tend to see a highly authoritarian top-down governance system in China, where commands are followed to the letter. This is not the whole picture, and in fact might say more about Western observers themselves than China per se (Pan, 2012). Both within China domestically as well as abroad (in Africa, in the case here), a multitude of 'Chinese' actors exist with motivations that more often than not do not converge, but in practice all end up representing 'China' (e.g. see Taylor and Xiao, 2009). Although observers tend to believe that Beijing could control these actors, in fact it cannot. This situation is further complicated by the fact that the CCP wants to make it seem *as if* they are in control, which is then symbolically reciprocated by actors on the ground (Rosemont and Ames, 2016). As a result, binaries between 'the West' and 'China' have been hardening in recent years. Nevertheless, this is not caused by 'China' per se, but by a governmentality that puts a high premium on symbolic deference (Bunskoek and Shih, 2021).

Observers who mistake Chinese governance to be merely 'authoritarian' in the sense that central commands are implemented nationwide without questioning and along a certain blueprint naturally come to see the so-called 'China Model' of development as an exportation of Chinese-styled authoritarianism abroad (e.g. Rolland, 2020). It is paradoxical, however, that this presumably 'Chinese' model of development constitutes exactly how in fact the 'Washington Consensus' or, more accurately, neoliberalism, has been implemented by international financial institutions.[5] If developing nations wanted to borrow money from institutions like the International Monetary Fund or the World Bank, they had to adhere to certain 'conditionalities': implementation of a democratic system, free-market-promoting policies, and privatisation of many government institutions and enterprises (Stiglitz, 2003). In fact, they had to follow certain 'commands from above'.

Within the PRC's domestic development, the situation was and is rather different. In her 2016 book, *How China Escaped the Poverty Trap*, Yuen Yuen Ang proposes to look at development in China domestically as 'directed improvisation', in which 'central reformers direct', whereas 'local state agents improvise' (Ang, 2016: 17). The centre does *not* direct through providing fixed guidelines (top-down commands) that localities are not allowed to deviate from. Instead, it offers three types of guidelines, ranging from vague to less vague, within which local actors can improvise using the resources they have within their own context. This provides local actors with considerable room for 'adaptation' or 'experimentation', which can be summarised in three steps: (1) 'authorising yet delimiting the boundaries of localization (variation)', (2) 'clearly defining and rewarding bureaucratic success (selection)', and (3) 'encouraging mutual exchanges between highly unequal regions (niche creation)' (ibid.). Note that it also forces local (state) actors to scrutinise central policies to make sure their local amendments stay within central boundaries (Tsai and Tian, 2021). As for rewarding bureaucratic success post-1978, 'the two most important indicators of successful political performance in the appraisal of CCP cadres have been "economic development" and "social stability"' (Tsai and Dean, 2014: 345). The process that ensues is a 'coevolutionary process' between institutions and markets that provide mutual feedback to each other and can be summarised in three steps: 'Harness weak institutions to build markets → emerging markets stimulate strong institutions → strong institutions preserve markets' (Ang, 2016: 14).

Basing her analysis upon early successes in agricultural reform in China, Hsu (2015: 1761) concurs,

> [c]ontextualised within the perspective of the broader understanding and practice of development, a Chinese model of development suggests that local experimentation, such as accounting for local conditions in the area of agricultural reform, was crucial to early success. In particular, changes in agricultural production

had tremendous impact in the early phases of poverty reduction. A combination of past and present experiences and lessons thus constitute a Chinese model of development.

Moreover, the fact that Hsu (2015) refers to the importance of 'past experiences and lessons' highlights the point that merely focusing on the post-1978 period in China regarding Chinese models of development, as most observers tend to do, is problematic. As Heilmann and Perry (2011: 3) write, 'China's [contemporary] governance techniques are marked by a signature Maoist stamp that conceives of policymaking as a process of ceaseless change, tension management, continual experimentation, and ad-hoc adjustment'. Underscoring the alterity of the PRC regarding the Soviet Union or other Eastern European communist countries, 'Mao's China exhibited a trademark policy style that favoured continual experimentation and transformation (or 'permanent revolution') over regime consolidation', which they call 'guerrilla-style policymaking' (ibid.: 7). Heilmann and Perry (2011) show how such policymaking emerged from a situation during the Chinese Civil War (1927–49), when communication between different 'base areas' was nearly impossible. This 'decentralized initiative within the framework of centralised political authority' encouraged by Communists at the time 'proved highly effective when redirected to the economic modernization objectives of Mao's successors' (ibid.: 7). Reminiscent of Ang's 'directed improvisation', Heilmann and Perry coin the term 'experimentation under hierarchy' to refer to the 'model' implemented in China domestically. They also identify a key characteristic, which is that 'trial implementation of controversial or risky reforms in limited domains regularly precedes the enactment of national laws: risky policies are tried out first, spread to larger areas secondly, and only written into national law as a last step' (ibid.: 16).

In short, an important part of what the above and especially Heilmann and Perry indicate is that in the Chinese context new guidelines are followed by a period of experimentation, which is then again followed by adapted new guidelines and new experimentations (see also Sohn, 2011 for a demonstration of how this worked in the development of China's multilateral diplomacy). Only when these processes have stabilised a bit do the central authorities put these guidelines into national law.

Export of the 'China Model' to African countries

What then is exported from the so-called 'China Model' is not so much a model, but improvised and experimental development, with few prescriptions and with feedback loops. Nevertheless, Chinese actors do not come to African localities with a *tabula rasa*. In other words, they do take with them certain ideas about strategies that have worked before in other contexts (e.g. in China, but also in other overseas contexts, including Africa). Yet, they do not adhere to preconceived clear ideas about how development should take place. Chin and Gallagher (2019: 251), for instance, illustrate this by arguing that 'China's development finance push outwards has been a "coordinated" approach at two levels'. First, 'the highest levels of the Party-state in Beijing have set the overarching Chinese national objectives, and the global goals and aspirational parameters for the outward push' (ibid.). This corresponds to the 'directedness' in Ang's (2016) 'directed improvisation' and 'hierarchy' in Heilmann and Perry's (2011) 'experimentation under hierarchy'. Just as is the case in China domestically, however, such 'national objectives' often come in the form of relatively vague and multi-interpretable guidelines, providing room for adaptation and experimentation on the ground (Ang, 2016).

The second level (Chin and Gallagher 2019: 251) is that 'the Chinese state-guided coordinated investment approach mirrors the form of a "big push" approach that Rosenstein-Rodan (1943) examined as a corrective for a number of "coordination failures" that existed in the economy'. Nugent (2018), moreover, argues that this approach has come back in Africa, and can now be seen in the 'big push' of African governments and parastatal actors (e.g. port authorities with a high degree of autonomy) for infrastructure projects. Lixing Zou, former chief economist at the China Development Bank (CDB), for instance highlights the fact that the CDB played such a 'coordinating' role in China domestically (Zou, 2014). Part of such a 'big push' approach is the practice of providing funding for infrastructure in 'bundles' or in an 'all-inclusive' fashion (*yilanzi*). Meant to lower the risks and heighten success rates, the PRC's national development finance institutions 'operating abroad tend to lend in extraordinarily large lines of credit and loans for bundles of infrastructure and energy and other overseas national developmental projects, and do so in a coordinated fashion—with a number of different (Chinese) bank and non-bank corporate actors taking part in creating … "coordinated credit spaces"' (Chin and Gallagher, 2019: 247–8). Thus, 'Chinese financial institutions are exporting the coordinated financing model that has allowed Chinese banks to control credit risk, while boosting China's economic growth' (ibid.: 251).

Gelpern et al. (2021) provide evidence for the existence of these 'coordinated credit spaces' through their analysis of 100 contracts signed between Chinese actors and foreign governments in the period 2000–20, particularly their finding that '50 percent of CDB contracts … include cross-default clauses that can be triggered by actions ranging from expropriation to actions broadly defined by the sovereign debtor as adverse to the interests of "a PRC entity"' (ibid.: 7). In other words, the debt contracts assure that local governments do not give up (e.g. default) on one of the projects in a 'bundle', because this would have a detrimental impact on the feasibility and ability to make a profit of all projects belonging to the 'coordinated credit space'.

Still, this is not the whole picture. As Muyang Chen (2021) points out, Chinese policy banks also play an important 'enabling' or 'empowering' function. Traditionally, a 'major challenge of conducting infrastructure projects in underdeveloped regions … is that the owner of project, normally a government organ of the host country, does *not have* sufficient capital to pay contractors' (M. Chen, 2021: 847, emphasis by author). To deal with this problem, Chinese 'policy banks assist the owners by offering them loans, thereby indirectly helping Chinese construction companies acquire global contracts' (ibid.). This practice sets Chinese policy banks apart from earlier catching-up economies (e.g. Japan), where policy banks 'provided [domestic] exporters with much cheap, state-subsidised capital to rival foreign competitors' (ibid.: 831). Chinese policy banks instead tend to strengthen local (African) governments by enabling them to borrow money,[6] and Chinese companies then often benefit because they win public tenders due to their competitive pricing. This corresponds to Nugent's (2018) argument that Chinese involvement on the African continent tends to strengthen African state actors. And not only that, 'in many cases Chinese credits are not [even] disbursed to rival more advanced economies, as Chinese firms and firms of industrial economies are not necessarily interested and specialised in the same kinds of projects' (M. Chen, 201: 846). In other words, Chinese funding fills a gap.

Additional to these policies creatively facilitating investments and development in African localities where none was possible conventionally, an important means to both 'guide', 'direct', or 'coordinate' on the one side, and receive 'feedback' on practices in the African context on the other is the Forum on China–Africa Cooperation (FOCAC) (Sohn, 2011). Whereas during its inaugural Ministerial Conference, which took place in Beijing in October 2000, only four African presidents attended, this increased to 41 heads of state in 2006 during its first official Summit and third Ministerial Conference (Tang, 2020). The fact that in 2018, twice as many African presidents attended the FOCAC summit as the UN General Assembly further highlights the popularity of the forum (Dahir, 2018). As African observers (Shelton and Paruk, 2008: 84) point out, the FOCAC is so popular because it is 'not a Western-style donor talk-shop, but rather a robust dialogue system which produces concrete results and specific outcomes'. Data gathered by the China Africa Research Initiative and Boston University Global Development Policy Center (2022) clearly illustrates this by highlighting how Chinese loans to Africa started to build in 2006, right after the first FOCAC summit meeting, and reached a high point in 2016. Although after 2016 the number of loans decreased significantly, this does not mean less Chinese engagement on the continent. Rather, it highlights responses to both African demands for more people-to-people training (Benabdallah, 2020) and the US accusation of China practising 'debt-trap diplomacy' (Office of Policy Planning, 2020), as well as the finding of alternative financing mechanisms (e.g. public–private partnerships, or PPPs). Sohn (2011: 89) highlights that 'China's earlier experience [sic] of the ARF and the Shanghai Five … were critical for the Chinese feedback on multilateralism and subsequent multilateral offensive in the developing world'.

In terms of a model, little is being exported. In fact, it is (African) governments which tend to become strengthened in proposing and following their own visions and developmental programmes (e.g. Kenya Vision 2030, Cameroon Vision 2035, and Rwanda Vision 2050). Chinese institutions, for their part, constantly receive feedback both multilaterally and bilaterally through what Sohn (2011) coins a 'cognitive feedback model' and therefore constantly adapt their policies and practices. In other words, engagements with Chinese actors tend to enable/empower African governments. This stands in sharp contrast to the Western logic of exporting 'best practices' (e.g. democracy, free-market capitalism), recipes, standards, values, etc., because of their perceived superiority vis-à-vis local alternatives. As such, fundamental to shaping 'Chinese' development in African countries is the role played by African agency/ies.

African agency/ies

As other chapters in this volume illustrate empirically, the kind of development that eventually takes place on the ground is ultimately shaped by African actors (Gadzala, 2015). Or, more accurately, by the successful intermingling of Chinese and African agencies that leads to relationally co-constituted development. Whereas in Chinese contexts, local governments and institutions actively attracted and supported companies to jointly develop localities (Brautigam, 2015: 49, 125, 11; Driessen, 2019: 153–4), the same is (mostly) not the case in African contexts because the structural contexts differ so much, hence, the agency local actors exercise. Chiyemura et al. (2022: 4) argue that the 'political, economic, and legal-bureaucratic contexts within African states … crucially condition infrastructure projects with Chinese involvement'. To illustrate, they use the cases of Bagamoyo Port in Tanzania, Adama wind farms in Ethiopia, and Lamu Port in Kenya.

In the case of Bagamoyo, Chiyemura et al. (2022: 8–12) effectively highlight how a lack of flexibility and adaptation to local development policy on behalf of the Chinese investor, China Merchants Port Holdings, has caused the project to be stalled for the moment. China Merchants, conversely, effectively blamed the stalling of the project on the new demands by the Tanzanian side, which made the project neither 'commercially feasible' nor in line with 'win-win cooperation' (Reuters, 2019). Conversely, in the case of the Adama wind farms, they clearly illustrate not only how it was the Ethiopian side that first 'approached the Chinese government seeking financial and technological assistance to develop further wind farms' (Chiyemura, Gambino, and Zajontz, 2022), but also how the Chinese side successfully adapted to the local concerns by taking on an Engineering-Procurement-Construction + Financing scheme that diverted the project delivery risk from the Ethiopian Ministry of Water, Irrigation and Electricity to the Chinese contractor. This concern was particularly pertinent to Ethiopian state actors because it had led to previous construction delays working with the French firm Vergnet (ibid.). Finally, in the case of Lamu Port, Chiyemura et al. show how local Kenyan government actors ended up reshaping Chinese practices even though the centralised Lamu Port–South Sudan–Ethiopia Transport Corridor Development Authority was actually in charge. They point out that '[s]uch "peripheral" agency has prompted Chinese companies to formulate and then redeploy risk mitigation strategies with regard to controversies around local content requirements' (ibid.: 17).

It is thus the case that 'Chinese actors adapt their strategies to suit the particular histories and geographies of the African states with which they engage' (Carmody and Taylor, 2010: 497). Although Carmody and Taylor base their assessment on research on Chinese impacts on governance in Sudan and Zambia, Gagliardone (2015) further highlights the validity of their argument through a comparison of Chinese-backed information infrastructure construction in Ethiopia and Kenya. He 'shows that China has indeed adapted to the policy environments and the power dynamics of each state—sometimes [even] to its own (immediate) disadvantage' (Gagliardone, 2015: 45). Moreover, '[w]hile engagements of Chinese telecommunications firms and media outlets in both countries are in many ways similar, their disparity is a product of the approaches and policies of both governments, respectively, and of China's so far demonstrated ability to work in, and adapt, to both' (ibid.: 57).

The same counts for another project in Kenya, namely the Nairobi Expressway. Due to the Kenyan government's concerns about borrowing more money and, simultaneously, to avoid adding fuel to the 'debt trap' fire, actors involved set up the project as Build Operate Transfer (Koech, 2021), or a PPP (Olander, 2021). In practice, this means that the China Road and Bridge Corporation (CRBC), the same contractor that built the Mombasa–Nairobi Standard Gauge Railway (SGR), both finances and builds the expressway. Afterwards, in order to recoup its investments, CRBC will operate the expressway for 27 years, asking drivers to pay a toll per mile depending on vehicle type (see Koech, 2021), and then hand it over to the Kenyan government. This alternative financing strategy to the one used for the SGR clearly illustrates the risk taken by CRBC as well as the trust shown in Kenya's government under Uhuru Kenyatta and vice versa. Although Chinese state-owned enterprises are state-owned, they do have to remain financially viable themselves, and have quite considerable independence from the Chinese government. In fact, CRBC's long-term embeddedness in Kenya's political environment suggests a high degree of independence. As Lam (2017) underscores, the Chinese state tends to 'retreat' the longer companies are in a locality.

Now, based on the above, it is attractive to draw the conclusion, as Xiaoyang Tang (2020) does, that what Chinese actors do in African countries is just effectively capitalising on market opportunities and, hence, that the export of the 'China Model' is tantamount to the export of a '"model" with no model'. This, however, misses an important point. Tang proposes to see the relationships between Chinese and African actors as one of 'coevolutionary pragmatism', which he describes as a 'process' within which it is 'critical' that Chinese and African actors interact towards a 'common target' which he defines as the promotion of 'sustainable productivity growth' (Tang, 2020: 36). However, sustainable productivity growth is certainly not always the end goal of all African governments/ actors. Instead, African elites tend to prioritise projects that allow them to either remain in power, gain power, or increase their legitimacy, however that is defined in the local context (Large, 2021; Hodzi, 2018).

In fact, the 'common goal' of sustainable productivity growth probably says more about the context from which the Chinese actors have come, than about the African context per se. Therefore, by arguing in favour of coevolutionary pragmatism as a '"model" with no model', Tang might actually (unconsciously) be transplanting or imposing a Chinese development approach to African contexts— that is, one in which the extent to which 'economic development' and 'social stability' are achieved are the main means of assessing actors' performances (Tsai and Dean, 2014)—in the process implicitly highlighting the superiority of this Chinese approach. This is in line with Bunskoek and Shih (2021), who argue that because this approach to development 'worked' in China domestically, it underlined its 'moral superiority' from a Chinese point of view, especially vis-à-vis Western approaches, making it a responsibility of the Chinese government to export it to other localities. In other words, it constitutes a type of 'gift-giving'. Therefore, the idea of 'coevolutionary pragmatism' still highlights a certain amount of 'Chinese exceptionalism' (Zhang, 2013). As this section has shown, actual successful interactions between Chinese and African actors on the ground typically illustrate a much more relational type of development; not towards a pre-defined common goal, but to a relationally defined goal that has emerged out of a specific context.

A relational (re)making of the 'China Model'

Therefore, this situation requires the relational (re)making of the 'China Model'—whether that is 'directed improvisation', 'improvisation under hierarchy', or a '"model" with no model'. Flexibility, adaptability to change, and a decentralised political system that leaves local actors with high degrees of autonomy and freedom are deeply ingrained in the 'Chinese' worldview.[7] In fact, continuity can be observed here. Going from dynastic history to nationalist rule, to communist rule, and after 'reform and opening up'. As argued above, this contradicts significantly with 'Western' expectations of 'authoritarianism', which perceive authoritarian

China as strictly top-down and consisting of actors directly following the orders (or, 'commandments') of those higher in the hierarchy and in the centre. The Washington Consensus shares a hierarchical logic in this regard: universally valid models are expected to be implemented to the letter.

However, the Washington Consensus combined with the Western view of China is reflective of a particular tradition. As Giorgio Shani (2015: 2) argues, the 'language intelligible to "all citizens" is the language not of secular modernity, but of a "secularized" religio-cultural "tradition", which in the West takes the form of Judaeo-Christianity'. He also points out that the main characteristic of this tradition 'aims at salvation through *submission to God's commandments*' (Shani 2015: 3, emphasis by author). As Sun Yat-sen (1924) argued above, this Western situation required a revolution to acquire more 'freedom'. Yet, the approach to development we have seen above in both the Chinese and African contexts is arguably reflective of another 'secularised' religio-cultural tradition, one that is 'congruent with a long and influential line of traditional thought which stressed fluid, dialectical, and tactical approaches to managing ubiquitous tensions and contradictions' (Heilmann and Perry, 2011: 15). This alternative tradition, based upon 'Chinese' religio- or, in the Chinese case more apt, socio-cultural traditions (e.g. Confucianism, Daoism, etc.) that have been practised over time and are uninhibited by the Judaeo-Christian tradition,[8] provides actors with the idea that everything is relative and dependent on specific conditions, as a result of which high amounts of freedom to make decisions along 'local conditions' are seen as natural. Therefore, Tang's 'common goal' of 'sustainable productivity growth' is, in fact, still too 'top-down' and aligned with the Judaeo-Christian tradition.

Instead, rather than top-down, the various ways in which development actually takes place through the practices of African and Chinese actors on the African continent are far more bottom-up and relationally constituted. Helpful in explaining this is Shih et al.'s (2019) distinction between two 'modes of relationality', namely (1) prior relationality and (2) improvised relationality. Although all actors inescapably engage in both modes of relationality, the top-down commandments by Western development actors are reflective of one type of prior relationality, namely 'natural rights qua liberalism', which is a 'thick' form of relationality characterised by its relatively fixed 'norms and institutions' (Shih et al., 2019: 243). The implication of this form of relationality is that actors can relate only if their identities (consisting of norms, values, and institutions) correspond, and if this is not (yet) the case, 'development' consists of making this happen—hence, the 'conditionalities' attached to loans by Western development institutions. Conversely, Chinese actors tend to operate along a much thinner form of prior relationality, that is, *Tianxia*, which is not in favour of fixed institutions or norms but instead emphasises symbols and rituals, adherence to which, on a reciprocal basis is meant to enable harmony between actors. As a result, *Tianxia* 'requires improvisations of relationships in specific contexts, usually bilateral, to substantiate the sense of resemblance between actors' (ibid.). This 'sense of resemblance' then 'obliges reciprocity that is essential to self-actualization' (ibid.)—namely, self-actualisation within a specific context.

As for the mode of improvised relationality, it is reserved not only 'for those not sharing prior resemblance', but also for 'those in quest of specific relationships under a thin prior relation' (such as *Tianxia*) (Shih et al., 2019: 244). The most expedient way of establishing improvised relations is through gift-giving. According to Confucianism, gift-giving constitutes a demonstration of sacrifice to replicate awareness of a 'greater-self' (Yan, 1996). That is, between the self and the recipient of the gift, hence 'relating' both parties. Especially effective are 'sacrifices that answer a correctly perceived need of the other party [because they] symbolise resemblances of interest and identity between them' (Shih et al., 2019: 244). As such, practices such as providing loans (low-interest or not) where earlier no loans were available (Chen, 2021), sponsoring symbolic or prestige projects such as the African Union headquarters in Addis Ababa, or finishing projects on time or even ahead of schedule before (local) elections are all forms of creative gift-giving with the goal of establishing, maintaining, or strengthening relationships. Moreover, by adhering to particular contexts, they all make Chinese-styled development practices much more relational.

A particularly distinct characteristic of Chinese-styled development as opposed to Western-styled development, with the former exhibiting thin prior relationality and the latter thick, is the fact that the former does not seek to fundamentally effect the 'identities' of actors, whereas Western-styled development does. Chinese actors on the ground tend to improvise 'resemblance in accordance with the conditions of the other side [which] suggests that [their] Chineseness is constituted by dynamic processes rather than by any stable contents' (Shih et al., 2019: 244). As a result, this 'leads to a kind of Chineseness that is epistemologically undefinable and useless' (ibid.). In this sense, the idea of Chinese-styled development points to the situation on the ground in which both African and Chinese actors and their identities *in specific relations* are (re)shaped through practices into post-identities. Actors on the ground do not implement projects according to a blueprint coming from one side or the other. Instead, both actors are involved in creating a form of 'in-betweenness' which can also be referred to as a post-identity. This is significantly different from Tang's argument that there is a common goal of sustainable productivity growth, which highlights a fixed identity.

The idea of relationally co-constituted post-identities is, however, not only existent in 'Chinese' thinking, but can also be found in Western relational thinking (Nordin et al., 2019). For instance, according to the Austrian Jewish and Israeli philosopher Martin Buber, 'Man is a creature of the between' (Buber, 1965: xx) and therefore 'does not exist as a separate entity' (Yalom, 1980: 364). This is so because, according to Buber, people possess an 'innate' longing for relationships (Buber, 1970: 76–9). Buber points out 'two basic types of relationships', which can also be portrayed as 'two types of in-betweenness', namely 'I–Thou' and 'I–It'. Whereas 'the "I It" relationship is the relationship between a person and equipment, a "functional" relationship, a relationship between subject and object wholly lacking mutuality, [t]he I–Thou relationship [conversely] is a wholly mutual relationship involving a full experiencing of the other' (Yalom, 1980, 364–5). This distinction is reminiscent of Shih et al.'s (2019) division between thick prior relationality and thin prior relationality (or improvised relationality). 'When relating to

"It" (whether to a thing or to a person made into a thing) one holds back something of oneself: ... one categorizes it, analyzes it, judges it' (Yalom, 1980: 365) and, in fact, might even try to change it, as in Western-styled development which seeks to (re)create a thick prior relationality. Conversely, 'when one relates to a "Thou," one's whole being is involved; nothing can be withheld' (Yalom, 1980: 365). As a result, in an I–Thou relationship, 'the "I" is "betweenness"; the "I" *appears and is shaped* in the context of some relationship. With each "Thou," and with each moment of relationship, the "I" is created anew' (Yalom, 1980: 365).

In short, successful development by Chinese actors has tended to occur only when they have allowed their 'Is' to be shaped *in the context of some relationship*—hence, leading to a post-identity. This, however, does not mean that all Chinese actors on the African continent engage in successful development. No, failures abound. That said, the propensity to engage in effective development by Chinese actors tend to be higher due to their stronger adherence to a thinner form of relationality, e.g. *Tianxia*, which does not seek to transform the identities of local actors. In contrast, Western-styled development actors champion 'natural rights qua liberalism', which seek to tranform local identites into identities like the self.

Consequently, Chinese-styled development in effect takes into account the distinction Buber made between 'genuine' and 'pseudo' listening: '[i]f one is to relate truly to another, one must truly [i.e. genuinely] listen to the other: relinquish stereotypes and anticipations of the other, and allow oneself to be shaped by the other's response' (Yalom, 1980: 365). Since for effective development, 'genuine listening' to local actors involved is important, not 'pseudo', the Western-styled adherence to a thick form of relationality largely fails because it is seen as patronising. Conversely, Chinese actors have more often implemented effective development, both in China and in African countries, because they tend to genuinely listen to and adapt to local actors. It is exactly this that makes it so difficult to ontologically fix any kind of 'China Model'. Hence, this proposal for the relational (re)making of the 'China Model'.

As a result, rather than unilaterally being able to explain the behaviour of all Chinese actors on the African continent, effective

Chinese-styled development (as opposed to ineffective) might actually serve as an ideal to strive for, not only for Chinese actors, but also for Western ones.

Conclusion

This chapter zoomed in on development practices by Chinese actors in both China and in African localities. It then zoomed out to illustrate the broader patterns of Chinese-styled development, proposing a relational (re)making of the 'China Model'. In a nutshell, relationality in development is highlighted by the adaptation of Chinese development practices, which are anchored in relatively vague guidelines on how development should be conducted, to the visions of development by African actors by genuinely listening to them. Consequently, effective development in a specific locality is constituted by an intermingling of African and Chinese agencies. In practice, the Chinese agency/ies involved here often play an enabling function, making development along local visions possible where it was not before. From a Chinese perspective, however, this provision of the means for development can be perceived as 'gift-giving', which has as its goal the establishment of long-term reciprocal relationships. Nevertheless, from African perspectives, particularly the population (as opposed to elites), Chinese-funded projects are not always seen that way, leading to severe criticisms of specific development projects and, by extension, 'China' as a whole. This is further illustrated in Chapter 6 by Kilaka, and in Chapter 8 by Sambo and Bußler in this volume.

That said, perceiving Chinese-styled development practices in African countries as more relational can shed new light on the analysis of both Chinese and other development practices. By being both 'relational' and largely based upon 'non-Western' practices and epistemologies, it contributes both to the relational turn in IR as well as Global IR. That said, a limitation of this short chapter is that it could only paint Chinese-styled development with a rather broad brush. Further empirical evidence for this form of development is, however, provided in the chapters by Kilaka, Sambo and Bußler, and Gambino and Bagwandeen in this volume. Still, more work is needed to theoretically and conceptually develop such Chinese-styled development.

Another avenue of future research is to find out the extent to which development as practised by Chinese actors on the ground might actually influence approaches to development by 'Western' actors. Comaroff and Comaroff's (2012) work, namely, suggests that effective development when practised successfully by Chinese actors might constitute the future of 'Western' development rather than vice versa. At first sight, current US President Joe Biden's proposal of the *Build Back Better World* strategy, which essentially seeks to mimic China's Belt and Road Initiative, seems like an example of this. However, although actual practices have yet to be observed, its representation by the White House (2020) as 'a values-driven, high-standard, and transparent infrastructure partnership led by major democracies' that dominantly mobilises private capital seems more like a continuation of the conventional Western adherence to an identity-transforming thick relationality, rather than providing a type of development that 'genuinely listens' to the Other.

Last but certainly not least, more research is needed into the distinct and context-specific nature of the African agencies relationally shaping Chinese development practices on the ground. Questions such as 'what kind of epistemology/ies undergird(s) Tanzanian agency and how is it (re)shaping development in Bagamoyo?' or 'to what extent do Chinese and Kenyan epistemologies co-constitute each other and how does this (re)shape Kenyan visions on development?' provide fertile ground for further research to explore.

3

THE PRACTICES OF INDIAN AND BRAZILIAN INFRASTRUCTURE BUILDERS IN AFRICA

Barnaby Joseph Dye,[1] *Mathias Alencastro and Ricardo Soares de Oliveira*

Introduction

2016 marked a turning point for Indian and Brazilian infrastructure financiers and builders in Africa. Actors from both countries became increasingly established over the preceding decade, with state finance supporting a raft of firms entering or expanding across the continent. By 2015, India had lent USD 6.7 billion through its state-owned Exim Bank, with 161 projects spanning the continent, including Ghana's Presidential Palace, Rwanda's largest dam and international electricity transmission lines.[2] Meanwhile, Brazil had lent USD 2.9 billion to African states by 2013, with most investments going to Mozambique and Angola. In the latter, the Brazilian infrastructure giant Odebrecht was the largest private-sector employer for much of the decade. Its projects in Angola include Africa's then joint-largest dam,[3] airports and roads. Moreover, state-owned banks and companies from both countries supported further infrastructure schemes, including Sudan's major oil pipeline, financed by the Indian state-owned oil company,[4] and the Brazilian-orchestrated Mozambican Tete mining mega-scheme involving a new railway and port, known as the Nacala Corridor (see Chapter 8 by Sambo and Bußler in this volume). However, by 2016, Brazilian and Indian infrastructure-construction programmes were beset by corruption allegations and accounts of malpractice (Alencastro, 2020; Cezne, 2019; Dye, 2022a, 2022b). These were an order of magnitude bigger in Brazil, fuelling a wider political crisis that saw the fall of the Workers' Party (PT), entailing a rapid retraction of Brazil as an infrastructure player in Africa. India, in contrast, saw a changing of the guard. The companies previously dominating the governments' infrastructure-finance schemes were effectively banned and replaced by more established firms.

What remains remarkable is the limited degree of academic literature on either of these significant trajectories. Whilst Chinese companies, finance and political strategies are well researched, India and Brazil have built a significant profile of infrastructure lending and finance that remains largely under the radar. For example, the China Africa Research Initiative at Johns Hopkins University and the AidData programme at the University of William & Mary provide reliable and comprehensive datasets of China's engagement with Africa and, in the case of the latter, other developing countries. Meanwhile, a growing number of case studies examine the details of Chinese actors' operations and construction practices, for instance on the governance and impacts in dam projects (Hensengerth, 2013, 2018; Olorunfemi et al., 2017; Owusu et al., 2017; Chen and Landry, 2018; Yankson et al., 2018). Equally, there is a growing literature examining African agency in relations with China (Mohan and Power, 2008; Brautigam, 2011; Power, Mohan and Tan-Mullins, 2012; Mohan and Lampert, 2013; Chiyemura, 2019; Soulé, 2020). This was an important antidote to analysts placing 'Africa' as a passive continent unable to shape policy choices, ignoring the important role of political elites, civil society, migrants and communities. Indeed two of the authors of this chapter have argued elsewhere that this is under-appreciated in the literature on Brazil's ties with Africa, that too often the focus is on the Brazilian state, the agenda of President Lula and his Workers' Party, but not enough on how elites in Africa were key solicitors of investment and crucial shapers of its relative success (Dye and Alencastro, 2020). However, this stress on African agency can be taken too far, obscuring the inequality between elites and citizens in Africa and the structural constraints on governments on the continent (Phillips, 2019; Dye, 2022a) Gaps also remain in the literature on the 'Southern' powers' relations. This chapter contributes to filling three of these.

The first point contributes to the book's argument that there are significant differences between countries often lumped together under labels such as the Global South or rising powers. These labels can have academic merit in some contexts, but they can also hide key differences between the types of actors and the national political-economic relationships involved. Empirically, we demonstrate significant contrasts in the role of the state versus the private sector, and in the histories, investments, actors and political drivers involved in India's and Brazil's infrastructure-building in Africa. In the Indian case, a historically embedded diaspora and a longer history of trade and private-sector investment place corporations as key drivers of infrastructure-building on the continent. The Indian government has tended to play catch-up, providing an important, albeit somewhat passive, enabling role. In contrast to India's gradual rise and apparent foreign policy consensus, Brazil underwent a dramatic see-saw in relations and investment on the continent. This stems from the state's far more prominent role and the lack of embedded foreign policy consensus in the political elite. There is consequently a different balance of agency between the state and private sector, with activist companies leading development cooperation for India versus an activist Brazilian state working in partnership with an enthusiastic private sector. We also highlight the important differences in the size and experience of private-sector firms involved in infrastructure-building. For Brazil, large, established mining and infrastructure firms, chiefly Vale and Odebrecht, were at the forefront of realising the government's Africa policy. In contrast, for India, the first decade of the state's concessional credit scheme was dominated by inexperienced and initially small, or new, companies. This reinforces the argument for this book's globalities approach (see Chapter 1), which aims to capture the complexity and intersecting geographic levels of transnational 'Southern' infrastructure relations.

Our attention to the private sector is central to our second argument that stresses the importance of moving beyond state-centric analyses of South-South relations in Africa. As stated in this volume's introduction, the relations of Southern powers in Africa have too often remained singularly focused on the nation states as the key actors negotiating infrastructure and other investments. States are centrally important but we argue for a rebalancing in favour of treating corporations as key actors in their own rights, as capable of initiating investment deals, and as key players determining planning and implementing practices. For example, the new jack-of-all-trades firms that bagged the majority of Indian state-financed infrastructure schemes from 2004 to 2014 were frequently learning on the job, which affected infrastructure quality at times. Brazil's constructors were large, internationalised firms that built close, often corrupt, relationships with recipient governments and the Brazilian state. For both countries' African relationships, this attention to firms is important given their role in making key decisions about how projects were implemented and thereby about the outcomes of infrastructure construction for people, the environment, and the economy.

Our third assertion calls for greater appreciation of domestic state–society relations in the 'donor' country. There is an understandable tendency to address the global level of international deal-making and donor countries' foreign policy, or focus on recipient states and the particular places where infrastructure 'lands'. This book, for example, contains case studies of an infrastructure's locale affecting the national and international politics. These three geographical scales are important, but this chapter, alongside that by Bunskoek, demonstrates that political agendas and relations in the 'donor' country also require assessment. Bunskoek, regarding China, asserts the importance of the domestic relations to Chinese firms' practices abroad. We similarly find that political agendas and relations 'at home' determined the trajectory and practices of Indian and Brazilian infrastructure-building in Africa. This point is most overt in the shifts occurring around 2015–16. Political turmoil and electoral turnover that brought alternative political parties to power in both countries altered foreign policy in different ways, whilst corruption scandals discussed in the media created a backlash initiating policy transformation. In Brazil, in what became known as the Lava Jato (Car Wash) scandals, criminal prosecutions and a popular revolt against the questionable interweaving ties between businesses and political elites, forged through infrastructure investments in African and Latin American economies as well as in Brazil itself, resulted in shockwaves across the political landscape and the virtual withdrawal from overseas infrastructure projects. The new political establishment then largely abandoned development cooperation with Africa. Meanwhile, in India, a change in the companies receiving state finance occurred after a corruption scandal. Additionally, practices changed as a new government altered the degree of planning and qualifications necessary for corporations receiving infrastructure financing. Unintentionally, this led to a fall in infrastructure financing. Thus, 'domestic' political strategies and state–business relations are immutably tied to the international: experiences and relationships within both the financing and the 'recipient' countries interplay to forge the policies, actors and practices of South-South infrastructure projects.

The next sections flesh out these three points with comparative analysis of Indian and Brazilian infrastructure-building in Africa. We argue for an analytical approach that appreciates the multiple political geographies, incorporating the global with national decision-making in Brazil and India, alongside details of specific infrastructure project sites. We first trace the trajectories, key actors, and policies of each country with regard to the subsidised financing and constructing of infrastructure on the continent. The following section turns to examining the agency of the private sector in each case and the evolution of Indian and Brazilian infrastructure in Africa. This chapter is supported by eight years of research. The study of Brazil in Africa encompasses fieldwork in Angola from 2010, including in the northern regions where Odebrecht operated Angola's foremost kimberlite mine and the capital Luanda. All the authors have also conducted interviews in São Paulo, Rio de Janeiro and Brasília to reconstruct the trajectories of public- and private-sector Brazilian actors in Africa. To study India–Africa relations, the chapter draws on research conducted since 2012, featuring statistical analysis of governmental data on trade and financing of

India-Africa, and interviews with ministerial advisers, diplomats, civil servants and policy researchers in Delhi and Mumbai. Given the authors' focus on tracing the politics of policymaking amongst the relevant governments and companies, research followed a qualitative approach that used process tracing to construct a detailed understanding of events, actors, decisions and rationales. This more inductive approach was additionally necessary given the research subject, which included often sensitive investments and infrastructure projects and extractive activities. Our approach enabled a research nimbleness necessary in politically controversial contexts where data availability is limited. The triangulation of multiple sources and types of data is then necessary in the analytical process to ensure rigour.

Trajectories of Indian and Brazilian infrastructure construction in Africa

The following section highlights the contrasting trajectories of India and Brazil as major infrastructure builders. This analysis highlights India's steadier trajectory of engagement with Africa, where important shifts occur under broad policy continuity. Conversely, Brazil saw a rapid surge in infrastructure financing under the first two terms (2003-10) of President Lula of the Workers' Party. However, this governmental support was not strongly embedded in the wider political class and was abandoned after the Workers' Party's departure from power in 2016 amidst the Lava Jato corruption scandal that particularly harmed the infrastructure firms that were central to the Africa policy. The sections below also detail the contrast between the small, essentially new infrastructure firms of India, who took a majority share of state-infrastructure finance until 2015, against Brazil's larger corporate players.

India's steady rise as an infrastructure builder in Africa

India rose as an infrastructure builder in Africa through two mechanisms. The first involved the state's concessional lines of credit which are crucial for infrastructure that typically needs subsidised lending to pass economic feasibility tests. These subsidised financial arrangements have their roots in South-South cooperation, an agenda to support other newly independent former colonies with mutually beneficial loan deals (Mawdsley and McCann, 2011; Dubey, 2016). The earliest concessional credit line was confirmed in 1948. They were then incorporated into India's formal policies of South-South cooperation, to be made on an ad hoc basis through an officially agreed programme, initially with the government's State Bank of India, replaced by the Indian Exim Bank in 1982. Together, they made 83 loans to 23 developing countries between 1966 and 2005, totalling USD 498.56 million (Saxena, 2016).

However, with the turn of the twenty-first century, the government decided to scale up the amount of subsidised credit, introducing a single, standardised loan facility in 2003. By 2005 it had been fully institutionalised as the Indian Development and Economic Assistance Scheme (IDEAS).[5] From 2004 to 2020, the IDEAS scheme lent approximately USD 9.7 billion to Africa, the largest regional recipient of the scheme that is open to all developing countries.[6] Of these loans to Africa, most went to infrastructure projects, which received USD 6.72 billion, and of these, the largest sectoral recipient was the power sector, comprising 42% of the share (see Figure 3.1).

SECTORAL BREAKDOWN OF EXIM BANK
LOANS TO AFRICA

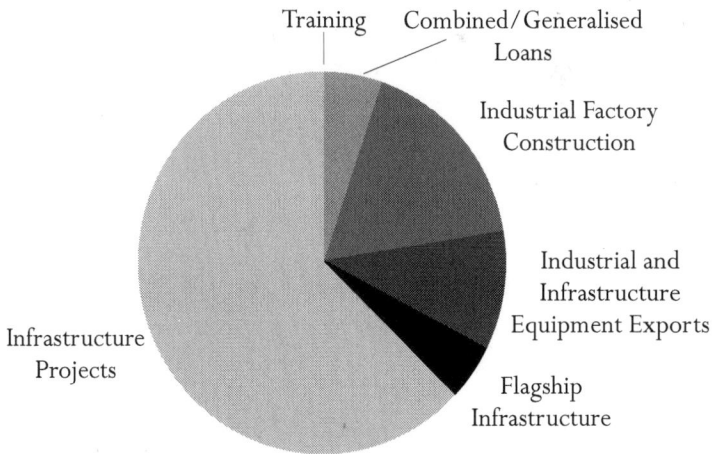

Figure 3.1: Infrastructure and infrastructure equipment 2004–20.

Source: Statistics from the Indian Exim Bank

The IDEAS scheme was publicly affirmed through the rhetoric of South-South cooperation (Modi, 2011), which justified the scheme's mutual benefit, with loans mandating Indian content (Dubey, 2016; Saxena, 2016; Dye, 2022a). India's strategic concerns drove the lines of credit (LoCs) push. Of primary importance was the Ministry of External Affairs (MEA), which provides the loan's subsidy from their budget and manages the process of approval. The MEA seeks to use the IDEAS to build ties with other governments and thereby boost support for policy goals like the reform of the United Nations Security Council, favourable trade governance and India's appointment to key positions in international organisations.[7] Additionally, Indian governments have expanded Exim Bank funding to support the internationalisation of businesses and exports, boosting the economy. Indian officials and businesses additionally sought ties with Africa given its increasing potential as a source for natural resources, particularly oil, and as a growing market for agricultural and pharmaceutical goods (Dye, 2022b). Thus, the Ministry of External Affairs is a key actor in India's infrastructure rise, instituting this key policy alongside its subsidiary Development Partnerships Administration that handles loan administration. They work closely with the Exim Bank to decide the terms for loans, conditions attached—primarily focused on Indian content—monitoring procedures and evaluation and reporting requirements. However, beyond the broad desire to support international business and particularly economic relations with Africa, the state plays a relatively passive, albeit crucially underpinning, role.

This left open-ended the practices by which Indian cooperation would work and the governance oversight of specific projects. To understand why individual projects came to involve India, and to understand the planning processes of projects, we must turn to the corporations themselves. The private sector had been lobbying the government for greater international support after a wave of internationalisation in the 1990s that accompanied the Indian state's liberalising of trade and investment regulations. Private-sector federations, and in particular the Confederation of Indian Industries and Federation of Indian Chambers for Commerce & Industry, are particularly important actors. They secured government funding from 2003 to facilitate new business ventures in Africa through the 'Focus Africa' programme, for example. As Taylor and two of this chapter's authors argue elsewhere (Taylor, 2016; Taylor, van der Merwe and Dodd, 2016; Dye, 2021b; Dye and Soares de Oliveira, 2022), India's private sector started significant investment and business operations before the government's twenty-first-century strategic interest in the continent. Perhaps the foremost example here is the Tata conglomerate, which built mining and car sales operations from the 1970s, giving the firm an established presence in countries like South Africa and Zambia. This enabled Tata to pick up infrastructure contracts, including the Itezhi-Tezhi Dam in Zambia. Additionally, Indian firms are heavily involved in the extractive sector. ArcelorMittal (which is Indian-owned, but headquartered in Luxembourg), for instance, has iron mines and processing plants in South Africa and Liberia, whilst Jindal Steel and Power owns coal mines in Mozambique, Botswana and South Africa.

These companies, as established international conglomerates, draw on international finance for their operations, often alongside Indian state banks and Exim Bank. Moreover, most of these mining ventures in Africa are not considered especially strategic by the Indian state, and there has not been any coordinated governmental concerted support. For example, the Indian government did not undertake public or high-level advocacy for Vedanta's copper mine when the Zambian government eventually forced its exit in 2020, or for Tata's stalled mining projects in Madagascar and Côte d'Ivoire.[8] These corporations involved in extractive activities constitute a significant proportion of the infrastructure associated with India on the continent, given their involvement in roads, railways and industrial machinery. This often involves Indian infrastructure companies such as Shapoorji Pallonji, Larsen & Toubro, Sterling & Wilson and Afcons. For example, the latter were involved in ArcelorMittal's Liberia mine. Therefore, these infrastructure activities occur largely out of the orbit of the state.

In addition to these private firms, state-owned corporations involved in infrastructure have expanded across Africa. The main example here is Bharat Heavy Electricals, which built power plants for oil, gas and hydropower stations. Additionally, government-owned coal and oil companies have struck deals, including oil-for-infrastructure agreements. Major examples here include ONGC Videsh Limited (OVL), the overseas arm of India's major oil company, constructing a USD 2 billion pipeline to Port Sudan (Patey, 2011). Additionally, in Mozambique, Indian state-owned firms Bharat Petroleum, Oil India and OVL are part of the consortium with concessions for off-shore gas and the contracts to develop off-shore gas platforms, a port and refinery. For both these private and state-owned ventures, state banks have been an important source of funding. The State Bank of India, for example, partially finances the aforementioned off-shore gas development, and Jindal's African ventures.[9]

India's engagement therefore fits a pattern whereby the state provides underlying financial support for private companies, who are then positioned as key drivers finding opportunities in Africa, getting deals over the line and building ties with recipient governments. Notably absent are Indian governmental officials and political leaders. The independence and strong drive of the private sector is further confirmed by the case of four companies that came to dominate the Exim Banks' IDEAS loans before 2015, being involved in approximately 60% of the LoCs from 2003 to 2016: Angelique International, Overseas Infrastructure Alliance (OIA), Jaguar Overseas and Lucky Exports. They are interesting given their limited previous experience in the infrastructure sector and general platform model that saw firms engage in disparate types of infrastructure. Angelique, for example, had its origins in an export business but started engaging in infrastructure in the 2000s through two Indian-financed dam projects in Afghanistan and Rwanda, then moving to build an IT park and water treatment facility in Tanzania (Confederation of Indian Industries, 2018; Dye, 2021b). OIA, for example, got contracts for a sugar factory, water supply project and rural electrification, but was only formed in 2005. This is a more extreme example than Bunskoek's case (see Chapter 2 in this volume) of Chinese state-owned enterprises that, whilst being large infrastructure firms, also undertook types of projects in Africa for which they had little direct specific experience.

The domination of the four firms, Angelique, OIA, Jaguar and Lucky Exports, of the IDEAS scheme, and the engagement in such a broad range of projects, was possible because of these firms' active practices. They would undertake unsolicited bidding and pursue memoranda of understanding with the recipient governments before the involvement of an Indian state. Governments in Africa would then submit a line-of-credit request to an Indian embassy, which then handed it to the MEA to approve. Indian firms sometimes went on to support preparation and planning and potentially lobbied the Indian government to speed along projects, but they could be assured that approval would eventually come. This is because approval for an Exim Bank deal has consistently come before the content of a proposal is reviewed; the MEA makes the call based on its political priorities, and with closer ties to Africa as a target, virtually no projects have been rejected (Dye, 2022a).

Table 3.1: List of key Indian infrastructure companies in Africa

Type of Infrastructure Company	Key Company Names	Notable Infrastructure Project Contracts
Larger Established International Infrastructure Companies	Tata (and subsidiaries Tata Africa and Tata Power)	• Zambia: Itezhi-Tezhi Dam
	Shapoorji Pallonji	• Ghana: Presidential Palace • Niger: International Convention Centre • Ghana: Railway line
	Afcons (subsidiaries of Shapoorji Pallonji from 2000)	• Ethiopia: Transmission lines and interconnectors • Mauritius and Gabon: Ports
	Larsen & Toubro	• Ethiopia: Transmission lines and interconnectors • Mauritius: Light transit project
	Econo Services (India)	• Wastewater and sewage treatment

Type of Infrastructure Company	Key Company Names	Notable Infrastructure Project Contracts
	International Consultants and Technocrats	• Various countries: Work on engineering design and feasibility studies (often for detailed project reports in the Exim Bank process)
	J. P. Mukherji & Associates	• Uganda: Sugar processing plant • Ethiopia: Sugar and biomass plant
	Jain Irrigation Systems	• Ethiopia: Finchaa sugar plantation
	Kalpataru Power Transmission	• Multiple equipment and construction contracts
	KEC International	• Also involved in transmission
	Praj Industries	• Tanzania: Distillery plant • Malawi: Ethanol plant
	Sterling & Wilson	• Guinea: Sheraton Hotel • Sierra Leone: Hilton Hotel • Power equipment supply through subsidiary
	Transrail Lighting	• Ethiopia: Transmission lines
	Uttam Sucrotech International	• Sudan, Ethiopia and elsewhere: Sugar factory construction
State-owned Infrastructure Companies	BHEL	• Libya, Sudan, Rwanda and Burundi: Power plants • Ethiopia: Sub-contractor in biomass plant

Type of Infrastructure Company	Key Company Names	Notable Infrastructure Project Contracts
New General Platform Companies	Angelique International	• DR Congo, Rwanda and Burundi: Dams • Tanzania: Water treatment plant • Kenya: Electrification • Mali: Transmission lines, IT park
	Jaguar Overseas	• Zambia: Health facilities • Zimbabwe: Power plant renovation • CAR: Two hydropower projects
	Lucky Exports	• Tanzania and Rwanda: Electrification projects
	Overseas Infrastructure Alliance (OIA)	• Ethiopia: Two sugar factories, transmission lines • DR Congo: Electrification

Source: Compiled from public sources and Confederation of Indian Industries (2018)

Shifting practices in response to experience: A change of the guard

However, the four smaller firms ran into controversy, resulting in a change to the LoC policymaking process and the companies involved in infrastructure. This change is significant as it evidences our argument about the intertwined nature of the domestic and international in state-backed infrastructure financing and its practices. Alongside successes, a number of the projects contracted to Angelique, OIA, Jaguar and Lucky Exports failed to reach construction, suffered major delays or faced questions over their quality. Some factors were beyond the firms' control, such as the violence in the Central African Republic that stalled two dams, but other problems stemmed from difficulties negotiating relevant project approvals, problems acquiring finance and resources or the lack of instituted quality control measures. The Nyabarongo Dam in Rwanda was, for example, Angelique's first major African venture and the scale of recruitment they needed to conduct to undertake the project delayed work. Additionally, sections of the dam had to be redone because of quality control issues (Aecom (RSW Inc), 2015; Dye, 2022a). Elsewhere, OIA's sugar factories in Ethiopia were flooded during construction, reportedly due to poor design, meaning that work had to be redone.[10] Projects involving the larger, established, experienced firms also faced issues in some cases. Whitfield (2018: 173) records a USD 35 million factory in Ghana that was not sufficiently capitalised and had insufficient land to supply materials for manufacturing, causing the project to stall within a year. Another example concerns an irrigation project in Rwanda with the Indian state consultancy WAPCOS. It received IDEAS finance of USD 120 million in 2013–14 but is yet to be completed.

The practices of India's infrastructure in Africa, and their potential to cause delays and quality concern, worried Indian diplomats and strategists. A key purpose of state-subsidised finance was diplomatic—to build closer ties with governments on the continent. Additionally, it was intended to internationalise infrastructure firms, establishing their activities and reputation. If infrastructure projects were low quality, these goals would be undermined. These fears were furthered by concerns raised by African delegates to the annual India–Africa coordination forum. Interviewed diplomats reported African counterparts raising concerns, particularly about the timeliness of LoC projects.[11] These issues came to a head in late 2015. Exim Bank, the government agency handling this concessional credit, raised a 'red flag' over the role of the smaller, inexperienced firms receiving most loans to Africa. This was picked up in the press and led to public speculation about corruption. Indeed, in February, a few months later, India's Enforcement Directorate raided the homes of former ambassador Deepak Vohra. He worked with the largest of the four companies, Angelique, to secure contracts in Africa. Although no cases were pursued in India, the World Bank later blacklisted Angelique given evidence of corruption in Ethiopia (*The Economic Times*, 2018).

Concerns were therefore raised on both sides of the Indian Ocean and the suspicion of scandal pushed an evolution of the finance programme. A new set of regulations in November of 2015 for IDEA LoCs focused on improving the technical quality and timeliness of projects, with funding for project conceptualisation, policies instituting greater scrutiny, an open and competitive tendering process, and close project monitoring (Ministry of Finance Department of Economic Affairs Bilateral Cooperation Division, 2015; Saxena, 2016; Dye, 2022b). This evolution demonstrates the way bottom-up processes, informed by experience, public media and political pressures, filter up to decision-making processes in infrastructure projects.

Elections also appear to have influenced the post-2015 changes. After 2016, the four, newer, less-experienced infrastructure firms received no new Exim Bank finance. This is somewhat surprising as, from a technical perspective, by 2016, the four had built operational networks in Africa and had experience of delivering infrastructure on the continent. In some cases, they had delivered more projects, and had a wider geographical footprint, than larger internationalised Indian firms like Larsen & Toubro and Tata. Interviewees therefore explained the exclusion of these firms as a political motive,[12] with reports that Angelique and OIA, in particular, were backed by financiers from the Congress Party. With a new Bharatiya Janata Party administration arriving in 2015, the implementation of the new 2015 rules may have been conducted to damage the rival Congress Party's funding. Again, this demonstrates the different geographies in the making of India–Africa infrastructure. Domestic party-political concerns and foreign policy strategy combine with domestic impressions of what has happened in Africa to influence government policy. African states' concerns also fed into the rationale for the LoC policy change.

Overall, this underlines the argument that the domestic context in both 'donor' and 'recipient' countries forms a major driver for Southern powers' Africa ties and the way they evolve. Political strategies concerning development practices, elections, and foreign policy in both countries combine to shift policy and therefore actors and activities. Infrastructure financing therefore has many interlocking geographical levels. Moreover, evidence here underlines the importance of the private sector to India's infrastructure-building in Africa. They are the actors who are largely responsible for driving the financial support provided by the Indian state through open-ended subsidised LoCs to infrastructure projects. Indian firms have pursued infrastructure construction independently of the Indian state. The private sector, not just the Indian government, is consequently key for initiating, implementing, and negotiating India–Africa relations. The de facto and de jure policymaking of the Indian LoCs therefore demonstrate a disconnect between the public rhetoric of South-South cooperation, of development-focused governmental assistance, and a more complex and corporate reality of infrastructure-building drivers and actors. Analysis here also highlights the important variety in this active corporate group with state companies, established firms, those working through India's diaspora, and new start-up, inexperienced firms.

Brazil's concentrated infrastructure boom in Africa

The triangle of companies, politicians and financiers in Africa

Brazil's infrastructure-building in Africa contrasts with India in terms of the trajectory it has taken, the actors involved and the practices of finance and project governance. These practices again underline the degree to which policymaking and domestic politics in the 'donor' country combine with other geographical scales to shape infrastructure projects. Unlike India, the Brazilian infrastructure sector saw consolidation in the second half of the twentieth century resulting in the establishment of four powerful conglomerates that played a comparably important role for the state, such as Odebrecht, Camargo Corrêa, Andrade Gutierrez, and Queiroz Galvão. Their internationalisation has been supported by two key institutions, the Brazilian Development Bank (Banco Nacional de Desenvolvimento Econômico e Social (BNDES)) and state-owned Banco do Brasil. Originally named BNDE, the bank was created in 1952 to finance domestic projects aimed at accelerating 'national development', under instructions from the Ministry of Planning. From 1974, the Bank's focus expanded to include the private sector alongside public corporations and, in 1982, was rebranded BNDES to incorporate a social dimension into its mandate. However, it was only in 1994 that BNDES began funding exports, as part of a broader liberalisation programme implemented by the Fernando Collor de Mello (1990–92) and Fernando Henrique Cardoso presidential administrations (1994–2002). During that period, the BNDES support for foreign operations was conducted indirectly on an ad hoc basis. The Financing Programme for Machinery and Equipment Exports (Programa de Financiamento às Exportações de Máquinas e Equipamentos), set up in 1991, and later renamed BNDES–EXIM, supported specific projects including infrastructure schemes such as electro-mechanical components for the Three Gorges Dam in China. The other major institution involved in financing such exports and supporting the internationalisation of Brazilian firms was the Banco do Brasil. However, Banco do Brasil was also primarily focused on Latin America. Thus, in the 1990s, Africa barely appeared in either bank's strategy.

The administration of President Lula and the Workers' Party (Partido dos Trabalhadores, PT) rapidly changed Africa's importance in Brazil's foreign policy from 2003. Under PT rule, all state institutions were instructed to build ties with Africa, whether through development cooperation, knowledge exchange or by supporting corporate internationalisation. Between 2003 and 2010, trade between the two regions expanded more than six-fold, increasing from USD 4.9 billion to USD 26.5 billion. During the same period, Lula made 33 official visits to African states and, in order to achieve a stronger diplomatic presence, 19 new embassies were opened on the continent. Lula's government essentially exported Brazilian social and infrastructure practices to countries in Africa. Cooperation projects used the same agencies, whether in health or agriculture, in Africa. Flagship initiatives included the Cotton-4 initiative with Mali, Chad, Burkina Faso, and Benin, the establishment of an African outpost of the leading agricultural research institute Embrapa, and health agency Fiocruz extended domestic programmes, for instance around maternal health (Seibert, 2019b). Thus, Brazilian actors assumed they could simply use the same techniques and economic models as they used domestically. These practices were publicly affirmed in the language of South-South cooperation, emphasising solidarity, non-interference, and the importance of multipolar global governance, in common with longstanding principles of the Non-Aligned Movement and institutions like the G77 (Milani and Klein, 2021). This rhetorical framework, and the building of international strength through ties with developing countries, has featured as a prominent school of thought in Brazil's foreign policy since 1988, resulting in the creation of the Brazilian Cooperation Agency (ABC) under Brazil's foreign ministry, the Itamaraty (Seibert and Visentini, 2019; Dye and Alencastro, 2020).

The other major export from Brazil was infrastructure, always a key component of the Africa policy, receiving the most resources. The first major actor here was the state-owned Banco do Brasil. It has a longer history in Africa and specifically Angola, as it created Brazil's first foreign oil-for-credit deal to fund Odebrecht's construction of Angola's Capanda dam in 1984. This expanded, with the bank hosting two routine credit lines for the country by 1988, one short-term, 180-day loan, for financing consumer goods between USD 50 million to USD 90 million; and another medium-term, five-year loan for capital goods between USD 60 million and USD 120 million, such as infrastructure equipment and machinery (Ribeiro, 2008). Both were part of an oil-backed deal whereby Angola could repay Brazil's state-owned Petrobras with petroleum. The bank's activity expanded under the Lula administration with the *Internacionalização* programme for expanding corporations, launched in 2005. Lending reached a peak in 2006 of USD 248 million, with a total of USD 1.4 billion lent between 1997 and 2009, but this rapidly dropped off after 2007, crashing from USD 189 million to just USD 32 million in 2008 (Viana, 2016).

This decrease occurred because BNDES took over the key financing role, domestically and internationally. Between 1999 and 2006, 92% of the operations of the BNDES were directed to capital goods and only 8% concerned infrastructure but this flipped so that by 2014, the latter accounted for half of the BNDES portfolio.[13] The bank's international ventures began in 2002 when Fernando Henrique Cardoso's government approved new directives. It was furthered by an internal task force, formed in 2000, which concluded that even companies established abroad needed 'financial, operational and technical' support to continue internationalisation (Além and Cavalcanti, 2005). BNDES made three types of credit line available to Brazilian companies, one for foreign direct investment, and another for export trade finance, whilst the BNDESPAR, a subsidiary of the BNDES, provides corporate investment.[14] At first, such finance primarily went towards Latin America, and was that region's largest regional lender by 2007 with an investment volume of USD 14 billion.[15] However, the PT government directed the bank to contribute to its Africa policy and so, by 2007, lending grew to Africa, from USD 200 million annually in 2005–06 to almost USD 600 million annually in 2007, and more than USD 1 billion annually between 2009 and 2014, with the exception of 2010.[16] Angola far outpaced the other major African recipients, Ghana and Mozambique, with a total of USD 3,273 billion. This amounted to 31% of all BNDES international loans between 1998 and 2019 in contrast to Mozambique and Ghana, that took a combined share of 3%.[17] Two thirds of the Angolan loans went to Odebrecht, which received USD 2.4 billion. Elsewhere, BNDES financed an airport hangar, market and national road in Ghana to Mozambique's Nacala airport. Additionally, BNDES opened a USD 3.5 billion line of credit for agriculture in Ghana and Mozambique, particularly targeting biofuels and including the Northern Sugar Resources scheme with USD 260 million to plant 30,000 hectares and a sugarcane plant built by Odebrecht. As Table 3.2 demonstrates, construction companies therefore dominated the BNDES's export finance to Africa, with spending on infrastructure thereby taking pole position amongst the flow of resources from Brazil to Africa.

Table 3.2: Listing BNDES operations and spending in Africa

Country	Company	Number of Operations	Total Spending (USD millions)
Angola	Odebrecht	43	2,455
	Andrade Gutierrez	14	277
	Queiroz Galvão	18	314
	Camargo Corrêa	8	203
Mozambique	Odebrecht	2	124
	Andrade Gutierrez	1	64
Ghana	Contracta	2	17
	Andrade Gutierrez	1	137

Source: Compiled from BNDES public sources

The balance of state and private-sector agency

As the analysis above suggests, the state was key to this extension of finance for African infrastructure and thus played a major role in determining the process of finance extension and its (limited) governance. The decision-making process starts with negotiations between the Brazilian company and the foreign partner. Once concluded, the Brazilian partner approaches BNDES, and if it meets competency tests and fits operatives from the Ministério do Desenvolvimento, Indústria, e Comércio Exterior (MDIC) (Directives for Foreign Trade Policy), the proposal is passed to the Brazilian Committee for the Financing of Exports (COFIG). Created in 2004, COFIG is the technical body responsible for approving loan parameters (interest rates, subsidies, timelines and guarantees). They then submit an opinion to the Council of Ministers of the Chamber of External Commerce (Camex), which is composed of ministerial-level appointees and gives final political approval, with Banco do Brasil providing the interest rate subsidy. By controlling the appointments to these committees, and by sending out directives, the government pushed BNDES to ramp up financing of infrastructure companies in Africa. This drive overrode technical analyses drawn up by these committees, with the Parliamentary Inquiry Commission on the BNDES identifying several instances where COFIG and Camex recommendations were overturned.

There was therefore a strong political directive to boost infrastructure financing for Africa and funnel it particularly to the 'national champion' infrastructure firms. This political support extended beyond financing, with Brazil's diplomacy instructed to find projects for companies to engage in. This is detailed, for example, by our analysis of efforts to establish Brazilian firms, chiefly Odebrecht and Quiroz Galvão (Dye and Alencastro, 2020; Dye, 2021a), in Tanzania. Seibert and Stolte (Stolte, 2015; Seibert, 2019b) also assert the importance of presidential and ministerial trips of Brazilian and African leaders, because of their ability to generate meetings between corporations, BNDES and African counterparts (Stolte, 2015; Dye, 2021a). The Brazilian state was therefore an active facilitator and initiator for infrastructure in Africa, largely overlooking the developmental positive and negative impact of projects in the rush to find and implement any project.

Such support continued, albeit not at the same level, after Lula left office in 2010. President Dilma Rousseff pushed a diversification of BNDES beyond Angola, and with the aim of spreading beyond Lusophone Africa, resulting in a new Africa strategy and regional office in Johannesburg in 2013. A key priority for BNDES was Mozambique, where Brazilian mining conglomerate Vale had just made a major investment in the coalmines of Moatize, Tete Province. In 2013, Rousseff met with Mozambican President Armando Guebuza to discuss a USD 320 million credit line for the construction of the Moamba Major dam. Internal Camex documents[18] show Fernando Pimentel, then Minister of MDIC, approving the loan against the advice of BNDES representatives. Again, this underlines the degree to which BNDES finance was enrolled in a political project, aggressively backing infrastructure companies to internationalise.

The balance of state to private-sector agency is therefore different here compared to the Indian case. Internationalising infrastructure firms specifically across Africa was a deliberate, politically led drive, which Brazil's 'big-4' infrastructure firms willingly embraced in a partnership with the state. The big-4 responded to the state's push and invested significant resources, time and energy in engaging in infrastructure ventures across the continent, including projects that did not reach implementation (e.g. the dams in Tanzania (Dye, 2021a)). An active government thus worked in tandem with companies, lubricated by state-subsidised finance without significant governance oversight or examination, on the Brazilian side, of what the finance was contributing to. This stands in contrast to India's more private-sector-led infrastructure-building, as does the concentration of Brazilian support on a small group of larger, established infrastructure companies. Unlike Indian firms' independent initiatives, there is a relatively equal balance of agency between companies and the state in driving initiatives, with the corporations working with African governments to determine the process of implementation and pattern of benefits.

However, there is one major example of corporate initiative leading cooperation: Odebrecht in Angola, sub-Saharan Africa's second largest oil producer. Odebrecht's leaders built close personal ties with President Dos Santos's Movimento Popular de Libertação de Angola (MPLA) and as Angola came out of a civil war in 2002, Odebrecht worked with the MPLA regime to deliver a state-building strategy that spent significant petro-dollars on an array of reconstruction and development projects (Soares de Oliveira, 2015). The company implemented a range of strategic projects, from irrigation schemes and large hydroelectric dams to housing projects and the creation of a supermarket chain (Stolte, 2015; Seifert, 2016; Croese, 2017; Dye and Alencastro, 2020). Angola's elevated position was recognised internally in Odebrecht's bureaucracy, where it was incorporated into their Latin American division, rather than the smaller African unit, and the Odebrecht family owners held annual meetings with Angola's former President Dos Santos. Thus, officials in Brazil commented that Odebrecht had closer insider knowledge of Luanda than Brazil's embassy,[19] something also observed in fieldwork.

Rather than seeing this as a major exception, Odebrecht–Angola could be seen as one of the models that the Brazilian state sought to develop in Africa, where a company would fully integrate into the political project of the host state. That degree of integration was never achieved by the other big-4 infrastructure firms, nor by Vale in Mozambique, although Queiroz Galvão attempted this in Ghana. Moreover, the Brazil–Odebrecht–Angola case demonstrates that regardless of external states and private sector, African states still retain a significant degree of agency. Thus, agency is not necessarily a zero-sum game; on the contrary, the Brazilian government and particularly its subsidised finance, and the Angola state, reinforced each other via the investments made by Odebrecht. This tripartite description of agency underlines an important contribution of the chapter: the need to tease apart the multiple agencies spearheading infrastructure investment in Africa.

The collapse of Brazil–Africa: Combined international and domestic drivers

Unpacking agency also reveals important differences between India and Brazil. Brazilian cooperation is smaller overall but also more geographically concentrated in Lusophone countries. The role of corporations is also distinct, with a more even balance of agency and initiative with the state. An activist government and diplomacy pioneered Brazil's infrastructure-building in Africa, but companies then acted on the state's initiative, investing in project planning, contract negotiations and then construction. Private and state agencies were therefore relatively balanced, in contrast to the degree of Indian firms' independence.

Brazil also markedly differs from India because of the collapse in governmental relations and corporate activity since 2016. This has earlier roots as, despite noteworthy efforts such as the opening of the BNDES Africa office in Johannesburg, Brazil's diplomatic drive to Africa began to decline under Lula's successor Dilma Rousseff (2011–16); (Marcondes and Mawdsley, 2017; Alencastro and Seabra, 2021). This decline in attention accelerated under President Michel Temer (2016–18), with Africa practically disappearing as a foreign policy agenda under President Jair Bolsonaro (2019–22) (Coletta, 2021). This has roots in the degree of state activism and particularly the presidentialism of Brazil's foreign policy. Historically, the country's diplomatic priorities have swung between different presidents, with some favouring relations with the USA and Europe, and others seeing Brazil's strategic interest lying in Southern alliances, in South America, Africa and the BRICS (Seibert, 2019a; Dye and Alencastro, 2020). The PT administrations were strong advocates of the latter, but governments since 2016 reverted from a focus on South-South relations, cutting development-cooperation spending, closing embassies in Africa and focusing attention on the USA, especially during the years of President Trump (Lopes, 2020; Casarões and Barros Leal Farias, 2021). Given the leading role of diplomats and ministerial visits in sustaining the Africa push and expanding ties beyond a select number of Lusophone countries, the swing of foreign policy priorities against Africa markedly reduced activity in Africa, including in infrastructure investment.

The collapse was exaggerated in the case of Brazil because of the degree to which the PT's Africa policy essentially extended their domestic political-economic strategy. For the Lula government, raising Brazil's profile on the continent was seen as a complement to its domestic agenda of reducing inequality, which involved poverty reduction policies and affirmative action for the country's large Afro-Brazilian population (Gala, 2019). Given the different power bases of right-wing governments this voting constituency has not figured significantly since the PT. This demonstrates the degree to which foreign policy principles are weakly institutionalised in Brazil, and therefore swing in different directions under different governments. Such an abrupt change stands in contrast to India, whose elite and diplomatic service appear more unified in foreign policy priorities and clear priorities.

Another element that led to the depth of withdrawal post-2016 was the effect of the Lava Jato corruption investigation on the four main infrastructure companies that were key to the Africa policy, namely, Odebrecht, Andrade Gutierrez, Queiroz Galvão and Camargo Corrêa. They were tasked with implementing the domestic programme of large infrastructure-building, also with BNDES funding. This relationship paid off, with the companies becoming key financial backers for the PT for the first time, alongside the other main political parties. Thus, Brazil's political economy was partly defined by an 'iron triangle'—whereby politicians, state finance and corporations worked hand in glove to pursue institutional and personal benefits. Such relationships bled into corruption. The Lava Jato investigations revealed the close nexus between all of Brazil's major political parties and the four big infrastructure firms, which involved an implicit bargain involving illegal kickbacks and legal political donations in exchange for infrastructure contracts and finance at home and abroad. Although BNDES has never been implicated explicitly in corrupt deal-making, its finance was a key element in these implicit bargains. The Brazilian state wasn't the only important actor here, with the Lava Jato investigations showing how Odebrecht forged similar corrupt deals around the world. Angola was perhaps the foremost example. The company's close ties to the Angolan presidency gave it an advantage over competitors, with the Angolan state lobbying Brazil to rapidly approve finance through established oil-for-credit agreements, arguing that it would otherwise turn to geopolitical rivals like China.[20] Odebrecht then supported Dos Santos's presidency by rewarding the ruling elite after the civil war with sub-contracts in infrastructure projects. As Chief Executive Officer Emilio Odebrecht stated, Dos Santos asked the company to help 'recycle generals into entrepreneurs' and incorporate his allies in local business deals (Alencastro, 2020). Thus, a relationship of convenience became well established, with vast infrastructure projects serving domestic and international agendas for Brazil and recipient states like Angola.

Revelations of these relationships were a key trigger for dwindling political support and popular unrest, which in turn facilitated the downfall of the PT and resulted in key PT figures being arrested, not least President Lula, despite implicating almost the entire political class and revealing that opposition parties were involved in a greater volume of corrupt deals. The corruption allegations thus resulted in a dismantling of the policies, which had underpinned Brazil's infrastructure-building at home, and in Africa. The big-4 infrastructure companies were forced to retreat under severe negative public perceptions, with senior leadership arrested and record fines levied. BNDES was forced to temporarily suspend infrastructure finance for a time and end loans to Africa.[21] Additionally, significant for Brazil–Africa was the political change within Angola's ruling party in 2017, from President José Eduardo dos Santos to current incumbent President João Lourenço, which dented Odebrecht's pre-eminence given the company's deep personal ties to the former regime (though the company is now experiencing something of a return to high-profile activity in Angola). Infrastructure project practices rested on 'iron-triangle deals' that spanned international borders, but eventually unravelled, causing further erosion of Brazil's presence in Africa.

Beyond these linkages in the practices of infrastructure project financing and decision-making and between domestic policies and political economy relations with infrastructure-building in Africa, similarities and crossovers occur in critiques of Brazilian infrastructure and in networks of resistance against these projects. As in Brazil, the four infrastructure firms were conscious of socio-environmental impacts, something learnt especially from Amazonian mega-dams. Corporate social responsibility efforts used 'at home' were replicated internationally. For example, Odebrecht officials, in interviews and through media presentations, demonstrated their spending on mitigation policies and corporate social responsibility initiatives, such as housing, livelihood, and training schemes for those displaced by the Belo Monte Dam in Brazil, the Lauca Dam in Angola, and infrastructure associated with the Vale Tete mining project in Mozambique.[22] However, such experience and longer-standing international operations did not result in these companies having necessarily positive, developmental impacts—as Odebrecht's Nacala airport has been little used since construction (with two commercial flights per week in 2017) and Mozambique defaulted on the airport's loan in 2017.[23] Moreover, Odebrecht played an instrumental role in the revival of a dam in Tanzania's World Heritage Site, the Selous Game Reserve, despite experts warning the project would end the site's Outstanding Universal Value given its ecological destruction (Dye, 2017). Odebrecht carried out feasibility studies and design assessments for the dam, which is now under construction, albeit by Egyptian companies. Another notable episode is the successful 2014 lawsuit[24] accusing Odebrecht of human trafficking and of maintaining workers in slave-labour conditions in Angola. This reinforced the impression that Odebrecht had a poor human-rights record in Africa, with widespread displacement and negligence of environmental impacts. Such outcomes replicate controversies in Brazil, with Amazonian infrastructure, including large dams, like Belo Monte, having major socio-environmental impacts and questionable development impacts (Fearnside, 2014; Atkins, 2020). Indeed, the Amazon's Belo Monte Dam, the Mozambican Tete mine, and Tanzanian mega-dam have all been critiqued for specific common practices, including insufficient assessment and mitigation of social and environmental impacts and insufficient benefit-sharing with affected peoples. In the Mozambican case there were some joined-up campaigns by African and Brazilian civil society, but overall, such instances of collaboration and solidarity are rare (see Waisbich,[25] including Chapter 4 in this volume).

Conclusion

In conclusion, this article has analysed the trajectories of Brazil and India as infrastructure financiers and builders in Africa. These two countries have been frequently overlooked in the literature, which has focused on studying China (see Chapter 1 by Hönke et al., as well as Chapter 2 by Bunskoek). Our analysis demonstrates major shifts taking place in 2015 to 2016 in both countries' infrastructure-building in Africa, in terms of the volume of finance invested, the governmental policies and the actors involved. We also demonstrate important differences between the two countries in African infrastructure. The balance of agency between the state and the private sector, for instance, varied significantly between Brazil and India. The government played a key role in Brazil–Africa infrastructure, initiating a major set of financing and diplomatic activities because of foreign policy, internationalisation and economic growth objectives. The agenda pushed BNDES and the wider Brazilian state to aggressively support infrastructure ties with Africa, a mission that large corporations fully embraced: an activist state worked in tandem with activist companies, fuelled by subsidised finance. This more equal balance of state–private sector relations contrasts with India. The Indian state has been comparatively passive, with the historically embedded business diaspora playing a key role. Financial support by the state, chiefly through the IDEAS scheme, crucially underpinned infrastructure projects, but private companies have tended to lead the push towards infrastructure as opposed to other types of cooperation, and have forged the specific deals with governments in Africa.

The comparative study of India and Brazil brings two further lessons for the study of South-South relations. First, the private sector must be treated as an actor in its own right. State-centric analyses often omit that companies consistently play a key role in determining and implementing practices (see also Chapter 1). Second, given this importance of the private sector, the public-spirited rhetoric of mutual development cooperation hides a more private-sector reality. Private companies lead the initiation or implementation of Indian and Brazilian ties. Third, as other chapters also show, the political geographies of infrastructure-building in Africa travel through multiple, entangled layers that take in the strategies devised in offices in São Paulo or Mumbai, the corridors of power in capital cities and financial market centres, as well as within and around individual construction sites. As demonstrated above, domestic governmental strategies and political relations are reflected in the policies and practices of South-South cooperation. This is most overt with Brazil, where its policies for Africa essentially exported domestic economic growth and poverty-reduction policies. Thus, the deals struck with infrastructure companies domestically transcended national boundaries, with corporations securing contracts in exchange for kickbacks to politicians and their parties. This is also true for the impacts of infrastructure projects and protests against them, with dissonance between Brazilian discourses on corporate social responsibility and poverty reduction contrasting with the lived impact of projects in the Amazon or Tete Province, Mozambique.

PART TWO

CONTESTATIONS

4

SOUTH-SOUTH COOPERATION
MONITORING MOVEMENTS

ENGAGING SOUTHERN POWERS IN AFRICA
'FROM BELOW'

Laura Trajber Waisbich

Civil society mobilisation is a longstanding feature of international development cooperation politics. Transnational civil society campaigns have widely acted upon and contested large infrastructure projects in developing countries, notably those backed by international financial institutions and multilateral development banks (Fox and Brown, 1998; Park, 2019). Similarly, civil society-led 'aid monitoring movements' (McGee, 2013) have also contested development finance and assistance led by Northern/Western governments to promote development elsewhere in the Global South, and particularly in Africa. Activism within so-called (Northern/Western) 'traditional donor countries' of the Development Assistance Committee of the Organisation for Economic Co-operation and Development was aimed at shaping development aid policies and initiatives, influencing its geographical and sectorial priorities, as well as promoting greater aid transparency and accountability towards taxpayers at home and towards local communities in partner countries in the South (Eyben and Ferguson, 2004; Jensen and Winthereik, 2013; McGee, 2013).

With the (re-)emergence of South-South cooperation (SSC) in the early 2000s attention has also turned to social mobilisation in the context of Southern powers' rise as global development actors, with greater interest in their footprint in Africa (e.g. Pomeroy et al., 2016; Chichava and Alden, 2017; Cezne, 2019; Yeophantong, 2020; Shipton and Dauvergne, 2021; Waisbich, 2021b). This chapter contributes to this bourgeoning field by investigating SSC accountability-related mobilisation by civil society organisations (CSOs) from Brazil, China and India in domestic and transnational arenas in the 2010s, many of which in partnership with African actors or in relation to Africa-based initiatives. It provides a comparative analysis of the framings and repertoires used by Brazilian, Chinese and Indian civil society actors, and the issues citizen-led action brings to the forefront. Methodologically, the chapter relies on scholarship and documental analysis, on interviews and participant observation conducted in the three countries, as well as in global policy arenas, between 2017 and 2020.[1]

The focus on social mobilisation dynamics in the context of SSC contributes to understanding the ways citizens demand and forge alternative citizen-led forms of participation and political control over this burgeoning political field of state action, policies and/or practices within Southern powerhouses. While doing so, it connects the SSC-related mobilisation dynamics to evolving state–society relations in the context of foreign policymaking in the three countries, and to the broader African infrastructure globalities unpacked in this edited volume.

Three particularities of this study must be openly discussed before moving forward. First, the present chapter focuses on the intricacies and sociopolitical dynamics of pro-accountability national and transnational mobilisation by civil society actors in/from Brazil, China, and India. More often than not, this mobilisation happened in partnership with other civil society groups in Africa and beyond.[2] The explicit focus on *mobilisation dynamics* and on *civil society groups from/in 'rising powers'* departs from (as much as it complements) other studies looking at contestation spatially situated in/around projects in Africa (see Chapter 5 by Sändig and Hönke, Chapter 6 by Kilaka, and Chapter 8 by Sambo and Bußler).

Second, any analysis on civil society mobilisation must consider the different meanings, manifestations and practices it takes in Brazil, China and India, beyond the more frequently mobilised (Western) assumptions of civil society as a separate political and social sphere and their liberal-democratic mobilisation practices. Any given time, space and context-sensitive analysis on SSC-related social mobilisation dynamics should also acknowledge the diversity of state–society relations across the three countries due to variations in political regimes and historical sociopolitical trajectories (see Waisbich, 2021c) and the always evolving state–society relations (both in terms of the shirking and opening of civic spaces) in all three countries.[3]

Finally, it is also important to recognise the limitations of (primarily/exclusively) tracing 'organised' civil society activism in Brazil, China and India, which is by no means exhaustive of the variety of contentious politics in and around SSC. Additional forms of citizen contestation include social mobilisation led or driven by African stakeholders *in* Africa (see, for example, Chichava and Alden, 2017; Shipton and Dauvergne, 2021; (see also Chapter 5 by Sändig and Hönke, Chapter 6 by Kilaka, and Chapter 8 by Sambo and Bußler)[4] and popular citizenship politics such as citizens' online activism (for a discussion on online activism inside China, see Ma, 2019; Waisbich, 2022).

The chapter offers three main contributions. First, new forms of social activism on Southern-led development cooperation have emerged. Social mobilisation reflects not only conflicting worldviews and preferences of a range of social actors on SSC projects and policies, but also the unfolding negotiations between states and citizens over rights and/or entitlements to accountability in this particular policy field. These accountability-related negotiations speak to broader constructions of citizenship and to the evolving agreements on the social contract in a particular time, space, and policy realm (Grant and Keohane, 2005; Hickey and King, 2016). Second, the chapter argues that while some particularly contentious development cooperation initiatives have generated cross-regional campaigns that connected civil society groups from Brazil, China and/or India to peers in other Global South countries, notably in Africa, intense mobilisation has taken place at the policy level, at home. Third, the chapter shows how civil society groups adopted a continuum of 'insider–outsider' mobilisation strategies and 'collaboration–confrontation' modes of engagement with national 'SSC bureaucracies' and implementing actors (public entities and public/private companies) while having to reinvent strategies to engage Southern powers in the terms of their SSC initiatives. The most prevalent mode of engagement in Brazil was 'critical collaboration' and 'friendly critique' in India. In turn, China-based groups pursued 'constructive engagement' with the Chinese state and companies, largely around the environment–development nexus of China's global footprint.

In the coming sections I first discuss the emergence of 'SSC monitoring movements' in Brazil, China and India. Next, I provide a comparative analysis of the main mobilisation dynamics across the three countries in and around development cooperation in Africa. In the concluding section, I locate these instances of mobilisation in the context of SSC inside Brazil, China and India as part of broader discussions around participating in foreign policymaking and shaping rising powers–Africa relations in the twenty-first century.

The 'SSC boom' and the rise of SSC monitoring movements

SSC has gained in political, material and symbolic importance in the last two decades (Mawdsley, 2012; Gu, Shankland and Chenoy, 2016). This expanded role has, at the same time, generated new forms of development cooperation politics and new social expectations (from domestic and foreign constituencies) on the so-called 'Southern providers', particularly the larger ones like Brazil, China and India (see Chapter 1 by Hönke et al.).

Emerging debates and social activism in and around Southern-led development cooperation reflect not only the worldviews and policy preferences of a range of social actors, but also unfolding negotiations between states and citizens over rights and/or entitlements to accountability in this particular policy field. These accountability-related negotiations reflect broader constructions of citizenship and the always evolving agreements on the contours of the social contract in a particular time, space and policy realm (Grant and

Keohane, 2005; Hickey and King, 2016). Development cooperation, and foreign policy more broadly, are policy fields with their own citizenship dynamics, their own forms of negotiated entitlements to explanations, justifications or redress, and their own expectations of 'good', 'just' and/or 'appropriate' state behaviour (Hill, 2003; Eyben and Ferguson, 2004; Waisbich, 2021a). How these rights, entitlements and expectations play out in the context of SSC, I contend, responds to a series of confounded dynamics. First, the disputed and incomplete institutionalisation of SSC in most Southern countries, including Brazil, China and India (Waisbich and Mawdsley, 2022). Second, the uneven and contested nature of development in these 'SSC champions' and the interconnectedness between social expectations on the state role in promoting development at home and abroad (van der Westhuizen and Milani, 2019; Waisbich, 2021a). Third, the nature and practices of interaction between actors within rising powers (including governments, civil society and businesses) and governmental and non-governmental actors elsewhere in the Global South, and in this case in Africa (see Chapter 5 by Sändig and Hönke).

In the early days of SSC (re-)emergence, in the 2000s, rising powers' global development ambitions received strong support from several domestic constituencies: from domestic businesses to rights-based and development groups (Mawdsley and Roychoudhury, 2016; Shipton and Dauvergne, 2021). Many CSOs hoped rising powers' diplomatic rhetoric to reform global governance would (or could) bring about greater 'justice among states' but also 'justice within states' (Mawdsley, 2014a). They also expected Southern-led development cooperation in Africa to be different (and better) than traditional North–South development aid. As official SSC engagements increased, however, tensions and contradictions became more visible and civil society groups adopted more critical engagement with, when not in open resistance to, official Southern-led development cooperation initiatives.

Social mobilisation in and around SSC expanded significantly throughout the 2010s. Civil society groups based in (or working on) Southern powerhouses came together—in more or less formal national and transnational networks—to try shaping the policy-institutional frameworks for managing and delivering SSC, influencing SSC initiatives on the ground, and participating in policy debates around development cooperation and foreign policy (Pomeroy et al., 2016; Waisbich, Pomeroy and Leite, 2021). SSC monitoring movements, as I label them, emerged as key actors in demanding greater transparency, accountability and participation in the context of South-South relations, in particular with Africa. They did so by building—to employ a notion widely used in participatory studies—'spaces for participation' (Gaventa, 2006) and spaces for the contestation of SSC policies and projects at the national and transnational levels. These spaces had to be crafted both emulating and departing from existing mobilisation and participation repertoires found in the so-called 'North–South cooperation'.

From 'aid monitoring movements' to 'SSC monitoring movements'

Social mobilisation in 'traditional/Northern donor' countries, often in partnership with groups in 'Southern/recipient' countries, has been an integral part of the development cooperation landscape since the 1990s. Social mobilisation challenged the purposes and impacts of North–South development aid, contested projects negatively impacting on the lives and livelihoods of local populations and championed greater transparency (in particular budgetary transparency) in the sector through the use of information technologies and information politics as a tactic (Jensen and Winthereik, 2013; McGee, 2013). Among most Northern/Western aid donors, civil society groups crafted spaces for participation along the intertwined policy realms of foreign policy and development assistance, usually gravitating towards the latter. Indeed, throughout the twentieth century, development assistance grew as an autonomous policy field within Northern/Western countries with specialised 'aid bureaucracies' (Lancaster, 2006). Despite the recent wave of institutional changes and mergers of foreign relations and development cooperation bureaucracies in countries like Australia, Canada and the UK, civil society international development accountability-related mobilisation in most 'traditional aid donors' is still largely shaped by somewhat aid-specific policy dynamics. There are well-defined aid-related budgets, programmes and institutions, and even aid-specific accountability mechanisms, such as the UK Independent Commission for Aid Impact, Japan's non-governmental organisation (NGO)—Japan International Cooperation Agency Desk, or the World Bank Inspection Panel.

In this context, social mobilisation within aid donors has often revolved around three major understandings of donorship-related state duties and responsibilities. First, domestic accountability to taxpayers in donor countries for spending in development abroad. Second, international accountability to global non-binding commitments donor countries agreed on, notably the 0.7% of gross national income target for their official development assistance. Third, legal and para-legal responsibility for 'doing-no-harm' and eventually redressing socio-environmental damages and misconducts incurring from development projects abroad.[5] Mobilisation and participation dynamics in large SSC providers exhibit, nonetheless, their own set of underpinning accountability logics. CSOs based in rising powers had to develop their own ways to engage Southern providers in the particularities of their (re-)emerging global developmental roles.

Monitoring rising powers' global development footprint in Africa

An important feature of SSC monitoring movements is the interconnectedness between foreign policy and SSC in the context of the engagement in Africa of major Southern providers, like Brazil, China and India. Networks of activists across Brazil, China and India have joined existing global 'aid monitoring groups' and used the political opportunities provided by transnational networks (Keck and Sikkink, 1998; Tarrow, 2005) to boost SSC/foreign policy-related advocacy at home and in partner countries. Africa has been a major site for this transnational activism. The African continent not only harbours an ever-expanding multidimensional presence of rising powers (Alden, 2019; Moyo, Yeros and Jha, 2019; also see Chapter 1 by Hönke et al.) but is also the quintessential site of attention and concern for many in the international development industry (Roy and Crane, 2015).

During the early 2000s, CSOs from Brazil and India (and to a lesser extent from China) have actively participated in global 'Aid Effectiveness' debates alongside many others in Asia, Africa and Latin America. Around the same time, some organisations also turned to monitoring their own countries' foreign policy and development engagements abroad, with great attention to their participation in what many called a 'new scramble for Africa'. Their activism benefitted from a surge in global attention to (and even obsession with) BRICS countries (Brazil, Russia, India, China, South Africa) (Gomes and Esteves, 2018; Zarakol, 2019) and to the (potential and actual) negative impacts of BRICS-led major infrastructural development projects in countries and communities elsewhere in the Global South (Mohan, 2014; Moyo, Yeros and Jha, 2019). In countries like Brazil, monitoring development cooperation and its negative impacts in the region and in Africa also fed into growing civil society mobilisation around 'democratising foreign policymaking' (Cabral and Leite, 2015). Activism there revolved around foreign policy (and Brazil–Africa relations) as much as around development and development cooperation per se (Waisbich, 2021b).

Debunking SSC myths: Transparency, accountability, and participation claims

Social mobilisation by CSOs in Brazil, China and India monitoring their countries' official development engagements in other Southern countries combines transparency, accountability and participation claims.

Demands for transparency have been a central tactical 'rally point' (Gheyle and Ville, 2017) and sometimes even 'the lowest hanging fruit' for activism in and around rising powers-led development cooperation. The lack of transparency and participation of the Mozambican communities affected by the triangular agricultural development programme ProSAVANA (jointly implemented by Brazil and Japan in Northern Mozambique, see Chapter 8 by Sambo and Bußler) were major issues for the 'No to ProSAVANA' transnational campaign from the start. Civil society groups from Brazil, Japan and Mozambique denounced, for instance, the absence of official communication on the project to local communities in Nampula and the mismatch between the information publicly available and what was being shared with potential investors (Shankland and Gonçalves, 2016). Transparency claims were used not only to support civil society claims (in the three countries) around a right to participate in project design but also to dispute the meaning of South-South and triangular agricultural cooperation. Mobilisation over project transparency reinforced civil society contestation of ProSAVANA's overall agricultural transformation model, based on concerns with land displacement and resettlements.[6] Advocating for greater transparency was equally important for activists as a discursive tool to unveil and challenge a perceived 'state–capital nexus' driving the project and Brazilian SSC more broadly (Aguiar and Pacheco, 2016; Durán and Chichava, 2017; Funada-Classen, 2019). By doing so, anti-ProSAVANA mobilisation echoed global debates on agricultural development opposing smallholders / family farming and agribusiness on both sides of the Atlantic, as well as on land-grabbing and the Green Revolution in Africa (Shankland and Gonçalves, 2016; Milhorance and Bursztyn, 2017).

Transparency was also a major entry point in the case of mobilisation related to national and multilateral Southern-led development banks. Brazilian and Indian groups exhorted national public banks, such as the Brazilian Development Bank (Banco Nacional de Desenvolvimento Econômico e Social, BNDES) and India's Exim Bank, to abide by the highest transparency and socio-environmental standards when granting national companies credit to export services and implement projects abroad (Sierra and Hochstetler, 2017).[7] Civil society activism on the Shanghai-based BRICS-led New Development Bank (NDB) also perceived the issue of transparency as a major priority.[8] Transparency (i.e. disclosure policies and public availability of project documents) was both a goal in itself and a prerequisite for CSOs to be able to influence and participate in NDB's decision-making processes during its set-up phase and first operational cycle (2016–20). Fighting for greater transparency was strategic to activists from BRICS countries and their peers in other parts of the world also interested in shaping the 'BRICS bank' in order to open up dialogue with NDB since its inception while waiting for projects to be actually implemented on the ground (Waisbich, 2021a). It was also a necessary entry door for CSOs to initiate the dialogue and enable other procedural and substantial issues, including participation in decision-making and the negative impacts of NDB-funded projects on local communities, to emerge.

Moreover, activists have also mobilised around (and denounced) what they saw as SSC-specific transparency politics. In Brazil, the non-monetary/non-grant nature of SSC technical cooperation exchanges made Brazilian development cooperation with other Southern countries almost invisible in national policy debates and budgets and thus very hard to track (Lopes and Costa, 2018). Along similar lines, in India, the economic and trade-based South-South exchanges (conceived to foster the internationalisation of national companies and services) were deemed not easy to discern and account for in national budgets and policy debates (Mitra, 2018).

Overall, the way the transparency issue has been framed and claimed in the context of SSC, particularly for Brazilian and Indian organisations, has revolved not only around the more traditional budgetary concerns with 'taxpayer money being spent abroad' but also around a 'right-to-know' and a 'right-to-participate' in (foreign/SSC) policymaking. Such an approach relates to the very nature of SSC as a policy field in these countries, which is not necessarily perceived by domestic constituencies as 'unchecked large sums of taxpayer-funded grants' to help beneficiaries abroad or meet international poverty alleviation obligations (as in the traditional aid policy debates within Northern/Western donors). The reasons for that are manifold. First, the fact that South-South exchanges are not exclusively about aid-like 'concessional grants' and are moreover coated in official 'mutual development'/win-win cooperation' narratives. Second, the lack of internationally agreed-upon financial obligation from 'Southern providers' towards meeting global poverty alleviation targets (Bracho, 2017). Third, the (so far) invisibility of SSC flows and initiatives in domestic politics in the three countries, making it a subject mostly for professionalised CSOs rather than the general public (Cabral and Leite, 2015).

As for participation claims, the very notion of participation in the context of SSC exchanges encompasses several distinct country-specific expectations on state–society relations and civil society practices. As a result, civil society groups have claimed and negotiated participation in SSC differently across the different countries and within countries depending on the nature of the issue or the civil society coalition. While civil society demands to act as implementers of official SSC initiatives on the ground, including in Africa, were present in the three countries (Waisbich, Pomeroy and Leite, 2021), claims to participate in policymaking were more visible in Brazil and India, though these are equally growing within China. When challenging specific initiatives located in African frontier zones, claims to participation in policymaking meant having local communities ('in the other Southern country') being consulted about and having a say on initiatives immediately affecting their lives and livelihoods. This was the case of Brazil's ProSAVANA programme, Brazilian giant Vale's mining operations in Mozambique, or the China-funded Lamu coal-power plant and port in Kenya (Cezne, 2019; Njunge, 2019; Lesutis, 2020; Shankland and Gonçalves, 2016; see also Chapter 5 by Sändig and Hönke, Chapter 6 by Kilaka, and Chapter 8 by Sambo and Bußler). In other cases, such as in the context of NDB-related advocacy efforts, participation meant having a seat at high-level policymaking tables (Waisbich, 2021a).

Different conceptions of participation and different perceptions about the normative and strategic value of institutionalised participation (in other words, of seating at the table with 'SSC bureaucracies' and policymakers) impacted on the tactics and repertoires employed. Brazilian and Indian CSOs adopted what Mdlalose and Thompson (2018) termed 'tree shakers and jam makers' mobilisation strategies and carved, not without tensions, both (insider) institutionalised spaces for dialogue with those in charge of SSC initiatives and (outsider) autonomous spaces for contesting when not resisting them. Chinese organisations, on the other hand, have mainly adopted an insider and largely non-confrontational approach, along the lines of 'embedded activism' (Ho, 2007), to carefully foster a space for their (critical) participation on perceived safe(r) issues such as the ever-growing 'green agenda' in China's international relations (Waisbich, 2022).

India is the country where CSOs have secured the most formalised space for participation. In 2013, the Indian Ministry of External Affairs (MEA) through its affiliated think tank Research Information System for Developing Countries (RIS) created the Indian Forum for International Development Cooperation (FIDC). The Forum came to existence a year after the set-up of India's development agency, the MEA-affiliated Development Partnership Administration. FIDC has worked since as an 'invited space' (Gaventa, 2006), hosted by RIS, that gathers key representatives of MEA and of a selected group of CSOs' representatives and academics.[9] While some FIDC participants recognise it as a unique space in a context where social participation has become more challenging, others believe the space remains limited and controlled.[10] Other development experts in Indian civil society believe the Forum is somewhat co-opted and insufficiently radical. They believe FIDC is 'too civil', 'too civilised', alluding to other formal governmental-led participation processes, like the C20 (at the G20) or the Civil BRICS (at BRICS Summits).[11] Such critique echoes Chatterjee's (2004: 33) own seminal characterisation of 'civil society' as 'sanitized and palatable' forms of participation in the Indian context, as opposed to other popular forms of mobilisation in what he calls 'political society'. Another critique by outsiders is that FIDC lacks representativeness, as it remains very elite-dominated and reproduces engrained gender and caste dynamics found elsewhere in Indian politics.[12]

Such multi-layered views on FIDC and its value as a participation space illustrate even deeper divisions within the already small group of CSOs monitoring India's global development role (Mawdsley and Roychoudhury, 2016). Diversity in terms of political views and tactics mirror, on the one hand, the plurality of voices and conceptions of development, development cooperation and social participation in India. On the other, divisions were also reflective of evolving political views on whether and how to engage the Indian state under Narendra Modi's Bharatiya Janata Party rule. Altogether, divisions hindered the creation of a larger SSC monitoring movement in India during the past decade. Organisations like Oxfam India, Action Aid

India, VANI, PRIA (as well as informal coalitions like the BRICS Feminist Watch and the People's Forum on BRICS) became leading voices on matters related to India's development cooperation during the second half of the 2010s. They were actively mobilising at the policy level during the 2015 India–Africa Forum Summit and also in the context of particular projects, such as the Indian agricultural investments in Ethiopia (Chenoy and Joshi, 2016; Mawdsley and Roychoudhury, 2016). In the most recent years, however, citizen engagement seems to be fading away. Demobilisation is a result of a combination of factors, including a slowdown in India's official development finance and cooperation since 2017 (see Chapter 3 by Dye et al.), growing domestic social turmoil and pressure over the voluntary sector under Modi's second term (Chacko, 2018), and shrinking international funding for Indian groups to work on and monitor 'Global India'. All together, these factors contribute to further rendering invisible India's development cooperation footprint in Africa among national groups already overburdened with domestic developmental issues.

In Brazil, the coalition monitoring the country's SSC has secured fewer institutionalised spaces for participation but encompassed a wider range of actors and networks (professionalised NGOs, critical academics, social movements, labour unions and/or foundations). These groups tracked different dimensions of 'Global Brazil', including Brazilian multinationals in the extractive industry and agribusinesses, Brazil's bilateral relations with Africa and Latin America, or Brazil's internationalisation of its 'successful' social policies (Waisbich, 2021b). For most of the 2010s, these groups self-identified as a coalition of 'progressive social voices' and acted along the dual line of 'critical collaboration' and 'contestation' of official initiatives (Waisbich, Pomeroy and Leite, 2021). As critical collaborators, activists worked for certain policy issues and policy instruments to be included in Brazilian SSC cooperation (Milhorance and Bursztyn, 2017) and partnered with state institutions (including the Brazilian Cooperation Agency, the BNDES and line ministries) to design, implement and evaluate SSC initiatives. Such 'insider-like' forms of mobilisation had an impact on SSC accountability dynamics in Brazil, as they helped forge and/or strengthen incipient transparency and accountability mechanisms, including official quantification and reporting tools such as the Brazilian International Development Cooperation Report (known as the COBRADI report) or ad hoc external evaluations of South-South cooperation initiatives.[13] As for 'outsider-like' forms of mobilisation, they included open contestation, 'naming-and-shaming', and resistance repertoires, like the 'No to ProSAVANA' or the 'Affected by Vale' campaigns in Mozambique (Durán and Chichava, 2017; Cezne, 2019). Just like in India, activism on international issues, including on the Brazil–Africa agenda, also decreased considerably since 2016, mirroring the retreat of Brazil's official SSC and a growing sense of urgency, among CSOs, to look and work domestically (see also Chapter 3 by Dye et al.).

The breadth and diversity of Brazilian civil society engagement with SSC finds no parallel in the other two countries. It also strongly contrasts with the dynamics in China, where a small group of development and environmental CSOs, China-based international non-governmental organisations, think tanks and independent journalists have been carving spaces for participation around China's 'Going Out' policy and its developmental and environmental initiatives and impacts. Unlike Brazil and India, the trend since the mid-2010s for China-based organisation seems to be upwards. There is a growing demand by Chinese NGOs, such as the China Foundation for Poverty Alleviation, to act as implementers of state projects (Hsu, Hildebrandt and Hasmath, 2016; Qiang, 2019). Besides acting inside China, the foundation currently works in a few countries in Asia and Africa, such as Ethiopia and Uganda. There is also an official acceptance, and even encouragement, by China's political leadership for Chinese civil society to participate in China's official international development initiatives. Xi Jinping's congratulatory letter to the International Civil Society Solidarity Conference on the Beijing-led Global Development Initiative, organised by China-based CSOs in 2022, is an example of a rapidly evolving and somewhat enabling environment for certain kinds of social mobilisation within China.[14]

There are also more and more organisations willing to monitor and participate in 'Global China' policymaking, including in the context of the Belt and Road Initiative (BRI). Chinese and China-based organisations (like the Beijing-based Greenovation Hub, the International Institute for Green Finance, World Resource Institute China and the World Wild Fund for Nature China) have, for instance, secured a place at the Green Belt and Road Initiative, launched by the Chinese government in 2019. This multi-partner initiative, which includes United Nations agencies, academic institutes in China and from overseas, businesses and other partners such as the German development cooperation agency, aims at achieving green development in the context of BRI investments and assisting BRI countries in integrating sustainable development goals-related environment and development concerns into their BRI-related connectivity projects. So far most of the BRI-related engagements are still fairly policy-related and largely concentrated in Chinese / China-based think thanks and research centres. An example is the recently launched Green Development Guidance for BRI Projects (from 2021).[15] Yet, this could potentially evolve to project monitoring on the ground, including in Africa, in case there is appetite for this kind of role among other China-based and / or Africa-based CSOs.

While certainly growing, mobilisation in and around China's SSC initiatives has its own particularities. Contrasting with Brazil and India, Chinese organisations do not advance rights-based advocacy framings, such as the 'right-to-scrutinise' China's international development. They have neither centred their activism on a right to demand state officials to explain policy choices or to gain access to foreign policy-related decisions; nor have they chosen to publicly dissent. Rather, and following the 'embedded activism' paradigm, organisations took longer to mobilise and have cautiously done so by acting closer to the state and framing their role as civic partners helping Chinese state institutions and companies to 'improve' their international development engagements, making them greener and eventually more responsive to local communities' needs (Waisbich, 2022).

Chinese organisations are also latecomers to BRICS/NDB mobilisation, having adopted a very low profile. This is visible inside the Coalition for Human Rights in Development, in the context of the NDB advocacy, but also in the fact that groups in China have had a very limited participation in the more radical BRICS-related grassroots mobilisation by networks of activists under the loose umbrellas of the BRICS-from-below or the People's Forum on BRICS. This is not unique to BRICS-related dynamics, as China-based NGOs have been largely absent from major solidarity campaigns taking place in other developing countries in Asia or Africa against China-led or China-funded initiatives, notably in the extractive sector (Yeophantong, 2020; Shipton and Dauvergne, 2021). Whether this is due to lack of interest or capacity (including political constraints and language barriers), the truth is that without Chinese organisations transnational advocacy coalitions will most probably struggle to navigate Chinese institutions and actors on the ground and back in China, limiting the potential of campaigns for policy and project change (see also Chapter 5 by Sändig and Hönke).

Against all the odds, however, organisations in China have shown growing appetite to build politically safe ways to mobilise around Chinese overseas investments in recent years, notably within China. China's new international development cooperation agency CIDCA might also facilitate this dialogue with certain ('more palatable') civil society groups in China in the years ahead, creating a single focal point for organisations to engage.

Politicising SSC 'from below' and the challenges of speaking 'from within'

How to make sense of more than a decade of mobilisation by SSC monitoring movements in Brazil, China and India and what it can offer as insights of (critical) engagement dynamics both at home and on the ground, alongside African peers?

Despite the many practical challenges faced by monitoring movements to track SSC initiatives on the ground and forge dialogue spaces at home, an important achievement of SSC monitoring movements so far has been at the level of discursive politics. In other words, changing the agenda and the terms of the debate around SSC, notably at home. As mentioned before, pressure groups in rising powers have joined other critical voices, including in/from Africa, to debunk some of the myths around SSC. While doing so they brought politics back to SSC: 'from within' and 'from below', evoking a way of being in the world differently and doing SSC differently (Fiddian-Qasmiyeh and Patricia Daley, 2018;Yeophantong, 2020).

Activism by CSOs based in rising powers, alongside partners in other countries in Africa and beyond, brought to the forefront challenges to policymakers of 'whose demands count' in South-South relations, exposing tensions, fractures and inconsistencies in official SSC 'win-win' framings. In many ways, civil society-led campaigns and advocacy efforts exposed the limits of what Rottenburg (2009) calls the 'official script' that, in the case of Southern providers, equated the differential nature of SSC vis-à-vis traditional Northern-led development aid with its alleged benign effects on the ground (see also Chapter 1 by Hönke et al.). Particularly in Africa, civil society mobilisation made visible the tensions between official South-South narratives around 'horizontality' and 'transferability' and their practices on the ground. It also openly questioned rising powers' own domestic and exported developmental models, be that export-led agricultural transformation or coal-based energy development (Shankland and Gonçalves, 2016; Waisbich, Pomeroy and Leite, 2021; Shieh, 2022).

Social mobilisation revealed, moreover, a range of unfolding national/global social justice battles and their connection to persistent forms of national/global inequalities. Acting on SSC and forging ties with African-based stakeholders allowed for certain domestic issues (such as land dispossession or state and business-driven environmental degradation) to be rendered global and for actors based across the North-South divide to generate common forms of resistance. Civil society challenges to the SSC socio-economic and environmental footprint were seen as part of an interconnected discussion between development and dispossession at home and abroad across the Global South.

This became visible in different project-specific mobilisation instances in the 2010s (be that Brazil-sponsored agricultural and mining activities in Mozambique or India–Ethiopia agricultural partnerships) or regarding infrastructure initiatives funded by Southern-led development finance institutions (including national and multilateral development banks like BNDES, India Exim Bank, China Exim Bank, the BRICS-led NDB, and the China-initiated

Asian Infrastructure Investment Bank (AIIB)). In all those cases, social mobilisation helped create discursive and symbolic bridges between groups self-identifying as 'those who lose' from large infrastructure developmental processes in both rising powers and Africa, as many activists in Brazil, China and India had experienced (or still experience) similar projects at home (Cezne, 2019).

When bringing to the forefront the voices of those 'negatively affected' by certain South-South initiatives, activists explicitly or implicitly asked for 'democratic ownership' of SSC, discursively countering state-centred understandings of 'national ownership' in development cooperation. They did so by positioning themselves in global development debates as critics of both North–South and South-South cooperation. Rather than solely mimicking existing 'aid accountability' framings, repertoires and tools, Southern-based CSOs acting transnationally have generated their own forms of SSC accountability politics.

While their pro-accountability mobilisation generated new dynamics within existing global advocacy networks and new ways to think about accountability in development cooperation, their activism was inescapably shaped by specific power dynamics and dilemmas of speaking 'from within'. Southern activists found themselves having to navigate what they thought were fair political claims about the 'differential' and 'transformative' role of rising powers-led development initiatives (vis-à-vis 'traditional aid') and Brazil, China and India's practices on the ground, which largely deviate from what they believed to be 'good' development cooperation practice or even universal social-environmental justice values.

From a mobilisation tactics point of view, it also meant having to reinvent their own 'theories of change'. Activists had, for instance, to find ways to discuss (national/international) public responsibilities that would resonate with how rising powers conceived their roles and identities in global development. The case of Southern-led development banks lending and/or operating abroad (such as the BRICS-led NDB) offers an example of these tactical challenges. Here, civil society activists—who had historically criticised the World Bank's 'weak' or 'tokenistic' socio-environmental safeguard system—ended up finding themselves taking these safeguards as a benchmark. Indeed, they started to look at existing safeguards systems as a minimum denominator of existing international standards for the newly created Southern-led multilateral banks. This included making project documents available, setting up civil society liaison focal points and consultation procedures, adopting socio-environmental frameworks and operational safeguards to ensure 'doing-no-harm' and creating independent accountability mechanisms where affected groups could file complaints and seek redress.[16]

Besides having to negotiate standards and responsibilities, another set of practical challenges relate to the always evolving, and still very much under consolidation, nature of the policy realm of development cooperation inside large Southern providers like Brazil, China and India. Such an incipient policy field not only creates obstacles for CSOs to forge spaces to engage (and question) state policies and actions but also hinders their ability to use strategic communication. Mobilising the media or general public opinion on SSC-related issues remains complex, as these initiatives are rarely perceived as relevant enough or, worse, as a waste of public resources when there is still a great amount of poverty and inequality at home.[17]

Not unrelatedly, mobilisation around SSC remained limited to specific sections of civil society, which already worked internationally or on international affairs, and to specific issues that fluctuated across the years (Waisbich, Pomeroy and Leite, 2021). While CSOs in Aidland have over time developed a clear identity and mobilised resources to work as 'aid watchdogs', this is not the case for national CSOs mobilising around SSC issues. Brazil-, China- and India-based CSOs (knowledge groups, development and environmental NGOs, rights groups, labour unions, social movements and representatives of 'affected communities') do not necessarily self-identify as 'SSC monitoring movements' or have the means (including human and financial) to institutionalise a work stream around SSC or relations with Africa.

Whereas the more professionalised national groups within rising powers were able to secure funds with existing thematic transnational networks (not uncommonly Northern-led/Northern-funded networks and foundations) to sustain some kind of advocacy work, to monitor the BRICS countries or their development banks' footprint (notably in Africa), others only participated in fewer instances. Overall, engagement has been largely limited to a few issues and instances: BRICS Summits and other high-level summits with African head-of-states (e.g. China–Africa Forum on China–Africa Cooperation or the India–Africa Summit); Southern-led international financial institutions (e.g. the BRICS-led NDB or the China-led AIIB); or project-specific transnational campaigns (e.g. the 'No to ProSAVANA Campaign' in Mozambique and the campaign against Indian agricultural investments in Ethiopia).

Mobilisation around SSC also failed to involve and consolidate stronger and lasting transnational linkages with groups based 'in the other Southern partner', including in African countries. Not only have there been few sustained joint-campaigns, but also Africa-based civil society voices were rarely present in domestic policy debates and in autonomous civil society spaces within Brazil, China and India. The ties between Brazilian and Mozambican organisations were perhaps the major exception to this during the 2010s but even then, there were power imbalances and problematic assumptions about shared struggles and aspirations (Cabral and Leite, 2015; Chichava and Alden, 2017), including a somewhat patronising approach of 'activist coaching' along the lines of 'we need to teach them' how to contest.

A last element of the challenges to re-invent 'theories of change' includes funding for monitoring movements working in/on Brazil, China and India. Southern-based CSOs have decades of experience in participating in global debates, alongside peers and partners from the Global North, and have in many ways successfully navigated the implications of doing so. However, building SSC monitoring movements in the 2010s has generated its own set of politics. Brazil-, China- and India-based CSOs' close connections to, and strong reliance on, foreign funding from the traditional development apparatus created different degrees of governmental resistance and suspicion. Although Southern governments themselves receive funds from industrialised countries to improve their development cooperation systems (see Waisbich, 2021c), SSC monitoring movements' (alleged) proximity to Northern/Western donors was often used to de-legitimise or curb social mobilisation. In different ways, either during the anti-ProSAVANA mobilisation or in the context of recent legal restrictions for not-for-profits to operate in India and China while receiving foreign funding, governments challenged activists' ties to 'the North/West' and accused them of being 'anti-national'. More than ever, over-dependence on 'foreign' (Northern/Western) funds and networks is now a hindrance for Southern-based groups. Hence the challenge to build domestic support for this kind of citizen oversight role within Brazil, China and India and to sustain SSC as a policy and political field in the years ahead.

Conclusion

This chapter has discussed how civil society groups from Brazil, India and China sought to engage and contest official South-South cooperation initiatives in a rapidly growing policy field within rising powers. It revisited emblematic social mobilisation instances since the 2010s to show that pro-accountability mobilisation on SSC initiatives taking place in Africa is inseparable from two sets of policy and political dynamics: mobilisation on foreign policy issues inside rising powers and social disputes over 'development models' (see Chapter 2 by Bunskoek), and over how rising powers share them with other countries in the South.

SSC-related civil society activism by groups based in Brazil, China and India brings to the forefront context-specific questions of social accountability and state–society relations in the context of global development cooperation policymaking in rising powers. Over the last decade, mobilisation has not only engaged with prevalent issues for traditional 'aid monitoring movements' (such as aid measurement, budgetary transparency, development cooperation ownership by 'aid beneficiaries', and 'do-no-harm' approaches) but also contributed to politicising SSC 'from within and from below'. Rendering SSC and rising powers' relations with Africa problematic, from a national civil society point of view, meant questioning the very assumptions of 'horizontal' or 'win-win' cooperation embedded in official narratives around South-South relations, in general, and South-South development cooperation between rising powers and African counterparts, in particular.

These SSC monitoring movements, as I called them here, also represent emerging 'constituencies' for SSC in Brazil, China and India that carry their own inter-subjective perceptions of the growing socio-political and material effects of SSC initiatives inside rising powers. By unpacking the nature of social mobilisation, the chapter underscores that SSC pro-accountability mobilisation has not always grown out of clearly shared expectations by citizens (in Brazil, China and India) of their governments fulfilling international development-related commitments or responsibilities (such as a duty to reduce global poverty or help least-developed countries in Africa). Rather, mobilisation happened out of a sense of social entitlement to engage with foreign policy priorities and impacts on the ground (notably in frontier zones in Africa) and to shape the very content and contours of official development cooperation initiatives.

On the issues of contention, I have suggested that certain SSC modalities have generated more contestation, enabled by the material and political visibility of South-South infrastructure-building and agricultural development, and the role of Southern-led national and multilateral development banks in Africa. Salience in those cases was also due to the presence of transnational networks already mobilised around these very issues *in* Africa. Growing disputes around South-South development finance, particularly for infrastructure-building, points to a direct link between the *materiality* of this form of South-South exchange and its national and global *political salience* (and significance) to a range of stakeholders inside rising powers, in Africa and in other countries. Moreover, disputes related to South-South infrastructure-building abroad, and notably in Africa, were not treated by rising powers-based civil society groups as standalone issues. Rather they fed into broader internal and global policy and public debates on the developmental state, private–public collusion and corruption, or on sustainable/green development models. Through different strategies, civil society organisations in Brazil, China and India have challenged overly optimistic 'win-win' narratives of Southern development finance being able to deliver 'much needed infrastructure' to Africa while also supporting key economic actors or creating jobs inside rising powers. While modest in size and impact and not always capable of penetrating mainstream political and policy debates, these critiques 'from within' and 'from below' are already shaping the debates regarding several SSC initiatives and tend to grow in tandem with SSC's own expansion.

At the same time, the chapter shows variation across the three countries and within countries in mobilisation practices. It highlights that mobilisation has occurred along a continuum of embedded or institutionalised collaboration and contentious politics, with Brazilian and Indian landscapes being more internally diverse than the Chinese one in the ways different organisations engage the state on SSC issues. While some groups aligned with local communities in Africa 'negatively affected' by projects based on transnational solidarity, others employed rights-based policy transparency and accountability language. Many, however, self-identified as watchdogs and even more so as (critical) partners in making Southern-led development cooperation with Africa better. In India, the most prevalent mode of engagement was the one of 'friendly critique', in Brazil of 'critical collaboration' and in China of 'constructive engagement'. In all three countries, however, there are several groups willing to partner with the state and SSC implementing actors to promote accountability reforms, through what Fox and Brown (1998) once described as 'internal-external reformist alliances'. This meant, in all three cases, having to navigate the tensions of acting both through showing disagreement and, at the same time, acting as partners in 'improving' SSC institutions to enhance outcomes on the ground and consolidate the field domestically. This is the case of Brazilian think tanks and CSOs partnering with 'SSC bureaucracies' to improve their development cooperation sectoral policies and monitoring and evaluation frameworks. This is also the case of Indian organisations in FIDC or Chinese NGOs and think tanks working alongside policy banks and companies to improve socio-environmental regulations for overseas operations or partnering with the Chinese government to 'green BRI'.

Finally, the dynamics of social mobilisation analysed here provide a window into the unfolding politicisation and consolidation of SSC, and South-South relations more broadly, *inside* rising powers. They illustrate the socially contested nature of foreign policy in emerging powers and its intersections with Africa's global infrastructures, amidst significant variation in opportunities and tactics for national civil society groups to articulate their expectations and objections, alongside or without peers in Africa. In some cases, like Brazil–Mozambique relations, national configurations and bilateral relations allowed numerous contentious issues to be publicly articulated and disputed. However, this was rather the exception, and many others remained rather invisible in public debates. What is more, after having expanded in the early 2010s, SSC-related social mobilisation itself is going through its consolidation phase. This downturn mirrors the relative slowdown of rising powers' Africa relations due to various national circumstances and the Covid-19 pandemic, but also a reverse in the initial attention to / obsession with South-South relations from 'traditional' donors and 'aid watchdogs' worried about the negative footprint of rising powers in Africa.

This brings a new set of challenges for mobilisation 'from below' from rising powers-based CSOs, alongside their African counterparts, in the years ahead. First, to sustain and expand activism in times of change and uncertainty going beyond the professionalised development and rights-oriented NGOs and increasing the popular basis of domestic SSC-related debates. This is a key element for the continuity of SSC-related mobilisation in the years to come, as most CSOs within rising powers are not exclusively devoted to acting on SSC or Africa-related matters. Rather they seem to advance the identities and *modus operandi* of highly transnationalised social justice groups, which have encountered 'Global Brazil, China and / or India' acting in Africa as part of their work and will keep acting on and reimagining domestic and global justice simultaneously. Second, to connect with local African groups 'negatively impacted/ affected' by Brazil, China and India in a more sustained manner. This is particularly important for China–Africa relations, as the Chinese presence in the continent continues to expand and ties between organisations remain insufficiently developed to be able to exert pressure and influence both sides of the South-South cooperation equation, and to read and navigate China in an increasingly China-dominated SSC landscape.

5

CHALLENGING CHINESE MINING COMPANIES

NGO ADVOCACY PRACTICES AND THE 'BOOMERANG MODEL'

Jan Sändig and Jana Hönke

Introduction

Since 2013, China has been the largest foreign investor in Africa, surpassing the US. Chinese actors spent USD 4.2 billion in foreign direct investment (FDI) to Africa in 2020, which is a striking rise from USD 100 million in 2003 (SAIS–CARI, 2022).[1] These investments comprise headline-grabbing projects from the Belt and Road Initiative (BRI), like the Addis Ababa–Djibouti Railway, the Standard Gauge Railway in Kenya, or Bagamoyo Port in Tanzania. Some involve controversial resources-for-infrastructure swaps, wherein raw minerals are exported to China in exchange for Chinese loans and infrastructure construction. But there are also thousands of small and medium-sized Chinese enterprises in virtually all sectors of African economies (Chen, Dollar and Tang, 2018).

With Chinese investments on the rise, we ask in this chapter how this affects the playing field for activism in Africa and transnationally. Looking at Chinese mining investments, affected communities in Africa regularly complain about issues such as land grabbing, pollution, loss of livelihoods, jobs shortages, and exploitative working conditions. As these problems abound in mining operations in general (Conde, 2017), it is not clear whether Chinese mining projects have worse social and environmental consequences than Western and other Southern mining investments (Irwin and Gallagher, 2013; Wegenast et al., 2019). However, the political context for activism differs in important regards.

For structural differences in political opportunities, there could be a shortage or even absence of contention against Chinese mining investments. Many, though certainly not all, of these investments in Africa occur in autocratic political contexts. The political authorities in these countries often derive substantial revenues from extractive industries and therefore remain unresponsive to local demands and repressive of protest. In such a context, activism has often followed the 'boomerang model' (Keck and Sikkink, 1998): when facing repression and unresponsive opponents (notably including their government), Southern activists usually ask international NGOs (INGOs) for assistance. INGOs, which are mostly from the Global North, then lobby their own governments and/or international organisations on the locals' behalf to exert pressure that will eventually affect change locally. There is ample evidence for the boomerang model in cases of Western companies that operate in the Global South (McAteer and Pulver, 2009; for a critical view see e.g. Waites, 2019). Yet considering that INGOs need leverage over their campaign targets, they prefer challenging companies from their own country and region (Hatte and Koenig, 2020). Hence, INGOs may disregard Chinese investment projects, given the distance to China and the lack of access to the Chinese public and policymakers. Building transnational alliances with NGOs from China also remains difficult. China's NGOs operate under constrained political and civil rights and tend to pursue cautious practices of 'embedded activism' (see Chapter 4 by Waisbich). When action opportunities are closed like this, both domestically and transnationally, advocacy becomes unlikely (Sikkink, 2005).

We therefore interrogate advocacy practices against Chinese investments in Africa, with a particular focus on the mining sector and non-governmental organisations (NGOs).[2] We ask: how do

NGOs respond to the new presence of Chinese miners, and does advocacy affect Chinese business practices? These questions relate not only to advocacy research but also to the still brief literature on how Chinese mining investments become contested abroad (Christensen, 2019; Shipton and Dauvergne, 2021). Relatedly, understudied is how Chinese mining companies respond to contentious actions (SOMO, 2021).

As a case in point, we examine mining investments in the Democratic Republic of the Congo (DRC). The DRC has become the foremost Chinese investment destination in Africa, at an FDI volume of USD 2.5 billion from 2017 to 2020 (SAIS–CARI, 2022). Our focus is on the Katangan Copperbelt in the Southeastern DRC—a key African mining hub with global significance for cobalt mining. Based on acquisitions and new projects, Chinese mining companies now hold most of the mines in the region (Ericsson, Löf and Löf, 2020). To examine how NGOs have responded to this, we draw on NGO documents (reports, petitions, press releases) from online repositories, websites, and social media accounts.[3] Moreover, we rely on recent advocacy research, which has put many of the 'old' assumptions, especially regarding the boomerang model, into question. These studies show how advocacy structures and practices have evolved in our globalised world. Southern civil society[4] has come to the forefront (Fadaee, 2016) and local actions increasingly have global effects (Pallas and Bloodgood, 2022). Northern NGOs are moving towards assisting rather than replacing Southern struggles, which amplifies Southern agency (Schramm and Sändig, 2018). Hence, in many ways the action opportunities have been shifting.

Far from inaction, our case will show significant advocacy efforts against the Chinese mining companies that operate in the Southeastern DRC. These actions do not correspond to the boomerang model: in a repressive setting, which could qualify as domestic blockage, DRC-based NGOs have challenged Chinese mining companies on the ground. At the same time, NGOs from China have not advocated—through the boomerang model—on behalf of affected Congolese people. Instead, we find some of the 'new' modes of advocacy, also including transcalar effects that reach into China (Pallas and Bloodgood, 2022). Yet, the case also illustrates that the world of advocacy has only gradually changed: 'old' advocacy players from the Global North remain important for transnational actions in this case (Prause, 2020). These advocacy pathways reflect political, legal, and economic opportunities as well as constraints within the DRC, China, and the INGOs' home states. Especially within the DRC, advocacy opportunities—and thus actions—regarding Chinese, Western, and other Southern mining companies are appearing, but there are notable differences in the conditions for transnational advocacy. One is the lack of involvement of Chinese NGOs in transnational mobilisation, and the other is the reluctance to engage with societal actors by the Chinese government (Liu, 2021; see also Chapter 2 by Bunskoek). Thereby, the chapter seeks to contribute to the study of how South-South, particularly Chinese, large-scale investment projects have become contested. Moreover, we aim to elucidate how advocacy practices are changing, how non-Western transnational practices are remade in Africa, and how African civil society actors are exerting agency in the face of foreign capital inflows and repressive rule.

Advocacy practices against large-scale investment projects

Since the early 2000s, there has been a rise in large-scale investment in the Global South. Thousands of projects are under way for new ports, railways, plantations, mines, pipelines, special economic zones, and more. Governments, international organisations, and development banks typically promote these investments for furthering development and fighting poverty, but they also have detrimental impacts that lead to conflicts, particularly involving affected local communities. Virtually all investment projects become contested in one way or another by means such as everyday resistance or collective action (Sändig, 2021). Beyond the local arena, NGOs and transnational social movements often advocate on behalf of local groups. Advocacy can be defined as efforts of seeking change for actors who are affected by poverty, pollution, discrimination, or other issues. Advocacy organisations that struggle against large-scale investment projects typically pursue 'naming-and-shaming' campaigns, lobby the government and other actors through petitions, and file formal complaints with investment-regulating bodies. These strategies often complement collective action and other forms of activism.

Considering that there is an established repertoire of advocacy means, we treat them as practices. In line with this volume, practices denote fairly coherent, routine ways of going about things (Hönke, 2013: 30) that are 'organized around shared practical understandings' (Schatzki, Knorr-Cetina and Savigny, 2001: 2). But these practices can also change, as actors modify existing or develop new advocacy means.

Advocacy practices have been extensively researched. In what now appears as the 'old world' of transnational advocacy, scholars highlighted the relevance of transnational advocacy networks with INGOs at the forefront (Keck and Sikkink, 1998). Prototypical INGOs like Amnesty International, Greenpeace, or Friends of the Earth are mainly based in the Global North, considering their organisational structures, history, and membership. Following the classic literature, INGOs have dominated the advocacy networks, whereas Southern activists were short of resources, skills, and political opportunities (Bob, 2005). Therefore, INGOs often advocated on behalf of the Southern activists who could not exert their agency due to repression and unresponsive local opponents. Southern activists thus sought to bypass the domestic blockage by alerting (i.e. 'throwing the boomerang' to) INGOs (Keck and Sikkink, 1998: 12–13). The latter would then call on foreign governments or international organisations to take up the issue and seek remedy. The corporate boomerang model specified the logic for Northern corporations that invest in the Global South (McAteer and Pulver, 2009). In this variant, INGOs seek to mobilise shareholders or public pressure against Northern-based parent companies for them to address human rights violations at their Southern branches.

Yet, advocacy networks have evolved over the past two decades. In the 'new world' of advocacy, Southern civil society groups and networks have expanded and become resourceful and skilled (Fadaee, 2016; Sändig, Bernstorff and Hasenclever, 2020). Powerful advocacy networks have arisen within some Southern countries. For example, Indian NGOs and local social movements have led the struggle against a bauxite mining project in Northern India (Kraemer, Whiteman and Banerjee, 2013). Southern activists have also pursued transnational advocacy, e.g. when Brazilian and Mozambican activists jointly contested the operations of the Brazilian mining company Vale in Mozambique (Cezne, 2019). NGOs from the Global North still play important roles in many of these struggles, but their approach has shifted. Rather than replacing Southern activism through the boomerang model, they increasingly act in partnership with Southern groups, providing them with technical assistance, media outreach, and funding (Schramm and Sändig, 2018). Tackling long-standing practices of Northern paternalism, this aims to amplify the agency of Southern activists at the frontline of the struggles. Furthermore, advocacy increasingly transcends scales from local to global. In transcalar advocacy, actions at one level have impacts at others (Pallas and Bloodgood, 2022). A key example is domestic advocacy that impacts norms, policies, or corporate practices at the international level. This complements but also puts into question the 'old' distinction between domestic and transnational advocacy. In this chapter, we define domestic advocacy as the actions of NGOs that operate and have effects mainly within the national arena. Transnational advocacy cuts across borders: it involves domestic and international advocacy organisations that either jointly target domestic actors, or international actors.

A major theoretical strand, which we connect with, is political opportunities theory. This refers to contextual factors that enable or constrain activism and its chances of success, e.g. through access to political institutions, available allies, and repression (McAdam and Tarrow, 2019). Activists thus orient their strategies along the political context to minimise the risk of repression and win power to achieve change. Research on large-scale investments for agriculture and mining widely demonstrates how political opportunities shape contention and its outcomes (Prause and Le Billon, 2020; Sändig, 2021). This logic is also central to the boomerang model, which sees closed domestic opportunities, known as domestic blockage, as a precondition for the engagement of INGOs. When closure prevails both domestically and transnationally, even advocacy actions become unlikely (Sikkink, 2005). Yet, scholars have much debated how to conceptualise opportunities, alongside constraints for action (McAdam, Tarrow and Tilly, 2001). We distinguish political, legal, and economic opportunities. Political opportunities derive from access to political institutions and state actors. Legal opportunities are based on the law, legal arguments, and access to courts and 'soft law' mechanisms such as human rights commissions and grievances complaints bodies (Schramm, 2020). Economic opportunities allow actors to inflict costs on their opponents, for example through boycotts or public shaming of brands (Wahlström and Peterson, 2006). In practice, advocacy organisations thus can have or win leverage over companies and state actors by using various political, legal, and economic opportunities. Crucial is proximity to the corporate target and relevant regulators as well as access to the public sphere in which the company operates (Hatte and Koenig, 2020).

Drawing on this theoretical framework, we examine the practices and scales of advocacy regarding the Southeastern DRC. Our analysis further explores the opportunities and leverage of the NGOs and the impacts of their actions. But first, we briefly introduce the case study.

Mining and the political context in the Southeastern DRC

The DRC is the largest copper miner in Africa and an exceptional place for cobalt mining. Seventy per cent of the global cobalt supply, which has become a critical mineral for the 'green transition', comes out of the Katangan Copperbelt in the Southeastern DRC (Matthews, 2020). This peripheral area is a typical frontier zone with limited statehood (Hönke, 2013). Yet, the region is extraordinarily relevant for the DRC's political economy. The mines, which run along the axis from Kolwezi (Lualaba province) to Lubumbashi (Haut-Katanga), generate 46% of the national budget and 99% of export earnings (ITIE RDC, 2021: 260). Despite a separatist movement and manifold local conflicts, the region has been stable and state-controlled. This differs from the Eastern DRC where armed conflict has persisted since the late 1990s, partly fuelled by artisanal and small-scale mining (Vogel, 2022).

The Southeastern mining industry has been undergoing multiple transition processes over the past twenty years. After devastating wars between 1996 and 2003, President Joseph Kabila sought to attract foreign investment to rebuild the infrastructure and reduce poverty. Therefore, the mining law of 2002 liberalised the sector and allowed investors to acquire the assets of the state-owned Générale des Carrières et des Mines (Gécamines). Subsequently, prominent international mining companies entered the DRC, including Glencore (Switzerland) and Freeport McMoRan (USA). Chinese investments took off with the USD 3 billion deal for Sino-Congolaise des Mines (SICOMINES) in 2008 (Maiza-Larrarte and Claudio-Quiroga, 2019). The foreign mining corporations invested heavily to modernise the decaying industrial mines. However, their arrival displaced tens of thousands of artisanal miners who now live and mine under precarious circumstances at the margins of the industrial mines (Katz-Lavigne, 2019). For years, the DRC's government has pledged to create artisanal and small-scale mining (ASM) zones, abolish child labour, and enforce health, safety, and environmental standards. Yet, the reality is bleak. There are very few designated ASM zones, and thousands of artisanal miners trespass into company grounds daily to extract ore (Nkumba, 2020). The formalisation of ASM is stuck, mainly because political elites themselves own ASM cooperatives and profit from them. For the industrial sector, a stricter mining law was adopted in 2018. It seeks to increase development benefits, in line with the trend towards resource nationalism and local content policies in Africa (Wilhelm and Maconachie, 2021). Still, the mining regulation remains poorly enforced, administrative bodies lack capacities, and rent-seeking practices are pervasive (Wakenge, 2018). Ever since the Mobutu regime (1965–97), the mining sector has fuelled the patronage-based political system of the DRC (Global Witness, 2017).

Among the transition processes was the arrival of Chinese miners. While Western mining companies were present in the DRC during the 2000s, they have increasingly left since the early 2010s for economic and other reasons, including reputational concerns and fears over sanctions on conflict-related minerals. In these years, the bust in mineral markets and rising financial pressures forced companies to sell their shares, and Chinese companies in particular were able to step in. Chinese actors now hold 17 out of the 25 largest copper mining and trading companies in the Southeastern DRC (our calculation, based on Ministère des Mines, 2021). This includes major players like Tenke Fungurume Mining (TFM), SICOMINES, Compagnie Minière de Musonoi (COMMUS), Congo Dongfang Mining (CDM), MMG Kinsevere, Société Minière de Deziwa (SOMIDEZ), Huachin Mabende, and Ruashi Mining.[5] Most of these copper miners also extract cobalt. By its size, the Swiss-based Glencore still stands out. It operates Mutanda, the world's largest cobalt mine, and the flagship Kamoto Copper Company. But some Chinese operations are not far behind. TFM operates the world's second-largest cobalt mine, and CDM and Ruashi Mining are also among the world's top eight cobalt mining companies (Matthews, 2020: 9). The parent companies comprise several of the foremost Chinese miners, including China Molybdenum (TFM), Zijin Mining (COMMUS), Zhejiang Huayou Cobalt (CDM), China Nonferrous Metal Mining Group (SOMIDEZ, Huachin Mabende), and the China Minmetals Corporation (MMG Kinsevere). Chinese construction companies are also present, particularly in SICOMINES. Some of these companies are state-owned (like China Nonferrous Metal Mining Group), whereas others are publicly listed (China Molybdenum, Zijin Mining).

Referring to these companies as Chinese may overemphasise particularities and hence should be treated with some caution. Through the typical joint venture structure, the DRC state usually holds about 20% within them. Like their peers, the Chinese usually employ domestic subcontractors and recruit almost all workers within the DRC. Since several of the companies were acquired, there are legacies left from former Western (e.g. TFM, MMG Ltd.) and Southern owners (Ruashi Mining). Moreover, these very large and internationally operating corporations from China have much replicated 'Western' environmental, social, and corporate governance (ESG) standards (Ericsson, Löf and Löf, 2020: 166). While there is no sharp divide, in some regards Chinese mining companies do have distinct business practices and their funding often has the strings of the Chinese state attached (Lee, 2017). Moreover, as we show below, the Chinese background of these companies has impacts on the contestations.

Advocacy practices against Chinese mining companies in the Southeastern DRC

Considering the domestic context of Chinese mining investment in the DRC, this could be a case for the boomerang model. Political and civil rights, such as the freedom of assembly and expression, are regularly infringed in the DRC. Opposition groups, journalists, and human rights defenders face intimidation, obstruction of their lawful activities, and high risk of arbitrary arrest, unfair trials, bad prison conditions, or outright killing (Amnesty International, 2022: 147–8). The run-up to the 2018 presidential elections saw a harsh crackdown on opposition parties, young activists, journalists, and others critical of the Kabila government. Since the mining industry has high national relevance, repression of mining activism is likely. Indeed, the Katangan Copperbelt is awash with police, private security firms, and by now even armed forces to protect the mining companies (Katz-Lavigne, 2020). Artisanal miners who trespass into company grounds are often beaten up. Moreover, the companies co-opt local elites and use 'soft' means such as funding for community projects within corporate social responsibility (CSR) programmes to undercut local protest (Hönke, 2013, 2018c). At the same time, affected groups regularly complain that the companies make insufficient efforts to remedy the problems that they cause, such as pollution, displacement, or worker exploitation. State agencies, in turn, lack capacities and tend to pursue self-interest through patronage politics (Wakenge, 2018). In short, there is a repressive context and low responsiveness, which could motivate local activists to 'outsource' contention to INGOs via the boomerang model.

Yet, local activists pursue manifold protests and advocacy actions within the DRC. Artisanal miners use everyday resistance and occasionally engage in vandalism and riots (Katz-Lavigne, 2020). Local communities regularly write petitions, march in protest, or block roads to put pressure on the companies. The company workers and their trade unions occasionally go on strike.

And NGOs complement these actions through numerous reports, media statements, and petitions. The opportunities for action are certainly constrained but not closed within the DRC's competitive authoritarian system (Matti, 2010).

Systematising our observations, we identify multiple pathways of advocacy: domestic actions, transnational interactions, and transcalar effects (see Figure 5.1). As we will detail in the following, there is a strong national advocacy network in the DRC and transnational action is partly possible, especially vis-à-vis Western consumer publics and the supply chain. Moreover, we find transcalar effects that reach into China, whereas the potential pathway of direct access to the Chinese government and Chinese consumers is largely blocked.

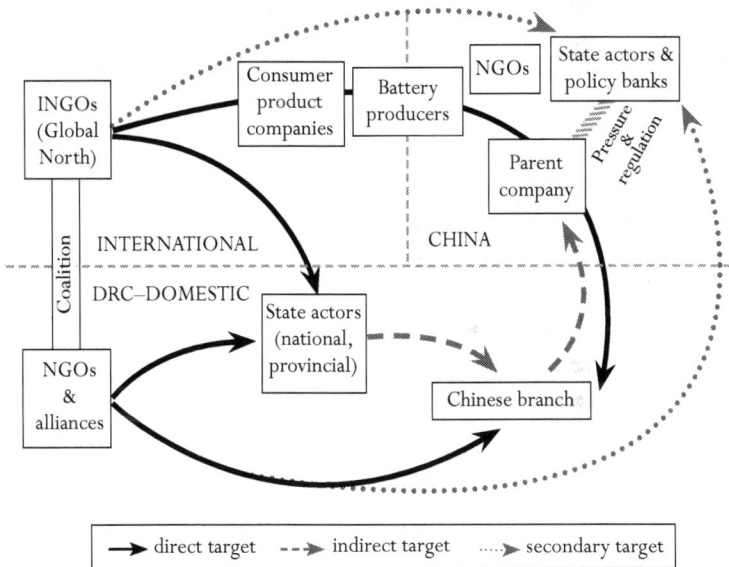

Figure 5.1: Advocacy pathways

Source: Authors' representation

Domestic advocacy and transcalar reach

In many instances DRC-based NGOs petitioned the local branches of the Chinese mining companies and raised public awareness both domestically and beyond through research reports and press conferences. The involved NGOs include African Resources Watch (AFREWATCH, based at Lubumbashi), Action contre l'Impunité pour les Droits de l'homme (ACIDH, Lubumbashi), Initiative pour la Bonne Gouvernance et les Droits Humains (Kolwezi), Association Congolaise pour l'Accès à la Justice (Lubumbashi), Southern Africa Resource Watch (SARW, Kinshasa), and the Carter Center (Lubumbashi). These organisations occasionally cooperate within ad hoc alliances and joint platforms such as the Synergie des Organisations de la Société Civile du Lualaba or the Cadre de Concertation de la Société Civile du Lualaba. They are also connected with NGOs from other parts of the DRC, especially from Kinshasa, but hardly connected with NGOs from the Eastern DRC.[6] Some of the NGOs are not strictly domestic, though. For instance, the Carter Center at Lubumbashi is a branch of the US-based Carter Center, headquartered at Atlanta. SARW has a regional structure with offices in various southern African capitals and its headquarters in Johannesburg.

Congolese NGOs address the Chinese mining companies mainly on the ground. Their reports and petitions either directly target the company (see black arrows at the DRC level in Figure 5.1) or mobilise indirect pressure by calling state actors for action over the company (dashed grey arrows). Typical addressees comprise the mining ministries at the provincial and national level, the province governors, and the prime minister and president at the national level. For leverage and to shield themselves from repression, the NGOs have relied on political and legal opportunities within the national arena. They have invoked mining, environmental, and labour regulation, the constitution, and occasionally human rights conventions (e.g. Cadre Provincial des Concertations de la Société Civile, 2020; AFREWATCH, 2022). For example, the mining law of 2002, despite being investor-friendly, already contained provisions on compensation, environmental impact assessments, and environmental management plans. The environmental protection law (2011) and reformed mining law (2018) provided stricter regulation. These laws serve the NGOs to justify their demands towards the companies and state actors. For instance, in mid-

2020, an NGO alliance challenged TFM for violating the reformed mining law by not involving the local communities around the mine in the drafting of its new community development programme (Coordination des Actions de Plaidoyer de la Société Civile, 2020). Another opportunity for advocacy has been Lualaba's Provincial Commission on Relocation, which was created in 2017 following abundant conflicts over displacement and compensation. The Commission, albeit often criticised as ineffective, has become a site of contention where people seek remedy, especially for involuntary displacement by COMMUS.

There is transnational NGO involvement in some of these 'domestic' actions. AFREWATCH and ACIDH have particularly strong international cooperation. The international partners include major organisations, which are based mostly in the Global North, such as Amnesty International, Human Rights Watch (HRW), Friends of the Earth (FoE), Rights and Accountability in Development (RAID), or the Centre for Research on Multinational Corporations (SOMO). Congolese NGOs partly receive technical or financial assistance for their reporting. Since reports are then usually reposted on the websites of the INGOs (e.g. AFREWATCH, 2017), this increases the reach and blurs the domestic–international divide.

'Domestic' NGO actions can also have transcalar effects into China. Most importantly, the companies' internal reporting procedures can carry the NGOs' appeals, made towards the DRC-based branches, 'upwards' to the parent companies in China. In this indirect advocacy pathway, the local branch may ask the parent company for action and assistance. Some NGO reports and petitions also address the parent company, state actors, and the so-called policy banks in China. For instance, NGO reports from the DRC have invoked the investment safeguards of the China EXIM Bank or the China Chamber of Commerce of Metals, Minerals and Chemicals Importers & Exporters (e.g. PremiCongo, 2018). These are secondary targets in our understanding (indicated through the dotted grey lines in Figure 5.1): the NGOs make recommendations for action to these actors and occasionally invoke their investment guidance but do not mainly and directly address them (e.g. through sending letters to them). In such transcalar advocacy, domestic actions within the DRC may have implications for the parent companies and others within China.

These pathways of advocacy resemble those used for challenging Western and other Southern mining companies in the DRC. Irrespective of the investors' country of origin, domestic NGOs typically address the same targets (mainly the company, state actors, and Congolese public) and use the same means (particularly research reports, petitions, and press conferences). The similarity rests on the opportunity structures: mining and environmental laws, access to political institutions, and the existence of social and environmental investment guidelines similarly applies to investments from various country backgrounds. As detailed below, significant guidance now also exists for Chinese overseas investment, and Congolese NGOs are becoming increasingly aware of this. Occasionally, domestic NGOs even address Chinese and non-Chinese mining companies simultaneously. For instance, one NGO report condemned similar environmental problems at mines run by Chinese, Swiss, and Canadian companies at Kolwezi (CODED, 2020). Hence, Chinese companies are not singled out, nor do the pathways and means of domestic and transcalar advocacy differ very much from non-Chinese cases. Differences do exist, however, regarding transnational opportunities for advocacy, in regard to collaboration with Chinese NGOs and action within China.

Transnational advocacy

The 'new' world of advocacy assumes more diverse forms of civil society and intra-Southern networking. Indeed, DRC-based NGOs are also connected within the Global South. Most importantly, AFREWATCH, ACIDH, SARW, and PremiCongo are members of the Alternative Mining Indaba network and the African Coalition for Corporate Accountability. However, these South-South networks have not specifically targeted Chinese mining companies, nor mining in the DRC. They tend to advocate more broadly on mining and its linkages with development, the environment, and governance in Africa.

Regarding Chinese mining companies in the DRC, we rather observe the presence of 'old' transnational advocacy players, especially prominent and mostly Northern-based INGOs, like Amnesty International, FoE, Global Witness, HRW, the International Crisis Group, RAID, and SOMO. They work with Congolese NGOs both bilaterally and through transnational campaigns like Le Congo n'est pas à vendre (Congo is not for sale) and the Mind the Gap consortium. Such transnational advocacy typically addresses the DRC state, the local mining company, and the parent company in China. For instance, accountability watchdogs (like Global Witness, The Sentry, and the Carter Center) have condemned the DRC state, Gécamines, and the mining companies for bad governance and corruption (e.g. Global Witness, 2020).

A major transnational advocacy pathway runs, as we call it, 'through the supply chain'. In highly mediatised reports and a litigation case in Washington, DC, INGOs have sought to leverage Western consumer power over mining companies in the DRC. Cobalt from the DRC is contained in the batteries needed for mobile phones, laptops, and electronic vehicles around the world (International Rights Advocates, 2019). INGOs document issues that arise locally from industrial mining (including pollution, displacement, and exploitative working conditions) and from artisanal mining (such as health hazards and child labour, see Amnesty International, 2016; RAID and CAJJ, 2021). They link these grievances 'upstream' at the Katangan mine sites with the products sold 'downstream' by consumer product manufacturers. This targets major brands from Western countries (like Apple, Microsoft, Tesla, and Volkswagen) but also from China (BYD) and Korea (Samsung). Along the supply chain, parent companies in China, as well as cobalt trading and refining companies (mostly based in China), are targeted too. Zhejiang Huayou Cobalt has been particularly in the spotlight for initially buying cobalt from the poorly regulated ASM. The advocacy mechanism, thus, hinges on economic opportunities. Although Northern NGOs are distant both from the DRC and from miners from China, they can influence the choices of Western consumers. This gives them power over electronic consumer goods manufacturers and by extension the mining companies.

But these transnational advocacy pathways are neither limited, nor specific to Chinese mining companies. In fact, there has been outstanding attention by Congolese and international NGOs on Glencore, the world's largest cobalt miner. The company has a shattered reputation, mostly over corruption allegations (Pain pour le prochain and Action de Carême, 2018). Alongside Glencore, accountability watchdogs have regularly condemned corruption by Kazakhstan's Eurasian Resources Group, the Chinese mining companies, and other miners in the DRC (Carter Center, 2017). The advocacy pathway 'through the supply chain' also works for non-Chinese mining companies (RAID and CAJJ, 2021). But it requires NGO access to consumer publics, which implies limitations. There are an increasing number of Chinese brands that cater mostly for the domestic market in China. Here the pathway would work less well, considering the domestic context within China.

NGOs and the limited space for action in China

NGOs from China remain disconnected from the above-mentioned transnational advocacy networks. In principle, there are numerous NGOs in China, particularly in the environmental sector. These organisations have often lobbied political actors to prevent the construction of large-scale infrastructure within the country (Steinhardt and Wu, 2016). However, only a few hundred Chinese NGOs work internationally and only a handful address China's foreign investment (Global Environmental Institute, 2016). These include the Global Environmental Institute, Social Resources Institute, or Greenovation Hub. The latter, for instance, reported on environmental and social issues from the operations of Zijin Mining in Peru and MMG Ltd. in Laos (Greenovation Hub, 2014). Both companies also run major mines in the DRC. But the focus of these NGOs has been mostly on Southeast Asia, which receives more FDI from China than Africa. Within China, these NGOs evidently operate in a challenging context where public protest is not impossible but regularly repressed (Göbel, 2019). Therefore, the Chinese NGOs tend not to confront state actors but to cooperate with them (Dai and Spires, 2018; see also Chapter 4 by Waisbich). Forging transnational connections with these NGOs remains extraordinarily difficult, not least because of the language barrier. We found no joint advocacy and nearly no connections between NGOs from the DRC and China. Rare organisational links exist through two networks that also work on mining conflicts: the Mind the Gap consortium and the grassroots lawyers' association Namati, which comprise NGOs both from the DRC and China.

The absence of Chinese NGOs from these transnational advocacy networks undercuts the opportunity for the boomerang model. Thus, action opportunities for challenging Chinese mining companies differ to some extent from Western cases. The vast advocacy networks in Western countries, which also benefit from civil and political freedoms, have more opportunities to mobilise the public over damaging corporate conduct in the Global South. This contributes to the disproportionate advocacy that we observe regarding Glencore, the largest Western mining company in the DRC. In contrast, only a few Chinese NGOs address overseas investment at all. They are poorly connected, and they evade publicly highlighting issues and rallying people, for instance, for consumer boycotts. In the cases of state-owned enterprises, the pathway of shareholder activism is also missing. Hence, there are limited transnational advocacy opportunities in the Chinese case, and 'throwing the boomerang' to NGOs in China is hardly possible.

Another limitation concerns access to investment grievance mechanisms. Affected communities, concerned citizens, and NGOs often use such complaint procedures to voice their grievances and challenge Western investment projects. This is possible for all investments from companies based in member countries of the OECD or with funding from the International Finance Corporation. For example, Swiss NGOs appealed to Switzerland's state prosecutors and Canadian security exchange commissions to inquire into corruption allegations in Glencore's investments in the DRC. NGOs also complained to the OECD's National Contact Points regarding Glencore's operations in Colombia and Chad. Yet, these international grievance mechanisms cannot be called upon in the case of most Chinese mining investments. Complaint procedures regarding Chinese investment projects remain opaque, despite extensive CSR guidance that now exists by the Chinese state, policy banks, industry associations, and state-owned enterprises (IDI, 2019). Existing grievance mechanisms are often less open and formalised than in Western cases, and grievances can only be voiced behind closed doors.[7] The effectiveness of these complaint procedures and their relevance for transnational advocacy in China–Africa relations remains limited for now.

Advocacy impacts: Do the Chinese miners change?

Having shown ample advocacy actions, but also their limitations, we wonder if these efforts contribute to remaking Chinese business practices. At the company level, we indeed find anecdotal evidence of changes. After Congolese NGOs challenged TFM in mid-2020 for violating the new mining law regarding community participation, the company started cooperating with SARW to consult communities. A prominent report by Amnesty International (2016), researched together with AFREWATCH, led Zhejiang Huayou Cobalt, Apple, and Samsung to scan their supply chains for human rights violations, particularly child labour. In response, Zhejiang Huayou Cobalt developed CSR policies, abandoned buying cobalt from unregulated local miners, joined responsible international mining initiatives, and developed labour standards for its artisanal mine at Kolwezi (S. Chen, 2021). Hence, major Chinese mining companies in the DRC do feel the pressure that results from NGO advocacy and from the rising public expectations for ESG in the West and beyond. China Molybdenum, for example, stated that its branch 'TFM is also audited by customers, including major automobile and electronics manufacturers, who seek assurance that the products used in their supply chain originate in a socially responsible manner' (CMOC, 2017: 25).

Yet, other Chinese mining and mineral processing companies remain reluctant to change. In particular, the battery manufacturers from China have lacked due diligence actions (Amnesty International, 2017). In the DRC, for instance, COMMUS has been slow to endorse CSR practices. Such reluctance mostly results from the lower international visibility and lower vulnerability to supply-chain pressure (Wang and Hu, 2017). The battery producers are a rather invisible part of the supply chain, and COMMUS seems less vulnerable to NGO advocacy because its parent company Zijin mainly supplies the Chinese market. In contrast, the more responsive companies, like TFM and Zhejiang Huayou Cobalt, have more global customers, which increasingly expect responsible sourcing practices.

Besides exposure to global markets, the Chinese state has been a key driver for more responsible practices within Chinese investment projects (Liu, 2021). Since the mid-2000s, numerous ESG guidelines have been issued for outbound investments. This includes policies by the State Council, Ministry of Commerce, State-Owned Assets Supervision and Administration Commission, China Banking and Insurance Regulatory Commission, and CCCMC (IDI, 2019). There is guidance for 'greening' the massive infrastructure projects from the BRI. Also, China's policy banks that fund projects in Africa, particularly China EXIM Bank and China Development Bank, now require environmental and social impact assessments. These social and environmental standards are partly voluntary but partly also binding.[8] Whereas Western CSR relies much on voluntary commitments, China is going further than many countries in making a range of corporate guidelines for outgoing business mandatory (UNDP China, 2019). Hence, Chinese corporations and particularly state-owned enterprises have both obligations as well as incentives to respect voluntary CSR guidance.

Chinese investment regulation and guidance is particularly developed in the cobalt sector, and thus regarding the DRC. In 2016, the CCCMC introduced the Responsible Cobalt Initiative and offered training to align the sector with the OECD's due diligence standards. State-led efforts mainly aim at improving China's international reputation, especially in the much-monitored cobalt industry (Breslin, 2020; Liu, 2021). Exposure to international markets has also triggered some diffusion and socialisation processes in this sector. Chinese companies have learned from their customers and competitors abroad and from each other, which has diffused due diligence practices, also within China (Wang and Hu, 2017; S. Chen, 2021). Institutions like the CCCMC, in turn, have learned from the experiences of the companies and from interactions with the OECD. Behind these processes is pragmatism (Tang, 2020) but a pragmatism that also goes beyond adapting to the diffusion of 'Western' practices. Chinese state actors and corporations also pragmatically endorse practices such as gift-giving, social spending, and other measures to respond to local demands drawing from older Confucian, Daoist, and socialist traditions of thought in China (see Chapter 2 by Bunskoek, also Bunskoek and Hönke, forthcoming). By promoting 'relational development' (ibid.), they seek to improve their reputation and address problems that they encounter in their relations with the hosting countries and communities.

Advocacy actions and supply-chain pressure are among the multiple drivers of the Chinese state regulation of overseas investment. NGOs from outside China have exposed the malpractices of Chinese mining companies, which has contributed to the bad reputation of China's presence in Africa. NGOs have also shaped increasing public demand for responsible investment practices and supply chains that are free from human rights violations. This has put Chinese corporations and the Chinese state under pressure. Still, the outlined processes that push Chinese state and corporate actors to change business practices towards CSR are complex and go beyond the effects of NGO actions.

Conclusion

We started with the assumption that advocacy against Chinese mining investments could be very limited in African contexts like the DRC. There are ample constraints in these settings: repression at the mines and the companies' headquarters in China, the paucity of Chinese NGOs that address overseas investment, and the presumed lack of leverage of Western NGOs over far-away Chinese companies.

Far from inaction, however, we observe significant advocacy along multiple pathways. Our case partly reflects nascent advocacy research, which has gone beyond the classic boomerang model to highlight the rising relevance of Southern civil society actors and transcalar advocacy (Pallas and Bloodgood, 2022; Routledge, Nativel and Cumbers, 2006; De Waal, 2015; see also Chapter 4 by Waisbich). We observe that NGOs from the DRC, occasionally with

INGO assistance, have addressed the Chinese mining companies on the ground and called upon the DRC state to act. There is a powerful national advocacy network here, as in other countries of the Global South (Kraemer, Whiteman and Banerjee, 2013). Western-based NGOs have contributed to these actions, amplifying the agency of domestic NGOs (Schramm and Sändig, 2018a). In addition, we observe transcalar effects of the local actions at the mining frontier: as the Chinese branches report complaints back to their parent companies and as Congolese NGOs invoke investment guidance from Chinese state actors and policy banks, local actions reach into China. Given the strong domestic actions and the lack of involvement of China's NGOs, the case does not follow the boomerang model— rather it shows varied possible advocacy pathways aside from the boomerang model, the relevance of which is diminishing in today's advocacy world. Yet, some 'old' patterns of transnational advocacy persist. Rather than 'new' South-South coalitions that bring NGOs from the DRC and China together, we observe that prominent INGOs from the Global North still play important roles. They have targeted the DRC state and exerted pressure 'through the supply chain' by raising consumer awareness, mainly in the West, over the human rights violations involved in the mining of cobalt for electronic goods and vehicles. INGOs thus use the vulnerability of major brands, such as Apple and Volkswagen, to put pressure on mining companies, battery producers, and others along the supply chain (Prause, 2020).

These advocacy pathways largely reflect political, legal, and economic opportunities as well as constraints within the DRC, China, and the INGOs' home states. Especially for domestic advocacy practices, which depend on the laws of the DRC, whether a mining company is from China or elsewhere plays little role. In transnational advocacy, Northern NGOs similarly expose bad governance and exert pressure 'through the supply chain' to target Chinese and non-Chinese mining companies alike. Nevertheless, opportunities for challenging Western-based corporations are larger. There are dense advocacy networks, publics that scrutinise corporate conduct, and numerous investment grievance mechanisms in the West. Unsurprisingly, we observe a disproportionate number of advocacy efforts on Switzerland's Glencore. Several of these advocacy opportunities are missing within China, amongst other reasons, due to the lack of involvement of Chinese NGOs. Outside NGOs have little means to mobilise Chinese publics or use the increasing number of investment grievance mechanisms within the country. The playing field for advocacy thus differs in important regards (Shipton and Dauvergne, 2021). And as argued in the introduction to this volume, China's growing global relations are transforming transnational (advocacy) practices from the ground up.

Despite the constraints, advocacy actions also have impacts on Chinese business practices. In response to NGO advocacy, some Chinese mining companies in the DRC have increased their CSR efforts, and some parent companies have taken steps towards due diligence. But exposure to global markets and Chinese state regulation have also been catalysts for these changing business practices. Since the mid-2000s, China has introduced both voluntary but also mandatory CSR guidance, which goes beyond the investment regulation in most Western countries. Moreover, socialisation and diffusion processes, as well as the typical pragmatic and relational approach of Chinese actors (see Chapter 2 by Bunskoek) drawing from domestic traditions contributed to the recent mainstreaming of CSR practices. But to be sure, some Chinese miners have lagged behind, due to their limited international visibility and focus on the Chinese domestic market where the pressure for ESG has been lower.

Our findings corroborate recent advocacy research, which is increasingly putting the boomerang model into perspective. The literature is showing ever more diverse advocacy pathways and rising Southern civil society involvement (Pallas and Bloodgood, 2022). The boomerang model, alongside the insider-outsider coalition perspective (Sikkink, 2005), represents the optimism of the late 1990s and early 2000s about how a liberal global order was to help constrained domestic Global South activism. As our case shows, the limitations of this have become more and more visible since. The boomerang model and especially its assumption about domestic blockage tends to neglect that, meanwhile, Southern activists can seize advocacy opportunities even in repressive contexts. Moreover, we show that transnational advocacy is still possible—in our case 'through the supply chain'—even when outside opportunity structures are largely closed, as in China.

We have also furthered understanding of how large-scale Chinese investments become contested in Africa's frontier zones of multiple infrastructure globalities. So far, scholars have hardly examined how the investor's country of origin impacts such contestations (Christensen, 2019). While the means of domestic NGO advocacy do not seem to differ for investments from different country origins, differences emerge at the transnational level. Here our findings align with Shipton and Dauvergne (2021: 246), who find that 'China remains largely inaccessible to the boomerang strategy.'

There are, of course, limitations to this chapter and avenues for further research. We wonder about the advocacy opportunities regarding smaller Chinese investments and companies that mainly supply the Chinese domestic market. They may face less NGO scrutiny than similarly sized Western investment projects. In terms of advocacy impacts, we present anecdotal evidence, but a more thorough analysis is needed regarding the varied factors that make Chinese companies respond to advocacy, regulation, and public pressure. Several caveats of our analysis result from space constraints. For example, more could be said about contextualisation of advocacy (regarding other forms of activism) and political opportunities (regarding potentially available opportunities where no action was taken). Also, we could only superficially explore the dynamics between advocacy organisations, corporations, state actors, and publics that interact in various arenas and iterations, which reshape opportunities for action. In any case, we encourage further research by showing that Chinese mining companies, like other Global South investors, are becoming much more contested and held accountable in various and unique ways for corporate conduct at Africa's global mining frontier.

6

CONTESTED PRACTICES

CONTROVERSIES OVER THE CONSTRUCTION OF LAMU PORT IN KENYA

Benard Musembi Kilaka[1]

Introduction

In the last two decades, China's economic engagement in Africa has significantly increased and has subsequently attracted widespread attention from many quarters (Alden, Large and Soares de Oliveira, 2008; Gill and Reilly, 2007; Kamoche and Siebers, 2015). Perceptions and opinions of China's increasing forays into Africa have greatly differed largely between sentiments that see the trend as a form of neo-colonialism, or a win-win situation (Alden, Large and Soares de Oliveira, 2008; Lorenz and Thielke, 2007; Mead, 2018). Despite widespread notions that the renewed engagement by China in Africa is largely predatory and driven by its demand for Africa's abundant natural resources, this is far from the reality as such engagements are much more complex (Alden, Large and Soares de Oliveira, 2008; Anthony, 2013; Bhamidipati and Hansen, 2021; Drogendijk and Blomkvist, 2013; Kragelund, 2009). This complexity is particularly visible in Chinese engagements in infrastructural development (Anthony, 2013; Eom et al., 2017). In this case, Chinese companies and funding can be seen through their involvement as funders, contractors and even investors in many big infrastructure projects in many African countries, which have emerged as key frontier zones for Chinese capital and expertise. The launch of the Belt and Road Initiative (BRI) added further impetus to China's investments in infrastructure projects in Africa.

Despite China's massive and increasing involvement in infrastructure projects, much of the scholarly debate has focused on their engagements in countries with abundant natural resources such as Zambia, Angola and Sudan where they are engaged in high-profile infrastructures, which are largely intended to cement relations between China and the respective African states (Alden, Large and Soares de Oliveira, 2008; du Plessis, 2016). Although this focus has helped highlight issues such as the drivers and manifestations of Chinese involvement in Africa, such accounts are not exhaustive since they mostly present a partial view of the situation. In most cases, the primary focus is on Chinese actors. This is despite assertions by several scholars that Chinese involvement in Africa is complex as it involves many players (Gill and Reilly, 2007; Alden, Large and Soares de Oliveira, 2008; Kragelund, 2009). This understanding is particularly noteworthy since it recognises the complicated environments that Chinese actors constantly navigate as they attempt to consolidate their positions in the burgeoning construction industry in most African countries.

One aspect that warrants more scholarly attention concerns the interactions between Chinese companies and host communities, especially in areas where Chinese companies are involved in construction infrastructure projects that have the potential for massive social, economic, and environmental disruption. This empirical angle helps to illustrate a key aspect of an emerging infrastructure globality, seen through the introduction of new and sometimes controversial practices and the consolidation of Afro-Sino ties, following the entrenchment of Chinese capital and practices in the African continent (see Chapter 1 by Hönke et al.). As noted in numerous news articles and scholarly sources, several Chinese companies have ended up being embroiled in controversies with local communities due to a litany of grievances (BBC, 2012; Martorano et al., 2021;

Ryan, 2019; Zhao, 2014). Such events therefore point to the need to take instances of local agency seriously since they not only affect the activities of Chinese companies, but also have an implication in how their involvement is perceived by communities. As such, this study seeks to account for the local agency of community members who in most cases bear the brunt of the adverse implications arising from infrastructure projects. More specifically, the focus on African agency, particularly that of local communities, is important since it sheds light on the intricate and complicated relations between local communities and Chinese companies. It also brings to the fore the discursive and material practices that local communities employ as they engage with Chinese companies, even when the odds are against them. By illustrating the nuanced interactions between the communities and Chinese actors, the study contributes important knowledge about the complexities and lived experiences that local communities endure in their interactions with Chinese companies. More importantly, the focus on local agency further provides a deeper understanding of the communities' resilience vis-à-vis implications of Chinese activities on their lives and the power dynamics that are inherent in the engagements between local communities and Chinese companies.

This interest in illustrating the agency of communities in their interactions with Chinese companies follows arguments by a number of scholars who caution against looking at African actors as passive in China–Africa relations (Brown, 2012; Brown and Harman, 2013; Giles Mohan and Lampert, 2013; Mohan, 2015; Otele, 2016; Bhamidipati and Hansen, 2021; Chiyemura, Gambino and Zajontz, 2022). For instance, Brown and Harman (2013) are particularly critical of dominant perceptions that often portray African actors as victims of exogenous forces that are strongly conditioned by immobile structural constraints. This chapter therefore seeks to challenge assertions that often portray local actors as helpless victims and at the mercy of external actors. Such accounts only provide a partial and sometimes misleading understanding of situations since they ignore the myriad ways in which some African actors shape their interactions with external actors. Focusing on the practices of engagement by local communities brings to the fore the strategies and actions that local actors use to respond to, engage with, adapt to, and resist the increasing involvement and presence of Chinese companies in their localities.

Although several scholars have in the recent past strived to overcome this anomaly by pushing for the acknowledgement of African agency in the interactions with external actors, such accounts have mostly focused on state-level actors and rarely on ordinary actors such as communities who in most cases are the most impacted by the activities of external actors (Brown, 2012; Mohan, 2015; Chiyemura, Gambino and Zajontz, 2022). This is particularly visible in the ongoing engagement of Chinese companies in the current infrastructural construction boom in most African countries, where several aspects of an evolving Chinese infrastructure globality can be discerned (see Chapter 1 by Hönke et al. and Chapter 2 by Bunskoek). By this, I refer to the unique practices and influences that Chinese companies bring to the contexts in which they operate and play a key role in shaping the interactions with different stakeholders.

Through the case of the new Lamu Port in Kenya, which is being constructed by several Chinese companies, this chapter seeks to account for the ways in which a section of the local community in Lamu has exercised their agency in their interactions with both Chinese contactors and state officials as they seek to safeguard their interests and wellbeing as well as the effectiveness of these attempts at remaking corporate practices. The chapter achieves this by zooming in on their engagements with the activities of a consortium of Chinese companies headed by China Communication Construction Company, hereafter referred to as CCCC,[2] whose subsidiaries operated under its name and constructed the port. The project is a key component of the Lamu Port, South Sudan, Ethiopia Transport Corridor (LAPSSET) mega-project that seeks to connect Kenya with South Sudan and Ethiopia through a network of infrastructure components. The focus on local agency is therefore important on two grounds. First, it foregrounds political and social concerns that have necessitated action. Secondly, it provides deeper insights into the intrigues and difficult choices that ordinary actors choose to assert their agency. Two issues are particularly pertinent in this regard, namely, the extent of the influence that the host community has over the Chinese contractors and what issues enable or constrain their actions and practices. As I argue, whereas the ability of a section of the Lamu community to tap into transnational networks of environmental activism, mainly non-governmental organisations (NGOs) from the Global North, came with certain advantages, the close ties between Chinese contractors and state officials, coupled with the enclave nature of the project, greatly constrained the agency of local actors.

The emphasis on local agencies provides additional insights into Chinese companies' increasing engagement in Africa's infrastructure industry. It highlights the actions of local communities, who in most cases are the most aggrieved by the activities of Chinese companies. The 'seeing as the community' perspective is therefore important in expanding our understanding of the growing involvement of Chinese companies in Africa since it reveals a body of knowledge that is often overshadowed by dominant narratives that focus on Chinese investments in Africa.

In fact, one aspect without proper elaboration concerns the unique practices that Chinese contractors bring to the African context as they undertake infrastructure projects. As noted in several studies, China's engagement in the infrastructure sector is particularly favoured by political elites and a section of the population in Africa due to their practices, such as the swift and timely implementation of projects, efficiency of work performed and their strict policy of political non-interference[3] (Gill and Reilly, 2007; Hofmann et al., 2007; du Plessis, 2016). For a continent with a complicated history and relationship with the Western world, these attributes and practices that Chinese companies bring stand out and have altered long-standing relations between African countries and their traditional allies from the West (Hofmann et al., 2007; Drogendijk and Blomkvist, 2013). Yet, interestingly, it is also these distinctive practices that have attracted intensive criticism and controversies in several contexts where they operate. For instance, critics of infrastructure projects undertaken by Chinese companies often note that their fast implementation of projects in Africa often comes at the expense of controversial labour practices, environmental degradation, and strained corporate relations with the host communities.

As such, drawing inspiration from scholarly works on the concept of 'travelling models' by scholars such as Behrends et al. (2014) and Reyna (2007), this chapter will illustrate how the practices of Chinese companies undertaking infrastructure projects in Africa travel and trigger disputes and controversies as they get translated in the contexts where Chinese companies operate. My focus on controversies follows conceptual debates by Barry (2013) and Hönke and Cuesta-Fernandez (2018), which direct me to focus on disputes between actors. Such controversies exemplify a clash of realities, and their non-resolution often leads to a deleterious perception of Chinese companies. As such, the focus on controversies is important, for it not only helps to unmask key aspects of growing Chinese involvement and practices in Africa but also amplifies the voices of local communities, who so far have been neglected in much of the scholarly discourses around the increasing engagement of China in Africa. Additionally, the approach is important in illustrating how local actors draw inspiration from practices of resistance in other contexts, where communities and civil society groups have successfully challenged mega-projects. By 'travelling models', I follow Reyna's (2007) argument, which sees them as 'procedural cultural plans of how to get something done elsewhere'.

For this study, data was collected from members of local communities and civil society activists in Lamu. While the views of the local community have provided valuable insights into their experiences and perspectives, it is also important to acknowledge that there were limitations in accessing Chinese contractors working at the Lamu port due to a myriad of issues, namely, the enclaved and securitised nature of the Lamu port and language barriers. The security measure around the port particularly hindered access to Chinese contractors, thereby limiting access to their perspectives which would have been crucial for understanding the ongoing dynamism of South-South encounters (see for instance, Hönke et al.'s discussion of field entrance in their conclusion). Consequently, this has shaped both the nature of knowledge that this study produces and the voices that are amplified.

Lamu county in context—A history of problematic centre-periphery relations

In examining local agencies in Lamu, this study particularly takes into account the problematic and complicated centre-periphery relations between the national government and inhabitants of Lamu county since independence. Just like other counties traversed by the LAPSSET project, Lamu county experienced a long period of marginalisation by the national government, which deliberately opted to channel resources to areas within Kenya that were perceived to be productive (Republic of Kenya, 1965). In essence, the post-independent regimes pursued a policy of continuity with previous practices of the colonial regime by investing in the former white highlands (Odhiambo, 2014). As a result, when compared to other areas of Kenya, Lamu lagged behind on many socio-economic indicators of development, such as inadequate infrastructure development, low literacy levels, high levels of unemployment and elevated maternal mortality rates (County Government of Lamu County, 2016). Matters were complicated by the Shifta War, soon after Kenya's independence, between the Kenyan government and Somali irredentist forces which wanted Somali-inhabited regions in Kenya to secede and be part of the Republic of Somalia (Whittaker, 2012; Ndzovu, 2014). Due to the activities of the 'Shifta' in Lamu, the county became a theatre of security operations by Kenyan security forces, who heavily militarised the region. In the ensuing military operations, Lamu residents experienced gross human rights violations and displacement from their ancestral homes. To date, many have been unable to return to their lands. This experience, together with the constrained political space in Kenya at the time, seriously undermined local agency as communities had few opportunities to agitate for their interests.

However, three events since 2010 have reorganised centre-periphery relations in Lamu by presenting opportunities that allowed communities and actors including activists to engage with the national government and other private actors. These events include, first, the promulgation of a new constitution in 2010 that ushered in a devolved system of government and created a special fund for formerly marginalised counties. Second, the unveiling of Vision 2030, Kenya's blueprint for long-term development, committed to address the historic marginalisation that some counties experienced. The Vision replaced Kenya's initial policy on long-term development at independence, Sessional Paper No.10 of 1965, that favoured the development of areas perceived to be productive (Odhiambo, 2014). Third, the launch of the LAPSSET mega-project in 2012 was presented as a game-changing investment that would not just open the region to investments but rather integrate Lamu and northern Kenya into the rest of Kenya and global value chains (Bremner, 2013; Mosley and Watson, 2016; LCDA, 2017; Chome, 2020).

These developments not only provided new opportunities for engagement between the national government and residents in Lamu, especially through the new county government, but also led to community mobilisation especially in anticipation of the LAPSSET project, which had generated mixed feelings among Lamu residents (Laher, 2011; Bremner, 2013; Chome, 2020; Chiyemura, Gambino and Zajontz, 2022). Whereas a section of the Lamu community welcomed the project due to its anticipated positive impacts, another section of the Lamu community, especially those who consider themselves 'native' to the county, voiced concerns. They feared that the project would entrench marginalisation owing to its perceived negative impacts as well as a prevailing belief that the project would only serve the interests of national elites and outsiders (Laher, 2011; Bremner, 2013; Chome, 2020). Previous experiences with the national government such as the Shifta War, illustrated above, and the government-sponsored resettlement of migrant communities in Lamu in the 1970s, informed these positions. It is within this context that this study explores the local agency of communities in their engagement with the Chinese-constructed port in Lamu.

This chapter has three sections. The first section begins by highlighting the growing involvement of Chinese companies in Kenya, with the project sites evolving as frontier zones. I argue that the growing engagement by Chinese companies in Kenya's infrastructure sector in general, and the Lamu Port more specifically, is driven by unique practices that Chinese companies have perfected at home and ride on to illustrate their competitiveness as they entrench their presence in the country. The second part accounts for the specific controversies that have surrounded the activities of CCCC, contractor of the Lamu Port. I chiefly focus on three controversies surrounding the activities of CCCC in Lamu, namely, the environmental concerns of their activities, poor labour conditions and the displacement of fisherfolk from their traditional fishing grounds. This is then followed by the third section that illustrates the local agency by aggrieved community members in their attempts to deal with controversies emanating from CCCC's activities.

For the empirical material in this study, I rely on both primary and secondary data. The primary data was collected between January 2019 and March 2021 during fieldwork exercises in Lamu. In this exercise, I interviewed government officials, community members and representatives from civil society organisations (CSOs). The secondary data emanates from official reports by both state and non-state actors and newspaper articles.

Chinese investments in Kenya and Lamu Port

In recent years, Kenya has emerged as a key partner for China on the African continent. This is particularly well illustrated by the growing trade ties between the two countries and the significant presence of Chinese companies in the country. Indeed, in the last two decades, trade between the two countries has dramatically increased but is imbalanced in favour of China (Kamoche and Siebers, 2015; Githaiga and Bing, 2019). For example, in 2002, trade between the two countries was worth USD 186.37 million,[4] but had significantly increased by 2017, when China emerged as the main source of Kenya's imports, amounting to USD 3.37 billion, while Kenya's exports totalled USD 100 million (Githaiga and Bing, 2019). In addition, ties between Kenya and China have further been driven by Kenya's strategic location as the gateway to the greater East Africa region as well as the Great Lakes Region (Wissenbach and Wang, 2017; Githaiga and Bing, 2019). It is partly due to this that Kenya has emerged as a key partner in the massive BRI being undertaken by the Chinese government as illustrated by the Chinese funding to the 472-km Standard Gauge Railway (SGR) that connects the coastal city of Mombasa to the capital Nairobi (Wissenbach and Wang, 2017; Githaiga and Bing, 2019). For a country that lacks vast natural resources, the engagement of Chinese companies is enormous and spans several sectors of the Kenyan economy such as security, construction, real estate and the telecommunications sectors (Onjala, 2018). This deepening of Chinese engagements in Kenya has elicited mixed reactions not only from Kenyans but also from the Western diplomatic community, which has for a long time been Kenya's traditional ally (Njiraini, 2010; Guguyu, 2022).

Although Chinese investments in Kenya cover many aspects of the Kenyan economy, their involvement in infrastructure projects is the most conspicuous and has subsequently generated the most interest (Wissenbach and Wang, 2017; Onjala, 2018; Wang and Wissenbach, 2019). This is partly because this type of activity makes the Chinese presence in the country more visible and also due to the different practices they bring along. In fact, Chinese companies have been and continue to be involved in the construction of major infrastructure projects in Kenya, with their most conspicuous engagement being the construction of the 472-km SGR between Mombasa and Nairobi at an estimated cost of USD 380 million. To date, the project is the biggest and the most expensive project ever undertaken in the history of Kenya (Jiang, 2020). Other notable infrastructure projects undertaken by Chinese companies include Thika Superhighway and the upgrading of Jomo Kenyatta International Airport (*China Daily*, 2018; Onjala, 2018).

It is also noteworthy that Chinese investments in Kenya involve a wide range of actors such as state-owned enterprises, private companies, and individuals. In addition, contrary to widespread assumptions, not all infrastructure projects that involve the Chinese are financed by China. As several studies note, Chinese activities in Kenya, like elsewhere in Africa, take three main forms: financing of infrastructure projects, participating as contractors, and lastly as investors (Foster, Butterfield and Chen, 2009; Cheung et al., 2012; Giles Mohan and Lampert, 2013; Arewa, 2016). To illustrate, whereas Chinese funding has been key in projects such as the SGR, Chinese companies have also won tenders for the construction of major infrastructure projects, even when the funding does not come from China, thereby leading to concerns that their involvement is pushing Kenyan firms out of the market (Guguyu, 2022). The role of CCCC in the construction of Lamu Port, which is entirely funded by the Kenyan government, exemplifies this dimension of Chinese engagement. Additionally, other Chinese companies' involvement in infrastructure projects is driven by investment rationales since the key goal is to generate profits. In Kenya, a good example is the new 27.1-km[5] expressway (toll road) in Nairobi, which was constructed by the China Road and Bridge Corporation (CRBC) at an estimated cost of USD 560 million through a Build, Operate and Transfer framework.[6] As part of the agreement with the Kenyan government, CRBC, through its subsidiary, Moja Expressway, will recoup its investments by collecting tolls for 27 years.[7]

The involvement of a Chinese company in the construction of the Lamu Port illuminates the growing dominance of Chinese firms in Kenya. The port is a key pillar in a major mega-project unfolding in northern Kenya known as the LAPSSET project, which seeks to connect Kenya to South Sudan and Ethiopia through a series of highways, pipelines, airports, railways, and resort cities. In contrast to the SGR, which was predominantly financed by Chinese loans, Lamu Port, or at least the first three berths currently under construction, is entirely funded by the Kenyan government (Githaiga and Bing, 2019). Although it is not clear whether the tendering process for the port's construction was open and competitive, a USD 487 million tender was eventually awarded to CCCC, thus entrenching its involvement in major infrastructure projects in Kenya (Anthony, 2013; Mwende, 2013). CCCC is a major Chinese construction company, that is majority-owned by the Chinese state and has operations all over the world, sometimes through its subsidiaries. Although the company is a contractor for the Kenyan government, it wields enormous influence over several aspects of the port such as the hiring of personnel and control over who can access the port. As such, the company has repeatedly found itself entangled in some of the controversies rocking the port's ongoing construction. However, the port's enclave nature, together with its close engagement with the government, has shielded it from adverse publicity that other Chinese companies have had to endure.

As a result, whereas it is common to see reports of confrontations between local communities and Chinese companies in other areas of Kenya, such reports on Lamu are rare (Zhao, 2020; Bhamidipati and Hansen, 2021). However, this does not mean that Chinese corporate operations at Lamu Port are smooth. As I illustrate below, some of their practices have elicited mixed responses from the local community, leaders, and a range of NGOs.

Controversial practices

Chinese companies often base their competitiveness on attributes such as efficiency, the timely implementation of projects and their affordability (Hofmann et al., 2007; Deutsche Welle, 2020; Jiang, 2020). This is also the case for Lamu Port where government officials repeatedly praised CCCC operations for working within the project's timelines.[8] In interviews with government officials, the 24-hour working model by CCCC workers has been particularly highlighted, on numerous occasions, as a practice that Kenyan contractors can emulate from their Chinese counterparts.[9] However, these positive attributes have been overshadowed by several concerns from a section of community members in Lamu and CSOs. Three concerns have particularly emerged as the most prominent. They include concerns over the environmental impact of the construction activities, poor labour conditions at the port, and forced displacement and human rights violations. Indeed, as a number of studies on Chinese investments in Africa note, these concerns are not unique to the situation at the Lamu Port (Akorsu and Cooke, 2011; Mohan, 2013; Plummer, 2019).

In Lamu, critics such as fisherfolk and hoteliers note that the rapid construction of Lamu Port has come at an enormous cost to the environment, which has in turn affected their livelihoods[10] (High Court of Kenya, 2018). To illustrate, the port is being constructed in a spot considered a key traditional fishing ground and the main transport channel by residents around the Lamu archipelago.[11] Given that earlier work for the port's construction entailed the clearing of over two hectares of mangroves and dredging works, several residents and activists complained that such activities adversely affected fishing activities,[12] water transport and the tourist sector, which are key industries in Lamu that support thousands of residents (High Court of Kenya, 2018). Despite assurances that CCCC would pursue less intrusive dredging techniques as it constructs the port, a number of fishermen and environmental activists particularly decried that dredging activities by the company had adversely affected the environment, thereby depriving fisherfolk of their sources of livelihoods (Ministry of Transport Republic of Kenya, 2013: ii). Such activities were noted to have destroyed mangrove forests, sea grass and coral reefs which serve as nesting areas for fish and other sea animals[13] (High Court of Kenya, 2018). In addition, given that dredging works were being undertaken in a channel that acts as a key transport route within the Lamu archipelago, residents and boat operators raised concerns about their safety as the dredging activities had not only deepened the sea but had turned a large section of the sea water murky and therefore unsuitable for fishing.[14]

Secondly, CCCC activities at the Lamu Port have been marred by complaints of poor labour conditions, especially for locally recruited workers.[15] In this case, current and previous CCCC employees complained that they were paid meagre wages and were often subjected to poor working conditions, thereby overshadowing the common assertion from both the government and CCCC that the port's construction had created hundreds of jobs.[16] Claims of poor working conditions are diverse and encompass complaints such as long working hours, harassment and subpar living conditions for workers residing within the port. For instance, formerly employed youths by CCCC on Lamu Island complained that other than being forced to work extended hours, the company also pays extremely low wages (around USD 3.68 per day) that barely met their daily expenses and transport to their workplaces. For instance, one parent-cum-activist on Lamu Island expressed this concern as follows:

> When they announced those jobs, the children crossed the sea and went. When they reached there, they were given KES 400 in a day without being provided with transport to and from work. At that time, a boat ride from here to Mokowe used to cost KES 100 for the boat, which came to KES 200 if you go back and forth. And that was from here to the jetty. Not even to the port. So, it was like

they were being paid the transport money. (Interview with activist/ parent, Lamu Island, 8 February 2019)

As I illustrate below, a section of the youths on Lamu Island have reacted by boycotting work at Lamu Port. Due to their reluctance to work under such difficult circumstances, CCCC has been forced to source employees from the Lamu mainland and other parts of Kenya, mostly former employees from its subsidiary CRBC that constructed the SGR from Mombasa to Naivasha, through Nairobi (Xinhua, 2015). However, this move has elicited another round of controversy from local politicians, especially those representing indigenous interests, who contest the fact that many jobs at the port have gone to 'outsiders' (Mohamed, 2018). Despite threats by local politicians that they would lead protesters to disrupt operations in the port if their demands are not met, no meaningful remedies have been undertaken and, as a result, controversies over the labour practices persist. The concerns over poor working conditions at Lamu Port are illustrative of a common concern that cuts across many Chinese firms operating in Kenya (Opondo, 2009; Zhao, 2020). Although CCCC has managed to create jobs and construct the port within acceptable timelines, the reputation of the company in the eyes of the local population has suffered, thus entrenching the perception that China's increasing engagement in Kenya is predatory.

Thirdly, CCCC has also been embroiled in controversy over the displacement of fisherfolk from their traditional fishing grounds and the lack of spillover benefits to the local community from its operations in Lamu. The former concern emanates from the ongoing construction activities which have meant that fisherfolk are prohibited from fishing around the port area due to both safety and security concerns.[17] The latter concern emanates from the enclave nature of the port which has led to minimal interactions between CCCC activities and the host community. It is particularly a key concern for the business community which had anticipate cashing in on new opportunities that would come with the port's construction.[18] As such, members of the business community in the nearby townships of Lamu Island, Mokowe and Hindi have emerged as one of the most vocal critics of CCCC. According to one activist in Lamu, this concern was further accentuated by 'CCCC's failure to implement any corporate social responsibility project in Lamu'.[19] However, senior national government officials serving in Lamu have emerged as CCCC's key defenders, thereby signifying the close relations between CCCC and the national government. In this case, senior government officials often downplay concerns raised by the local business community by pointing out that local entrepreneurs lack both the capacity and skills to supply the enormous material needs at Lamu Port.[20] The grievance of the displacement of fisherfolk from key fishing grounds is closely tied to human rights violations that fisherfolk have had to endure on two levels. The first one touches on their rights to compensation, which is enshrined in Kenya's constitution. Up to date, fisherfolk are yet to be compensated for their losses despite the 'fact that the port is already operational (Bachmann and Kilaka, 2021). Secondly, accidents between fishing vessels and big ships supplying construction material at the port have seen several fisherfolk not only lose their fishing gear and boats, but also be left with injuries and trauma. According to several affected fisherfolk, their attempts to report and seek compensation for their losses have always been frustrated by different government officials who have often been reluctant to intervene on their behalf.[21]

Taken together, these complaints have therefore undermined the carefully curated image by both Chinese diplomatic officials and companies that their companies come with unique and progressive practices that are transforming the infrastructural landscape in Kenya and beyond. In fact, these controversies have greatly perpetuated growing anti-Chinese sentiments among aggrieved members of the community, such as fisherfolk and businesspeople. More importantly, a section of the host community has demonstrated their agency through attempts to engage and resolve the controversies. In this case, aggrieved members of the community have engaged with the Chinese contractor and state officials in several ways with different levels of success. As I illustrate now, such engagements have included court action, boycotting work at Lamu Port and constant demands for opportunities at the port, which are fused with threats of protests.

Unmasking local agency in Lamu: Contestations and intrigues

Aggrieved community members, activists and local politicians have exhibited local agencies in three main ways, namely lobbying to be included in the port's activities, litigation, and boycotting working at Lamu Port. As I illustrate, the initiatives have not only attracted different responses from both CCCC and the national government but have also been deeply entangled in local politics, thereby leading to mixed outcomes.

Negotiating local involvement

One of the areas where a section of the Lamu community exhibited local agency centred on their efforts to be included in the planning and implementation process of Lamu Port. Their efforts were particularly driven by concerns that the national government had sidelined them in the port's rollout. As a result, landowners in the area where Lamu Port was supposed to be situated, together with political leaders, fisherfolk and activists, put up a spirited campaign to be included in the planning process to take care of their interests.[22] These efforts took the form of protests, lobbying and even disrupting earlier works linked to the port, such as the construction of a new road towards the port's location on land that was yet to be acquired for the LAPSSET project.[23]

To avert community disruptions and guarantee the launch of the project by the three presidents of Kenya, South Sudan and Ethiopia in March 2012, the government established the Lamu Port Steering Committee[24] in January 2012 to act as a medium of communication between the national government and sections of the Lamu community (UNHCR, 2012). This move is illustrative of developments in other sites along the LAPSSET corridor where communities have not only anticipated the infrastructure project differently but have attempted or managed to fight for their inclusion in LAPSSET's rollout (Elliott, 2016; Aalders et al., 2021).

The committee was chaired by the County Commissioner and had 50 members who represented various community interests.[25] Apart from government officials and representatives of civil society, a representative of CCCC also sat on the committee, which was a significant development since it was one of those rare moments where Lamu-based activists had direct access to the company. For the short duration of its existence, the committee played a crucial role in mitigating conflicts between the national government and CCCC on the one hand, and sections of the Lamu community on the other. For instance, the committee was particularly involved in the selection of beneficiaries of the LAPSSET presidential scholarship scheme and agitating for compensation for affected landowners and fisherfolk. One of its major achievements was the compensation of landowners in the areas where the current port stands. Although the landowners lacked title deeds to prove their ownership of the land, the Steering Committee lobbied hard for their compensation.

Regardless of its achievements, the Steering Committee faced several challenges in the brief period that it existed. Not only was the committee constituted hurriedly, but it also marginalised some sections of the community. Given that the committee was not gazetted, it also faced funding challenges that hampered its ability to conduct activities effectively. Additionally, the committee not only had a bloated membership, but also lacked decision-making powers (Sena, 2012; Kituo Cha Sheria, 2014). The big most formidable challenge, however, came from political rivalry among Lamu's political elites, more specifically, from the first county government of Lamu under the leadership of Issa Timamy that came into office in 2013. The new governor insisted that the county government was the legitimate representative of community interests and therefore challenged the involvement of the Steering Committee on issues related to Lamu Port. For example, in 2013, the county government ignored the initial list of beneficiaries for the LAPSSET presidential scheme by coming up with their own list (Kituo Cha Sheria, 2014). To avert a stalemate, the then County Commissioner disbanded the Steering Committee and chose to work with the county government. A former member of the Steering Committee summarised the situation as follows:

> So, when the county government came, the governor said that the county was not represented. The governor perceived the people on the Steering Committee as not his supporters, so politics came

in and he insisted that the Steering Committee be disbanded. And honestly there were some good works that the Steering Committee did like the farmers' land valuation. They had said they were doing valuation on the land and not the crops, that is when a private valuer was brought in who valued it at 2 million per acre whereas they were saying 1 million per acre, so there were negotiations that brought an agreement at 1.5 million per acre. But when the county government came, it forced the Steering Committee to be abolished. (Interview with a former member of the Lamu Port Steering Committee, 6 February 2019)

From the above quote, political struggles played a key role in undermining the existence of the Steering Committee and clearly illustrate some of the challenges that hamper local agency. In this case, the governor perceived the Steering Committee to be full of loyalists for his political rival, Fahim Twaha, who had been the area Member of Parliament when the Steering Committee was established. The county's decision not to join forces with the Steering Committee effectively deprived other actors and activists of a formal platform where they could articulate their issues. Additionally, it meant that CCCC was no longer accessible, as engagements were now between the county and the national government. Yet, in spite of these challenges, the committee's influence on the final valuation of actual compensation to landowners is a clear testimony of how local actors managed to exert their influence and safeguard the interests of a section of community members.

Environmental activism and navigating transnational networks

Court action by activists and selected members of the Lamu community challenging the port's construction has emerged as another prominent demonstration of local agency (High Court of Kenya, 2018). In this case, in January 2012, a few community members in Lamu, with the support of one Kenyan and two international organisations that specialise in public-interest litigation, filed a court case challenging the port construction and the LAPSSET project on three key grounds (Center for International and Environmental Law, 2012; High Court of Kenya, 2018). First, the petitioners asserted that the project's design and implementation violated several constitution and statutory laws that touch on project implementation and environmental considerations. Secondly, the petitioners highlighted the adverse effects of the port construction on the marine ecosystem in the larger Lamu archipelago in the form of the destruction of mangrove forests, discharge of industrial waste into the environment and adverse implications for fish species and marine life in general. Thirdly, the petitioners further argued that the port and other components of the LAPSSET project posed a major danger to Lamu's cultural heritage, way of life and livelihoods (High Court of Kenya, 2018).

The concern over the environmental consequences of the port's construction and its implication for the livelihoods of many fisherfolk was greatly influenced by the nature of CCCC activities since it started constructing the port. Environmental activists were particularly critical of CCCC's ecological intervention, for instance, the decision to clear around two hectares of mangrove forest to pave the way for construction activities and ongoing dredging works, which were noted to have increased the water's turbidity and murkiness.[26] As such, these activities not only destroyed crucial coral reefs and affected the population and location of the fish, but also negatively impacted many fisherfolk who relied on the areas around the port for fishing due to its strategic location. Faced with these merits, the court ruled in favour of the petitioners and ordered the state to compensate around 4,700 fisherfolk with KES 1.7 billion (USD 17 million). In addition, the court returned the environmental impact assessment licence for the first three berths of the Lamu Port back to the National Environment Management Authority and ordered the project proponents to strictly address the environmental shortcomings that were identified by the petitioners (High Court of Kenya, 2018).

A keen focus on the court's ruling together with the petitioners' decision to pursue litigation reveals several insights into their local agency. First, by going to court, the petitioners avoided direct confrontation with both the national government and CCCC, both have enormous resources at their disposal. Secondly, the court therefore presented a neutral ground where they raised their concerns without fear of intimidation or harassment, which several environmental activists had previously endured in their advocacy work on LAPSSET-related issues (Human Rights Watch and National Coalition of Human Rights Defenders Kenya, 2018). Other than that, the petitioners pursued legal avenue, cognizant of the fact that court rulings, unless appealed, are binding on all involved parties. Thirdly, their agency is also demonstrated in the framing of grievances. By depicting the concerns as violations of their constitutional rights and that of the environment, the petitioners not only made the courts take their concerns seriously but also attracted the attention and support of national and international environmental activists, mostly from the Western world.

On this note, it should also be noted that the local agency of the petitioners was greatly aided by external support, mostly from environmental and human rights organisations located in Nairobi and abroad, and from the previous county government of Lamu under the leadership of Governor Issa Timamy. Four notable organisations that provided support to the petitioners were the Katiba Institute, Natural Justice, the Global Initiative for Economic, Social and Cultural Rights and the Center for International Environmental Law, which all specialise in public interest litigation. As Gloppen (2008) argues, public interest litigation has over the recent past emerged as a key strategy by activists to amplify the voices of the poor in the legal-political system and as a mechanism for making the state more responsive to their needs and concerns. Such support is often driven by a mix of factors, including ideological, the international human rights movement, and a liberal reform agenda. Public interest litigation therefore becomes a strategy for effecting social change by empowering the vulnerable to challenge powerful actors and social injustices.

The involvement of activists, especially those based in the West, presents another layer for understanding how practices travel. Most of the international groups that support Lamu-based activists operate in different contexts all over the world, especially where communities are perceived to be vulnerable to grand infrastructure projects. Most of the strategies that these international organisations pursue travel from one locality to another, especially if they have been successfully deployed in the past. One of these strategies can be seen in the choice of litigation as a strategy of contention. For example, this is particularly visible in the activities of Natural Justice, which has specialised in providing legal help to communities to challenge the environmental impacts of big projects (Natural Justice, 2021). In Lamu, this type of support was not only limited to the Port. For instance, external support played a key role in halting plans for the construction of the proposed Lamu coal power plant in 2019. With the support of external actors, mostly from the West, Lamu-based activists not only managed to successfully push for the cancellation of the environmental licence for the coal project, but also piled pressure on major financiers as well as contractors to abandon the project with success (Boulle, 2019; Ayhan and Jacob, 2022).

In Lamu, support from these organisations was crucial since it provided the petitioners with much-needed resources, such as funding, legal and environmental expertise, moral support, and publicity, whose absence could have seriously undermined their efforts to find a solution to problems bedevilling them. For instance, Katiba Institute not only provided pro bono services to the petitioners, but also facilitated the participation of renowned experts from both Kenya and abroad in the court proceedings.[27] Their involvement was particularly helpful in providing expert opinions on the concerns raised by the petitioners and challenging testimonies from government lawyers and experts. On its part, the support of the previous county government played a key role in legitimising many of the concerns that were raised by the petitioners. Although the county government did not explicitly support the court process, its altercations and engagements with the national government over port-related issues mirrored the concerns raised by the petitioners in court.

Negotiating local content

However, even with a favorable court ruling, the controversy did not end, but rather took a new twist due to disagreements concerning compensation modalities and a decision by the Kenya Ports Authority (KPA) to appeal the court ruling.[28] Such developments constrain local agencies and hence illustrate the structural impediments that local actors face in their attempts to settle controversies. According to one senior county official in Lamu who is actively involved in this controversy, KPA's decision to appeal the ruling was driven by the need to avert the stoppage of ongoing construction work by CCCC. KPA's move, which is solely intended to facilitate the port's construction, sheds light on the extent to which government agencies shield and support CCCC in its activities. As I elaborate below, the support that CCCC gets from the government has indeed been a key factor constraining the local agency of affected Lamu residents. As such, this has only served to perpetuate existing controversies, thereby contributing to increasing anti-Chinese sentiments.

A section of aggrieved members of the community in Lamu have also demonstrated their local agency by resigning or boycotting working for CCCC in protest over the poor working conditions at the port.[29] A key observation was that the boycott was taking place amidst high unemployment rates in Lamu. Lamu youths, especially those coming from Lamu Island and claiming to be indigenous to the county, pointed out that boycotting work in the port's construction was a demonstration of their resistance towards exploitative labour practices being perpetrated by the Chinese company. Several former CCCC employees who had previously worked as fisherfolk, particularly perceived the daily wage from working at port construction as ridiculously low compared to what they were making from the fishing industry.[30] By boycotting working for CCCC, the former employees therefore challenge the common narrative from national government officials and CCCC that their interventions in the construction sector are creating thousands of jobs. Whereas most individuals from the indigenous communities resist working at the port due to poor labour conditions, Lamu residents, especially those considered as migrant communities, dominate CCCC's labour pool and serve to illustrate the social divisions in Lamu, which have greatly hampered efforts at collective agitation by affected residents. Even though Lamu residents account for the highest percentage of CCCC employees, Lamu political leaders, especially those representing the interests of indigenous communities, consider this development unacceptable since it allegedly only benefits perceived outsiders. As a result, whereas local concerns that greatly shaped CCCC's move to employ workers from Lamu aimed at promoting local acceptance of the project,[31] the grievances by a section of the Lamu community, mostly those who consider themselves 'natives' to the region, have neither derailed construction activities, nor led to a substantial improvement in the labour practices at the port.

The failure by aggrieved community members in Lamu to influence the labour practices at the port stands out, especially when compared to other areas in Kenya where locally recruited labourers have protested unfair labour practices by Chinese companies and managed to extract deals. Two reasons may explain this. First, the port's enclave nature together with its heavy securitisation have made it difficult for aggrieved workers to stage protests or disrupt ongoing construction activities. The fact that all CCCC employees are non-unionised has also made it difficult for the aggrieved to collectively agitate for fair labour rights.

Secondly, given that CCCC is a contractor on a major state project, it enjoys strong support from national government officials, who in essence have emerged as the main defenders of their practices. In fact, senior government officials in the region often dismiss claims of poor pay as unwarranted and often base their assertions on a common stereotype that natives in the region are lazy and therefore unable to cope with the rigours and routines of formal employment[32] (Kazungu, 2019). With this position, government officials not only silence legitimate claims by affected youths but also block potential avenues for resolving grievances from workers. The perceived biases of the state in favour of CCCC have thereby fomented feelings of resentment against both the national government and the Chinese company. Therefore, whereas residents were able to demonstrate their agency by having CCCC employ most of its employees from Lamu, this did not translate to any influence on labour practices. As a result, complaints over poor pay and other labour malpractices persist. This reality has therefore entrenched the perception that the ongoing port construction is reproducing the long history of marginalisation that Lamu residents have endured in post-independent Kenya.

Attempts at remaking corporate practices

These three cases illustrate several aspects of Chinese-community engagements in Lamu. Although some of their practices have attracted criticisms from different segments of the Lamu community and even activists, the company remains unresponsive largely due to its close association with the government. It can therefore be argued that such a relationship has severely hampered the agency of local communities. As a contractor on a major flagship project for Kenya's government, this relationship is even stronger and is well illustrated by the spirited defence of the company's activities by the government officials serving in the region. By being partisan in such controversies, the government limits the avenues for resolving such disputes and inadvertently helps perpetuate the controversial practices.

Most importantly, such action also pushes aggrieved parties to seek alternative ways of addressing their complaints. As Lamu's case illustrates, when confronted with a constrained space for airing their grievances, litigation has emerged as the most common and visible approach that community members together with CSOs have adopted to challenge some of the practices that they consider harmful. As such the decision to go to court, despite the uncertainties that such an action presents, demonstrates that local communities do not consider the government as a neutral arbiter in their struggles with the activities of CCCC.

In addition, the level of local agency has been different depending on the specific issue areas in which grievances emerge. This is particularly the case for grievances around labour practices and environmental concerns. Regarding labour practices, the inability of aggrieved workers to challenge poor labour practices can be attributed to reasons such as the precarious contracts that local employees hold, the availability of a large pool of unemployed people who can easily be recruited and replaced to work in Lamu Port, and the strong ties between the Chinese contractor and the national government. These factors have therefore seen CCCC having little incentive to engage with controversies over poor labour practices, which has forced affected individuals to boycott working at Lamu Port. Conversely, agitation over environmental concerns has resulted in different outcomes. Here, community members who petitioned the court were able to demonstrate their local agency by successfully arguing the case. However, this was largely possible due to the support from external activist groups. The court action was particularly instrumental in forcing the national government to engage with fisherfolk on modalities of compensation.

Moreover, power dynamics between CCCC and the aggrieved parties have also played a key role in perpetuating the contested practices. As a contractor to a government project, CCCC enjoys enormous advantages over the local community and is shielded from direct engagement with the local community. In this case, CCCC requires the government to provide it with a conducive environment to undertake its activities. Therefore, aggrieved members of the community often find themselves battling both the government and CCCC whenever they have grievances. To illustrate, during my fieldwork, I encountered a group of fishermen whose attempts to be compensated by CCCC for a collision in the high seas with a ship supplying building materials to the port were frustrated by different government agencies, such as the police, the KPA, and even fishing officials, who refused to record and follow up on the accidents.[33] Furthermore, activists[34] who attempt to voice critical concerns over both the port and the activities of CCCC complain of intimidation and harassment by state officials and are often labelled as being 'anti-development' or accused of having ties to 'terrorist' groups (Kenya Human Rights Commission, 2015). Consequently, CCCC is rarely contested directly for its actions. Given that its activities are restricted to the port facilities, which are heavily protected, it is hard for aggrieved communities to express their dissatisfaction. Therefore, despite the controversies, CCCC remains unbowed and continues its activities undeterred, even when its reputation in the eyes of the local population is at stake. According to the affected communities, despite the project's magnitude, the company has yet to initiate any social events or social investment projects in Lamu as part of its outreach programme or corporate social responsibility.

Conclusion

As this study shows, some of the construction practices of Chinese companies have successfully travelled to many sites in Kenya where these companies are involved in big infrastructure projects. Through an analysis of their involvement in Lamu Port, this chapter has illustrated how certain practices are a key aspect of the growing Chinese infrastructure globality, as Chinese actors cement their presence in Kenya's construction industry. Some of the practices have been embroiled in controversies that involved aggrieved members of the community. In contesting the controversial practices by the Chinese company involved in constructing Lamu Port, local communities have exhibited their agency, albeit with different levels of success. Although aggrieved members of the community were able to raise their concerns and even attract the attention of the national government, their ability to achieve their intended outcomes was often hindered by political rivalry among the fractious political elites in Lamu, strong connections between the national government and the Chinese contractor, and a strong resolve by the national government to implement the project despite many unaddressed issues. These include compensation to fisherfolk and the launch of the project even without a proper environmental and strategic impact assessment report for the LAPSSET corridor project.

Despite the mixed results, the fact that communities reacted and managed to get favourable court rulings, and even spearheaded the creation of the Lamu Port Steering Committee indicates a level of local agency that has specifically been aided by political developments in Kenya since 2010, community concerns to safeguard their interests, and the involvement of international activist groups, mostly based in the West.

The involvement of external players demonstrates that practices of activism have equally travelled, just like the practices of construction by Chinese companies. In this case, activist groups with expertise in effectively challenging big projects through litigation have played a key role in challenging the controversial aspects of both Lamu Port and the Lamu coal plant. This assistance has greatly aided the local agency of communities and activists in Lamu since it provided them with both material and ideational support that was crucial in engaging with a powerful state that has exhibited its interest in implementing the project regardless of community concerns. The general absence of Chinese-based activist groups in the controversies, together with the heavy involvement of Western-based organisations, may point to geo-political dynamics at play that further complicated the situation, but that must be put into perspective given the overall limited activism by Chinese NGOs (see Sändig and Hönke in this volume).

PART THREE

EVERYDAY ENTANGLEMENTS

7

A GLOBAL SENSE OF WORK*PLACE*

LABOUR RELATIONS IN SINO-AFRICAN CONSTRUCTION SITES

Elisa Gambino[1] *and Mandira Bagwandeen*

Introduction

Since the development of the Lamu Port project in northern Kenya began in 2016, construction site noises—a combination of the busy engines of cranes and the constant rasping of the dredger—have resounded throughout the dense mangroves and calm waters of the Lamu archipelago. The Chinese state-owned company China Road and Bridge Corporation (CRBC), a subsidiary of China Communication Construction Company (CCCC), was contracted to build the port of Lamu, while the Kenyan government is financing the project's first phase, which is estimated to cost USD 480 million (LAPSSET Corridor Development Authority, 2020). The development of this port is part of a broader regional connectivity project, namely the Lamu Port–South Sudan–Ethiopia Transport Corridor, which aims to connect Kenya to its neighbours via cross-border infrastructures, such as brand-new highways and a railway. Lamu Port will play a vital role in the region's integration efforts as it is expected to become one of the largest ports in East Africa and an import-export hub

157

for South Sudan, Ethiopia, and the northern regions of Kenya (on the development of Lamu Port and LAPSSET see Browne, 2015; Chome, 2020; Gambino, 2020; Lesutis, 2020; Aalders, 2021).

Growing China–Africa economic engagement and the increase in Sino-African infrastructure projects have highlighted that China–Africa relations are increasingly unfolding beyond government-to-government agreements and elite relations (see Alden and Large, 2018). Since the late 1990s, the growing demand for infrastructure financing and construction in Africa (Nugent, 2018b; Goodfellow, 2020) has coincided with the 'outward' push given by the Chinese state, prompting an increase in Sino-African engagement in the infrastructure sector. Beyond the much-discussed financing mechanisms—and their implications—characterising Chinese-sponsored projects (Alden and Jiang, 2019; Jones and Zeng, 2019; Sum, 2019; Brautigam, 2020; Carmody, Taylor and Zajontz, 2022), Chinese contractors have significantly expanded their market share in Africa (Huang and Chen, 2016). In 2009, 50% of the overall projects built by Chinese companies were funded by non-Chinese actors (Chen and Orr, 2009), and recent estimates suggest that Chinese contractors' revenues increased from USD 28 billion in 2009 to a record USD 54.7 billion in 2015[2] (China Africa Research Initiative, 2021). As such, an examination of Sino-African engagement should include several different actors, such as construction workers and company managers.

In parallel, many scholars, policymakers, civil society organisations, and media organisations have questioned Chinese companies' labour practices. Labour relations, particularly in terms of contractual conditions (DfID and China Centre for Chinese Studies Stellenbosch, 2006; Rounds and Huang, 2017), management practices (Oya, 2019; Fei, 2020), skill transfer efforts (Meng and Bempong Nyantakyi, 2019; Bempong Nyantakyi, Meng and Palmer, 2022) and the localisation of labour (Kernen and Lam, 2014; Gambino, 2020) have been at the centre of these debates. In turn, the proliferation of Sino-African construction sites has prompted reflections on the ways in which (and the extent to which) Chinese domestic practices of labour governance are 'transported' to overseas projects. Specifically pertinent to this volume is questioning the extent to which practices are remade at the intersection of external engagement with Africa's infrastructure development, which resonates with concerns traditionally associated with the study of labour relations.

The geographical boundaries of the workplace, however, have often constrained the investigation of labour dynamics, particularly in the case of construction sites as the practice of 'living at work' is widespread. Yet, labour relations unfolding in Sino-African construction sites speak to broader debates on the intersection of diverse labour governance practices and the formation of 'ethnotechnical hierarchies' (Hecht, 2002) in Sino-African workplaces (Procopio, 2018; Links, 2021; Chiyemura, Gambino and Zajontz, 2022). For instance, Driessen's (2019) work on Chinese roadbuilders in Ethiopia through the lens of everyday resistance (Scott, 1985) highlights the need to investigate daily encounters amongst Chinese and African workers in the context of broader narratives and trajectories commonly associated with Sino-African engagement. In another prominent example, while exploring the practice of 'living at work', Fei (2020) draws connections between the spatial organisation within workers' dormitories in China and mining compounds in apartheid-era South Africa to analyse the implications of spatial techniques on managerial practices in Sino-Ethiopian construction sites.

As Oya (2019) also suggests, a multidimensional analysis of African and Chinese labour markets and political economies is needed to capture the various processes and outcomes of labour relations. Specifically, he posits that these can only be understood through the analysis of the fluid intersection between China and Africa's labour regimes, state–society and state–capital relations, as well as structural dynamics (ibid.: 257). Thus, in this chapter, we build on this premise to investigate workplace dynamics in Sino-African construction sites through the case study of Lamu Port in Kenya. Specifically, we focus on the practice of 'living at work' to capture the complexities of Sino-African labour relations and illuminate 'practices in the making' emerging from said encounters.

The practice of 'living at work' refers to spatial, material, and social dimensions characterising Sino-African workplace relations. Firstly, 'living at work' refers to the organisation of and nonreciprocal access to living spaces (see also Fei, 2020), which is strongly influenced by the 'ethnotechnical' hierarchical structures (see Hecht, 2002) regulating the construction site. Secondly, the practice of 'living at work' brings to light the material implications of structural constraints in Sino-African labour relations, such as the incentive/deterrent regime discussed in this chapter (see also Driessen, 2019). Thirdly, 'living at work' also implies another aspect of workplace dynamics, namely the trend whereby the construction site also becomes a space for social connections and brokerage. As a heuristic of workplace dynamics, 'living at work' embodies both how the inequalities and asymmetrical power relations in Sino-African construction sites are refracted into Chinese corporate practices, as well as the ways in which African workers secure their working lives by means of social relations gathered through the workplace.

This chapter draws from critical geographer Doreen Massey's conceptualisations of place to suggest that the study of Sino-African construction sites should rely on a dynamic understanding of the workplace. In this chapter, we posit that workplace dynamics, situated at the intersection of narratives 'within' and 'outside' Sino-African construction sites—such as labour control, managerial arbitrariness, aspirations of social mobility, and labour agency—have differentiated implications for Sino-African labour relations.

The chapter is based on qualitative data collected through ethnographic observations and interviews conducted by Elisa Gambino at the Lamu Port construction site between February and March 2019, complemented by single-day visits before and after the ethnographic research period. The ethnographic approach to research—in line with other authors' work (see Driessen, 2019; Fei, 2020)—was selected in order to understand the social, material, and ideational conditions of the construction site. This allowed us to explore a set of key themes emerging from previous visits and how they unfold in practice, to later be triangulated through in-depth interviews and follow-up site visits. This highlighted the relationship between labour relations on the construction site and specific social, material, ideational, political, and institutional contexts characterising Sino-African engagement.

The chapter is structured as follows. In the first section, we reflect on the boundaries of the workplace and put forward our conceptualisation of the workplace through the lens of Massey's theory of place. In the second section, we investigate the workplace dynamics at the Lamu Port construction site, focusing on the spatial organisation of 'living at work' in this Sino-African workplace. In the third section, we analyse the connections between China's political economy of work—particularly the 'virtue' of *chiku nailao*—and the workplace dynamics at the construction site. In the fourth section, we assess the 'brokerage' of labour controversies amongst Chinese and Kenyan workers, focusing on the figures of 'brokers' and connecting this to the broader discourse characteristics of labour relations in Kenya's construction industry and beyond. The conclusion highlights the different implications of work*place* dynamics.

The 'boundaries' of workplace dynamics

Like most construction sites around the world, the Lamu Port construction site in Kenya is gated. Only reachable through a non-paved road or by boat (and with the relevant authorisations) the boundaries of this workplace appear to be clearly marked by the perimeters of the construction site. Analytically, the workplace is indeed often defined by its material boundaries, a conceptualisation that inevitably produces a dichotomic relationship between what (and who) is 'inside' or 'outside' the perimeters of the workplace. In Lamu, this boundary—cordoned off and monitored to only allow the entry and exit of workers, goods, and resources—resonates with discussions around a practice commonly associated with Chinese overseas businesses.

Chinese companies have a reputation for building gated residential compounds and corporate enclaves governed as private entities with limited linkages to the local economy and society— similar to pre-colonial mercantilist *entrepôts* (see Mohan, 2013). The concept of enclaves echoes French colonial thinking of *l'Afrique utile* (usable/useful Africa), understood as 'noncontiguous "useful" bits that are secured, policed, and, in a minimal sense, governed through private or semiprivate means' (Ferguson, 2006: 39–40).

For instance, Bergesen (2013) discusses instances of China–Africa engagement as 'surgical colonialism', which is 'resource extraction by a foreign power that involves [minimal] local disruption, making the extraction almost surgical in nature' (ibid.: 302).

This concept is very much reminiscent of the static understanding of space (see Mohan, 2013). Yet, enclaves are connected 'not in a continuous, territorial national grid, but in transnational networks that link dispersed spaces in a selective, point-to-point fashion' (Ferguson, 2005: 380). Thus, 'sites of large-scale economic and infrastructure investment', as is the case for construction sites, can be viewed as '"frontier zones" in which well-known modes of governing are reproduced and reinforced, but in which contestation and new practices also become visible' (Hönke, 2018a: 348).

In this chapter, we aim to follow this line of inquiry by focusing on investigating labour relations beyond a bounded understanding of the workplace—until recently prominent in organisational studies (see Sergot and Saives, 2016). Instead, our analysis is inspired by the study of labour relations through the lens of labour agency (Herod, 2001; Castree, 2007; Coe and Jordhus-Lier, 2011), labour regimes (Lee, 1999; Knutsen and Hansson, 2010; Taylor and Rioux, 2018; Cezne and Wethal, 2022), and politics of production (Burawoy, 1985; Thompson, 1990; Rowen, 2015), which focus on the socio spatial relations characterising workplace dynamics.

With regard to Sino-African construction sites, Wethal (2017) borrows the concept of 'labour agency'—understood as the ability of individuals or collectives to advance their objectives of 'shifting the *status quo* in favour of workers, even if temporarily' (Coe and Jordhus-Lier, 2011: 216)—from labour geographers to study work dynamics in Chinese-built projects in Mozambique. Wethal analyses two parallel, yet divided, workplace regimes of Chinese and Mozambican workers on construction sites. She suggests that although Mozambican workers expressed their resentment for poor working and living conditions, they are 'locked in their current situation, with their agency heavily constrained' (Wethal, 2017: 399). This is primarily due to the lack of alternative job opportunities and support from Mozambican state and non-state organisations.

Furthermore, Wethal rightly points out that the organisation of life and work on the construction site—'the technical and social organisation of the labour process' (2017: 386)—and the politics of production—'the political apparatus of production and the institutions that regulate and shape workplace practices' (ibid.)—are inherently interlinked (see also Peck, 1996). As an example of this, Driessen (2019) shows that Sino-Ethiopian labour controversies— particularly the contestation of terminating employment—are mediated at the township level through *wereda* courts, which have become the '*de facto* mediators in relations between the Chinese employers and Ethiopian labourers' (ibid.: 150, italics added). These courts not only lie at the interface of Chinese and Ethiopian workers but also negotiate broader political, economic, and social practices and discourses that shape workplace relations. These township courts have become a way for Ethiopian labourers 'to keep their Chinese managers in check and to improve wage levels, employment conditions and contractual procedures' (ibid.: 132). Thus, *wereda* courts represent an instance of the intersection between the organisation of work at construction sites and the institutions that contribute to shaping transnational labour governance practices.

Workplace dynamics 'inside' the construction site are shaped by relations across multiple and interrelated scales and, in turn, broader trajectories 'outside' the material boundaries of the construction site. Similarly, Fei (2020: 9) suggests that relations amongst different actors, places, and scales need to be analysed. This means that the workplace dynamics of Sino-African construction sites should be investigated through the lens of 'relationships and processes emerg[ing] from both within and beyond the construction site' (ibid.). Here, we attempt to answer this call for a dynamic—and relational—understanding of the workplace and labour dynamics by building on Fei's (2020) and Sergot and Saives's (2016) work on the insertion of Massey's conceptualisation of place into the study of work*places*.

Starting from an understanding of space as 'constructed out of the multiplicity of social relations across all spatial scales', in which space is simultaneously the 'production of the social' and the product of said interactions (Massey, 1994c: 4), Massey proceeded in offering a reframing of the concept of 'place'. Countering static and bounded—or, as she phrases it, 'nostalgic' (see Massey, 1995)—understandings of place typically associated with locality studies in the late 1980s and 1990s (see for instance Cooke, 1986), Massey considers place as 'a particular articulation ... a particular moment in those networks of social relation and understandings' (Massey, 1994c: 5, 1994b, 1994a), or, in short, a 'spatio-temporal event' (Massey, 2005: 131).

In other words, a place is not understood through distinctions one can draw between a place and what is 'outside' of it, but instead 'through the specificity of the mix of links and interconnections *to* that "beyond"' (Massey, 1994c: 5, italics in original). According to this conceptualisation of 'place', a place is not unique per se, but its specificity is derived from the relations to broader dynamics and trajectories, in what Massey terms 'a global sense of place' (1994a: 156). This understanding of 'place' allows for the analysis of workplace dynamics in the context of broader—and often transnational—trajectories that characterise specific labour markets and political economies (see also Oya, 2019). More specifically, in our analysis, we focus on the encounter of narratives 'within' and 'outside' the construction site—such as labour control, managerial arbitrarity, aspiration of social mobility, and labour agency—to illuminate different outcomes of labour relations.

The following sections will present empirical vignettes from the Lamu Port construction site to analyse labour relations in the Sino-African work*place*. Although concerns over labour dynamics at the construction site are reminiscent of discussions emerging from Chinese construction sites—and Chinese engagement in other sectors (Jauch and Sakaria, 2009; Akorsu and Cooke, 2011)—across the African continent (Lee, 2009; Giese and Thiel, 2014; Fei, 2020), this chapter will specifically focus on the 'brokerage' of instances of labour controversy. Indeed, 'place' is closely related to the 'unavoidable challenge of negotiating [the] here-and-now' (Massey, 2005: 140), which is at the core of a dynamic understanding of 'place' as characterised by a multiplicity of outcomes (see also Castree, Featherstone and Herod, 2006).

The spatial organisation of 'living at work'

In addition to being gated, the perimeters of the Lamu Port construction site are also patrolled by security guards whose activities are monitored by Chinese heads of security through CCTV cameras. Through direct oversight over guards' activities on the perimeters, but also the activities of other workers through CCTV, Chinese security officers contribute to a multifaceted system of managerial control over the labour force. Fei (2020: 2) highlights that this practice 'offer[s] important insights into the mobilisation of spatial techniques to achieve managerial control over labour.' Specifically, the proximity of the worksite and the living facilities allows employers to have continuous and direct access to the labour force and simultaneously oversee employees at all times.

This is amplified by the practice of 'living at work', as social and working lives mainly occur within the construction site's gated boundaries. 'Living at work' can be traced back to the *danwei* (单位—work units) system, a form of hierarchical spatial arrangement institutionalised as part of the planned economy in Chinese urban areas (see Bjorklund, 1986; Lu and Perry, 1997; Bray, 2005). Yet, this remains a prevalent practice in the Chinese construction industry, both nationally (Pun and Smith, 2007; Swider, 2015) and internationally (Wethal, 2017; Fei, 2020), leading to questions around the implications of this practice for different dimensions of labour relations.

The spatial organisation of living arrangements is strongly influenced by the hierarchical management structures regulating the construction site and other factors, such as nationality and contract type. The hierarchical managerial structure sees Chinese managers and engineers overseeing the work of Chinese foremen and Kenyan supervisors, the latter of whom do not directly oversee the work of Kenyan manual labourers. This hierarchical organisation of the construction work applies to both Kenyan and Chinese workers (echoing Driessen's findings in Ethiopia, 2019) and, as discussed further later, suggests that Chinese and Kenyan workers alike can (re)negotiate workplace dynamics.

During the busiest construction period in 2019, the site employed around 1,200 people, about 1,000 of whom were Kenyan employees, and most of whom resided in the accommodation compound. Yet, at the time of research, no management position was held by Kenyan workers, and only a handful of them were supervisors. Similar to the findings of other researchers (Corkin, 2012; Auffray and Fu, 2015; Brautigam and Hwang, 2019; Driessen, 2019), opportunities for professional growth offered to Kenyan workers remain scarce.

The map provided (Figure 7.1) outlines the construction site, highlighting the spatial division between the accommodation of Chinese and Kenyan workers, which is disconnected from the rest of the site by gated walls. Access to these spaces is not often reciprocated. On the one hand, Chinese workers have access to the compound where Kenyan workers reside and often make their way to the small shop located there. The shop mainly sells snacks, cigarettes, alcohol, and toiletries, and was opened by a group of job seekers who— after arriving in Lamu—realised their entrepreneurial goals instead of waiting for employment as construction workers. The presence of a shop also speaks to another aspect of 'living at work', whereby workers carve out spaces for recreational or business activities (Fei, 2020) and develop support networks, which are discussed further below. On the other hand, Kenyan workers' experience of 'living at work' prominently features their limited mobility in the construction site. The limitations of Kenyan workers' mobility go well beyond access to the Chinese workers' compound, extending to several aspects of their work and recreational lives. For instance, differently from the gym and recreational facilities available to Chinese workers residing in Area 2 and 3 (see Figure 7.2), Kenyan workers turned a grassless open space into a dusty football field.

Additionally, the organisation of living arrangements is also demarcated by the difference in accommodation types. For instance, Chinese foremen are accommodated in portable blocks—whose temporary nature ironically echoes their employment contracts— while engineers reside in brick-walled buildings. Foremen are employed on a project basis,[3] which means they will soon have to look for other employment opportunities. Alternatively, as observed by Wu (2021) in Zambia, after taking part in construction projects, some workers might decide to remain there with the prospect of, in the long term, migrating again towards 'higher-status places'

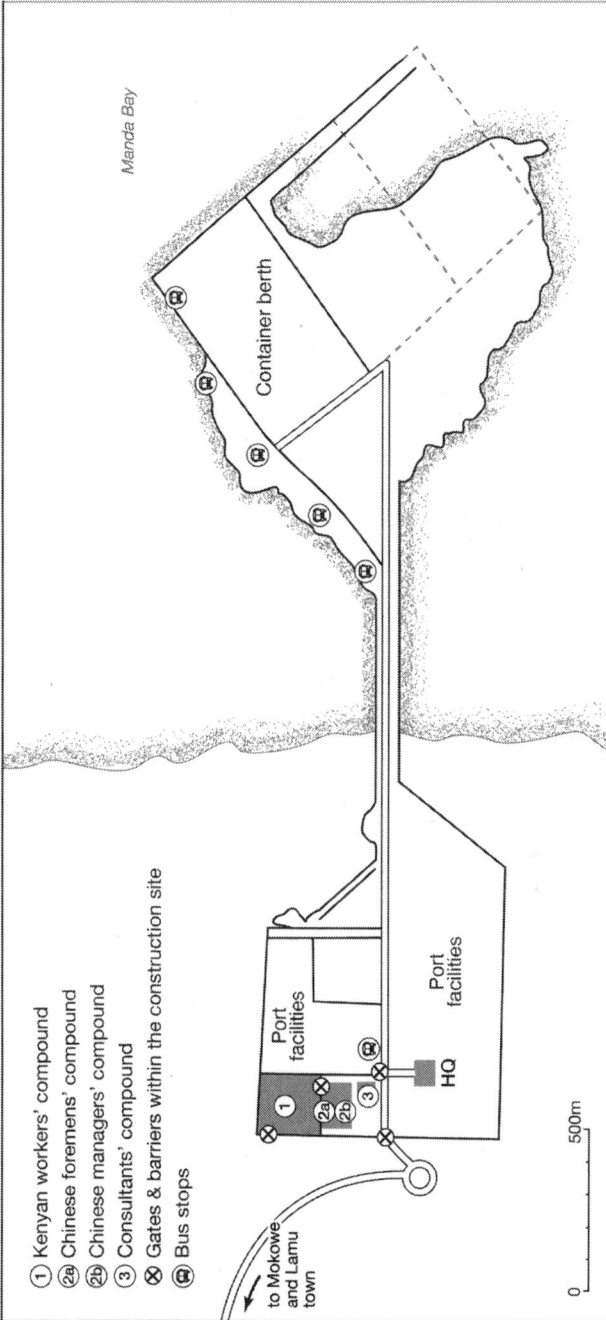

Figure 7.1: Map of Lamu Port construction site

① Kenyan workers' compound
②a Chinese foremens' compound
②b Chinese managers' compound
③ Consultants' compound
⊗ Gates & barriers within the construction site
⊛ Bus stops

Manda Bay

Container berth

Port facilities

Port facilities

HQ

to Mokowe and Lamu town

500m

0

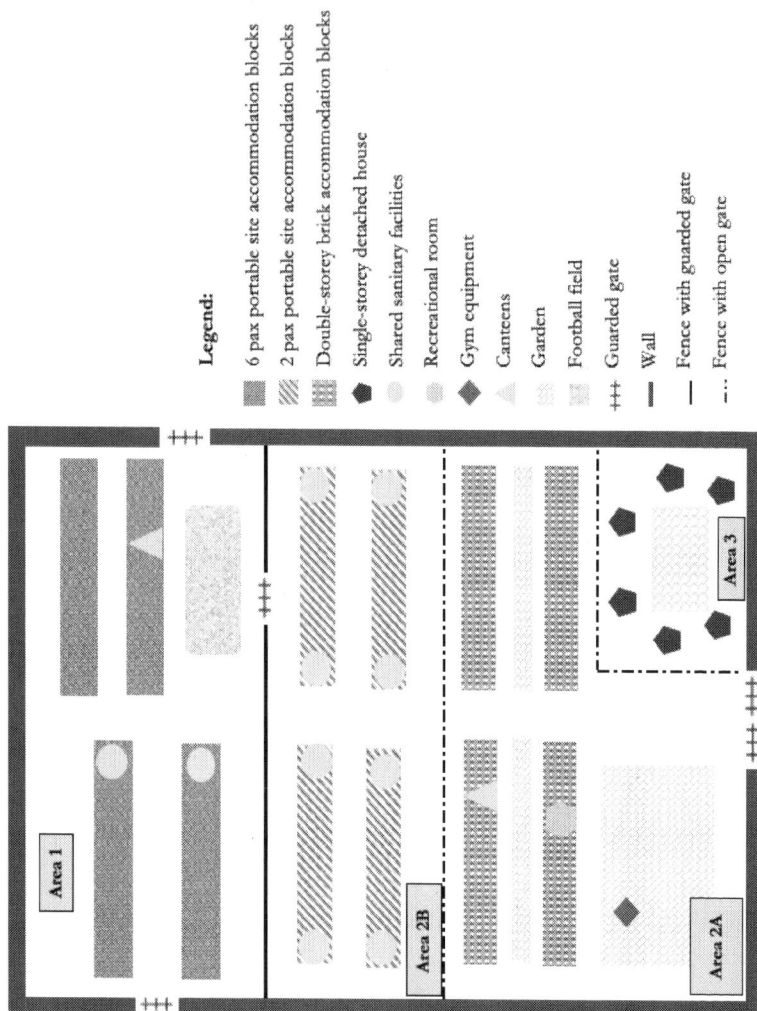

Figure 7.2: Lamu construction site living compound

Legend:

- 6 pax portable site accommodation blocks
- 2 pax portable site accommodation blocks
- Double-storey brick accommodation blocks
- Single-storey detached house
- Shared sanitary facilities
- Recreational room
- Gym equipment
- Canteens
- Garden
- Football field
- Guarded gate
- Wall
- Fence with guarded gate
- Fence with open gate

(ibid.: 14), usually associated with North America and Europe. As will be explored further, different employment contracts, amongst other factors, have different implications on Sino-African workplace dynamics. This offers some insight into how the workplace's spatial organisation and work structures are influenced by relations and processes that can be traced well beyond life and work at the construction site.

Lastly, how Kenyan and Chinese workers commute from the accommodation compound to the construction sites differs significantly. The distance between the housing and the furthest construction area is approximately 2.5 km. At the beginning of every shift, Chinese workers make their way to the construction areas by car, as several vehicles (and drivers) are available to them, as are the employees of the construction consultant residing in Area 3. For Kenyan labourers, a shuttle service consisting of one bus (supplied by CRBC) travels back and forth from the gate near the Kenyan workers' compound to the construction area, making several stops along the way (see the bus stops in Figure 7.1). The shuttle service was introduced to reduce commute time and, consequently, the likelihood of workers being late. Although the bus facilitates the commute of some workers, one bus alone cannot accommodate all the employees, and many make their way on foot to avoid delays.

Often, reporting late to work can result in employment termination, offering a first insight into the high job insecurity faced by Kenyan labourers. In the mornings, a very orderly queue can be found at the bus stop, which is overseen by a Chinese foreman. Amongst commuters, a silent agreement allows supervisors to jump to the front of the queue. A worker in the queue recalled that, when the bus was first introduced, arguments were very common amongst commuters, with some ending in physical fights. In response to this discord, CRBC managers decided to position a Chinese foreman on the other side of the road to prevent fights and issue 'fines'—in the form of suspensions—to those who jump the queue or are involved in brawls. This reflects the constant striving of Chinese contractors to improve productivity through the use of different types of deterrents and incentives, such as financial bonuses, or through the reframing of organisational processes, as demonstrated by the monitoring of

Kenyan workers queuing for the shuttle service to the Lamu Port construction site. This leads us to analyse practices unfolding in the workplace and their connections to narratives characterising the Kenyan and Chinese labour markets and political economies.

Workplace dynamics and the 'virtue' of chiku nailao (吃苦耐劳)

The incentive / deterrent regime briefly discussed above does not only involve Kenyan workers. Chinese foremen are similarly embedded in this workplace dynamic, which we consider to be closely linked to the practice of 'living at work'. In Lamu, Chinese foremen compete to complete sections of the project on schedule and produce good quality work to enjoy financial benefits in the form of bonuses. In turn, their Kenyan teams work under stressful conditions. They are pushed to work harder and faster or face repercussions, such as suspension or termination of employment. Job insecurity, which will be discussed further in the next section, translates into an environment of uncertainty. As such, workers fear repercussions if they were to openly criticise and defy the hierarchical management structure or question their working conditions (see also similar findings by Wethal, 2017).

Moreover, the arbitrary decision-making of Chinese foremen and managers (see Driessen, 2019: 106) deeply contributes to sustaining the high degree of job insecurity for African workers. This has a considerable impact on the relations between Chinese and Kenyan workers, similar to labour relations observed in other contexts across the African continent (Giese and Thiel, 2014, 2015). Kenyan workers are mainly employed in non-managerial positions, meaning that their work is organised and overseen by Chinese employees. This resembles what Hecht (2002: 699) calls an 'ethnotechnical hierarchy' whereby 'powers and privileges are unequally distributed by expatriate executives, national skilled employees, and local unskilled workers' (Rubbers, 2020: 194).

The language barrier between Kenyan and Chinese workers is significant and impacts daily encounters. Because of this, the organisation of work on the construction site relies on fragile lines of communication between Chinese and Kenyan workers. Most

Chinese foremen do not speak English upon arrival at the Lamu Port construction site. The languages most used for communication between Chinese and Kenyan workers on the construction site are a mixture of Kiswahili, Mandarin, and English—reminiscent of similar observations by Driessen (2020). Amongst Kenyan workers, who come from different regions of Kenya, Swahili and English are the most commonly spoken languages, while amongst Chinese workers, Mandarin is the language of communication. During the first few weeks at the construction site, workers familiarise themselves with how to communicate, negotiating a 'code' almost unintelligible to outsiders. Some Kenyan workers learn a few words in Mandarin, such as greetings and words such as 'no' or a few numbers. Chinese workers have also made similar efforts, learning English words such as 'tomorrow', 'no', or 'okay'. Since the English vocabulary of Chinese workers is quite limited, Kenyans often intentionally use incorrect grammar structures or make up new ways of expressing themselves to facilitate the communication with their Chinese counterparts. For instance, instead of saying 'the day after tomorrow', they say 'tomorrow tomorrow', which Chinese foremen understand because they are only familiar with the word 'tomorrow'.

Below is an example of an interaction between Bonny, a Kenyan supervisor, and a Chinese worker, the content of which will be the focus of analysis in the following section:

> [Bonny] is trying to reach the Chinese foreman at the end of the structure, where he is smoking a cigarette with another Chinese worker. We arrive, and [Bonny] greets him with a 早上好 [*zaoshang hao*, good morning in Mandarin], the worker smiles. [Bonny] points at the superstructure, the Chinese foreman points at a Kenyan worker and says, 'no work!'. There is an issue. The Chinese foreman says, '他 [*ta*, Mandarin for he/him] go home!' he is still pointing at the worker. (Fieldwork diary entry, Lamu, 15 March 2019)

In the initial construction phase in 2016, translators were hired by CRBC, but they only worked on the construction site for a couple of months before being relocated to another site. Amongst Kenyan workers, rumours have it that CRBC's decision was guided by the need to 'protect their secrets'.[4] Whatever the reason for the removal of translators, it highlights that smooth communication is not a priority for the contractor. Instead, the project's timely completion takes precedence over any other concern. In turn, pressure to carry out work speedily and effectively significantly shapes day-to-day interactions amongst workers and the broader workplace dynamics on the construction site.

The long working hours, the quest for improved productivity, and the incentive/deterrent regime represent the materialisation of the Chinese 'virtue' of 吃苦耐劳 (*chiku nailao*). This four-character expression encompasses two concepts. First, 吃苦 (*chiku*) 'eating bitterness', from 吃 (*chi*) 'to eat' and 苦 (*ku*) 'bitterness'. The Chinese idiom *chiku* refers to a life and work ethic characterised by enduring hardship, discipline and self-sacrifice in the hope of a better future. Second, 耐劳 (*nailao*) 'hard-working', from 耐 (*nai*) 'to be able to endure' and 劳 (*lao*) 'labour'. The concept of *nailao* is expressed daily through the more colloquial expression 努力工作 (*nuli gongzuo*), translated into 'work(ing) hard'. Thus, the four-character expression *chiku nailao* refers to the notion of 'biting the bullet', which is not only embedded within the management structure on the construction site but also in labour relations dynamics in China.

As Driessen (2019: 158) suggests, Chinese workers' *ku* (bitterness) is not limited to the hard work itself—especially as Chinese workers are now increasingly employed on overseas construction sites as managers or foremen—but represents a 'newly developed flavour inherent in their marginal position in an increasingly affluent China.' China's economic reforms have transformed the relations between the Chinese state and Chinese state-owned enterprises (SOEs) overseas (Brødsgaard, 2016) and have significantly impacted people's lives. Since the 1990s, the restructuring of SOEs has reshaped the geographies of production within China, whereby the coastal regions saw rapid industrialisation and urbanisation (Cai, 1999). In turn, temporary migrant workers from rural areas began to move to the cities to work on construction projects or in the manufacturing industry (Swider, 2011). For instance, in 2003 alone, rural migrant labourers amounted to 114 million people (Shaohua, 2005: 13). In turn, the income gap amongst workers in rural and urban areas widened (Biao, 2014) and, to this day, migrant workers in the urban areas continue to face a high degree of instability due to the household registration system.[5]

In other words, the work on construction sites in Africa is a 'bitterness' that Chinese workers—engineers and foremen alike—are ready to 'eat' in the hope of social mobility in China (Driessen, 2016; Lee, 2017: 100; Schmitz, 2020; Wu, 2021: 12). Higher salaries in overseas construction projects are often a decisive factor for Chinese foremen, as they enable them to provide prospects for their families to climb the social class ladder in China (Driessen, 2015). State-owned contractors—such as CRBC—also incentivise directly employed workers (mainly engineers) to go to Africa through the disbursement of an allowance (补助 - *buzhu*) for 'hardship and bitterness' (艰苦 - *jianku*), known as 艰苦补助 (*jianku buzhu*), which is calculated on the basis of an employee's ranking within the company and the assessment of a 'region's level of development and standard of living' (Wu, 2021: 13).

In addition to being away from home to earn higher salaries, state media often glorify the work of Chinese companies in Africa, which contributes to their obtaining respect at home (Driessen, 2019: 17). For instance, in Lamu, construction workers have been discussed in Chinese media, specifically on China Radio International (Yang, 2019), as '筑梦人' (*zhu meng ren*), translated into 'dream builders'. This concept is promoted by CRBC's mother company CCCC, on their official website (China Construction Communication Company, 2019). Lastly, *chiku* ('eating bitterness') also becomes a crucial part of workers' identity. This is closely related to the 'bitterness' that comes from Chinese workers finding themselves in a limbo of 'permanent temporariness' (Swider, 2011: 139). They are neither connected nor disconnected from their home networks and the communities in their place of work.

Yet, *chiku nailao* has a different meaning for Chinese managers and foremen. In Lamu, most Chinese managers are young, male (with a few exceptions), single, recently graduated engineers, while foremen, on the other hand, have perfected their skills through years of experience over formal education and are generally older married men. Unlike workers at other Chinese construction sites on the continent (see Fei, 2020), workers in Lamu are from different

Chinese provinces. This is likely due to the labour force transfer from other projects in Kenya, such as the Standard Gauge Railway, and the fluctuation of the number of workers at this construction site. Although both managers and foremen are employed temporarily on the construction site, engineers have a permanent contract with CRBC (Swider, 2015), and foremen's contracts are temporary.

In addition, during the length of construction projects, workers' mobility is restricted by the company. This is similar to Driessen's (2019: 104) example of Chinese migrant workers in Ethiopia being unable to make plans to visit China since the contractor was in possession of their passports. CRBC's employees in Kenya also reported similar travel restrictions in informal conversations, and some of them had not visited China for over two years (before the Covid-19 pandemic). However, in the case of Chinese engineers, overseas projects represent a stepping stone or fast-tracking opportunity for their careers within CRBC. For example, an engineer who had worked in Kenya during his first project in 2016 described his journey of 'slowly coming home' from Kenya to the Hambantota Port project in Sri Lanka, and then a bridge construction in Suzhou, China.[6]

Workplace dynamics and the brokerage of labour controversies

The previous section identified two hierarchies emerging from the 'living at work' practice, namely (i) the hierarchy amongst Chinese employees and (ii) the hierarchy existing within Sino-Kenyan labour relations. Here, we focus on the human resources (HR) processes of CRBC to illustrate different agential aspects of 'living at work'. To do so, we begin by highlighting one example of labour controversy at the Lamu Port construction site to speak to broader trajectories characterising and remaking labour practices.

The work at the Lamu Port construction site is organised in two shifts of 11–12 hours, which include a long downtime period during the hottest hours of the day. Due to unforeseen delays in the early stages of the project—caused by bad weather and a delay in payment (Gambino, 2020)—work is undertaken during the day and night, every day of the week. Often, the day shifts begin with controversy, as issues that arose during the night shift have to be dealt with. In an instance of this, at the beginning of the day shift on 14 March 2019, the shouting of a Chinese foreman rose above construction noises as he directed Kenyan workers to a corner of the construction area and intimated his team to hurry up and finish a task. Some of the work carried out the day before by John, a Kenyan manual labourer, had been washed away during the nightly pump cleaning process. This meant that the cement could not be poured into place before John, helped by other team members, had redone yesterday's work. The Chinese foreman checked the work closely and pushed John to increase his delivery speed, as the work had already been delayed by two hours.

Once John had finished, the Chinese foreman approached him and shouted, 'go home, home, go!' Hearing this raised voice, Bonny—the Kenyan supervisor for that construction section—approached the Chinese foreman to inquire about the issue that could get John fired. Bonny was attempting to negotiate an alternate solution before the incident was reported to the headquarters, at which point John's job security would have been in jeopardy. If an issue is not resolved in the construction area, the HR officers merely have a communication role. The hierarchical managerial structure of the construction site is also reflected within the HR department, where Chinese HR officers oversee Kenyan HR officers and, as such, the overall HR processes. One Kenyan HR officer described the decision-making process as follows:

If the problem is not resolved in the pit [the construction area], then it comes to the HR office. But things are not fair. The Chinese supervisor will give a reason to China HR, who will believe him, and the person who has an issue has to go home. They [the Chinese supervisors] call [their Chinese HR colleagues] before the [Kenyan] worker reaches the headquarters, and there's nothing else that the local HR [colleagues] can do. Once the decision is made by [the Chinese] HR, it is final; we [Kenyan HR] can't do anything. We went head-to-head with them at times, but it doesn't help at all. When we go to China HR, we know the decision has already been taken. (Interview, human resources officer, Chinese SOE, Lamu, 15 March 2019)

At the construction site, John—who had left Nairobi with a cargo clearance diploma hoping that working in the port could open opportunities for future employment in its operations—was standing a few steps behind Bonny, waiting for a verdict. Bonny and the Chinese foreman communicated—as workers do continuously during daily construction activities—in a mixture of gestures, English, Swahili and Mandarin words. Eventually, Bonny and the Chinese foreman reached an agreement whereby John was allowed to return to the site the day after, but he was suspended without pay for the day. Bonny's intervention and negotiation were critical in de-escalating a situation that could have cost John his job and livelihood. Later, Bonny explained that while talking to John, he was 'pretending to be on the side of the Chinese, so that he [John] learn[ed] his lesson.' This suggests that Bonny can deliberately—and temporarily—assume different identities to sustain his brokering strategies.

As highlighted by literature in political anthropology, 'brokerage' emerges in 'settings in transition' (James, 2011: 318) and 'brokers' 'shape the interactions amongst actors who have unequal power relations and diverging interests' (Koster and van Leynseele, 2018: 803). 'Brokers' were initially considered as mediating figures acting as an interface between marginalised, powerless or silenced communities and state power and market forces, but 'brokers' also encompass seemingly contradictory qualities as individuals, such as rent-seeking behaviour and moral drive (Mosse and Lewis, 2006; James, 2011). For instance, Raeymaekers (2014: 25) explored the 'brokerage' of traders in a context characterised by the 'modernising colonial practices and active resistance against (post)colonial rule ... formal political regulation and informal accumulation, and ... local dependencies and global economic engagements.' He highlighted the ambiguity of the traders' role as 'brokers', as they embodied both capitalist ideology and simultaneously suffered from 'its exploitative logic' (ibid.).

In the case of Bonny's role as a 'broker', his ability to mediate in the interests of both Chinese and Kenyan workers makes him an essential figure on the construction site, which, in turn, brings him some degree of influence over his own employment conditions. At the Lamu construction site, requests to increase the salary[7] of

Kenyan workers by 5 to 10 KES/hour can be submitted by Chinese foremen to the CRBC headquarters on site. Bonny, who plans to further his career by starting his own construction company, discussed this with his Chinese manager. Upon hearing about his entrepreneurial goals, Bonny's manager submitted a pay increase request to raise Bonny's salary from 125 KES/hour (about 1.25 USD/hour) to 135 KES/hour (about 1.35 USD/hour) to try to convince him to delay his business plans. Indeed, raises are often offered as an incentive to retain highly valued talent by Chinese workers, but do not translate into a promotion to a managerial role. As discussed in the vignette above, Bonny's ability to act as a 'broker' greatly impacts the construction site. In Bonny's own words, 'they call me, or I go, and I solve [issues] because I know how to work, how to talk with the Chinese. But me, I also know the needs of the workers … they come to me.'

This highlights another aspect of 'living at work', whereby the construction site also becomes a space for social connections, as Fei (2020) suggests. On the one hand, the construction site offers an opportunity for the building of social relations amongst Chinese and Kenyan workers. For instance, in the case of Lamu Port, some Chinese foremen defy company regulations to ensure their Kenyan team members are provided with food. This is done by adding fictional overtime (one hour per worker) so that the company must provide food free of charge to Kenyan workers. Doing so poses a risk to the Chinese foremen and those willing to take said risks fall in the minority, thus being unable to considerably shift the status quo of the incentive/deterrent regime.

On the other hand, within the space of the construction site, social relations amongst Kenyan workers go well beyond the social or recreational sphere, and, as suggested by Bonny, extend to the mitigation of practical challenges at work. This echoes Riisgaard and Okinda's (2018) findings on Kenya's smallholder tea farms and signals a continuum with broader trajectories beyond the reality of Chinese construction sites (as suggested by Oya, 2019). We trace specific aspects of social connection amongst Kenyan workers in Lamu Port to context-specific trajectories in the Kenyan the labour market, as well as wider shifts within the global economy to highlight the crucial role played by 'brokers', workers' leaders, or colleagues in remaking labour practices in Sino-African work*places*.

Historically, labour relations in Kenya have been characterised by the cultivation of personal and collective relations with 'patrons', within groups of workers and amongst unions (Sandbrook, 1972; Henley, 1976; Cooper, 1987: 42–144), or amongst migrant workers in tea plantations (Adagala, 1991). Similar dynamics can be observed in today's Kenyan construction industry, reflecting the significant changes in employment practices in the global construction sector. Indeed, construction companies worldwide have reduced their permanent labour forces in favour of employing workers temporarily; this correlates with the parallel trajectories of the precarity of work in other industries, such as logistics and distribution.

The supply of labour through intermediaries who recruit and control the workforce—a practice commonly referred to as labour contracting—is a well-established practice in the Global South's construction industry (van der Loop, 1992; Debrah and Ofori, 1997; Jha, 2002; Connolly, 2007; Wells and Jason, 2010). Intermediaries are known by various names, such as *mistri* or *jamadar* in India, *kepala* in Malaysia and Singapore, *oyaji* in Korea, *naikea* in Nepal, *gato* in Brazil, or *maestro* in Mexico, but their role is essentially that of 'supply[ing] labour for a construction site when it is needed and to take it away when it is no longer required' (Wells, 2009: 2).

As such, intermediaries serve as a bridge between labourers seeking work and contractors and subcontractors that can provide employment (Vaid, 1999). Similar dynamics can be observed in today's Kenyan construction industry. Contractors and gang leaders—in a continuum from the gangs of dockworkers in Mombasa Port during the colonial era (Cooper, 1987: 44–144)—still play a role in recruiting and supervising workers on construction sites. Amongst Kenyan contractors, hiring or contracting a gang leader— the distinction amongst which seems difficult to make (Mitullah and Njeri Wachira, 2003) but appears to be related to the degree of financial risk taken by the gang leader (Wells, 2009)—to provide workers and, at times, supervise the construction, continues to be a common practice.

Gang leaders primarily operate in Kenya's informal construction sector, which comprises 'unregistered and unprotected individuals and small enterprises that supply labour and contribute in other ways to the output of the construction sector' (Mitullah and Njeri Wachira, 2003: 7), both in terms of housing construction as well as larger construction projects (Wells and Jason, 2010). Gang leaders are 'usually artisans of many years of experience, good reputation and good contacts with potential clients who lead a group of skilled and non-skilled men who usually work together' (Mitullah and Njeri Wachira, 2003: 20), and it is their responsibility to seek and secure jobs for the gang members. Their role as 'brokers' in workforce provision translates into financial benefits (similar to what is discussed in James, 2011). They earn higher wages than the workers who are a part of their gang or receive commissions directly from the client. Mitullah and Njeri Wachira (2003) found that most informal construction workers in Nairobi aspire to be gang leaders because of their earning potential. At the same time, gang leaders also contribute to forming a network amongst workers, as construction gangs become social networks that play a crucial role in recruiting and sustaining labourers in the economy (Wells, 2009; see also Fei, 2020 on Sino-African construction sites).

Gang construction networks 'are a form of social capital and act as insurance for the comparatively poor urban workers who do not have any form of formal insurance'[8] (Mitullah and Njeri Wachira, 2003: 21). This aspect of the practice of labour contracting is particularly relevant to workplace relations at the Lamu Port construction site, as networks amongst workers serve several purposes. First, Kenyan workers keep track of the job opportunities arising within the construction site to report them back to those who have recently arrived in Lamu and are lodging in the Kenyan housing facilities waiting for employment. Second, newly hired Kenyan workers' training mainly occurs through interactions with colleagues and extends beyond the short training period—usually three days—required to obtain an employment contract. Third, as highlighted through the vignettes featuring Bonny, the 'brokerage' of workplace controversies is crucial to mitigating the high job insecurity that characterises work in the construction site.

Conclusion

This chapter analysed the workplace dynamics in the Sino-African construction site of Lamu Port in Kenya. In order to fully explore the embeddedness of workplace dynamics in multiple (social) relations beyond the interrelated concepts of workplace organisation and politics of production, we first argued for the inclusion of Massey's dynamic understanding of place in the study of work*place* relations (see calls from Sergot and Saives, 2016; Fei, 2020). Thus, through the analysis of the spatial organisation of 'living at work' and workplace dynamics involving both Chinese and Kenyan workers, we suggested that these are inherently linked to both labour relations within the construction site and broader trajectories beyond it. Specifically, we showed that different dynamics in labour relations in both China and Kenya are encountered in the spatio-temporal 'moment' of the construction site.

Second, we discussed the spatial organisation of the construction site, where disconnected spaces reflect the ethnotechnical hierarchy of the Lamu construction site delineating workers' roles within the company, the hierarchical managerial structures, as well as workers' nationality and contract type. This section offered insight into how the spatial organisation of 'living at work' is embedded in Chinese contractors' constant striving for productivity, consequently shaping the high job insecurity faced by construction workers. This sets the scene for the investigation of workplace dynamics.

Third, starting from a reflection on the arbitrary decision-making and the incentive/deterrent regime, we drew connections between these workplace dynamics and the Chinese 'virtue' of *chiku nailao*. Here, we highlighted the differentiated implications *chiku nailao* has for Chinese foremen and managers, even when the hope for social mobility 'at home' motivated both groups of workers to seek opportunities abroad. Mainly due to the difference in contracts— since managers have permanent contracts while foremen have temporary ones—foremen are often in a limbo of 'permanent temporariness' (Swider, 2011: 139), while overseas projects are a stepping stone for advancing the careers of managers.

Fourth, we shifted the analysis to how the competition for incentives amongst Chinese foremen and their arbitrary decision-making shapes the workplace dynamics of Kenyan workers employed in non-managerial positions. For instance, we highlighted how, when controversies arise and are reported to HR, the hierarchical management structure of the HR department (in which Chinese employees are ranked above their Kenyan counterparts) limits the manoeuvrability and authority that Kenyan HR officers can exert. As a result, most labour controversies that arise are not reported to the construction site's headquarters, which houses the HR department, as it would most likely result in the termination of Kenyan workers' jobs.

Instead, work-related disputes and issues are brokered within the construction site. These examples offered insights into brokers' strategies and relations with other workers. Indeed, the figure of the broker also highlights another crucial aspect of the construction site as a work*place*, where the forging of social relations occurs. The networks of Kenyan workers at the Lamu construction site are relatable to historical trajectories of labour relations within the country, particularly figures such as gang leaders, who have long been featured in the construction industry. By investigating instances of encounters amongst trajectories of labour control, job insecurity, labour agency, and aspirations of social mobility unfolding at a specific 'moment' of Sino-African relations, namely the work*place*, it becomes possible to connect practices 'within' the construction site to broader trajectories 'outside' this workplace.

Labour relations at the Lamu Port construction site thus speak to connections between this work*place* and pre-existing, yet evolving, geographies of power beyond its perimeters. These dynamics—often considered marginal due to their limited impact on the constraints on broader power imbalances that also echo South-South relations—are indeed shaping practices as part of current Sino-African economic engagement, thus becoming central to the understanding of contemporary world politics. As such, the work*place* represents a unique entry point to explore the making of global practices and how they are contested and reframed in the context of China–Africa engagement.

8

INVESTMENT AS COMMUNITY DEVELOPMENT?

BUSINESS–SOCIETY RELATIONS AROUND BRAZILIAN AND CHINESE PROJECTS

Michael Godet Sambo[1] *and Phyllis Bußler*[2]

Introduction

Despite the Mozambican government's long-held vision of agricultural development, economic growth in Mozambique is highly dependent on foreign direct investment (FDI) inflows, which concentrate more predominantly in the extractive industry than other sectors (Castel-Branco, 2010; Sambo, 2020). The agricultural sector, although designated as the foundation of development by the constitution, has been unable to attract a significant amount of investment. Rather, it only received 2% of the total FDI stock between 2011 and 2020, while 68% of it remained in the extractive industry (Banco de Moçambique, 2020; Sambo, 2020). Furthermore, FDI in the agriculture industry fell from USD 81.8 million in 2017 to USD 35.6 million in 2020. It may be argued that the government's high dependency on international aid prevents it from further intervention in the sector. Traditional donors' aid programmes tend to prioritise expenditures on areas such as institutions, governance, and social programmes rather than large-scale infrastructure projects in the agriculture sector (Mawdsley, 2018: 193). Thus, the global food crises of 2007–08 and 2010 became an opportunity for the Mozambican government to turn to new financial partners for agricultural expansion. China and Brazil were both considered to be promising and decisive contributors to an agricultural revolution.

In the diplomatic framework of South-South cooperation (SSC), the shared goals of the governments of China and Brazil to collaborate with the government of Mozambique culminated in the implementation of two large-scale agriculture-development corridor projects. These projects arrived in Mozambique in a similar fashion but ended up with different trajectories. The first is a Japanese-Brazilian project called the Tripartite Cooperation Programme for Agricultural Development of the Tropical Savannah in Mozambique (henceforth ProSAVANA). ProSAVANA was modelled after the PRODECER, an agro-development project between Japan and Brazil launched in 1979, which transformed Brazil's Cerrado region into one of the top world exporters of soy. The ProSAVANA Master Plan was to assist in drawing up the agriculture development plans and collecting investment and aid for materialising agribusiness projects to turn the region into a large-scale commodity production area. It covered 14 million hectares spanning the provinces of Zambezia, Niassa, and Nampula in northern Mozambique (Chichava, 2014a). Its linkage to the Nacala Growth Corridor was supposed to build synergies between Brazilian Vale and Japanese Mitsui's joint railroad investments in the region, implemented to serve their coal mining operations in the province of Tete. Despite its high-profile presence in the development cooperation landscape, ProSAVANA was formally terminated in 2020 (Da Silva, 2020). The second project is WANBAO Africa Agricultural Development Lda.—WAADL (henceforth WANBAO). Designed to promote China's image in Africa, WANBAO received financing from the China–Portugal Development Fund and the China–Africa Development Fund (Zhang, 2019). The project started in 2007 in Xai-Xai, the capital of Gaza Province in Southern Mozambique, comprising 20,000 hectares across the watering system of the lower Limpopo valley. In 2012, this project transitioned from a Hubei provincial initiative known as the 'Hubei–Gaza Friendship Farm', which was implemented by a Chinese state-owned enterprise (SOE), to a Chinese private investment company, WANBAO.

We highlight two similarities between ProSAVANA and WANBAO, which also extend to other South-South projects in Africa. First, both are sizeable projects that involve the construction of agricultural laboratories, demonstration centres, irrigation systems, and relevant logistical infrastructure. In this context, agricultural growth corridors planned throughout Sub-Saharan Africa are examples in which agricultural investment goes hand in hand with infrastructure and logistics (Weng et al., 2013 for an overview; Chome et al., 2020 for East Africa). Second, the Mozambican government negotiated both projects without involving, consulting or informing either potentially affected communities or civil society organisations (CSOs) in their respective planning and implementation processes. This is a widespread practice in many South-South projects in sub-Saharan Africa (Vaes and Huyse, 2013). However, in our study cases, this practice led to contestation throughout the encounters between both projects and the local communities, including CSOs.

Arguably, these initiatives, at least discursively, are typically presented as part of African states' efforts to drive national and community development. The official discourse in Mozambique for mobilising Chinese and Brazilian investments in agriculture is built around the goal (driving national economic development through agri-business), the status quo (tackling the problems of poor sectoral development and low productivity), and the potential (tapping into the availability of unused arable land and unlocking cost-effective business opportunities). Furthermore, the official discourse puts out a blueprint for community development, which will be accomplished through job creation, accessibility to food, technical transfer, and an active role in the global value chain.

This chapter, going beyond the euphoria of SSC (Bergamaschi, Moore and Tickner, 2017), questions whether and to what extent the initial prospects of these large-scale South-South investment projects have translated into 'community development'. Following Summers (1986: 360), the concept of 'rural community development' is defined as intentionally planned interventions aiming to improve people's living conditions in sparsely settled areas. In this chapter, we limit the scope of study to groups directly affected by these two projects. Furthermore, the chapter asks why these agricultural-infrastructure development projects had a similar start but took distinct trajectories. This contrast unveils how Africa's South-South relations are contested, remade, negotiated, and (de)materialised by different counterparts on the ground.

To address these questions, we approach business-community encounters around top-down development cooperation projects from two analytical angles. First, we draw attention to how actors and projects are embedded in political-economy configurations at regional and transnational levels where investments and their contestation happened. Such configurations include the existence of a robust CSO network, their alignment with or alienation from the government, and the political traditions in the regional context. We also highlight, among other things, diverse types of encounters between different project stakeholders and reverberance within a transnational network stretching between the Global North and the South. Second, we explore the extent to which encounters between different actors could (re)make transnational practices. Zooming in on how situations of the affected communities unfold, this chapter argues that the changing landscape of stakeholders throughout the process and varying degrees of co-adaptation have contributed to the different trajectories of the two projects (see also Tang 2022; and Chapter 2 by Bunskoek).

Comparative case studies are the main methodology of this chapter. It is based on qualitative empirical data collected separately in different time periods and research projects. For the case study of the ProSAVANA project, fieldwork was conducted in Mozambique (2016–17), Brazil (2017), and Japan (2018). The main methods included snowball sampling, semi-structured interviews with ProSAVANA proponents, CSOs and other stakeholders involved directly or indirectly in the contestation, and participant observation at the Third Trilateral People's Conference in 2018.

Given the degree to which the project was politicised, access to informants working in CSOs in Brazil and Mozambique was constantly negotiated; the outcome depended on the researcher's positionality towards a CSO's cause. In Brazil, for example, the researcher's membership in a German-Brazilian solidarity network facilitated the establishment of contact with CSO representatives. The Brazilian political context in 2017 proved challenging due to the turmoil generated by the trial against then former President Lula da Silva in April 2017. This happened on the heels of Brazil's Lava Jato (Car Wash) corruption investigations, which saw many of the country's political and economic elites facing controversial criminal charges and paved the way to President Dilma Rousseff's impeachment in 2016. The implication for fieldwork was that it was difficult to reach public representatives who had formerly been involved in Brazil's South-South engagement, as they were substituted after the impeachment. Moreover, ProSAVANA's politicisation also meant that the researcher's own positionality—as a German fluent in Brazilian Portuguese—played an active role in negotiating access. While the researcher's Brazilian accent prompted some informants to perceive the researcher as Brazilian, which might have opened the door for interviews, her German nationality combined with the research interest in ProSAVANA raised suspicion in others. Certain CSO representatives and ProSAVANA proponents suspected, for instance, that this research was carried out to serve the interests of ProSAVANA and/or on behalf of the German government, which had been in discussion about getting involved in ProSAVANA. These suspicions culminated in a quasi-denial of access during the researcher's stay in Tokyo, Japan.

Data collection for the case study of WANBAO was conducted by the other author in Xai-Xai, Gaza Province, in 2019. Key methods included snowball sampling, focus group discussions with small farmers and semi-structured interviews with key stakeholders such as provincial government officials, Chinese managers and staff at WANBAO, workers, local rice producers under the contract farming system in WANBAO, and small family farmers directly affected by but not involved with the project. The researcher also conducted participant observation during the season of cultivation to grasp dynamics at the farm. Grey literature—media reports and CSO publications—was also consulted to complement the primary data.

Comparable to the case study of ProSAVANA, field access to the WANBAO project was influenced by a number of factors. Some participants, due to negative experiences with other past research projects, declined interview requests over fears of being exposed and having their careers jeopardised. Such risks have been exacerbated by a dynamic of increasing political violence and repression in recent years in Mozambique, made worse by the insurgency in the gas-rich province of Cabo Delgado. At the same time, the researcher's own identity and positionality (Mozambican national working in Xai-Xai with research partners from the locality, and a researcher and lecturer affiliated with well-known Mozambican institutions) helped to overcome access limitations through the mobilisation of both personal and professional contacts to facilitate field access and research interviews (for a methodological reflection on doing research in challenging South-South settings, see the conclusion of this book in Chapter 10).

The remainder of this chapter provides an overview of Brazilian and Chinese investments in Mozambique, followed by a literature review that puts ProSAVANA and WANBAO in a comparative perspective. Then the chapter proceeds to the empirical analysis, before concluding.

Contextualising Brazilian and Chinese investment in Mozambique

Chinese and Brazilian investments in Mozambique are comparable at multiple levels. Both China and Brazil utilise strategic collaborations with Mozambique to display their respective models of development and partnerships with the continent. On the one hand, China has achieved food self-sufficiency at a rate of more than 95%, and China–Africa agricultural cooperation has entered a new stage, in which China aspires to play a proactive role in the rise of the 'going global' strategy (Cheru and Obi, 2011; Zhang, 2019). China's then President Hu Jintao demonstrated this intention by announcing 'eight key measures' to support Africa and the construction of ten Agricultural and Technology Development Centres (ATDCs) at the 2006 Forum for the China–Africa Cooperation Beijing Summit, increasing to 20 in 2009 and 30 in 2010 in subsequent forums (Zhang, 2019). Importantly, China has invested more in agricultural development in Mozambique than in any other African country

(Shaw, 2010; Cheru and Obi, 2011; Madureira, 2014; Ponguane, Mussumbuluco and Mucavele, 2021). On the other hand, Brazil had its success story when it emerged as an international development partner. It is widely recognised for its expertise in tropical agriculture (Chichava et al., 2013: 7) and the willingness to share its experience with African nations (Chichava, 2014b). In addition, due to closer political-cultural ties, Brazil has prioritized engagements with Mozambique and Lusophone Africa (Chichava et al., 2013). Apart from these similarities, nuances exist in the Chinese and Brazilian economic presences, especially in terms of FDI, trade, and loans. Despite having a larger trade volume with Mozambique, China's FDI between 2010 and 2020 accounted for one fifth of Brazil's cumulative investment in Mozambique, which amounted to 7% of all FDI reported in the same period. Nevertheless, Brazil's FDIs have decreased in the last few years, whereas Chinese investments have shown an increasing trend. China is currently the biggest bilateral lender to Mozambique, accounting for 20% of the total public debt on average between 2015 and 2021 (based on Ministério de Economia e Finanças, 2022).

At the grassroots level, the interactions between these emerging powers and local communities are often mediated by CSOs, which are crucial for understanding the (re)making of practices on the ground (see Chapter 4 by Waisbich and Chapter 6 by Kilaka). CSOs in the Global South are characterised by internal diversity rather than commonality (Kamruzzaman, 2018; and also Chapter 4 by Waisbich). This requires analytical attention to the specific political-economic contexts and postcolonial trajectories from which Southern CSOs emerge. These conditions are also relevant for understanding South-South encounters and their (potential) effects on civil society–state relations. We refer to CSOs as institutionally organised anti-hegemonic forces (Habermas, 1996; Kamruzzaman, 2018: 3) that seek to represent marginalised interests of a society. According to Cox (1999), CSOs are embedded in a field of global power relations, in which their role oscillates between being a stabiliser of status quo power relations (e.g. co-opted by states) and being resistant actors that contest the established hegemonic order (Kamruzzaman, 2018: 2). Empirically, CSOs are not necessarily

189

all anti-hegemonic. Some are more concerned with pursuing their interests than others (Moyo, 1993: 4). According to Ilal et al. (2018) in the authoritarian regime of Mozambique's ruling party Frente de Libertação de Moçambique (Frelimo),[3] CSOs are facing a shrinking participation space. Therefore, some CSOs attempt to work with, or be incorporated by, the government and ruling party as service deliverers. Such NGOs are usually donor-supported (local) NGOs created in the 1990s under the World Bank's Good Governance agenda and are usually not very influential politically (Ilal, Kleibl and Munck, 2018: 220; Kleibl, 2021). Others rely in turn on external financing, e.g. from cooperation agencies, to represent the interests of society's marginalised voices (see more in Johansson and Sambo, 2014).

In Mozambique, the heavy concentration of FDI initiatives in certain localities tends to have enclaving and marginalising effects; meanwhile, marginalised communities and CSOs have also gained experience over the years in contesting large-scale projects. This chapter argues that at the subnational and regional levels, the historical-political configuration in each location receiving FDI implies distinct modes of governance and patterns of mobilisation. These implicit conditions also play a role in remaking the outcomes of the investment projects and their contestations. In the Mozambican case, the regions that host the two infrastructural-agricultural projects in this chapter, namely, the Nampula Province and the Gaza Province, have distinct socio-political conditions. On the one hand, ProSAVANA is hosted by the Nampula Province, which is in the north and more than 2,000 km away from Mozambique's capital, Maputo. The region is characterised by a strong and established CSO community drawing on 20 years of mobilisation experience with a focus on governance issues (Topsøe-Jensen, 2015: 232). Furthermore, Nampula Province served as the geographical basis for Mozambique's National Resistance Party, Resistência Nacional Moçambicana (RENAMO), the main opposition party of Frelimo, and consequently has stable support among the local population (Sumich, 2010: 3). On the other hand, WANBAO is in Xai-Xai, the capital of the Gaza Province, around 220 km north of Maputo. Gaza Province has had a firm reliance on the Frelimo party and its policies since the independence of Mozambique in 1975. It has been the motherland of most of the Frelimo leaders (Roesch, 2014), and hence enjoys natural support from the local population against RENAMO. As a result, the kinds of CSOs that developed in this region are primarily aligned with the government. Most of them operated more as stabilisers of the status quo, according to Cox (1999), although a few emerged during contestations, such as Fórum das ONGs Nacionais de Gaza (FONGA). These historical-political dynamics at the subnational level, as this section argues, delineate the contours of projects' political lives from the outset. The following sections shall demonstrate how business-community relations and mobilisation unfold throughout each stage of the two projects.

Comparing ProSAVANA and WANBAO: Literature and approach

This section foregrounds our comparative approach in prior works on Brazilian and Chinese cooperation in Mozambique's agricultural sector (Chichava et al. 2013; Chichava, 2014b; Milhorance, 2015; Amanor and Chichava, 2016).

Regarding Mozambique's political-economic context, Chichava et al. (2013) discuss how FDI attraction to the agricultural sector via Southern partners is of enormous interest to Mozambique's business elite. Moreover, the literature has outlined different trends and model(s) between China and Brazil's South-South (agricultural) cooperation in Africa: China's strategy involves the installation of 20 demonstration projects in sub-Saharan Africa, many of which were constructed and operated by Chinese state-affiliated entities. Chinese agricultural models are implicit when transported to Africa; moreover, their implementation also depends on the executing Chinese company, which draws on development experiences from their home province (Cabral, 2018). In contrast to the case of the Chinese SSC, where both top-level design and fragmentation in practice are observed (see Chapter 2 by Bunskoek), the Brazilian SSC is more diverse regarding its stakeholders and rather divided at the political level. Brazil's agricultural sector is historically divided between agribusiness and smallholder proponents. Such division can be observed from the previous coexistence of two agricultural ministries during the government under Brazil's Workers' Party (Partido dos Trabalhadores, PT): the agribusiness-oriented Ministério da Agricultura, Pecuária e Abastecimento (MAPA) and the smallholder farming-oriented Ministério do Desenvolvimento Agrário (MDA). The MDA was revoked after the impeachment of former President Dilma Rousseff in 2016 and a change of government (Grisa, 2018). Importantly, each ministry has had its own SSC initiatives and agenda in the agricultural sector. Furthermore, whereas the Chinese state leads the design of its SSC framework, the strong position of Brazil's Landless Rural Workers Movement (Movimento dos Trabalhadores Rurais Sem Terra) and a well-established CSO landscape, formerly involved in SSC public policymaking, are further reflected in this division between agribusiness and smallholder farming.

In the case of WANBAO and China's engagement in Mozambique, Ponguane et al. (2021) contend that land grabbing, rather than successful rural and agricultural development, has taken place. Nevertheless, the project indeed boosted the productivity of participating farmers. Gu et al. (2016) analyse how Chinese state–business relations have impacted Chinese cooperation projects in Mozambique (and Zimbabwe). Zhang et al. (2019) demonstrate that micro-encounters between Chinese and Mozambican individuals have led to a process of mutual adaptation. These findings are confirmed by Scoones et al. (2013, 2016), who emphasise that the cooperation partners' embeddedness in their domestic contexts might shape transnational corporate or development practice in the 'recipient country'.

Transnational mobilisation and contestation have been the key themes of many studies on ProSAVANA and Brazil's engagement in Mozambique. For instance, Chichava and Durán (2016) reconstruct the origin of the contestation by tracing the diversifying stakeholder landscape and the elite interest driving the project. Shankland and Gonçalves (2016) analyse how spatial imaginaries and discourses referring to Brazil and Mozambique are employed strategically and transnationally in the contestation by proponents and critics. Moreover, Cezne's (2019) analysis of transnational contestation (also Chapter 4 by Waisbich) by the Vale Affected (AV) is a relevant predecessor for explaining the contestation. Monjane and Bruna (2020), in turn, focus on the Mozambican government, attributing ProSAVANA's failure and the fierce resistance to the Mozambican government's authoritarianism. While studies tend to treat the case as an instantiation of Brazilian actors' engagement in Mozambique, few publications have yet discussed Japan's engagement in this tripartite development project. One exception is Funada-Classen's (2019) analysis of Japan and the Japan International Cooperation Agency (JICA), which argues that both are manipulative actors. We argue, however, that the different project set-ups have implications for their latent trajectories and outcomes. Whereas WANBAO is a bilateral Chinese-Mozambican project linked to other Chinese agricultural projects such as ATDCs, ProSAVANA was a *trilateral* project involving Brazil, Mozambique, and Japan. In this regard, it is essential to consider how ProSAVANA has been embedded in the Japan-driven Nacala Corridor Development Programme (PEDEC-Nacala) on the one hand, and Vale/Mitsui's investments in coal extraction in the Moatize region on the other.[4] The involvement of Japan as a 'Northern partner' has crucial implications for the CSO mobilisation strategies, and is thus relevant for our understanding of South-South relations vis-à-vis existing North–South relations.

Local encounters with Brazilian and Chinese agro-infrastructural projects: ProSAVANA andWANBAO

Putting ProSAVANA and WANBAO in comparative perspective (Chichava et al., 2013), our study starts from the observation that the Mozambican government and respective proponents brought ProSAVANA and WANBAO to Mozambique in a similar and top-down manner without involving the local population and CSOs. However, the projects took different trajectories with varying outcomes over time. WANBAO underwent consolidation, whereas ProSAVANA faced intense transnational CSO contestation and was cancelled before the Master Plan component could be implemented.[5] Against this empirical backdrop, we start from Scoones et al.'s (2013) suggestion to study how transnational practices are entangled with the respective political-economic contexts in—and from—which South-South engagement happens (see also Chapter 1 by Hönke et al.). Furthermore, we suggest that understanding the respective encounters between stakeholders at the local level would help better understand projects' trajectories and outcomes. We identified three distinct phases that characterise each stage of a project's transnational political life, namely, 'arrival', 'controversy', and 'outcome of encounter'. 'Arrival' refers to all the events and processes prior to the establishment or in the early stages of each project's implementation in Mozambique. 'Controversy' characterises the turbulences arising from the encounters between each project and their stakeholders, especially the affected communities and CSOs. 'Outcome' elaborates on what has empirically emerged from the encounters between or among different stakeholders.

The first phase: Arrival

During the arrival phase for WANBAO and ProSAVANA, encounters occurred between governments and companies with little involvement of the local communities or CSOs. While ProSAVANA was well known prior to its deployment, spurring CSO mobilisation, WANBAO's implementation remained unknown to the public.

ProSAVANA (2000s–2015)

ProSAVANA started operating in 2011 in Nampula with its research component *Plano de Investigação* (PI) with the installation of the Japan International Research Centre for Agricultural Sciences (JIRCAS). Their Brazilian counterpart, Embrapa, joined in 2012. The other two components are the Master Plan *Plano Director*, which envisions the agricultural development of the Nacala Corridor over 20 years, and the extension component *Plano de Extensão e Modelos* (PEM) for the technology dissemination.[6]

Many scholars have commented on the consolidation of the transnational network between Brazilian, Japanese, and Mozambican CSOs (Chichava and Durán, 2016; Shankland and Gonçalves, 2016; Shankland, Gonçalves and Favareto, 2016; Durán and Chichava, 2017). As a result, these contestations have considerably delayed the rollout of ProSAVANA. The literature details five issues entangled with the controversy about ProSAVANA:

1. The lack of transparency on behalf of the Mozambican government towards the CSOs (Monjane and Bruna, 2020: 70).
2. The discursive reference to the allegedly successful development of the Cerrado region (Folha de S. Paulo, 2011)—a narrative inflected by the CSOs based on the Brazilian perception as traumatic in social and ecological terms (FASE, 2015; Shankland and Gonçalves, 2016).
3. The way CSOs view the colonialist approach of ProSAVANA, depicting the Nacala Corridor as an 'empty land' (Wolford and Nehring, 2015), although it is one of the most densely populated regions in Mozambique.
4. The construction of an infrastructure directed towards resource exportation while ignoring the infrastructural needs of the local population.[7]
5. Existing ties among Brazilian and Mozambican CSOs in the context of the international contestation of Vale in the Nacala Corridor contributed to fears of further conflicts (GRAIN and UNAC, 2015; Cezne, 2019).

We highlight three additional dynamics in the background that fuelled local scepticism of ProSAVANA. First, Vale's participation in ProSAVANA is critical for understanding the continuity of CSOs' strategies in contesting the project. In fact, Mozambican CSO initial impressions of ProSAVANA are heavily influenced by their experiences and encounters with Vale before the project's establishment in the country.[8] Vale's controversial entry into the Nacala Corridor is frequently regarded as a result of the company's tight relationship with the Mozambican government. Furthermore, this relationship recalls how the state deployed police forces against affected communities (ADECRU, 2013). Against this background, practices and strategies employed by the AV, such as shadow reports and 'caravans' (see also Cezne, 2019: 1180), were later reproduced in contesting ProSAVANA (FASE, 2015). The second factor contributing to the local scepticism against ProSAVANA is the perception of failing trilateral cooperation. CSOs criticise that agricultural research in Nampula by Embrapa and JIRCAS is conducted separately and partly on the same crop, hence the lack of credibility as a genuine cooperation. At the same time, the Mozambican counterparts were marginalised in the research and technical studies. For example, the Institute of Ararian Research of Mozambique (Instituto de Investigação Agrária de Moçambique) was barely present. Moreover, Mozambican staff were only employed for unskilled work.[9]

Finally, transnational networks were established as a result of notable events, correspondence, and reverberation (cf. the boomerang model in Sändig and Hönke's chapter). Such CSO networks have grown more consolidated over time. For example, Japanese CSOs[10] joined the cause in 2012 after a public statement by the National Peasants Union (União Nacional de Camponeses, UNAC) of Mozambique. Another example is the organisation of mutual exchange trips by UNAC and the Rural Association of Mutual Aid (ORAM) to the Brazilian Cerrado and Nacala Corridor, followed by public statements and an open letter to the three governments (Durán and Chichava, 2017: 281). Brazilian CSOs also use participatory spaces, such as the National Council for Food Security and Nutrition and the National Council for Sustainable Rural Development, as their platforms of activism. Other major events include the Trilateral People's Conferences held in August 2013 and July 2014, which allowed the gathering of more CSOs and eventually led to a network for more regular exchange of information. For example, an intensive study of the ProSAVANA Master Plan was presented by the 'No to ProSAVANA Campaign' (hereafter the 'No-Campaign') led by Mozambican CSOs. The No-Campaign is a transnational CSO network that launched in June 2014 in Mozambique and followed preceding activities. The campaign comprises CSOs, NGOs, grass-roots organisations, and scholars from Mozambique, Brazil, and Japan who criticise the ProSAVANA development model (FASE, 2015).[11] Academia was also engaged via, for example, discourse analysis (see Classen, 2013). Written and video materials were disseminated via this network (Schlesinger, 2014; ADECRU, 2015; FASE, 2015). Importantly, such documents not only problematised

ProSAVANA cooperation/investment, but also served to display each CSO's identity and positioning, thus creating a 'People's South-South Cooperation' (FASE, 2015) from below. For instance, while Mozambican CSO representatives emphasised that they learned by interacting with their Brazilian counterparts, Brazilian CSOs expressed their solidarity and commitment on level terms.[12]

WANBAO (2007–11)

WANBAO began operations in 2007. The Mozambican government granted Hubei Lianfeng Mozambique Company (HLMC) 300 acres of land for the 'Hubei-Gaza Friendship Farm' project, affiliated to Lianfeng Overseas Agricultural Development Company, a provincial-level SOE affiliated with the Bureau of State Farms and Land Reclamation under the Hubei Provincial Government of China (Chichava, 2014b; Madureira, 2014). The intention was, amongst others, to restore the high productivity of those fields, as in the former colonial period when Portuguese farmers occupied the land for rice farming.[13] The other intention was the technology transfer of rice production to local farmers. A WANBAO manager mentioned that during colonial times, rice productivity reached around 4 to 5 tons/ha.[14]

However, the residents had long forgotten the rice production around the lower Limpopo fields. With the end of colonialism, rice production in that area fell to the ground.[15] The irrigation infrastructure was damaged. Local peasants gradually seized the fields to produce a variety of local crops for self-sustenance, despite their limited financial capacity, low literacy rate, and lack of enthusiasm in rice farming.[16] Their production methods resorted mainly to rudimentary technology, depending on the crop rotation system, and were vulnerable to weather conditions. Moreover, land that was no longer being used for agriculture was used for cattle herding. Those were the only sources of livelihood for many in that community. Rice farming was a myth, at least in those areas of Xai Xai.[17]

Around 2007 and 2008, with the international cereal crises (Hossain et al., 2014; Brito et al., 2015), the government strategically matched its interest with China's going global strategy.

The government led by President Armando Emilio Guebuza seized the opportunity for an experimental collaboration with China in agriculture in Xai-Xai. Recalling past rice productivity levels in the region, the cooperation was presented as a means to increase agricultural productivity to former levels through Chinese expertise.[18] The objectives could be deemed positive in terms of community and country development, such as (i) attaining self-sufficiency in rice production, (ii) technology transfer to local farmers, and further (iii) creating export capacity. However, it failed to involve the local communities, who were neither consulted nor informed despite the potential effects on their livelihoods.

Significant changes took place within the project from 2007 to 2011. Management shifted from the SOE, HLMC, to a private entity, WANBAO. The new managing company, WANBAO, increased the investment significantly, with a promise of USD 289 million (Chichava, 2015) for the following five years. Meanwhile, the Mozambican government increased the land concession for the rice-growing project significantly in 2011. However, little is known about what exactly drove these changes. Two different explanations emerge from this period: the first, stated by the Mozambican researcher, Chichava (2014b), claims that financial problems at HLMC led to a managerial change to WANBAO (WAADL), a private company, in 2011 (Chichava, 2014b). The second assumption, developed by Chinese researcher Zhang (2019), suggests that both parties, Mozambique and China, were satisfied with the experimental results at the 'friendship farm', and thus decided to increase the scale of the project. In a similar fashion, little information had been released concerning the existence of the 'friendship farm'. The project seems to have no trace in the government's main agricultural production plan, as it is not acknowledged in the *Plano de Acção para Produção de Alimentos 2008–2011* (Ministério de Economia e Finanças, 2008). While the plan allotted an extra 22,000 hectares for rice cultivation across the country, Xai-Xai was not specifically mentioned as part of the territory that would be used for this purpose. The general public and CSOs in Gaza Province were kept in the dark about the government's goals in that area due to a lack of public information, which was later revealed to be at the heart of contestation. CSOs' general perception of the government's attitude is documented by Sousa (2011: 41): 'the lack of communication between the government and the citizens in Gaza tends to be the norm, except during the electoral period'. In the first phase, the public was thus unfamiliar with the 'friendship farm'.

The lack of vibrancy in the CSO network surrounding the WANBAO project is linked to subnational political dynamics. Gaza Province is a stronghold of the ruling Frelimo party, which makes it difficult for anti-hegemonic CSOs from outside to establish a foothold or mobilise support in the community. For example, the National Farmers' Union UNAC, headquartered in Maputo, is the country's largest national peasant movement. Meanwhile, Chokwe, a district in Gaza, is one of the principal agricultural product suppliers to the southern provinces. However, UNAC has no presence in Gaza Province, despite the geographical proximity between Maputo and Gaza. Meanwhile, while most CSOs in the province support the party's objectives, there was little cooperation between them. This isolation and co-optation of CSOs in Gaza may add to the widespread unwillingness to discuss or participate in the project.

The second phase: Controversies

The second phase is characterised by encounters between development partners and investors with CSOs and affected communities at the local level, which have been crucial in shaping the trajectory of both projects. In addition, we highlight that in the transnational frontier zones, frictions existed not only in business–community relations, but also among CSOs and investors (Tsing, 2004). Categories such as development partners or CSOs are not homogenous; actors have multiple interests and positionings even though they are engaged in the same project. In the case of ProSAVANA, the CSO landscape witnessed a division into two groups: those organised in the transnational 'No to ProSAVANA Campaign' (hereafter the 'No-Campaign')[19] on the one hand, and those who agreed to participate in the elaboration of the new Master Plan in cooperation with Mozambique's Ministry of Agriculture and Food Security (Ministério da Agricultura e Segurança Alimentar,

MASA),[20] the Japan International Cooperation Agency JICA, and the Brazilian Cooperation Agency ABC (Agência Brasileira de Cooperação) on the other. Moreover, there was also a shift of power regarding the protagonist role within ProSAVANA from Brazil to Japan. Brazil's initial leading role within the cooperation diminished with the impeachment of Dilma Rousseff in April 2016, resulting in the loss of participatory spaces and resources for Brazilian CSOs (see also Cezne, 2019) while Japan, represented by JICA, took over the lead. Consequently, Japanese CSOs became more engaged and, hence, more visible in shaping the transnational activist agenda. In the case of the WANBAO project, the second phase witnessed the rise of anti-hegemonic CSOs in Gaza and an open popular contestation led by community members and CSOs, mainly against the government. Hence, the hitherto relatively peaceful coexistence of affected communities and the 'friendship farm' was followed by the beginning of frictional encounters.

ProSAVANA (2016–17)

Early in 2016, a CSO coordination mechanism for the Nacala Corridor development, Mecanismo de Coordenação da Sociedade Civil para o Desenvolvimento do Corredor de Nacala (MCSC), was created on behalf of the ProSAVANA proponents. It was supposed to integrate Mozambican CSOs in the ProSAVANA implementation process and elaborate a new Master Plan version. Besides MASA, JICA and ABC, it involved the agricultural research institution Observatorio do Meio Rural (OMR) from Maputo and three CSO platforms from the respective provinces: PPOSC-N from Nampula, FONAGNI from Niassa, FONGZA from Zambézia, and the World Wide Fund for Nature Alliance of CSO Platforms for natural resource management.[21]

However, due to hierarchies and divisions among the groups, the mechanism failed (see also Funada-Classen, 2019). To start with, the No-Campaign refused to participate in the MCSC, criticising the top-down and non-transparent way in which the mechanism was created, e.g. CSOs belonging to the platform were automatically added to the MCSC. The No-Campaign members further explained that the funding scheme—funded and initiated by

JICA—has made an alternative outcome to the implementation of ProSAVANA impossible.[22]

Later on, the relationship between the No-Campaign and ProSAVANA representatives was further stiffened as both parties accused each other of refusing to communicate with one another. The No-Campaign tended to be a more centralised group of CSOs based in Maputo, therefore potentially better connected to the transnational CSOs and with relatively better access to funds. ProSAVANA proponents thus claimed that the No-Campaign was more powerful than the governments themselves, but its members were steered by foreign interests and unwilling to promote development in Mozambique. Meanwhile, No-Campaign members blamed the ProSAVANA proponents for their reluctance to provide official answers—in written and binding form—to CSOs' claims articulated in the No-Campaign. They also blamed the CSOs in the northern province of Nampula for joining the mechanism, hence being naive and prone to manipulation. CSOs in Nampula instead viewed joining the mechanism as an opportunity to participate in the elaboration of a new ProSAVANA Master Plan and positively influence the latter.[23]

Finally, issues such as transparency and mistrust within the MCSC eventually led to more fragmentation. CSOs participating in the MCSC also confirmed the lack of transparency regarding funding and access to information. Due to a close alliance between the mechanism's steering members, namely the ProSAVANA implementing agencies and the heads of respective CSO platforms, other participating CSOs were gradually marginalised. They suspected that the steering committee members had followed their personal interests and reproduced untransparent practices, instead of promoting meaningful public participation.[24] According to the No-Campaign, participating CSOs required MASA's consent to speak about the mechanism, resulting in their dropping out of the OMR as experts on rural development, further weakening the mechanism.[25]

A second finding is that controversial encounters between CSOs and the Mozambican state dominated much of the controversy. The Mozambican government's approach to the project—resorting to external actors while disregarding Mozambican domestic CSOs and communities—attracted critics from both sides. An interviewee claims that the pressure to implement ProSAVANA came from the Mozambican government, although it seems as though JICA was the body that rushed for another round of community consultation. Considering the local conditions, both the material and cultural perception of pace, communities would have preferred more time to prepare before the consultation. In line with this interviewee's perception, predominantly, the Mozambican government was hesitant, if not resistant, to recognise the CSOs' competencies.[26] Further, a CSO representative from the No-Campaign added that their offer of support and openness seemed to be of no interest to either MASA or to JICA.[27]

The problematic positioning of the Mozambican government became further apparent during the encounter of government representatives and civil society at the Third Trilateral People's Conference in October 2017 in Maputo.[28] MASA authorities flatly rejected the claims and arguments were brought forward by impacted peasants and No-Campaign members against ProSAVANA. This encounter reveals not only the polarised frontiers between the critical CSOs and the Mozambican MASA but also the latter's disrespect towards their peasant population and the country's CSOs. Moreover, the transnational CSO network is further restricted, as Naoko Watanabe, a Japanese CSO representative from Japan International Volunteer Center, who used to participate in these international gatherings, can no longer enter Mozambique, fearing for her life.[29]This is due to the Mozambican government's hostile attitude towards such critics.

Finally, how was transnational activism remade through the controversies of the second phase? Japan's move to the forefront was in fact reflected in the continued presence of JIRCAS and Japanese extensionists in the Nampula Provincial Directorate of Agriculture and Rural Development.[30] In the background, however, Japanese CSOs successfully intervened via Japanese institutions through a variety of practices on behalf of Mozambican CSOs. For example, advocacy practice in the Japanese parliament, as well as addressing an open letter to JICA's president in February 2017, resulted in the mechanism's financing being suspended[31](Funada-Classen, 2019).

Japanese CSOs also supported their Mozambican counterparts in anonymously filing an objection request based on JICA's Guidelines for environmental and social considerations. Thus, 11 peasants from the affected region made their claims to JICA. In July 2017, a delegation of a third-party commission started to investigate these allegations.

Although Brazil as a cooperation partner is less visible, the transnational exchange of knowledge and information via the No-Campaign, with a regional base in Maputo, continued across the three countries. Yet, CSOs from the mechanism in Mozambique's north are not in contact with their Japanese and Brazilian counterparts anymore; rather, transnational communication is maintained through the No-Campaign, which has its regional basis in Maputo. This reflects how the division among Mozambique's CSOs excludes part of them from the transnational network. Moreover, by rhetorically linking ProSAVANA to MATOPIBA, an agro-frontier located in the Brazilian Cerrado, the No-Campaign discusses ProSAVANA as a Brazilian domestic matter,[32] partly turning ProSAVANA and MATOPIBA into synonyms.[33] Nevertheless, the Brazilian government's actual engagement in ProSAVANA is opaque beyond their official participation: a Brazilian Embassy official representing ABC is responsible for ProSAVANA among 40 cooperation projects in total,[34] while the Brazilian representation in MASA's ProSAVANA office is vacant.[35]

On the ground, mismatches between the peasants' needs and the ProSAVANA programme became apparent in a pilot study conducted via the PEM component in the Monapo community (Nampula Province).[36] Under this component, peasants cultivate a plot with improved hybrid seeds, bought yearly. Although they confirm the increased quality of these crops, e.g. cabbage, they also report a higher demand for fertilisers, water, and labour. This links to the lack of water and a watering machine they thought would be granted by the project. According to a JICA official,[37] communities shall receive watering machines under the condition of refinancing them for other communities. Similarly, they are also expected to refund the fertiliser and seeds. Therefore, the source of financing needed to meet these obligations remains unclear. Furthermore, the peasants reported that they had been expelled from their original land plots before participating in the pilot study. The pilot study's land plot is also part of another land conflict in which the peasants are obliged to compensate the former users. These accounts reveal the discrepancy between Japanese ideas and Mozambican reality and show how the alleged South-South cooperation shifted towards an unsuccessful North–South endeavour with clashing realities.

WANBAO (2012–17)

The second phase of WANBAO began after the government transferred land to the private Chinese enterprise. It is characterised by the expansion of the company's operations beyond the 'friendship farm' in 2012, resulting in confrontations with the surrounding peasants and the emergence of anti-hegemonic CSOs in the controversies. The government assigned additional but previously occupied land to the firm without the approval or knowledge of the tenants. Instead, the agreement was struck in secret between the government and WANBAO, while the peasants went about their crop production routine. Their astonishment was palpable when, in January 2012, they unexpectedly discovered that machinery under Chinese operation was causing substantial damage to their nascent and yet-to-mature crops.[38] Consequently, they assembled and attempted to halt the degradation of their primary means of sustenance, all the while seeking to comprehend the unfolding situation. This situation marks the first encounter in which the Chinese become perceived as invaders on the local peasants' farmland.

Despite the language barrier, the peasants recognised that the Chinese were authorised by the government to do so because they were remitted to the latter. Efforts to obtain an explanation from the government and a new perspective for their livelihoods were futile. The continual destruction of the occupied lands by heavy machinery, on the one hand, and the persistent efforts of the peasants to regain their lands or receive compensation, on the other, set the stage for the confrontation.[39] The conflict gradually escalated as more people were affected by the company's expansionist activity, but no structured solutions were provided. Several meetings were held with government representatives through the Mozambican state-owned enterprise directly involved in land and water management, Regadio do Baixo Limpopo (RBL).[40] During these sessions, the government's interlocutor promised to assign land to peasants without specifying the type or location of the land, but the promise was not kept. They also suggested compensation, although the peasants frequently complained about not receiving any. In January 2013, a massive flood occurred in Gaza Province, affecting approximately 85,000 people. USD 13 million dollars were reportedly needed to restore the production capacity (see Júnior, 2013). Some claimed that when the flood occurred in 2013, the conversations and promises ended, but it had not.

The estimated number of the overall affected by WANBAO ranged from 500 (see additional details in Journal@Verdade, 2013; Wise, 2019) to 80,000[41] (see additional information in Issufo, 2012; Canalmoz, 2014). While the government limited its role to framing the narratives regarding the Chinese rice-production project, the Mozambican SOE RBL attempted to appease the affected communities.

The involvement of CSOs appears to have been driven in part by media coverage of the issue.[42] During what is known as the Xai-Xai peasant crisis, FONGA, a local CSO led by Gaza citizen Dr Anastácio Matavele, became vociferous about citizen issues, particularly in relation to the WANBAO project. FONGA picked up the case and continued representing the peasants, voicing their concerns, and mobilising the national CSOs based in Maputo and the academic community around this case. Apart from appearing as an interlocutor before the government and through the traditional media, the FONGA leader wrote letters denouncing the situation as a land grab, then sent them via email to academics and CSOs.

The conflict's visibility kept escalating after the flood in 2013, with more CSOs[43] joining and mobilising themselves in favour of the affected communities. They united their efforts in organising marches with the peasants and provided them with further support. Despite the communities' growing disputes and the involvement of the CSOs, however, the government did not publicly address the complaints. Instead, it remained silent and supported the project, disguising the community's concerns.

The third phase: Outcome (cancellation vs integration)

The third phase characterises the periods of consolidation and cancellation, respectively. While Japan initially increased its efforts to advance ProSAVANA, the project was cancelled in mid-2020. Japan's retreat was accompanied by Vale's announcement that they would divest from the coal business. In contrast, WANBAO project implementers, including Chinese professionals, appeared to gradually find mutual understanding with the local communities. However, disagreements and complaints from the peasants towards the local authorities prevail, albeit not being publicly demonstrated.

ProSAVANA—Cancellation (2017–20)

In this phase, Japan as a cooperation partner continues in the foreground, while Brazil's participation remains unclear (Funada-Classen, 2019). Beyond ProSAVANA, Japan continues to be involved in additional investment in the PEDEC-Nacala development programme via road and further infrastructure upgrading, also envisioning natural gas exploration in Palma, counting on the participation of Mitsui (Funada-Classen, 2019). In August 2018, ProSAVANA was condemned for human rights violations by the Administrative Court in Maputo due to a lawsuit by Mozambique's Bar Association, Ordem de Advogados de Moçambique, due to MASA's continued failure to provide information on ProSAVANA (GRAIN, 2018). In mid-2020, MASA announced the official cancellation of ProSAVANA (Da Silva, 2020). According to Funada-Classen (2019: 56), this is an indirect result of the 2017 objection request. Although the visiting committee did not confirm the objection request allegations, as a condition to continuing financing the participatory Master Plan elaboration, it recommended that all actors, including UNAC and the No-Campaign, be included in the ProSAVANA decision-making process. Nevertheless, critics are suspicious concerning that claim, expecting that ProSAVANA could continue under the label of SUSTENTA (ibid.).[44] It coincides with Vale/Mitsui's announcement that they would divest from the coal business, selling their investments to Vulcan Minerals, a subsidiary of the Indian Jindal mining company. According to the Vale Affected

(International Articulation of those Affected by Vale (AIAAV), 2021), Vale's withdrawal coincided with the end of the granting of tax benefits by the Mozambican government. Vale left behind vast social and ecological damage, for which the Vale Affected doubted that Vale would be held accountable. Indeed, Vale's withdrawal can be attributed instead to the company's strategic shift (Vale, 2022). Nevertheless, ProSAVANA's cancellation can be attributed to an overall failing of the trilateral cooperation strategy, as ProSAVANA's initial period comprised 20 years (Wolford and Nehring, 2015).

The encounters happened in the realm of the No-Campaign, e.g. in the context of the Fourth Trilateral People's Conference held in Tokyo in November 2018. As in previous trilateral gatherings, CSO and peasant representatives from all three countries were involved, denouncing violations and demanding the complete cancellation of ProSAVANA. The denunciations against Japanese public authorities regarding JICA and Mitsui included Japan's Ministry of Foreign Affairs and the Japan Bank for International Cooperation, particularly concerning the Nacala Corridor investments. Besides, the violations attributed to Japanese agents in Brazil were also denounced. They include violations in the context of PRODECER and MATOPIBA in the Cerrado region, as well as those committed by Vale in the context of the Estrada Ferrovia Carajás project in Brazil.[45]

In this context, Mozambican and Brazilian participants not only visited Japanese farmers but also emphasised their solidarity with them and the determination to continue in this common struggle. Japanese authorities are criticised for their colonialist views on Cerrado and Savana, as they are seen merely as a provider of resources without considering the necessities and demands of the affected communities in Brazil and Mozambique. In the Tokyo Declaration (Campanha Não ao ProSAVANA, 2018), CSOs further attached Japan's persisting wilful ignorance of these matters and its abstention from approving the peasants' declaration and rural worker protection at the UN General Assembly (2018). This meeting reveals the continued relevance of the Vale investments for the contestation of ProSAVANA and the further development of the Nacala Corridor, which represents another common ground on which the No-Campaign denounces human rights violations in both places (Aguiar, 2018). Joint publications on the future of the Nacala Corridor development, as well as the collective realisation of an online seminar in Mozambique on the Brazilian land reform, account for continued transnational CSO collaboration (FASE, 2021).

WANBAO—Integration (2014–20)

Integration here is used in two senses. First is the inclusion of peasants from affected communities into WANBAO's rice-farming project since there was no land to return to the peasants and their continuous resistance. According to community members, this phase started around 2014, even though conflicts from the second phase were not entirely solved but are instead rather latent.[46] Integration also refers to the gradual process of community acceptance of the project and a change of attitudes towards Chinese professionals on the ground.

The integration process of local farmers into WANBAO's rice-production scheme was somewhat unstructured and met with suspicion and criticism. Peasants, who were among the first batch members to join WANBAO, stated that they were invited to join the scheme when farming in disputed fields as a resistance gesture against Chinese occupation of the land since they had not been given an alternative source of livelihood.[47] Others mentioned that Chinese and RBL people were randomly walking in the neighbourhoods and asking for interested people to join the project.[48] From these descriptions, there were no clear criteria as to whom should be included in the rice-production scheme, thereby displaying a lack of planning and coordination on the part of RBL.

The unstructured integration process invited further suspicions over the nature of business-community collaboration. Indeed, the recruitment of peasants could be in alignment with WANBAO's goals of technology transfer and increased production. However, many suspected that it also served as RBL's tactic to silence resisting farmers who kept going to the occupied lands. For the affected peasants who responded to the call, joining the rice-production scheme appeared to be the only option, as it kept them occupied with some productive and 'safe' activities with a petty income from rice production.[49] These families became increasingly dependent on WANBAO's presence and subjected themselves to the working routine of the company. In addition, integration into WANBAO's rice-cultivation scheme means accepting the terms and conditions of the Chinese managers who would decide land usage and its output. As a result, participating farmers lose the freedom to apply alternative technologies or grow other crops to diversify their livelihoods in ways that mere integration into WANBAO's rice-production programme cannot provide. The dominance of rice cultivation further worsens their already low quality of life. Over time, however, the Chinese have begun to reconsider the possibility of allowing local farmers to produce more crops in WANBAO's contract farming system. This is supposed to improve their standard of living without affecting rice cultivation. This gesture can be seen as an adaptation of corporate vision to lived reality.

A significant number of people remained excluded from the rice-production scheme: some chose not to join the scheme in the first place or remained curious about how the scheme would work, while others gave up and opted out. With the years passing, some peasants have become more integrated into the WANBAO project than others. Meanwhile, different paths and experiences emerged among members of the affected communities. Given the demonstrated success of some participants, others who had previously declined to join the programme began to show an interest or a desire to join when the opportunity arose. Furthermore, although not universal, these interests were accompanied by a change in the perception of the Chinese presence, gradually shifting to a more accepting attitude that the Chinese on the ground are good people. Indeed, local peasants, both involved in and excluded from the WANBAO investment project, tend to slowly approach the Chinese workers, who are no longer seen as their enemies. Those remaining in the scheme believed that it was worthy of continuing to work with the Chinese despite complaints of injustice. These complaints were directed less towards the Chinese managers but more towards the chiefs from RBL, who only showed up at harvest time as mediators between the Chinese and the local peasants.

Affected communities, whether integrated into the rice-production scheme or not, pointed fingers at the government, although timidly. Integrated farmers complained that RBL chiefs inflated the production costs and performed other financial manoeuvres to extort them.[50] The non-integrated peasants who had lost their lands started to realise the importance of organising themselves in associations to gain more weight and negotiate with the government to reclaim their rights. Moreover, despite the prerogatives of alignment with the dominant party, the experiences these peasants had with the WANBAO establishment prompted them to be more open and welcoming to anti-hegemonic CSOs that defend their rights.

Comparison and conclusion

As this chapter shows, the case of ProSAVANA progresses from clash and contestation to further cancellation due to its embeddedness in the Nacala Development Corridor, Brazil's trilateral cooperation arrangement with Japan, and its strong association with the locally and internationally contested Vale. In comparison, the case of WANBAO progresses from silent experimentation to land-grab and contestation, then arrives at a new stage of mutual adaptation and coexistence, despite persisting conflicts. Beside the commonalities of both projects, such as the fact that they kicked off without CSOs or local community involvement, a 'silent' and non-frictional beginning of WANBAO's 'friendship farm' being relatively similar to the establishment of ProSAVANA's research laboratories, the following crucial differences were observed on the ground throughout the evolution of the projects.

First, this chapter highlights the embeddedness of both projects and actors in subnational political economy configurations, which have influenced stakeholders' perceptions and ability to draw repertoires from their respective networks. To illustrate, WANBAO is installed in the relatively appeased Gaza Province, with low local CSO engagement, and its implementation is connected to other Chinese investment projects such as ATDCs. ProSAVANA, on the other hand, was trilateral, involving the Northern actor Japan, and was embedded into Mozambique's Corridor Development Strategy. It was thus associated with Vale/Mitsui's investments in coal and railway infrastructure, which entailed local encounters perceived as violent, exploitative, and potentially negative to local community development. Moreover, the Mozambican government's alliance with Vale against the communities' interests (see Cezne and Hönke, 2022) became apparent, nurturing mistrust against Brazilian engagement in Mozambique and also marking a negative perception of the project.

Second, CSOs in the Nacala Corridor started off with strengthened links to Maputo CSOs and established transnational ties with their counterparts in Brazil, mediated first via the AV. Apart from having a common language, they also benefitted from the Brazilian CSOs' contestation history and their voice in Brazil's public policymaking, including South-South matters. The joining of Japanese CSOs contributes to further leverage. Besides, the relevant CSO communities in Maputo and Nampula are among the most substantial and most established in Mozambique, further facilitating resistance. However, those domestic ties suffered when the Mozambican government attempted to integrate the Northern CSOs via the dialogue mechanism into the ProSAVANA elaboration, with an unsuccessful outcome due to transparency matters. Conversely, in the case of Gaza CSOs, there is an emerging cluster of CSOs not aligned with the regime, instead contesting in defence of the community's rights. Furthermore, these emerging CSOs formed new alliances with the Maputo ones, showing promising results in their bonding with the affected communities.

Third, WANBAO was not mistrusted by CSOs in the beginning. As WANBAO underwent consolidation, the communities suffered direct impacts. With their lands and sustenance products taken, peasants found themselves contesting both the company and the government. However, such endeavours were challenging due to their lack of organisation and knowledge of their rights. Despite the region's political alliance with the ruling party, one particular CSO (FONGA) emerged, which in turn reached out to its counterparts. From there, a CSO network was gradually established at the domestic level but lacked transnational ties. Until the present, there is no evidence of transnational CSO engagement between China and Mozambique (see also Waisbich, and Sändig and Hönke in this volume).

The project's diverging trajectories, fourth, are shaped by how different stakeholders—states, CSO networks, and affected communities—have encountered each other, how such encounters have in turn shaped their practice, and whether mutual adaptation occurred. WANBAO is an illustrative example of how local encounters can positively change the practice of actors who are engaged in the encounters over time. On the communities' part, there is an emerging awareness of the government's faults and the need for community organisations to provide checks and balances. On the part of WANBAO project implementers, there is also rising awareness to better prepare for potential impacts and accommodate some peasants. Despite the observation that the communities and the project seem to have found a mode of coexistence, there is little improvement in peasants' livelihoods. It can even be argued that rather than improving, their conditions relatively worsened. Apart from having limited access to the rice they produce, they either need to buy or lose access to other foods they used to produce themselves.

We show, fifth, that fragmentation within the CSO landscape is likely to occur in an authoritarian context. Mozambique's government is held accountable not only for land grabs and crop destruction in WANBAO but also for its failure to actively involve (potentially) affected communities and local CSOs in the implementation process by providing information and protecting their citizens' rights. In both cases, the government attempted a (partly successful) appeasement policy with diverging outcomes. In WANBAO, some peasants who had lost their land became randomly integrated as contractors, while resisting CSOs were left at the margin. In ProSAVANA, attempts to integrate parts of the local CSOs into a dialogue mechanism failed, yet no attempt to integrate community members was made. This was flanked by the transnational No-Campaign, which, due to their counterpart's activities in Brazil and Japan, further contributed to the delay and final cancellation of ProSAVANA.

Similar to Sändig and Hönke's chapter we find, sixth, that political opportunities in the companies' home state matter. For instance, the involvement of Japanese CSOs was relevant for their Mozambican counterparts to access information from Japan, which would not have been available otherwise. Japanese CSOs were also crucial for accessing further participation, such as the objection request from 2017. In contrast, in the case of WANBAO, the transnational involvement of Chinese NGOs was absent (see Chapter 4 by Waisbich and Chapter 5 by Sändig and Hönke).

Finally, our two cases show the complex entanglement between South-South engagement and existing North–South (geopolitical) relations. This becomes apparent in the case of ProSAVANA, where South-South rhetoric in a trilateral configuration serves as a discursive strategy, blurring hidden interests of 'the North'. The trilateral cooperation contributed to ProSAVANA's lack of credibility when the non-cooperation became obvious. Brazil's partial withdrawal and Japan's protagonism from 2017 onwards turned ProSAVANA into a de facto North–South cooperation. This is exemplified in the PEM component implementation, where JICA's development concept failed to meet local peasants' needs. However, such a 'North' versus 'South' dynamic also translated into transnational contestation, where southern CSOs from Brazil and Mozambique blamed Japan as a northern cooperation partner for exploiting the South (Brazil and Mozambique).

PART FOUR

CONCLUSIONS

9

ON AFRICAN GLOBALITIES AND
FRONTIER ZONES

Vineet Thakur

Introduction

In a speech in the Ugandan parliament in July 2018, the Indian prime minister, Narendra Modi, outlined 'ten guiding principles' of India's engagement with Africa. His framing of India's African policy in a list of principles was somewhat uncharacteristic of the prime minister's speaking style. Modi has a penchant for pitching policies in acronyms and backronyms. For instance, defining the India–China relationship just two months before his Africa speech, in May 2018, Modi used a backronym 'Strength' (and in the process misspelling it) to assert key strengths of the relationship between the two Asian giants.[1] So, when he chose to list 'ten guiding principles' rather than some laboriously assembled acronym or a misfiring backronym, it was clear that the contours of India's Africa policy were shaped more by the need for sure-footed policies than for pleasing platitudes. Modi asserted that the India–Africa development partnership would be guided by African priorities and would be conducted on African terms (Viswanathan and Mishra, 2019).

Two months later, in September 2018, at the Forum on China–Africa Cooperation, China's President Xi Jinping was even more emphatic about Africa deciding its own priorities in relations with China. In the backdrop of not-so-hushed conversations on China's debt-trap diplomacy, Xi Jinping's 'Five No's' strongly emphasised that China will not impose its developmental policies on African countries (Yutong, 2018).

As these pronouncements make clear, Global South powers are acutely conscious of not replicating the European model of engagement through conditionalities with African countries. Countries like China, Brazil, and India are clear in their messaging about not wanting to interfere in the internal politics of the aid and in recipient countries (see Chapter 2 by Bunskoek).

For much of the Cold War period, relations among key Global South actors and African countries were high on solidarity but low on substance. This slowly changed at the start of the new millennium as three Global South powers, China, Brazil, and India, enlarged their cooperation with Africa. President Lula from Brazil visited the continent 33 times during his presidency between 2003 and 2010, while India began to leverage its long-standing diasporic links with the continent for larger economic cooperation (see Chapter 3 by Dye et al.). China, which was the first country to start a continent-wide ministerial conference with African countries, a model that had now been replicated by several other countries including India, Russia, and Turkey, placed Africa outreach at the forefront of its global power aspirations.

There is no dearth of literature today exploring the dynamics of relationships between key Global South actors and the African continent. Indeed, from an International Relations (IR) perspective, there is now a cottage industry of scholarship on 'rising powers' and Africa which explores the political, economic and diplomatic relationships (although a predominantly large quantity of this work focuses on China and Africa).

A lot of this scholarship has debated whether the rising powers are neo-colonial powers in Africa or benign actors fulfilling the grand emancipatory missions of South-South cooperation (Balasubramanyam, 2015; see also Chapter 1 by Hönke et al.). Such discussions have increasingly become trite, employed sometimes in propagandist ways, and as Folashadé Soulé (2020) argues, they grant little or no agency to African actors. Attendant to this is the old and cliched but always insightful caution, 'What is Africa?'. Any suggestion to treat a whole continent through the sweeping eyes of a roving academic or policymaker is fraught with issues which the convenience of categorisation can scarcely now hide. In turn, Raoul Bunskoek also raises the question in this volume: 'What is China?'. In other words, can we realistically speak of a 'China model', or for that matter, of an Indian or a Brazilian model, and so on?

The chapters in this book move away from the analytical certainties that the macro-frame of 'Africa's international relations' spawns in conventional IR literature. I trust that in the discussion below I will be able to alert the reader to aspects that make this book a worthwhile effort to reflect more deeply about Africa and its international relations. Drawing on various chapters, I reflect on the relevance of the Global South as an operative concept/category and discuss the various imaginaries of 'frontier zones' that come through in the book.

South-South interaction: The illusory promise of emancipation and difference

Emerging from a Goldman Sachs acronym for Brazil, Russia, India and China (which then excluded South Africa), the term BRIC(S) gained immense traction in the late 2000s to eventually coalesce into a political grouping. At the time of its emergence, some of the decolonial scholarship celebrated it for its emancipatory potential. In one such attempt, the decolonial theorist Walter Mignolo (2012) argued that the BRICS project was essentially one of 'epistemic disobedience'. Seeing BRICS as a historical successor to Bandung, Mignolo argued that BRICS was a power coalition with an anti-imperial ethic. It harnessed neoliberalism for the Global South through a process of delinking from Western institutions. All BRICS countries were ruled by 'people of colour'; 'the colonial/imperial wound' and a 'stigma of the skin' brought them together, 'even if their skin is white like Slavs in Russia or European migrants to Latin America from the second half of the nineteenth century' (Mignolo, 2012: 88–9). Indeed, he counselled countries in Africa, quoting

Lottin Welly Marguerite, to follow the 'BRICS model and find association of cooperation and mutual strengthening' (ibid.: 84).

Although Mignolo has progressively distinguished the BRICS form of 'de-Westernization' from a decolonial project of delinking from Western modernity, the latter is a utopia that bases itself on expectations rather than experiences. Substantively, 'de-Westernization' is what you get as a reality to compensate for the non-realisability of decolonial utopia.

However, one needs to be cautious about hearty hallelujahs around BRICS, and which the chapters in this book avoid. Indeed, juggling between de-Westernisation and decoloniality, Mignolo pays little attention to another possibility which has now progressively disappeared from public discourse. This was the vision of South-South cooperation advanced by the South Commission in the late 1980s. There are four key reasons why it is important to distinguish Mignolo's de-Westernisation from the less utopian but eminently more emancipatory vision of South-South cooperation.

Firstly, *The Report of the South Commission* which first proposed the development of a 'South Consciousness' had called for the need for a broader Global South coalition, a strategic alignment of countries of the Global South around common issues (Independent Commission of the South on Development Issues, 1990). And throughout the 1990s and 2000s, there did indeed seem to be a broader Global South sensibility which emerged around global equity and justice on issues as diverse as climate change, the World Trade Organization, nuclear disarmament, global health, and United Nations reforms (Hopewell, 2016; Plesch, 2016; Biehl, 2004). But by the late 2000s, a broader 'Global South' project had been effectively usurped by specialised coalitions of a few increasingly neoliberal and self-interested countries, such as the BRICS. On the issues above, the interests of these more powerful BRICS countries, such as China, Brazil and India, although not homogenous, are often at cross purposes with other Global South actors.

Secondly, the hopes riding on BRICS cooperation, such as those of Mignolo, were exponentially exaggerated. China and India are traditionally hostile to each other and given the geopolitical churning in the Indo–Pacific, India is more easily allied with the West than with China. Further, and it is increasingly evident, what brings Russia and China together is the geopolitical rivalry—and sense of threat—from the West rather than any 'solidarity of the colour'. Despite the rhetoric of Global South solidarity, public imagery is filled with 'Wolf Warrior'-like visions of BRIC countries acting as new saviours of Africa. Brazil under Jair Bolsonaro had turned its foreign policy focus away from the Global South though. In other words, the collective promise of BRICS for emancipation in the Global South is injudiciously amplified.

Thirdly, as various chapters in this book show, political rhetoric notwithstanding, the relationships between African actors and BRIC(S) countries are to a great extent driven by private actors rather than by political will. These private companies may originate from the Global South—although some of them, like Arcelor Mittal, operate from the Global North—they come under no illusions of being overly concerned about Africa or indeed emancipation.

And finally, as all four BRIC countries are, or have seen attempts to turn illiberal, de-Westernisation may increasingly serve as just a propagandist prop for their oppressive actions internally. Perhaps it is unfair to be critical of Mignolo more specifically for not ethically thinking through an event in the far future, i.e. the ongoing Russian invasion of Ukraine (as of this writing in 2023), but as Tamar Koplatadze (2019) has argued, the longstanding lack of engagement by decolonial/postcolonial scholars with Russia's own histories of internal colonialism perpetuates such blind spots towards Russia's 'subaltern imperialism'. Likewise, Dibyesh Anand (2012) has made the case for theorising China and India's policies in Xinjiang and Kashmir, respectively, as informal imperialism. Civil liberties for Muslims in Kashmir, more specifically, and the rest of India, in general, are under serious threat under Narendra Modi's right-wing regime.

In any case, this turn to illiberalism is not just an internal concern for these countries. As Laura Trajber Waisbich argues in the book (Chapter 4), illiberal policies foster less accountability towards Africa-focused projects in these countries. Civil society actors from the BRIC countries now play little or no role in devising and monitoring projects in Africa, shown also with regard to the absence of Chinese NGO activism around corporate projects by Sändig and Hönke (Chapter 5). We'll return to this point again later, but before moving on, it is important to reiterate that theoretical aspirations of a macro-level decolonial theory are fraught with counterproductive assertions and ingratiating apologia for illiberal regimes.

The Global South (non)models

Despite my hesitation about conceiving of the BRICS as an automatically benign grouping, I would not suggest—and this book and most other scholarship provides enough evidence of this—that the Western actors and non-Western actors have the same interests and modus operandi in Africa. But the question which motivates the three editors, Jana Hönke, Eric Cezne and Yifan Yang, 'do Global South actors bring a different model/distinct practices?', needs considerable unpacking. This may be broken down into a set of provocations.

To start with, do Global South actors bring different forms, sensibilities, and practices to what is often seen as a Western model? Yes, of course—that is inevitable. But as the editors and the authors in this book emphasise, there is also not one 'Southern homogenic' model to speak of. A Southern model is too far-fetched to consider when as Bunskoek shows, there is also, despite popular perceptions, no 'China model'. Indeed, the kinds of practices that finally concretise into policy outcomes evolve out of negotiated agreements between various stakeholders at multiple levels, including African stakeholders. To speak of one (or even several) Southern models may perhaps be heuristically convenient, but such characterisations come at the cost of understanding bottom-up and sideways processes. Furthermore, are all these policies from the Global South actors necessarily more beneficial to Africans than the policies of the Western actors? Again, answers that are arrived at through broad indicative generalisations would leave a lot out.

In addressing these issues through empirically rich studies, this volume raises important questions about how to think of South-South relations, albeit without necessarily spelling it out that way. It eschews a normative approach, and focuses on the materiality of relations and the agency of local(ised) actors. But importantly it provides invaluable insights on how we should think about 'the Global South' as a category.

Here, one pauses to ask: has 'the Global South' become an empty signifier? I must state the point with some caution: we certainly cannot disregard the colonial and historically racialised ways in which global inequalities are arrayed, or how in some of the Western literature, countries like China in particular are always suspected of evil designs. But despite that, when today key Global South actors are among the largest economies in the world, some of the most grotesque accumulators of weapons of mass destruction, purveyors of neoliberal policies, and oppressors of vast internal populations, focusing on their difference from the West serves limited normative or analytical purpose. Indeed, in works employing the term to connote a category of resistance with a promise of emancipation, the 'Global South' categorisation ends up reifying an inverse normative binary in which the Global South is already seen as a progressive agent.

Analytically, difference (as one of the editors reminded me here) may not be better but neither is it necessarily worse. Accordingly, a decade ago, in *Theory from the South: Or, How Euro-America Is Evolving toward Africa*, anthropologists Jean and John Comaroff (2012) suggested another way of thinking about the Global South and its difference from the Global North. Instead of looking at the Global South as a political entity doing action, they conceived of the Global South as a historical field which was at the forefront of modernity. The historical arc of modernity had bent towards the Global South, they argued. In other words, the world in general now looked more like the Global South than the Global North. Earlier, our theorisations about the world took the Global North as the primary field of action, for that was where all modern phenomena, such as industrialisation, progress, and nation state, played out. The Global South did the catching up to Global North modernity. Theory about the Global South could only be derivative. However, it was now quite evident that not only did modernity play out differently in the Global South, but it was the Global North which was doing the catching up. For example, European nation states are increasingly becoming 'polycultural postcolonies', mimicking the Global South template of nation states. This form of mimicking is replicated in several fields and zones from development (Mawdsley, 2018) to counter-insurgency (Camp and Heatherton, 2016). The Global South, the Comaroffs argued, was consequently the new global condition and hence a more privileged site for theory production.

Again, one could take issue with the Comaroffs: which 'Global South'? But to think of Global South as a space rather than as an agent, as Hönke et al. suggest with this book, helps to highlight the potential for creative work. It is here that the focus on African globalities in this book—seen neither as derivate of the West, nor as a universalising, thus normative, category of its own—presents a more engaging and fruitful way of thinking from and about the Global South. The focus on material sites, where we see politics in action, allows us to think through the entanglements of international political, social and economic life. Such sites (or 'frontier zones', soon discussed), are where ideologies are refined in actions, where idioms are chiselled into bureaucratic practice, where meanings are stitched in the raw and vibrant materiality of an infrastructural site that is composed of things, people, and institutions. If there is a 'Global South' sensibility or form or difference, it is through these sites that we must arrive at them. In other words, the task of decolonising knowledge must move beyond just focusing on Global South actors and incorporate analyses that centre the Global South as sites of knowledge production.

In general, as Hönke, Cezne and Yang remind us, broad-based analytical categories do not help with understanding the multifarious, plural, comprehensive and at times incomprehensible relations at these sites. A view of power as a top-down mechanism, flowing from one (state) into another, and, inversely, power as resistance which is necessarily bottom-up, does not comprehend the full scale of mechanisms and practices that are at play. Power, in the Foucauldian vein, manifests itself in the totality of its relations. It is a diffused, omnipresent force that relays through rather than originates from its subjects. For Foucault, this creates a paradoxical situation of subjectification: the process that makes a subject— one who is shaped by structural power—is the same process that creates an agent—one who shapes the structure. Power is always refracted, modulated, altered, and (dis)framed by the subject of its passing. Every subjective contact with power is simultaneously also an act of its amplification / subversion. When we focus our analytical eyes too much on clean categories of imposition, capitulation, or indeed resistance, we miss the multiplicities of its relay and their political potentialities. Might one then suggest a 'grounding' of theory: with people, with movements, and, as Ngũgĩ wa Thiong'o (2012) suggests, with the messy politics of everyday encounters. The 'frontier zone' as one such messy site of everyday encounter furnishes new conceptions of globalities.

Frontier zones

The term 'global' is in academic vogue. Indeed, there is a rush to adjectivise it into disciplinary vocabularies: Global History, Global Sociology, Global IR, and so on. But the term is an(other) empty signifier, at least in IR. 'Global International Relations' suggests doing what IR ought to be doing even without the word 'global', that is, to draw on the experiences of the whole world in our theorisations. 'Globalities', in contrast, as Hönke, Cezne and Yang argue, 'conceive the global in smaller, more pluralistic, and procedural terms.' Globalities cuts the global into manageable morsels, into active observable sites where one could make concrete analyses of the ways in which our world is being shaped. This approach necessitates taking an exploratory view of agency. Different chapters in this book argue for expanding our horizons of actorhood. In addition to states (and the decision-making state elites), private companies, civil society organisations in both receiving and granting countries, and local communities figure prominently as key actors who shape the contours of relationships in the book, although none of them operate completely autonomously.

Several chapters in the book zoom in on 'frontier zones' as concrete sites. Literally, the term frontier can mean two, sometimes contradictory, things. In one sense, the 'frontier' is a border or a limit—a space at the *end* of one's remit. The 'frontier' is where one's reach begins to end, the power begins to taper off; a space of discord between the intent and the reach of power; and consequently, a space that is sometimes fiercely vigilant against the possibility of subversion. In another, often complementary but also opposing way, the frontier is the space *just beyond* one's remit. An unexplored space whose uncertainty, abnormality, unpredictability and unboundedness fashion new horizons of compromise and creation. A frontier zone thus inheres contradictory possibilities. It encompasses zones of the contrived as well as the creative, and the managed and the messy.

In all, it seems to me that there are five ways in which these 'frontier zones' are manifested in this book. Each of these brings out new possibilities of research on African 'globalities'.

The first of these ways focuses on the materiality of these sites. As the editors explain, 'frontier zones' are 'sites [that] integrate expanding circuits of capital and (transnational) relations of exchange of various forms and destinations with Africa's long and multiple entanglements with various parts of the world' (Hönke et al.: 3). Objects as assemblage play a productive role in the creation of political relations. Infrastructures are not merely static objects but constellations of material and social relations. Thus, the port in Lamu cannot just be understood as a 'port', with a generic port function of acting as a node of supply lines, but as an assemblage formed through generic as well as specific ways in which circuits of people and things—both material and non-material—and their relations are produced. Here the port is conceived not as a static space, but one that consumes, observes, relays a surfeit of power relations. As Kilaka (Chapter 6) as well as Gambino and Bagwandeen (Chapter 7) show, Lamu is a political space, which to some degrees is distinct and irreproducible.

The second way in which 'frontier zones' appear in the book is in the form of what Mary Louise Pratt (1992) calls 'contact zones'. These are 'social spaces where disparate cultures meet, and grapple with each other, often in highly asymmetrical relations of domination and subordination' (ibid.: 4). The focus here is primarily on human relations, which although asymmetrical are still defined by relative indeterminacy. As Gambino and Bagwandeen show, what might appear at first sight as highly asymmetrical relations are themselves caught in what Bourdieu would call their respective 'fields'. The agency of individuals is constrained by the different fields they occupy. For instance, the Chinese supervisors and workers operate under disempowering constraints of the Chinese contract labour system and economy, even though they may seem to have immediate power over the African workers. But at the same time, the contact zone is a zone of mutual translation, a zone occupied by 'pidgin'— metaphorically and literally, which leaves more scope for assertive transfers of management practices but also subversive transgressions thereof (Driessen, 2020).

'Frontier zones' are also spaces of friction, spaces that contrive typical reactions from the 'clash' of ideas, motives, cultures. This is the third way in which frontier zones appear in the book. In a neoliberal world, the means and relations of transnational production are anchored in specifically exploitative ways. The focus on the subalterns, in this case, workers (in Gambino and Bagwandeen), host communities and advocacy networks (in Chapter 5 by Sändig and Hönke, Chapter 6 by Kilaka, and Chapter 8 by Sambo and Bußler) the outwardly political ways of their resistance is not merely a descriptive but also a political choice. The essays in the book take that choice seriously and by revealing the creative, innovative ways in which resistance is mounted, they restore political agency to the grassroots.

Fourthly, frontier also operates here as 'a zone of distinction': exceptionalised, even deterritorialised (such as special economic zones), often falling outside of the purview of normal legal mechanisms, gated time-spaces which produce distinctive sets of relations. In everyday encounters, frontiers appear as spaces of profusion and excess, as spaces in which the surfeit of interactions and the possibilities of their meanings exceed a certain permissible economy of their operations. African workers and Chinese/Brazilian/Indian supervisors are not supposed to talk much, limited by both the constraints of language, nationalities, and class positions, but the interactions produce their own dynamics—sometimes bringing order to structural chaos, and other times inserting manageable chaos into deliberately segregated spaces. The gated zone of this 'frontier' creates life-worlds of its own. In all this, the effort is not to suggest which of the ways does it best, but rather to point to a plethora of imaginations at the frontiers. The zooming in on these frontier zones allows us to see how power relations are sutured at specific sites (see Chapter 6 by Kilaka, Chapter 7 by Gambino and Bagwandeen, and Chapter 8 by Sambo and Bußler).

Finally, the 'frontier zones' allow for multiscale actorhood: these are spaces which involve governments—domestic and international, civil society actors—non-governmental organisations and community boards, companies (providing labour, machinery, and skills), specialised legal and financial regimes. The chapters in this volume do not take a unified view of agency, but instead point to different ways and means through which agency is exhibited by actors at different scales (see Chapter 2 by Bunskoek, Chapter 3 by Dye et al., Chapter 4 by Waisbich, and Chapter 5 by Sändig and Hönke). Going further, the 'frontier zones' in Africa, as we have argued with the Comaroffs, are now the privileged sites of theory production. This volume eschews that task somewhat, for it restricts itself to unearthing the practices, but one could suggest a further line of enquiry.

What do these 'frontier zones' of Africa's infrastructure 'globalities' tell us about modes of neoliberal governance? Operating at the crossroads of global finance, international and local governments, community life, and (racialised) cultural and labour practices, the 'frontier zones' proffer new modes of governance that integrate freedom and security, (political) rule and (market) management, dominance and resistance to produce racialised neoliberal subjects (on the racial capitalism of African infrastructures, see Kimari and Ernstson, 2020). Could one suggest that the 'frontier zone' is to the 2010s and 2020s what the factory floor was to the 1970s and 1980s?

Conclusion

I have made two broad points here: first that our discussions on the Global South must also increasingly problematise the term itself. The focus on the agency of Global South actors (largely key Global South states) tends to inscribe them with an emancipatory potential which is largely misplaced. Instead, it may be more fruitful to place the Global South, or rather the 'globalities' of the South, as concrete sites, at the centre of our analyses, which also helps to amplify the several other Global South actors who are on the ground. But going further, it is through a focus on these sites that we can appreciate the surfeit of actions, practices, movements, and structures that are being shaped and reshaped, and thus view these locations as sites for knowledge/theory production. This volume busies itself in excavating a rich tapestry of African infrastructure 'globalities'. As Global South powerhouses and their infrastructures (capital, labour, machines, practices) venture into new lands, including in the Global North, perhaps the next step, as I have indicated, is to query the extent to which these are generalisable.

10

SOUTH-SOUTH TRANSFORMATIONS
IN PRACTICE

CONCLUSIONS AND OUTLOOK

Jana Hönke, Eric Cezne and Yifan Yang

The 19th century was Europe's, the 20th century of the United States, and the 21st century must be ours.

We opened this book with Brazilian President Lula's upbeat assertion heralding a new dawn for South-South relations in the twenty-first century. It was conveyed during a state visit to Nigeria in 2006, when a global commodity supercycle set the tone for such optimism and drove the explosion of Global South-led infrastructure investments across Africa. After seeing several false starts since the Bandung Conference in 1955, many were convinced that this time would be different for the Global South. Prolonged high commodity prices, rapid resource-intensive growth, and the rise of a new tier of economic players significantly strengthened the political and business case for more Southern-led, polycentric development geographies. This was vested with transformative ambitions: opportunities for growth, modernisation, and poverty reduction through quantitatively and qualitatively enhanced ties among Global South countries at eye level—all while prompting diversification away from Western arrangements and dependencies. This book has shown how Africa's

231

global infrastructures tellingly captured such aspirations of South-South transformations at the turn of the twenty-first century.

Set in the context of Africa's multiple international relations, *Africa's Global Infrastructures* has emphasised the growing importance of Africa for understanding contemporary international and transnational relations (Death 2015; Harmann and Brown 2013). It goes beyond the usual engagement with the continent's relations with Europe and the Global North, and centres Africa's transnational South-South relations. In doing so, it also transcends state-centric accounts to instead analyse the diversifying transnational governance practices that emerge from South-South relations from the ground up. As such, it offers a unique window into the contemporary transformations of international relations and transnational practices more broadly.

With the passing of almost two decades since Lula's excited remarks, *Africa's Global Infrastructures* also discussed the tensions, complications, and misalignments that have emerged from the implementation, consolidation, and discontinuation of South-South infrastructural landscapes. After the boom of South-South relations in the 2000s, the enthusiasm and hopes of those years have cooled down, and the growth in FDI and development finance has somewhat as well. Over the years, with the end of the global commodity supercycle, a faltering euphoria for South-South cooperation, and the disruptions of the Covid-19 pandemic, the book highlighted the contingent, unstable, and complex (after-)lives of infrastructural interventions. Programmatic vocabularies of 'cooperation', 'friendship', and 'solidarity' the chapters contrasted with the ambiguities and controversies emanating from weak institutional oversight, business imperatives, and disregard of local needs.

At the same time, still, international relations keep transforming, away from Western hegemony. Global South countries such as China, Brazil, and India, plus their companies, professionals, and civil societies, have remained important actors on the continent and their presence continues to evolve. China has consolidated its close relations with African countries as the main investor and significant international partner for many states based on institutions such as FOCAC and the Belt and Road initiative. These relations are actively shaped on the ground, and remain contested in Africa and transnationally (see Chapter 2 by Bunskoek; and Chapter 5 by Sändig and Hönke). Despite the downward trend and disengagement of recent years, Brazil–Africa ties continued to take place among various forms of transnational activisms and people-to-people interactions (see Chapter 4 by Waisbich and Chapter 8 by Sambo and Bußler) and may experience another rebound as Lula's return to power pledges to rekindle relations with the continent. Finally, India is set to further increase its relevance as investor and political actor in African countries—and more widely on the global stage—as it becomes the world's most populous country. Hence understanding global transformations through South-South relations remains of crucial importance.

To contribute to such an understanding, this book has approached the 'global' in smaller, more pluralistic, and procedural terms. Globalities, we have shown, can be fruitfully studied through the many ways in which actors use diverse ideas of 'the global' to sustain connections to other localities, and the practices and technologies that travel and construct those connections. Nevertheless, very few things or processes that are described as 'global' are everywhere (literally all over the globe). Therefore, the global is more an ambition, an idea of something having a far extent, rather than a very clearly delimited space or a single political and social space at planetary scale (Bartelson, 2010: 219). The notion of globalities the book has proposed allows for being sensitive to those limitations. Indeed, transnational relations and practices require a lot of work (Latour, 1987: 137) and need to be constructed and sustained by situated actors, tools and practices across, but also within specific localities.

Therefore, the chapters have demonstrated the analytical relevance of scaling down South-South relations to project sites in which 'global' relations and practices are forged. These project sites, we have argued, are frontier zones in which expanding circuits of capital from different sources build relations and engage in ordering practices. Taking them as a starting point offers a more situated and relational vantage point that goes beyond methodological nationalism but also institutionalist accounts of Southern actors' engagement in Africa (for instance, Gu et al., 2016: 25–6; see also Thakur in this volume). Although the impact of home country and institutional factors—such as home country policies, headquarter-subsidiary dynamics, and ownership structures—are important for understanding Southern companies and projects,[1] we have demonstrated in this book the strengths of centring globalities, pursuing a practice methodology, and using frontier zones as entry points for analysis. Our approach offers a more inclusive, multiscalar analysis of transnational practices situated and grounded in projects and their relations and making, rather than the (mother) company and corporate-centric analytics as a remedy of state-centrism.

The chapters in this book have worked from these analytical starting points to understand emerging practices in the context of Africa's South-South, infrastructure-mediated transnationalisms. While each contribution is unique both in terms of disciplinary origins and empirical evidence, they all engaged the idea of globalities and used frontier zones and practices as entry points as relevant for their cases, actors, and processes under study. Taken together they demonstrate a multiplicity of global practices that draw from a larger set of histories, relations and rationalities than assumed in the literature on neoliberal government and its expansion across 'global' or 'technological' zones (see Chapter 1).

In the following, we first summarise key findings across chapters that attend to corporate and activist practices. The discussion revolves around the following core themes: beyond models/ towards multiple globalities, African agency, change in the domestic contexts of Global South countries, continuities of postcolonial hierarchies, and methodological contributions. Second, we discuss the implications of the fundamental transformations of our time— climate change and energy transformations, the outbreak and lasting effects of Covid-19, the Russo-Ukrainian war, and the growing US– China geoeconomic rivalry—and propose possible future research directions on Africa's global infrastructures and evolving globalities amid these challenges.

Africa's global infrastructures and South-South transformations: Findings

All contributions to the book have shown that several layers of development rationales and practices are at work in Africa's frontier zones of South-South relations. These rationales and practices have travelled and intertwined over time (Behrends, Park and Rottenburg, 2014). During the implementation of large-scale projects, different practices are assembled and adapted—in building elite relations and relationally shaping development (see Chapter 2 by Bunskoek and Chapter 3 by Dye et al.), in contestation (see Chapter 4 by Waisbich, Chapter 5 by Sändig and Hönke, and Chapter 6 by Kilaka), and in business–society encounters (see Chapter 7 by Gambino and Bagwandeen, and Chapter 8 by Sambo and Bußler). As argued in Chapter 1, infrastructure hubs are global zones that are differently made and characterised by situated practices, shaped in the manifold transnational relations of Africa's economic hubs.

In this regard, *Africa's Global Infrastructures* contributes to understanding Global South-South relations beyond binarisms, such as success versus failure. The chapters show how target populations, professionals, activists, investors, and governments creatively re-appropriate knowledge, skills, and agency. 'South-South transformations' from the ground up and in practice are thus about relational, negotiated processes. They have important economic and socio-spatial consequences that present both opportunities and challenges along multiple avenues, from diplomatic engagement to financial lending, to activism. While such transformations are often attributed to the existence of specific, pre-conceived models that travel from the emerging powers to Africa (see Chapter 2 by Bunskoek), this book demonstrated how official blueprints and scripts lose their grip when transplanted to ground-level realities, being transformed in the process, including through several forms of African agency.

A central question in the literature has been whether such distinct practices amount indeed to travelling 'models' of an alternative Chinese, Brazilian or Indian approach set to shape the global governance of business–society relations. We find evidence for tangible, distinct rationalities and practices that have travelled to Africa from China, Brazil, and India, but argue that they are not adequately captured as counter-models (see Chapter 2 by Bunskoek) or 'objectified models' disconnected from their domestic context (Behrends et al., 2014). To give one example, the Chinese construction industry is one of the pillars of China's economic growth and showcases its institutional strengths to rapidly mobilise resources and create infrastructure. By exporting labour (such as foreworkers) from China, Chinese construction companies exported their labour management practices to Africa. As the political significance of flagship projects can only be harvested within a specific time frame, African elites in turn use developmental repertoires to justify their fast-tracking of large infrastructure projects to garner popular support for elections. As Kilaka's chapter shows, the Chinese company CCCC responded to this practice by adopting a 24-hour working pattern to build the port in the shortest feasible time. This travelling model replicated the contingent labour arrangement in China and created 'permanent temporariness' (Swider, 2011) and precariousness in the Kenyan context. It relied on migrant labourers from other parts of Kenya while indigenous youth from Lamu were marginalised. Gambino and Bagwandeen's chapter delineated the spatial dimension of the Chinese labour compound and practices of brokerage in a global workspace. It also highlights the discursive practice of iterating Chinese virtues, such as 'eating bitterness and enduring hardships' (*chi ku nai lao*, 吃苦耐劳), which can be seen as soft tools to improvise Chinese-style management, making African labour more adaptable to their working conditions (see also Lee 2017; Driessen 2019).

But while an infrastructure-led growth model has been branded as a Chinese approach to international development in the Global South (Zhu, Mwangi and Hu, 2022), it is important to highlight African reworkings of these practices and African agency, alongside the historical conditions underlying the boom of infrastructure construction in China itself. China's construction sector has traditionally depended on contingent labour arrangements (Cooke, Wang and Wang, 2018) by using rural temporary workers sanctioned by the state (Swider, 2011). This regime of practice emerged in China between the 1980s to the 2000s (ibid.), when the total migrant population was around 144 million, accounting for 25% of the total working population (Liang and Ma, 2004). The construction sector was the largest employer of migrant workers, recruiting 30–50% of the migrant population (Solinger, 1999). Chinese migrant workers were hired on an informal per-job basis rather than on a year-long contract basis. Working conditions and employment relations were socially embedded in and governed by relational mechanisms, such as bounded solidarity, enforceable trust, social capital and reciprocity (Swider, 2011: 147).

However, the very question about counter-models implicitly rests on the idea that there would be projections of clearly distinct, even competing policies from Beijing, Brasília or New Delhi to African sites of engagement. Yet the chapters demonstrate flexible modes of governing business–society relations—referring to 'tropical technologies' from Brazil (see Chapter 8 by Sambo and Bußler; also Cezne and Hönke, 2022) and Chinese contingent and compounded regimes of labour (see Chapter 6 by Kilaka and Chapter 7 by Gambino and Bagwandeen), while also situationally referring to the standards of the International Finance Corporation and elements of Anglo-American 'global' CSR. As Bunskoek shows in his chapter for the case of Chinese companies, a Chinese model is often claimed but that claim suffers from Eurocentric assumptions about models as codified and fixed recipes. Behrends et al.'s (2014) discussion of how such models get translated is equally focused on this particular idea of a model as a starting point. Bunskoek's chapter shows though that there is no model in the first place, rather a range of experiences made from experiments and adaptations to distinct contexts. Hence while regulatory frameworks and bureaucratic procedures can provide guidelines to guarantee operability, improvisation and relational development are the overriding guiding principles in how Chinese professionals operate. Hence practices are shaped by the specifics of local situations, with reactions depending, amongst others, on actors' degree of embeddedness (see Chapter 3 by Dye et al.; Lam, 2017). The book therefore demonstrates the dynamism, changing nature, and heterogeneity of 'Southern' transnational practices. Global South companies do not only affect

African economic, social and political processes; they are themselves subject to processes of change.

Neoinstitutionalists have argued that we should expect growing adaptation to globally diffused Anglo-American business models, notwithstanding frictions and contestation along the way. Others have, instead, stressed divergence due to great power competition, or to different national business models and cultural exceptionalisms (the latter especially in the case of China). The chapters in this book find evidence for both, and hence a more complex story. This story calls on International Relations scholarship to step out of the implicit binaries inherent in asking how the Global South may challenge or converge on the global liberal order. If we understand China, Brazil, and India as 'fractured' (Hameiri and Jones, 2021) and also as embedded in the world and made by their relations, it becomes possible to appreciate nuanced narratives based on empirically grounded evidence pointing to the co-existence of multiple globalities and multidirectional processes of translation and change.

The book finds, furthermore, that like corporate practices, activist practices also travel and are combined and reworked in multiple ways. On the one hand, chapters in the section on contestation showed how local actors draw inspiration from practices of resistance from contexts where communities have successfully challenged mega-projects. External support, mostly from environmental and human rights organisations in the capital city (for instance, Nairobi and Maputo respectively in Chapter 6 by Kilaka and Chapter 8 by Sambo and Bußler) and abroad provided much-needed resources, such as funding, legal and environmental expertise, moral support, and publicity. Their involvement was particularly helpful in providing expert opinions to the concerns raised by the petitioners, challenging the testimonies from local elites, such as government lawyers and experts. In this case, activist groups with expertise in challenging big projects through litigation have played a key role in challenging the controversial aspects of both Lamu Port and the Lamu coal plant with impressive results. As Gloppen (2008) argues, such support is often driven by a mix of factors such as ideological factors, the international human rights movement and a liberal reform agenda. However, African NGOs don't have equal access to these resources.

Sambo and Bußler in Chapter 8 show this fragmented landscape with CSOs of multiple interests and positioning towards the same project.

Hence, while in many ways the advocacy opportunities regarding Chinese, Western, and other Southern companies are similar, there are also notable differences. This is especially the case for strongly state-controlled and -dependent NGOs, such as Chinese NGOs, which remain weakly engaged. Local grievances about Chinese companies therefore cannot be addressed to a (consumer) public in the company's home country. What has classically been described as the 'boomerang' route (Keck and Sikkink, 1998) remains closed (see Chapter 5 by Sändig and Hönke). Waisbich's chapter equally shows that Chinese organisations stand out as they exclusively seek to position themselves as insiders and partners of the Chinese state, helping companies and the government to improve in 'being partners' or 'greening' their activities. This decidedly non-confrontational approach towards their government is reflected in the absence of Chinese organisations from more controversial issues (see Chapter 5 by Sändig and Hönke; and Chapter 6 by Kilaka). In sum this demonstrates the challenges to engage home state governments and publics where an authoritarian regime is in place.

The chapters also identify challenges that arise from the evolving nature of the policy realm in the domestic context. States themselves change and adapt, as Gu et al. have put it, 'both to globalization and the inexorable logic of [their] own market-oriented reforms' (Gu et al., 2016: 24). In their engagement with transnational policy contexts, there is not only a need to translate and negotiate different political framings and normative expectations, while also building capacity to fully participate in transnational processes. Processes are in flux and entry points for NGOs still need to be carved out. Worse perhaps, mobilising public opinion or the media back home is rather complex when far-away problems are not considered relevant enough given the challenges and levels of poverty and inequality domestically (see Chapter 4 by Waisbich, Chapter 5 by Sändig and Hönke, Chapter 6 by Kilaka and Chapter 8 by Sambo and Bußler). Transnational and many other forms of mobilisation are also often constrained by collusion of state and business. However, this can also lead to campaigns that jointly address domestic and foreign issues with corporate practices, as demonstrated for the case of Brazilian multinational company Vale (see Cezne, 2019).

Consequently, NGOs in general adapt to the more diverse landscapes of infrastructure investment and governance. Waisbich's chapter shows that when CSOs/NGOs demand accountability from major Southern providers in their engagements with other Southern countries, they both emulate and depart from existing mobilisation and participation repertoires found in the so-called 'North–South cooperation'. Ironically, many NGOs historically used to criticise the World Bank and the IMF for the weak standards they set and criticised them for tokenism—paying lip service to socio-environmental standards without deeply entrenching protective measures as a legal requirement. They now had to reframe their agendas to make them resonate both with Global South governments and publics. As a result, some found themselves propagating the same weak safeguards criticised as benchmarks for Chinese, Brazilian, and Indian governments and companies to follow (see Chapter 4 by Waisbich).

This also shows—another main take-away—that South-South projects are embedded in the given global development architecture rooted in North–South relations, all while being shaped by local political traditions. South-South projects are not invented out of thin air, nor do they take place in a power vacuum.

Hence, on the one hand, global capitalism needs to be understood as always produced through local actions, discourses, and meanings (e.g. Tsing, 2004). Dye et al.'s chapter shows, for instance, how Indian and Brazilian performances of infrastructural practices are rooted in national trajectories and elite politics. The other chapters show how African agency matters, producing layered, situational globalities adapted to and shaped by the specific histories of localities and relations. Most projects covered in this book have mapped onto existing national development strategies and knocked open the door with their anticipated positive impacts for local and regional development, e.g. the Kenyan case of Lamu in Kilaka's chapter, and the Mozambican cases of ProSAVANA and WANBAO in Sambo and Bußler's chapter. Actors also cope with the local outcomes and legacies of the rise and downfall of different projects from different origins over time. These various layers remain fundamental (and contentious) points of reference in the expectations of people and communities (see Chapter 5 by Sändig and Hönke; and Chapter 6 by Kilaka). Whether and how companies adapt as such—how more generally they globalise and learn how to work and obtain resources in local contexts—depends on factors such as time and experience (see Lam, 2017), but also on the extent to which the project is contested (see Chapter 8 by Sambo and Bußler). Chapter 3 by Dye et al. also demonstrates how Indian firms muddle through as relatively inexperienced newcomers to Africa, as opposed to more experienced Brazilian companies.

On the other hand, relations and practices remain embedded in long-established hierarchies of North–South relations of aid and investment. In addition to consecutive phases of various corporate engagements, Southern actors are subject to dominant, globally circulating models of neoliberal management (see also Rubbers, 2021). Projects are imbued by the postcolonial hierarchies of North–South relations, and hence the narratives, institutions, and unequal material structures of North–South relations, and the (remnants of the) liberal global order.

Methodological contributions

A further contribution is methodological. The book brings fieldwork-based analysis of practices from the frontier zones of emerging, non-Western globalities to the fore. By zooming in on such localities and practices, it contributes to shifting the geographical focus of the practice literature beyond more often-studied communities of practice deeply rooted in a global liberal order dominated by 'the West' (Bueger, 2013; Sending, 2015; Pouliot, 2016; Goetze, 2017; Sondarjee, 2020). This book traced instead how managers, politicians, NGO activists and local communities in and across Kenya, the DRC, Mozambique, China, Brazil, and India, understand, contest and practise transnational politics and the governance of large-scale economic infrastructure. The chapters showed how economic infrastructure is linked to statecraft and to transnational assemblages of extraction. They hence transport rationales of governance but also serve as sites of struggle over those rationales and practices.

The book also illustrates—if rather implicitly and against our plans—how negotiating access to and doing research on Global South players in Africa has become more difficult. During the Covid-19 outbreak, most Chinese firms and institutions resorted to a closed-door approach. It remains to be seen whether increased access restrictions will be removed, or may become the new normal, not least considering China's increasingly authoritarian outlook. While research in closed and secretive contexts (De Guevara and Bøås, 2020; de Goede et al. 2019; Glasius et al. 2017) has always been challenging to conduct, emerging trends in international relations and domestic politics in many countries contribute to make theorising from the bottom-up an even more demanding task than it used to be. For one, many African contexts have seen the resurgence of armed conflicts, violence and political instability. This is exemplified by developments such as Mozambique's protracted Cabo Delgado insurgency, Sudan's clashes between rival military factions and the surge of military coups in West Africa, considerably limiting access and increasing the risks of doing research in several locations. In addition, public and private actors from the Southern emerging powers have grown increasingly resistant to critical scrutiny by international and domestic publics. The rise of Bolsonaro in Brazil and Modi in India, marked by heightened populist-nationalist appeals and discourses, has been revealing in this regard, contributing to less transparency, increased backlashes against science-based evidence, and diminished spaces for dissent and critical engagement with governmental policies and activities, both domestically and abroad (Casarões and Barros Leal Farias, 2021; Sinha, 2021).

Such dynamics pose significant methodological obstacles for researchers and scientific communities, who are subjected to greater suspicion, political scrutiny, and access constraints. Concurrently, however, this has also inspired methodological creativity and plurality to overcome emerging impediments, navigate power relations, and adapt to shifting circumstances. Examples of methodological resourcefulness across this book include the mobilisation of personal relations to embed and obtain access (Chapter 6 by Kilaka; and Chapter 8 by Sambo and Bußler), the turn to digital resources such as online news websites and social media to compensate for physical access constraints (Chapter 5 by Sändig and Hönke), and forms of transboundary research collaborations that productively allowed for knowledge co-creation, diversity of thought, and more symmetric partnerships between Northern and Southern scholars (such intents are reflected in Chapter 3 by Dye et al.; Chapter 7 by Gambino and Bagwandeen; and Chapter 8 by Sambo and Bußler). In doing so, despite old and new challenges, the flexible, adaptable, and relational methodologies embraced in this book contribute to create room for capturing the plurality of contemporary South-South experiences that are observable in Africa—and do so amid changing politics of knowledge production. Future publications would be welcome to experiment and engage with methodological pluralism and innovation in studying the complexity of South-South relations further. Overall, it is necessary to reflect collectively about ethical and feasible research methods in the context of the increasing challenges and limitations of knowledge co-creation today, within and beyond academia.

Africa's global infrastructures and South-South relations in a transforming world

It is pertinent for this conclusion to also reflect on the above in light of fundamental recent ruptures, as well as long-term fundamental transformations, of our contemporary world. Since Lula's defiant remarks in 2006, a great deal has changed in global affairs, with important consequences for Africa and other Southern emerging economies. The climate crisis, the outbreak and lasting effects of the Covid-19 pandemic, and the ramping up of geopolitical tensions (for instance, the Russian-Ukrainian war and the growing United States-China rivalry) are but some key developments that bring profound implications to the future of Africa's global infrastructures and South-South relations. They not only highlight (re-)emerging trends and challenges for existing geographies of cooperation, investment, and struggle but also lead to new and fresh questions that scholars will need to grapple with in the years and decades to come, in the realm of infrastructure and beyond.

If the commodity supercycle that marked the period between the 2000s and early 2010s—financing much of Africa's infrastructural boom—has ended, a new, more complex era of commodity market dynamics has begun. Some of the settings investigated in this book, such as the mining sites of the DRC (see Chapter 5 by Sändig and Hönke) are increasingly crucial frontiers for so-called 'energy transition resources' like cobalt, copper, and lithium, required to produce renewable energy and decarbonisation apparatuses (e.g. wind turbines, solar panels, and electric vehicle batteries). These minerals have seen growing investor interest in recent years, both from private and state actors, leading to the emergence and institutionalisation of 'green extractivism' in Africa: broad forms of resource extraction and infrastructures that are linked to or justified by the green economy (Dunlap and Jakobsen, 2020). Yet, critics underscore how such dynamics merely replicate and reinforce familiar socio-ecological harms and neocolonial dependencies under supposed 'green' labels (Jerez, Garcés and Torres, 2021) thus casting doubts over their transformative potentials to Africa's existing extractive geographies.

Still, despite this 'green' momentum, the current energy crisis and the consequent supply shortages exacerbated by the Russian invasion of Ukraine bring renewed covetousness to Africa's hydrocarbons and hasten the development of new fossil fuel projects, particularly in the realm of natural gas and coal, where Chinese and Indian actors are becoming increasingly central. This is to say that extractivism—whether 'green' or traditional—will remain central to the continent's economic and infrastructural landscape. This calls for continued research attention to monitor and understand changing patterns and new trends around state–business relations, models for extractive-based development strategies, and distributive pressures on host societies in current energy transitions—not least those involving what are now, in several respects, well-established Southern presences in Africa.

The Covid-19 pandemic, an important facet of the times in which this book was written, also merits consideration. Africa's global infrastructures cannot be disentangled from the implications of a similarly global health emergency, which yet again illustrates how infrastructural arrangements intersect with current globalities. The pandemic has fundamentally affected the range of practices we have covered in this book: governance modalities, labour and livelihoods, and forms of struggle. This has been the case, for example, through the imposition of further restrictions on workers' mobility (see Chapter 7 by Gambino and Bagwandeen), hindrances to civil society activism (see Chapter 4 by Waisbich and Chapter 6 by Kilaka), the disintegration and termination of existing projects (see Chapter 8 by Sambo and Bußler), and negative impacts on development cooperation finances (see Chapter 3 by Dye et al.). In this regard, the current phase of post-pandemic recovery, combined with the compounding implications of the climate crisis (manifested on the continent through more frequent and disruptive hazards like droughts, floods, and heatwaves), highlights the urgency for re-assessing and restructuring global production networks, financing regimes, and socio-environmental protection systems, including in South-South economic relations. There is a critical need for more multidirectional learning and closer coordination among countries to deal with ever-pressing transboundary challenges posed by health and climate emergencies. As such, future research can help us to re-think how global infrastructures' potential can be harnessed to deliver more inclusive pathways towards development in an increasingly vulnerable world.

The outbreak of Covid-19 also brought to the fore arguably neglected instances of racism and discrimination in South-South relations. For example, the widely covered case of maltreatments dispensed towards African diasporas residing in China—based on dubious pretexts of combatting the virus—sparked discussions of 'Chinese racism' (Visser and Cezne, 2023). However, such dynamics have never been absent from the daily realities of Africa's South-South infrastructure projects, being markedly manifested, for instance, in workplace encounters (see Chapter 7 by Gambino and Bagwandeen). Considering the range of associations with 'race' across the Global South, in Africa's broader South-South relations (see for example, Shankar, 2021; see also Chapter 9 by Thakur) and that South-South racialisations often transcend and complicate commonly discussed blackness-whiteness binaries, this opens up a range of thought-provoking and intriguing research questions that could benefit from more systematic research attention.

Another noteworthy development was the widespread 2022 Covid-19 protests in China against the government's severe and restrictive measures, which remarkably contributed to the easing of restrictions. In a context characterised by otherwise curtailed spaces for civic dialogue and social protests, this raises questions on whether there can be new openings and opportunities for effective transnational activism (see Chapter 4 by Waisbich and Chapter 5 by Sändig and Hönke) in Africa's infrastructure-mediated relations with China (and other politically restrictive contexts).

Finally, a scenario of heightened geopolitical competition, most vividly captured through the escalation of US–China tensions (sometimes called the 'Second Cold War') and the Russian-Ukrainian war, has strongly reverberated on the world's political organisation and multilateral cooperation. For one, while labels of global difference such as 'Global North' or 'Global South' are necessarily flawed, these developments have rekindled their importance and inevitability. Whether imagined or perceived, 'North–South' and 'West–East' demarcations continue to shape security and economic relations, influence bloc politics, and posit complex balancing acts. As of this writing in 2023, current developments linked to an expanding BRICS grouping – amid shared ambitions of increasing influence for Southern and non-Western countries—stand as a revealing indication. This book's focus on the 'South-South' thus provides insights to apprehend the co-constructed, performative, and dynamic nature of such labels in a changing world more broadly (see also Cezne and Hönke, 2022; Hönke, Cezne and Yang, 2023). In this sense, we hope our contributions can help to equip future studies towards more relational, less rigid and deterministic understandings of these (world-)ordering categories.

Nonetheless, many policy and media analyses of Africa's—and by extension the Global South's—positioning in such conjunctures have continued to display parochial and at times bigoted understandings, reviving traditional theorisations in International Relations that perceive the continent as a mere pawn in a great game driven by the geo-economic competition and security concerns of superpowers (for examples of this treatment, see Sheehy, 2022; Brands, 2023; Soy, 2023; Stremlau, 2023). Such takes often fundamentally neglect a key premise of this book. That is, African agency—in several forms, guises, and scales. At the strategic and diplomatic levels: the ability of African entities to negotiate relationships, advance strategic interests, and contest unfavourable outcomes (see Chapter 3 by Dye et al.). This ranges from efforts of seeking the most beneficial deals (for instance, next-generation communication networks amid a US–China technology race) or calls for enhancing energy transition minerals' value chains on the continent, to formulations of non-aligned yet constructive positions in multilateral fora on the Russian-Ukrainian war. At project and grassroots levels: the ability of African workers, civil society groups, and communities to re-think infrastructure spaces in their own terms, challenge official discourses, and address injustices and vulnerabilities, from confronting labour precarities through creative forms of dispute settlement and brokerage at the workplace (see Chapter 7 by Gambino and Bagwandeen), to instrumentalising transnational contestation alliances to further their own causes (see Chapter 8 by Sambo and Bußler).

What such dynamics do overwhelmingly highlight, in our view, is the continued and increasing relevance of African states, actors, and settings to the structures of international order and to meeting global challenges, such as climate change, global health, and security threats. Recently, increasing and bold efforts by world leaders to shore up relations with the continent stand as revealing indications in this regard. This includes dignitaries like US Vice-President Kamala Harris and Russia's Foreign Minister Sergey Lavrov touring Africa on week-long trips. It also extends to the more familiar actors discussed throughout this book, such as Brazil's Lula's renewed attempts, in his third term, to restore ties with Africa after the undoing of previous administrations and Narendra Modi's determination to grow trade and investment links with the continent as India has become the world's most populous country.

Not least, as the continent's largest trading partner and investor, China's footprint in Africa remains remarkable and wide-ranging, in a relationship which has long moved away from a narrow focus on commodities and now includes a diverse basket of cultural, security, technological, and health cooperations. At the same time, as highlighted in this book, the rapid expansion of Chinese projects has also met their growing share of challenges: indebtedness, murky political deals, social anger, and technical shortcomings, which will require continued monitoring and scrutiny in the coming years. We should also not forget about what Soulé (2020) aptly called a plethora of 'Africa+1' arrangements, as African countries forge and diversify their relationships with a broad array of partners, some of which, like Turkey, Israel, and the Gulf States, have become increasingly visible in recent years. Though this book was focused on actors from China, Brazil and India, the large amplitude of Africa's global relations opens several research questions and empirical perspectives that could potentially compare to and complement the findings of this book. Further research should trace these makings of multiple 'globalities' today, in and well beyond Africa's global infrastructures.

NOTES

1.   INFRASTRUCTURE GLOBALITIES

1. We would like to thank the European Research Council (ERC) for making this book possible through grant #759798 'Africa's Infrastructure Globalities' (INFRAGLOB), 2018–2025. Please see the dedicated section at the beginning of the book for full acknowledgments.
2. We thank Barnaby Dye for contributing these paragraphs on India's involvement in Africa.
3. Statistics in this paragraph were collected by Barnaby Dye from public sources.
4. Achille Mbembe's 2022 talk at the Africa Multiple research cluster at the University of Bayreuth emphasised this point (see also Hönke and Cuesta-Fernandez, 2017).

2.   BEYOND THE 'CHINA MODEL'

1. I would like to thank the European Research Council (ERC) for supporting this study through grant #759798 'Africa's Infrastructure Globalities' (INFRAGLOB). Moreover, I am thankful to Elisa Gambino (LSE) for her helpful comments on earlier drafts of the chapter.
2. Sun Yat-sen was the first president of the Republic of China and is now widely respected in both mainland China and in Taiwan.
3. He preceded this by the words, '[o]ur territory is so vast, our population is so large and the conditions are so complex that it is far better to have the initiative come from both the central and the local authorities than from one source alone' (Mao, 1965).

4. What I mean by 'Western' is the trained perspectives of IR theories based on primarily European and US experiences and the resulting practice of using them to explain the world.

5. This is underscored, for instance, by John Williamson, who first proposed the existence of a 'Washington Consensus' in 1989. 'In September 2004, Williamson joined 27 other economists, including Stiglitz, in issuing the 'Barcelona Development Agenda', which carried the warning: 'Encouraging developing nations to copy mechanically the institutions of rich countries—as international financial institutions tend to do—is not guaranteed to yield results, and can do more harm than good' (in Kennedy, 2010: 465–6).

6. As Chen (2021: 851) points out, they do so through several 'credit enhancing' strategies, such as allowing states to 'tak[e] over extra risks from the market—without government-provided guarantees or collateral, many of the infrastructure projects would not have been funded, since they could not pass financial appraisal on a pure commercial standard'.

7. It is, however, not essentially 'Chinese'. Nugent (2018: 31), for instance, points out how '[i]n most cases, [African] governments have established port authorities (PAs) that are granted a high degree of autonomy and maintain overall regulatory oversight'. They have done so because it tends to increase their efficiency and, hence, their ability to generate profits.

8. Naturally, these 'Chinese' traditions have their own limitations.

3. THE PRACTICES OF INDIAN AND BRAZILIAN INFRASTRUCTURE BUILDERS IN AFRICA

1. The research for this chapter was conducted from 2014 to 2020 and, in the case of Barnaby Dye, was supported by the UK's Economic and Social Science Research Council (ESRC) under a Grant [Grant No. ES/J500112/1] through a 3+ Doctoral Scholarship, the FutureDAMS research (UK Research and Innovation–Economic and Social Research Council [ES/P011373/1]) project. Further research support was provided by the India–UK Development Partnership Forum.

2. Authors' statistics collated from Exim Bank official releases.

3. The Lauca Dam in Angola.

4. GNPC and its overseas branch OVL (Patey, 2011).

5. A specific set of interest rates was set out in 2010 in line with the World Bank's categorisation of developing countries. Interviews with senior officials at MEA and Exim Bank, 2016 (Saxena, 2016).

6. Author's statistics based on Exim Bank data.
7. Dye (2021b, 2022a).
8. In Côte d'Ivoire, the deal was negotiated in 2007 with mining supposed to start in 2016. In Madagascar the deal was announced in 2010–11, with little seeming to have occured since.
9. https://www.livemint.com/companies/news/cbi-books-videocon-chairman-for-causing-losses-to-banks-in-mozambique-assets-11592929673140.html; https://economictimes.indiatimes.com/industry/indl-goods/svs/steel/jindal-steels-south-africa-units-file-for-business-protection/articleshow/64745693.cms.
10. Interview with former OIA official, 2020.
11. Interviews with former and current senior officials, MEA, 2019.
12. Interviews with senior OIA officials, Delhi, 2020, and with an academic in Mumbai, 2020.
13. Sub-Relatorio Congresso Nacional do Brasil, Deputada Christiane Brasil (2015), BNDES (2019).
14. One might argue that the BNDES played an important role, albeit indirectly, on the international projects of Vale and Petrobras (as well as some minor ones) via BNDESPAR.
15. CAF (the Development Bank of Latin America) lent USD 4 billion and the Venezuelan Economic and Social Development Bank (BANDES), USD 4.5 billion.
16. BNDES data published online (BNDES, 2019).
17. Ibid.
18. 97th meeting of the Council of Minister of the Chamber of External Commerce.
19. Field research in Luanda, October 2012.
20. Interview with the former head of government affairs at Odebrecht, 15 September 2018.
21. BNDES (2019).
22. Viana (2016), Viana and Capai (2016).
23. Described as a 'ghost airport' (Rossi, 2017).
24. See record by Business and Human Rights Centre (2014) (https://www.business-humanrights.org/en/latest-news/odebrecht-lawsuit-re-forced-labour-in-angola/).
25. Waisbich (2021c) and in this volume.

4. SOUTH-SOUTH COOPERATION MONITORING MOVEMENTS

1. This chapter draws largely on the author's doctoral research at the University of Cambridge (2017–21). Empirical data centres on actors

and dynamics within Southern powerhouses (notably Brazil, India and China). African perspectives were mostly sourced from documental and media reviews and a few additional interviews and ethnographic observations in South Africa, Mozambique and Ethiopia (see Waisbich, 2021c). Parts of this research are published elsewhere and thus cited here, when appropriated.

2. A similar approach can be found in Fox and Brown (1998) and Newell and Wheeler (2006).

3. Contemporary dynamics include a perceived 'de-democratisation' wave in Brazil and India and a more challenging environment for social mobilisation and dissent within both countries moving towards more 'illiberal democratic' configurations (Chacko, 2018; Hunter and Power, 2019). As for China, more recent configurations include both the expansion of public and social engagement on 'China in the world/China Going Out'-related affairs and not-for-profit groups expanding their own work beyond borders (Hsu, Hildebrandt and Hasmath, 2016; Qiang, 2019), as well as renewed forms of state control of society under Xi Jinping (Kuhn, 2018).

4. For a similar discussion in South East Asia, see Yeophantong (2020).

5. For a comprehensive discussion on the genesis of these conceptions of 'aid accountability' within Aidland, see Waisbich (2021c).

6. See Aguiar and Pacheco (2016).

7. See Chakrabarti and Bandyopadhyay (2017) and Conectas Direitos Humanos (2018).

8. See Coalition for Human Rights in Development (2017).

9. For more on FIDC, see https://fidc.ris.org.in/.

10. Interview with Indian development experts, working mostly for Delhi-based civil society organisations (2018–19).

11. The Civil BRICS, proposed and held for the first time by the Russian government in 2015, was set up mirroring the 'civil-society track' or 'civil-society summit' increasingly found in other intergovernmental processes like the C20 in the G20. For a discussion on the Civil BRICS and other autonomous civil society spaces related to BRICS, see Waisbich (2021a) and Bond and Garcia (2015).

12. Interview with Indian development experts, working mostly for Delhi-based civil society organisations (2018–19).

13. See Lopes and Costa (2018).

14. See China, The State Council Information Office. 'Xi calls on int'l community to build development partnership, 13/08/2022. Retrieved at http://english.scio.gov.cn/topnews/2022-08/13/content_78370628.htm (last access: 08/09/2022).

15. On the Guidance, see Green Finance and Development Centre. 'News: International Roundtable on the Green Development Guidance for BRI Projects', Green BRI Centre, 24/05/2021. Retrieved at https://greenfdc.org/news-international-roundtable-on-the-green-development-guidance-for-bri-projects/ (last access: 10/06/2022).

16. See Coalition for Human Rights in Development (2017), Kaushik (2018), NGO Forum on ADB (2015) and Sampaio (2019).

17. See United Nations Development Programme China (2017).

5.   CHALLENGING CHINESE MINING COMPANIES

1. We would like to thank the European Research Council (ERC) for making this study possible through grant #759798 'Africa's Infrastructure Globalities' (INFRAGLOB). Moreover, we are thankful to Felix Anderl (University of Marburg), and Raoul Bunskoek (University of Bayreuth) for helpful comments.

2. NGOs are not easily defined. By NGOs, we refer to professionalised civil society organisations that have a bureaucratic apparatus, permanent staff, established funding sources, a thematic focus, and media channels to raise public awareness (Edwards, 2019).

3. The repositories include congomines.org, the Environmental Justice Atlas (ejatlas.org), and the Business & Human Rights Resource Centre.

4. Civil society is a challenging and contested concept, especially in the context of Africa and China. We understand civil society as social groups who organise to defend common interests vis-à-vis the state and corporate actors (Edwards, 2019). While civil society comes in many forms (e.g. community-based organisations, foundations, trade unions, or social movements), we focus on NGOs because these are the main advocacy actors in our case study.

5. The following information on operations and ownership structures of these companies was collected from their websites, congomines.org, and the Extractives Industries Transparency Initiative (EITI) (ITIE RDC, 2021).

6. Differences in the mining technology and context likely impede the cooperation. There is little industrial mining in the East and the 'conflict minerals' framing of the region does not fit the Southeast (Katz-Lavigne and Hönke, 2018).

7. See for related literature on China e.g. Cooke et al. (2016). On the culture of anti-litigiousness see e.g. Jiang and Wu (2015).

8. Regarding the latter, see MOFCOM (2005) and SASAC (2011).

253

6. CONTESTED PRACTICES

1. The research for this chapter was enabled by a generous grant of the Swedish Research Council (grant 2016-05797_VR). I also extend my heartfelt thanks to the participants of the workshop 'Infrastructure Globalities. The Remaking of Transnational Practices in Africa' at University of Bayreuth for their invaluable insights and comments.

2. 'Kenya says Chinese firm wins first tender for Lamu Port project' (Drazen, 2013) https://www.reuters.com/article/kenya-port-lamu-idUSL5N0CX38D20130411. Accessed on 25 January 2022.

3. The timely delivery of projects by Chinese contractors is also echoed in several Chinese policy positions such as the 1964 speech by Zhou Enlai in 1964 in Accra, Ghana, while on a tour to several countries (Enlai, 1964) and also in the 1983 Zhao Ziyang's Four Principles of Economic and Technological Cooperation (n.a., 1983: 19). When outlining the eight principles for China's foreign aid to Africa Zhou Enlai stated that China will strive to undertake projects that require less capital but yield quicker results. In Ziyang's four principles, the second one states 'efforts will be made to achieve good economic results with less investment, shorter construction cycle and quicker returns' (Yan, 1988).

4. Kenya (Chinese Foreign Ministry, 2006) http://www.china.org.cn/english/features/focac/183441.htm. Accessed on 20 January 2022.

5. 'Erection of Box Girder for Nairobi Expressway Project in Kenya Launched' (CRBC, 2020b) https://www.crbc.com/site/crbcEN/381/info/2020/46883833.html. Accessed on 2 February 2022.

6. 'Construction of Nairobi Expressway Project Is in Full Swing' (CRBC, 2020a) https://www.crbc.com/site/crbcEN/381/info/2020/46883499.html. Accessed on 2 February 2022.

7. 'Weakening shilling drives up Nairobi Expressway toll fee ahead of launch' (Mutua, 2022) https://www.businessdailyafrica.com/bd/economy/weakening-shilling-drives-up-nairobi-expressway-toll-fee-3793036. Accessed on 20 August 2022.

8. Although the project has been behind schedule, the government attributes it to delays in disbursing funds, security challenges and now Covid-19.

9. Interview with the County Commissioner, Lamu County, Lamu Island, 5 February 2019.

10. Interview with an activist and member of Save Lamu in Lamu Island, 2 February 2019.

11. Interview with a fisherman in Lamu Island, 11 February 2019.

12. Interview with the chairperson of the Lamu County Beach Management Unit in Lamu Island, 6 February 2019.

13. Interview with a county official, Fisheries Department in Lamu Island, 18 March 2021.

14. Interview with the chairperson of the Lamu County Beach Management Unit in Lamu Island, 6 February 2019; interview with an activist in Lamu Island, 8 February 2021; interview with a fisherman in Lamu Island, 11 February 2019.

15. Interview with two former CCCC employees in Mokowe, 3 April 2019; interview with an activist, 8 February 2019.

16. Interview with two former CCCC employees in Mokowe, 3 April 2019; interview with an activist, 8 February 2019.

17. Interview with a fisherman in Lamu Island, 11 February 2019; interview with the chairperson of the Lamu County Beach Management Unit in Lamu Island, 6 February 2019; interview with a county official, Fisheries department in Lamu Island, 18 March 2021; interview with the County Commissioner, Lamu county in Lamu Island, 5 February 2019; interview with the Lamu Port Officer Commanding Station at Lamu Port, 12 February 2019.

18. Interviews with four businesspeople in Mokowe, Hindi and Lamu Island in February 2019.

19. Interview with an activist in Lamu Island, 6 February 2019.

20. Interview with the County Commissioner, Lamu County in Lamu Island, 5 February 2019.

21. Interview with a fisherman in Lamu Island, 11 February 2019.

22. Interview with the chairperson of the Lamu County Beach Management Unit in Lamu Island, 6 February; interview with a former councillor in the now defunct Lamu County Council, Mombasa, 24 January.

23. Interview with an activist in Lamu Island, 6 February 2019.

24. Interview with the chairperson of the Lamu County Beach Management Unit in Lamu Island, 6 February.

25. 'Lamu Port team demands legal backing and training' (*Business Daily*, 2012) https://www.businessdailyafrica.com/bd/economy/lamu-port-team-demands-legal-backing-and-training--2001776. Accessed on 10 October 2021.

26. Interview with a fisherman in Lamu island, 11 February 2019; interview with the chairperson of the Lamu County Beach Management Unit in Lamu Island, 6 February 2019.

27. Interview with the chairperson of the Lamu County Beach Management Unit in Lamu Island, 6 February 2019; interview with an activist in Lamu Island, 6 February 2019.

28. Interview with a county official, Fisheries department in Lamu Island, 18 March 2021; interview with the chairperson of the Lamu County Beach Management Unit in Lamu Island, 6 February 2019.

29. Interview with two former CCCC employees in Mokowe, 3 April 2019; interview with an activist, 8 February 2019.

30. Interview with two former CCCC employees in Mokowe, 3 April 2019; interview with a fisherman in Lamu island, 11 February 2019.

31. Minutes by the LAPSSET Corridor Development Authority on 19 November 2013. Minutes of the LAPSSET Corridor Project Oversight Technical Coordination Committee on Implementation of LAPSSET Corridor Project Held on 19th November 2013, 2nd Floor Board Room, at the Office of the Deputy President Building.

32. Interview with the County Commissioner, Lamu County in Lamu Island, 5 February 2019.

33. Interview with a fisherman in Lamu Island, 11 February 2019.

34. Interview with an activist in Lamu Island, 4 February 2021; interview with an activist in Lamu Island, 6 February 2019.

7. A GLOBAL SENSE OF WORKPLACE

1. Elisa Gambino's research was conducted under a European Research Council (ERC) advanced grant for the project 'African Governance and Space: Transport Corridors, Border Towns and Port Cities in Transition' (AFRIGOS; ADG-2014-670851).

2. Revenues of Chinese contractors in Africa currently amount to around 28% of their global revenues, the majority of which—about 50%—continue to derive from projects in Asia (China Africa Research Initiative, 2021).

3. This practice gained prominence in China after the reform programme known as 'separation of management from field operations' of 1984. Guided by this reform, state-owned construction companies began to reduce their permanent workforces; most construction workers in China are now employed temporarily (Lu and Fox, 2001; Sha and Jiang, 2003).

4. Interview with a construction worker, Lamu, 27 March 2019.

5. Also known as *hukou* (户口), the household registration system is a means of population and movement control, which entails the assignation of urban or rural status to individuals according to their place of birth, effectively limiting the access of rural-based individuals to urban-based welfare systems (i.e. schooling and healthcare) (Cai, 2003).

256

6. Interview with a senior engineer, Chinese SOE, Beijing, 20 May 2019.

7. Kenyan workers' salaries range between 60 and 200 KES (0.55 and 1.80 USD) depending on the workers' technical skills, their prior experience in Chinese-built infrastructure, and their employment contracts. Most Kenyan employees within the Lamu construction site have (i) temporary contracts with subcontractors, (ii) casual labour contracts with CRBC, or (iii) temporary contracts with CRBC. In the first case, CRBC subcontracts companies or individuals specialising in procuring a labour force, but the main contractor, in this case, CRBC, still decides the workers' salaries. Casual labour contracts with CRBC entail reporting to work when requested by the foreman or team leader. These contracts do not have a set length and are mostly unwritten; this is a common practice amongst Chinese-built infrastructure projects in Africa (Lee, 2017: 84). Similarly, a study comparing Chinese and American firms' contractual employment coverage shows that more than half of Kenyan employees working in Chinese companies do not have a contract of employment (Rounds and Huang, 2017). Temporary contracts with CRBC last for a minimum of three months, which is usually secured after a three-day trial period, and workers enjoy higher salaries than those of workers hired through labour contractors.

8. Workers that are a part of construction gangs rely on welfare associations, credit groups, personal networks, including church groups, and *jua kali* associations to take care of welfare matters or secure financial support (Wells and Jason, 2010).

8.   INVESTMENT AS COMMUNITY DEVELOPMENT?

1. We would like to express our gratitude to Sérgio Chichava (IESE) and the Embassy of China in Mozambique for providing invaluable contacts in Gaza Province for this research. Additionally, we would like to express our thanks to Kaleidoscopio—Research in Public Policy and Culture for generously hosting the research stay of Phyllis Bußler. We thank the editors for their valuable comments and support in developing this chapter.

2. The author was affiliated to Kaleidoscopio—Research in Public Policy and Culture during her research stay in 2017 in Maputo.

3. Frelimo was established after the independence at the 3rd Congress of the liberation movement FRELIMO (Frente de Libertação de Moçambique/Liberation Front of Mozambique) from where it

arises. The now established party was a single, ruling party-state that remained in power after the establishment of the multi-party democratic system by the new constitution of 1990 (Cuco, 2016; De Brito, 2019). This is reflected in the case sensitiveness of the writing. Therefore, we refer to the writing of the party in lower case.

4. Note that from the start onwards, Mitsui's share in the Vale investments was 50% in the coal extraction and 15% in the railway operation, demonstrating the Nippo-Brazilian cooperation at the company's level.

5. Whereas the PI component was concluded, the PEM component was partly implemented. However, the Master Plan implementation failed.

6. Interview with an Embrapa practitioner, Brasilia, 26 April 2017.

7. Interview with an ORAM representative, Maputo, 24 March 2016.

8. Interview with a former researcher at PACS (Instituto para Politicas Alternativas para o Cone Sul) Research Institute for Alternative Politics for the Southern Cone, Rio de Janeiro, 22 March 2017.

9. Interview with a representative from the No to ProSAVANA Campaign, Maputo, 30 August 2017.

10. They include, for example, ATTAC Japan, Japan International Volunteer Center and Africa–Japan Forum.

11. The number of involved organisations reduced over time in Mozambique due to political pressure.

12. Interview with a FASE representative, 8 March 2017, and Livaningo, Maputo, 30 August 2017.

13. Interview with a Chinese WANBAO Manager on 13 November 2018, in Gaza Province. Interview with a high government official at the provincial level on 19 November 2018.

14. Interview with a WANBAO Manager from China on 13 November 2018, in Gaza Province.

15. In the near districts of Chokwe, it fell considerably. Still, it remained low throughout the period after independence, with few remarkable recoveries mainly due to rice production fomented by a private agribusiness company called Mozfer Industrias Alimentares.

16. FGD (focus group discussion) with local peasants on 15 November 2018, in Gaza Province. Interview with resident affected by the project on 15 November 2018.

17. In the interview with a neighbourhood chief, who also lost his land and did not join the rice production scheme, he mentioned denying entering the WANBAO rice-production scheme because of fear: 'Eu Nunca soube o que era produzir arroz …, eu pensava que era um Bicho de sete cabeças', he said and laughed intensely, alleging that

he knew nothing about rice production, later showing regret for not entering. (Interview with neighbourhood chief in Bairro 3, Xai-Xai, November 2018.)

18. Interview with provincial high official government member, November 2018.

19. In 2018, the No to ProSAVANA Campaign comprised the following civil society organisations in Mozambique: Acção Académica Para O Desenvolvimento Das Comunidades Rurais—ADECRU. Comissão de Justiça e Paz da Arquidiocese de Nampula—CAJUPANA, Comissão Diocesana de Justiça e Paz de Nacala—CDJPN, Fórum Mulher—Coordenação para a Mulher no Desenvolvimento, Marcha Mundial das Mulheres Moçambique, Justiça Ambiental (JA!)—Amigos da Terra Moçambique, Liga Moçambicana dos Direitos Humanos—LDH, Livaningo, União Nacional de Camponeses—UNAC.

20. In Mozambique, MASA is not only represented at the national level, but has its top-down respective representations at the provincial level, e.g. the Provincial Directorate for Agriculture and Rural Development in Nampula (and counterparts in other provinces), as well as on district and administrative post levels.

21. The complete denominations are: for Nampula: Plataforma Provincial das Organizações da Sociedade Civil de Nampula (PPOSC-N), for Niassa: Fórum das Organizações Não Governamentais do Niassa (FONAGNI), for Zambézia: Fórum das Organizações Não Governamentais da Zambézia (FONGZA).

The World Wide Fund for Nature Alliance of CSO Platforms for Natural Resource Management is Aliança das Plataformas da Sociedade Civil que Trabalham na Gestão de Recursos Naturais.

22. Interview conducted with a representative from the No to ProSAVANA Campaign, 7 August 2017.

23. Interview conducted with a former member of the MCSC, Nampula, August 2017.

24. Interview with a CSO representative formerly belonging to the dialogue mechanism, Nampula, August 2017.

25. Interview with a representative from the No to ProSAVANA Campaign on 7 August 2017.

26. Interview with a former member of the MCSC, Nampula, August 2017.

27. Interviews with a representative from the No to ProSAVANA Campaign on 7 August 2017.

28. Notes on participation at the 3rd Trilateral People's Conference, Maputo, October 2017.

29. Naoko Watanabe, the representative of the Japan International Volunteer Center, was already denied access to Mozambique in September 2017 in the context of the Ministerial TICAD meetings based on an interview conducted with a Japanese CSO representative in Tokyo on 24 September 2018. There was even a petition on Change. org requesting the granting of a visa to her. Interview with a Japanese CSO member, Tokyo, 18 September 2018.

30. Interview with ProSAVANA 'focal point' and visit of Nampula Provincial Directorate of Agriculture and Rural Development, 11 August 2017.

31. Interview with a JICA representative, Maputo, 29 August 2017.

32. Interview with a CPT representative, Goiania, 24 April 2017.

33. Interview with a CIMI representative, online via Skype, 3 May 2017.

34. Interview with a representative from Brazil's International Cooperation Agency ABC—Agencia Brasileira de Cooperacao, Maputo, 27 July 2017.

35. Interview and visit a MASA, Maputo, 1 August 2017.

36. Notes on field visit on 17 August 2017.

37. Interview with a JICA representative, Maputo, 29 August 2017.

38. Interview with different peasants directly involved and uninvolved in the new contract farming with WANBAO, Xai-Xai, November 2018.

39. Multiple accounts from community members and peasants, Xai-Xai, November 2018.

40. FGD with peasants affected by the project and involved in the contract farming system with WANBAO, Xai-Xai, November 2018.

41. The vast difference is due to the absence of peasant association or registration of their activities. Their activities were informal and practised individually.

42. Fieldwork notes based on interactions, November 2018.

43. Amongst the involved CSOs are Justiça Ambiental, Liga Moçambicana dos Direitos Humanos, Centro de Integridade Publica, Acção Académica para o Desenvolvimento das Comunidades Rurais, União Nacional dos Camponeses (UNAC) as well as FONGA.

44. An agricultural development programme aimed at integrating small-scale farmers into value chains. (FNDS 2020.)

45. Estrada Ferrovia Carajás refers to an open pit mine located in the south of Pará state, operated by Vale for the extraction of bauxite, and connected to that the logistical infrastructure for material export via the Estrada Ferrovia Carajás.

46. Interviews with peasants in Xai-Xai, November 2018.

47. Interview with women farmers involved with WANBAO in November 2018 and FGD in November 2018.
48. Interview with local neighbourhood chief, who also lost his land for the WANBAO, November 2018.
49. FGD with local farmers involved with WANBAO, November 2018.
50. FDB and interview with local peasants involved with WANBAO, November 2018.

9.   ON AFRICAN GLOBALITIES AND FRONTIER ZONES

1. He said: 'And when I talk about STRENGTH, for me, "S" stands for Spirituality, "T" stands for Tradition, Trade and Technology, "R" for Relationship, "E" for Entertainment like Movies, Dance, Music and Art, "N" stands for Nature, "G" for Games, "T" for Tourism and "H" for Health and Healing and we can make all our plans with these alphabets'; see, https://www.boomlive.in/video-of-pm-modis-speech-in-china-misspelling-strength-goes-viral/

10.   SOUTH-SOUTH TRANSFORMATIONS IN PRACTICE

1. For example, Reilly and Na (2007) and Xu (2014) have argued that corporate ties with Chinese political and financial institutions are key to understanding corporate success and performance in Africa.

REFERENCES

Aalders, J.T. (2021) 'Building on the Ruins of Empire: The Uganda Railway and the LAPSSET Corridor in Kenya', *Third World Quarterly*, 42(5), pp. 996–1013. Available at: https://doi.org/10.1080/01436597.2020.1 741345.

Aalders, J.T. et al. (2021) 'The Making and Unmaking of a Megaproject: Contesting Temporalities along the LAPSSET Corridor in Kenya', *Antipode*, 53(5), pp. 1273–93. Available at: https://doi.org/10.1111/anti.12720.

Abegunrin, O. and Manyeruke, C. (2020) *China's Power in Africa: A New Global Order*. Cham: Springer International Publishing.

Adagala, K. (1991) 'Households and Historical Change on Plantations in Kenya', in E. Masini and S. Stratigos (eds) *Women, Households and Change*. Tokyo: United Nations University Press, pp. 206–41.

ADECRU (2013) 'Nota das Organizações e Movimentos Sociais sobre a violência e criminalização de manifestantes em Moatize com pedido de medidas urgentes', *ADECRU*. Available at: https://adecru.wordpress.com/2013/04/19/nota-das-organizacoes-e-movimentos-sociais-sobre-a-violencia-e-criminalizacao-de-manifestantes-em-moatize-com-pedido-de-medidas-urgentes/ (Accessed: 26 August 2022).

ADECRU (2015) 'Campanha Não ao Prosavana denuncia as irregularidades do processo de Diálogo sobre o ProSavana', *ADECRU*. Available at: https://adecru.wordpress.com/2016/02/22/campanha-nao-ao-prosavana-denuncia-as-irregularidades-do-processo-de-dialogo-sobre-o-prosavana/ (Accessed: 26 August 2022).

Aecom (RSW Inc) (2015) *Final Appraisal Report for the Completion of Nyabarongo Hydro-Electric Project*. Markham, Canada: Aecom.

AFREWATCH (2017) *The Sino-Congolaise des Mines Facing the Challenge of the Millennium: How Sicomines Deprived Communities of Their Rights*

REFERENCES

after Polluting the Environment. Lubumbashi. Available at: https://goodelectronics.org/wpcontent/uploads/sites/3/2019/03/AFREWATCH_Report_AFR_Sicomines_EN_2018.pdf (Accessed: 2 June 2022).

AFREWATCH (2022) *Tears of Hardship: Mining Operation by Congo Dongfang International SPRL (CDM), and Its Impacts on the Environment and the Health of the Kasapa, Kamatete and Kamisepe Local Communities.* Available at: https://afrewatch.org/wp-content/uploads/2022/02/Rapport_cdm_anglaise.pdf (Accessed: 2 June 2022).

Aguiar, D. (2018) *Conferência Triangular dos Povos Moçambique-Brasil-Japão inspira caminhos a seguir, FASE.* Available at: https://fase.org.br/pt/artigos/conferencia-triangular-dos-povos-mocambique-brasil-japao-inspira-caminhos-a-seguir/.

Aguiar, D. and Pacheco, M.E.P. (2016) *A Cooperação Sul-Sul Dos Povos Do Brasil e de Moçambique: Memória Da Resistência Ao ProSavana e Análise Crítica de Seu Plano Diretor.* Rio de Janeiro: Fase.

Akorsu, A.D. and Cooke, F.L. (2011) 'Labour Standards Application among Chinese and Indian Firms in Ghana: Typical or Atypical?', *The International Journal of Human Resource Management*, 22(13), pp. 2730–48. Available at: https://doi.org/10.1080/09585192.2011.599941.

Alden, C. (2019) *Emerging Powers and Africa: From Development to Geopolitics.* Text 19/23. Istituto Affari Internazionali. Available at: https://www.iai.it/en/pubblicazioni/emerging-powers-and-africa-development-geopolitics (Accessed: 29 August 2022).

Alden, C. et al. (2017) *China and Africa: Building Peace and Security Cooperation on the Continent.* New York: Springer. Berlin: Heidelberg.

Alden, C. and Jiang, L. (2019) 'Brave New World: Debt, Industrialization and Security in China–Africa Relations', *International Affairs*, 95(3), pp. 641–57. Available at: https://doi.org/10.1093/ia/iiz083.

Alden, C., Large, D. and Soares de Oliveira, R. (2008) 'China Returns to Africa: Anatomy of an Expansive Engagement'. Available at: https://www.realinstitutoelcano.org/en/work-document/china-returns-to-africa-anatomy-of-an-expansive-engagement-wp/ (Accessed: 14 August 2022).

Além, A.C. and Cavalcanti, C.E. de S. (2005) 'BNDES e o apoio a internacionalização das empresas brasileiras: algumas reflexões', *Revista do BNDES*, 12(24). Available at: http://web.bndes.gov.br/bib/jspui/handle/1408/12595 (Accessed: 28 August 2022).

Alencastro, M. (2020) 'A Odebrecht e a formação do Estado angolano (1984–2015)', *Novos Estudos —CEBRAP*, 39(1), pp. 125–41. Available at: https://doi.org/10.25091/S01013300202000010007.

REFERENCES

Alencastro, M. and Seabra, P. (eds) (2021) *Brazil–Africa Relations in the 21st Century: From Surge to Downturn and Beyond*. Cham: Springer International Publishing.

Amanor, K.S. and Chichava, S. (2016) 'South-South Cooperation, Agribusiness, and African Agricultural Development: Brazil and China in Ghana and Mozambique', *World Development*, 81, pp. 13–23. Available at: https://doi.org/10.1016/j.worlddev.2015.11.021.

Amnesty International (2016) *'This is What We Die For': Human Rights Abuses in the Democratic Republic of the Congo Power the Global Trade in Cobalt*. London. Available at: https://www.amnesty.org/en/documents/afr62/3183/2016/en/ (Accessed: 3 June 2022).

Amnesty International (2017) *Time to Recharge: Corporate Action and Inaction to Tackle Abuses in the Cobalt Supply Chain*. London. Available at: https://www.amnesty.org/en/documents/afr62/7395/2017/en/ (Accessed: 25 August 2022).

Amnesty International (2022) *Amnesty International Report 2021/22: The State of the World's Human Rights*. London. Available at: https://www.amnesty.org/en/documents/pol10/4870/2022/en/ (Accessed: 20 May 2022).

Anand, D. (2012) 'China and India: Postcolonial Informal Empires in the Emerging Global Order', *Rethinking Marxism*, 24(1), pp. 68–86. Available at: https://doi.org/10.1080/08935696.2012.635039.

Anand, N., Gupta, A. and Appel, H. (2018) *The Promise of Infrastructure*. Durham, NC: Duke University Press.

Ang, Y.Y. (2016) *How China Escaped the Poverty Trap*. Ithaca, NY: Cornell University Press.

Anthony, R. (2013) 'Infrastructure and Influence: China's Presence on the Coast of East Africa', *Journal of the Indian Ocean Region*, 9(2), pp. 134–49. Available at: https://doi.org/10.1080/19480881.2013.847553.

Appel, H. (2012) 'Offshore Work: Oil, Modularity, and the How of Capitalism in Equatorial Guinea', *American Ethnologist*, 39(4), pp. 692–709. Available at: https://doi.org/10.1111/j.1548-1425.2012.01389.x.

Arewa, O.B. (2016) 'Constructing Africa: Chinese Investment, Infrastructure Deficits, and Development', *Cornell International Law Journal* [Preprint], (49).

Atkins, E. (2020) *Contesting Hydropower in the Brazilian Amazon*. New York: Routledge.

Auffray, C. and Fu, X. (2015) 'Chinese MNEs and Managerial Knowledge Transfer in Africa: The Case of the Construction Sector in Ghana', *Journal of Chinese Economic and Business Studies*, 13(4), pp. 285–310. Available at: https://doi.org/10.1080/14765284.2015.1092415.

REFERENCES

Ayhan, S.H. and Jacob, T. (2022) 'Competing Energy Visions in Kenya—The Political Economy of Coal', in M. Jakob and J.C. Steckel (eds) *The Political Economy of Coal Obstacles to Clean Energy Transitions*. Oxford; New York: Routledge, pp. 171–87.

Bachmann, J. and Kilaka, B.M. (2021) 'Kenya launches Lamu Port. But Its Value Remains an Open Question', *The Conversation*. Available at: http://theconversation.com/kenya-launches-lamu-port-but-its-value-remains-an-open-question-161301 (Accessed: 14 August 2022).

Balasubramanyam, V.N. (2015) 'China and India's Economic Relations with African Countries—Neo-Colonialism Eastern Style?', *Journal of Chinese Economic and Business Studies*, 13(1), pp. 17–31.

Banco de Moçambique (2020) *Estatísiticas Gerais—Balança de Pagamentos*. Available at: http://www.bancomoc.mz/fm_pgLink.aspx?id=222.

Barry, A. (2013) *Material Politics: Disputes along the Pipeline*. Chichester, West Sussex: Wiley-Blackwell.

Bartelson, J. (2010) 'The Social Construction of Globality', *International Political Sociology*, 4(3), pp. 219–35. Available at: https://doi.org/10.1111/j.1749-5687.2010.00102.x.

BBC (2012) 'Zambian Miners Kill Chinese Manager during Pay Protest', *BBC News*, 5 August. Available at: https://www.bbc.com/news/world-africa-19135435 (Accessed: 14 August 2022).

Behrends, A., Park, S.-J. and Rottenburg, R. (2014) *Travelling Models in African Conflict Management: Translating Technologies of Social Ordering*. Leiden/Boston, MA: Brill.

Bempong Nyantakyi, E., Meng, Q. and Palmer, M.T. (2022) 'Local Skill Development from China's Engagement in Africa: Comparative Evidence from the Construction Sector in Ghana', *Comparative Economic Studies*, 64(1), pp. 68–85. Available at: https://doi.org/10.1057/s41294-021-00154-3.

Benabdallah, L. (2020) *Shaping the Future of Power: Knowledge Production and Network-Building in China–Africa Relations*. Ann Arbor: University of Michigan Press.

Beresford, A. (2015) 'Power, Patronage, and Gatekeeper Politics in South Africa', *African Affairs*, 114(455), pp. 226–48. Available at: https://doi.org/10.1093/afraf/adu083.

Bergamaschi, I., Moore, P. and Tickner, A.B. (eds) (2017) *South-South Cooperation Beyond the Myths*. London: Palgrave Macmillan.

Bergesen, A.J. (2013) 'The New Surgical Colonialism: China, Africa, and Oil', in G. Steinmetz (ed.) *Sociology and Empire*. New York: Duke University Press.

Besharati, C.N., Rawhani, C. and Rios, O.G. (2017) 'A Monitoring and

Evaluation Framework for South-South Copperation'. Network of Southern Think-Tanks, Africa Chapter. Available at: https://saiia.org.za/wp-content/uploads/2017/05/saia_NeST-Working-Paper_20170515.pdf (Accessed: 22 February 2022).

Best, J. (2014) *Governing Failure: Provisional Expertise and the Transformation of Global Development Finance.* Cambridge; New York: Cambridge University Press.

Bhambra, G.K. (2014) *Connected Sociologies.* London: Bloomsbury.

Bhamidipati, P.L. and Hansen, U.E. (2021) 'Unpacking Local Agency in China–Africa Relations: Frictional Encounters and Development Outcomes of Solar Power in Kenya', *Geoforum*, 119, pp. 206–17. Available at: https://doi.org/10.1016/j.geoforum.2020.12.010.

Biao, X. (2014) 'The Would-Be Migrant: Post-Socialist Primitive Accumulation, Potential Transnational Mobility, and the Displacement of the Present in Northeast China', *TRaNS: Trans-Regional and -National Studies of Southeast Asia*, 2(2), pp. 183–99. Available at: https://doi.org/10.1017/trn.2014.3.

Biehl, J. (2004) 'The Activist State: Global Pharmaceuticals, AIDS and Citizenship in Brazil', *Social Text*, 22(3), pp. 105–32. Available at: https://doi.org/10.1215/01642472-22-3_80-105.

Bjorklund, E.M. (1986) 'The Danwei: Socio-Spatial Characteristics of Work Units in China's Urban Society', *Economic Geography*, 62(1), pp. 19–29. Available at: https://doi.org/10.2307/143493.

Blok, A. (2010) 'Mapping the Super-Whale: Towards a Mobile Ethnography of Situated Globalities', *Mobilities*, 5(4), pp. 507–28. Available at: https://doi.org/10.1080/17450101.2010.510335.

Blok, A. (2013) 'Comparative Globalities: Actor-Network Theory and the Topologies of Japanese "Research" Whales', *East Asian Science, Technology and Society: An International Journal*, 7(2), pp. 185–204. Available at: https://doi.org/10.1215/18752160-2145260.

Bob, C. (2005) *The Marketing of Rebellion: Insurgents, Media, and International Activism.* Cambridge: Cambridge University Press.

Boone, C. (1998) '"Empirical Statehood" and Reconfigurations of Political Order', in L.A. Villalón and P.A. Huxtable (eds) *The African State at a Critical Juncture: Between Disintegration and Reconfiguration.* Boulder, Colo: Lynne Rienner Publishers, pp. 129–42.

Boulle, M. (2019) 'The Hazy Rise of Coal in Kenya: The Actors, Interests, and Discursive Contradictions Shaping Kenya's Electricity Future', *Energy Research & Social Science*, 56, 101205. Available at: https://doi.org/10.1016/j.erss.2019.05.015.

Bowen, S. (2015) *Divided Spirits: Tequila, Mezcal, and the Politics of Production*. Oakland, California: University of California Press.

Bowker, G.C. (2015) 'Temporality', *Theorizing the Contemporary, Fieldsights* [Preprint]. Available at: https://culanth.org/fieldsights/temporality.

Bowker, G.C. and Star, S.L. (2000) *Sorting Things Out: Classification and Its Consequences*. Cambridge, Massachusetts: The MIT Press.

Bowman, A. et al. (2021) 'Mining in Africa after the Supercycle: New Directions and Geographies', *Area*, 53(4), pp. 647–58. Available at: https://doi.org/10.1111/area.12723.

Bracho, G. (2017) *The Troubled Relationship of the Emerging Powers and the Effective Development Cooperation Agenda: History, Challenges and Opportunities*. 25/2017. Bonn: Deutsches Institut für Entwicklungspolitik.

Brands, H. (2023) 'The Global South Owes America Some Thanks', *Bloomberg.com*, 27 April. Available at: https://www.bloomberg.com/opinion/articles/2023-04-27/the-global-south-owes-america-some-thanks (Accessed: 3 May 2023).

Brautigam, D. (1998) *Chinese Aid and African Development—Exporting Green Revolution*. London: Palgrave Macmillan.

Brautigam, D. (2011) *The Dragon's Gift: The Real Story of China in Africa*. Reprint edition. Oxford; New York: Oxford University Press.

Brautigam, D. (2015) *Will Africa Feed China?* Oxford: Oxford University Press.

Brautigam, D. (2020) 'A Critical Look at Chinese "Debt-Trap Diplomacy": The Rise of a Meme', *Area Development and Policy*, 5(1), pp. 1–14. Available at: https://doi.org/10.1080/23792949.2019.1689828.

Brautigam, D. and Hwang, J. (2019) 'Great Walls over African Rivers: Chinese Engagement in African Hydropower Projects', *Development Policy Review*, 37(3), pp. 313–30. Available at: https://doi.org/10.1111/dpr.12350.

Brautigam, D. and Tang, X. (2012). 'Economic Statecraft in China's New Overseas Special Economic Zones: Soft Power, Business or Resource Security?', *International Affairs*, 88(4), pp. 799–816.

Bray, D. (2005) *Social Space and Governance in Urban China: The Danwei System from Origins to Reform*. Stanford: Stanford University Press, 137–55.

Bremner, L. (2013) 'Towards a Minor Global Architecture at Lamu, Kenya', *Social Dynamics*, 39(3), pp. 397–413. Available at: https://doi.org/10.1080/02533952.2013.842340.

Breslin, S. (2020) 'China's Global Cultural Interactions', in D. Shambaugh (ed.) *China and the World*. Oxford: Oxford University Press.

Brito, L. de et al. (2015) 'Revoltas da fome: protestos populares em Moçambique (2008–2012)', in L. de Brito (ed.) *Agora eles têm medo de nós! Uma colectânea de textos sobre as revoltas populares em Moçambique (2008–2012)*. Maputo: Cadernos IESE, no. 14P/2015, pp. 1–47.

Brødsgaard, K.E. (2016) '"Fragmented Authoritarianism" or "Integrated Fragmentation"?', in K.E. Brødsgaard (ed.) *Chinese Politics as Fragmented Authoritarianism*. Abingdon: Routledge, 137–55.

Brown, W. (2012) 'A Question of Agency: Africa in International Politics', *ThirdWorld Quarterly*, 33(10), pp. 1889–908. Available at: https://doi.org/10.1080/01436597.2012.728322.

Brown, W. and Harman, S. (2013) *African Agency in International Politics*. London: Routledge.

Browne, A.J. (2015) *LAPSSET: The History and Politics of an Eastern African Megaproject*. London: RiftValley Institute.

Buber, M. (1965) *Between Man and Man*. NewYork: Macmillan.

Buber, M. (1970) *I and Thou*. NewYork: Charles Scribner's Sons.

Bueger, C. (2013) 'Practice, Pirates and Coast Guards: The Grand Narrative of Somali Piracy', *ThirdWorld Quarterly*, 34(10), pp. 1811–27. Available at: https://doi.org/10.1080/01436597.2013.851896.

Bunskoek, R. and Hönke, J. (forthcoming) Worlding Orders of Worth. Unpublished manuscript.

Bunskoek, R. and Shih, C. (2021) '"Community of Common Destiny" as Post-Western Regionalism: Rethinking China's Belt and Road Initiative from a Confucian Perspective', *Uluslararası İlis̜kiler/International Relations*, 18(70), pp. 85–101. Available at: https://doi.org/10.33458/uidergisi.954744.

Burawoy, M. (1985) *The Politics of Production: Factory Regimes under Capitalism and Socialism*. London; NewYork: Verso.

Burges, S.W. (2012) 'Strategies and Tactics for Global Change: Democratic Brazil in Comparative Perspective', *Global Society*, 26(3), pp. 351–68. Available at: https://doi.org/10.1080/13600826.2012.682272.

Cabral, L. (2018) 'South-South Relations in African Agriculture: Hybrid Modalities of Cooperation and Development Perspectives from Brazil and China', in E. Fiddian-Qasmiyeh and P. Daley (eds) *Routledge Handbook of South-South Relations*. London; NewYork: Routledge.

Cabral, L. and Leite, I. (2015) 'ProSAVANA and the Expanding Scope of Accountability in Brazil's Development Cooperation', *Global Policy*, 6(4), pp. 435–45. Available at: https://doi.org/10.1111/1758-5899.12274.

Cadre Provincial des Concertations de la Société Civile (2020) *Situation inquiétante de la communauté de la GCM Kolwezi victime des minages de l'entreprise Compagnie Minière de Musonoie (COMMUS)*. Petition.

Available at: https://mobile.twitter.com/Lamekimike01/status/1290899190172864512.

Cai, F. (2003) *Migration and Socio-economic Insecurity: Patterns, Processes and Policies*. Geneva: International Labour Organization. Available at: https://www.ilo.org/public/english/protection/ses/info/publ/migration.htm (Accessed: 19 September 2022).

Camp, J.T. and Heatherton, C. (2016) 'Total Policing and the Global Surveillance Empire Today: An Interview with Arun Kundani', in J.T. Camp and C. Heatherton (eds) *Policing the Planet: Why the Policing Crisis Led to Black Lives Matter*. London; New York: Verso.

Campanha Não ao ProSAVANA (2018) *Declaracao de Tóquio*.

Campbell, B. (2012) 'Corporate Social Responsibility and Development in Africa: Redefining the Roles and Responsibilities of Public and Private Actors in the Mining Sector', *Resources Policy*, 37(2), pp. 138–43. Available at: https://doi.org/10.1016/j.resourpol.2011.05.002.

Canalmoz (2014) *Polícia acusada de impedir marcha de camponeses em Xai-Xai*. Available at: https://macua.blogs.com/moambique_para_todos/2014/05/pol%C3%ADcia-acusada-de-impedir-marcha-de-camponeses-em-xai-xai.html.

Carmody, P. (2013) *The Rise of the Brics in Africa: The Geopolitics of South-South Relations*. London: Zed Books Ltd.

Carmody, P. (2017) *The New Scramble for Africa*. Hoboken: John Wiley & Sons.

Carmody, P. and Taylor, I. (2010) 'Flexigemony and Force in China's Resource Diplomacy in Africa: Sudan and Zambia Compared', *Geopolitics*, 15(3), pp. 496–515. Available at: https://doi.org/10.1080/14650040903501047.

Carmody, P., Taylor, I. and Zajontz, T. (2022) 'China's Spatial Fix and "Debt Diplomacy" in Africa: Constraining Belt or Road to Economic Transformation?', *Canadian Journal of African Studies / Revue canadienne des études africaines*, 56(1), pp. 57–77. Available at: https://doi.org/10.1080/00083968.2020.1868014.

Carrai, M.A. (2021) 'Adaptive Governance along Chinese-Financed BRI Railroad Megaprojects in East Africa', *World Development*, 141, 105388. Available at: https://doi.org/10.1016/j.worlddev.2020.105388.

Carrozza, I. and Benabdallah, L. (2022) 'South-South Knowledge Production and Hegemony: Searching for Africa in Chinese Theories of IR', *International Studies Review*, 24(1). Available at: https://doi.org/10.1093/isr/viab063

Casarões, G.S.P. e and Barros Leal Farias, D. (2021) 'Brazilian Foreign Policy under Jair Bolsonaro: Far-Right Populism and the Rejection of the Liberal International Order', *Cambridge Review of International*

Affairs, pp. 1–21. Available at: https://doi.org/10.1080/09557571.2 021.1981248.

Castel-Branco, C.N. (2010) *Economia extractiva e desafios de industrialização em Moçambique*. 01/2010. Maputo: IESE. Available at: https://www. iese.ac.mz/lib/PPI/IESE-PPI/pastas/material_iese/Cadernos_ IESE/N1.pdf.

Castree, N., Featherstone, D. and Herod, A. (2006) 'Contrapuntal Geographies: The Politics of Organising Across Difference', in K.R. Cox, M. Low, and J. Robinson (eds) *The Handbook of Political Geography*. Los Angeles; London: SAGE Publications Ltd., pp. 299–306.

Center for International and Environmental Law (2012) *International NGOs Intervene to Prevent Human Rights Violations and Environmental Damage in Kenya*. Available at: https://www.ciel.org/news/international-ngos-intervene-to-prevent-human-rights-violations-and-environmental-damage-in-kenya-2/ (Accessed: 14 August 2022).

Cezne, E. (2019) 'Forging Transnational Ties from Below: Challenging The Brazilian Mining Giant Vale S.A. across the South Atlantic', *The Extractive Industries and Society*, 6(4), pp. 1174–83. Available at: https://doi.org/10.1016/j.exis.2019.10.007.

Cezne, E. and Hönke, J. (2022) 'The Multiple Meanings and Uses of South-South Relations in Extraction: The Brazilian Mining Company Vale in Mozambique', *World Development*, 151, 105756. Available at: https://doi.org/10.1016/j.worlddev.2021.105756.

Cezne, E. and Wethal, U. (2022) 'Reading Mozambique's Mega-Project Developmentalism through the Workplace: Evidence from Chinese and Brazilian Investments', *African Affairs*, 121(484), pp. 343–70. Available at: https://doi.org/10.1093/afraf/adac019.

Chacko, P. (2011) *Indian Foreign Policy: The Politics of Postcolonial Identity from 1947 to 2004*. London: Routledge.

Chacko, P. (2018) 'The Right Turn in India: Authoritarianism, Populism and Neoliberalisation', *Journal of Contemporary Asia*, 48(4), pp. 541–65. Available at: https://doi.org/10.1080/00472336.2018.1446546.

Chakrabarti, K. and Bandyopadhyay, K.K. (2017) *India's Development Cooperation with Bangladesh: A Focus on Lines of Credit*. New Delhi: PRIA/ Oxfam India.

Chalfin, B. (2010) *Neoliberal Frontiers: An Ethnography of Sovereignty in West Africa*. Chicago; London: The University of Chicago Press.

Chatterjee, P. (2004) *The Politics of the Governed: Reflections on Popular Politics in Most of the World*. New York: Columbia University Press.

Chaturvedi, S., Fues, T. and Sidiropoulos, E. (2012) *Development Cooperation and Emerging Powers: New Partners or Old Patterns?* London: Zed Books.

REFERENCES

Chen, C. and Orr, R.J. (2009) 'Chinese Contractors in Africa: Home Government Support, Coordination Mechanisms, and Market Entry Strategies', *Journal of Construction Engineering and Management*, 135(11), pp. 1201–10. Available at: https://doi.org/10.1061/(ASCE)CO. 1943-7862.0000082.

Chen, M. (2021) 'Infrastructure Finance, Late Development, and China's Reshaping of International Credit Governance', *European Journal of International Relations*, 27(3), pp. 830–57. Available at: https://doi. org/10.1177/13540661211002906.

Chen, S. (2021) 'The Emerging Role of Chinese Transnational Corporations as Non-state Actors in Transnational Labour Law: A Case Study of Huayou Cobalt in the Global Cobalt Supply Chain', *Journal of Asian Sociology*, 50(1), pp. 143–78.

Chen, W., Dollar, D. and Tang, H. (2018) 'Why Is China Investing in Africa? Evidence from the Firm Level', *The World Bank Economic Review*, 32(3), pp. 610–32.

Chen, Y. and Landry, D. (2018) 'Capturing the Rains: Comparing Chinese and World Bank hydropower Projects in Cameroon and Pathways for South-South and North South Technology Transfer', *Energy Policy*, 115, pp. 561–571. Available at: https://doi.org/10.1016/j. enpol.2017.11.051.

Cheng, H. and Liu, W. (2021) 'Disciplinary Geopolitics and the Rise of International Development Studies in China', *Political Geography*, 89, 102452. Available at: https://doi.org/10.1016/j.polgeo.2021. 102452.

Chenoy, A. and Joshi, A. (2016) 'India: From Technical Cooperation to Trade and Investment', in J. Gu, A. Shankland, and A. Chenoy (eds) *The BRICS in International Development*. London: Palgrave Macmillan, pp. 93–117.

Cheru, F. and Obi, C. (2011) 'De-coding China–Africa Relations: Partnership for development or "(neo) colonialism by invitation"?', *The World Financial Review*, pp. 72–5.

Cheung, Y.-W. et al. (2012) 'China's Outward Direct Investment in Africa', *Review of International Economics*, 20(2), pp. 201–20. Available at: https://doi.org/10.1111/j.1467-9396.2012.01017.x.

Chichava, S. (2014a) 'Africa and Brazil: Controversy Surrounds Brazil's Most Ambitious Agricultural Project to Date in Mozambique', *Africa at LSE*. Available at: https://blogs.lse.ac.uk/africaatlse/2014/02/05/ africa-and-brazil-controversy-surrounds-brazils-most-ambitious-agricultural-project-to-date-in-mozambique/ (Accessed: 26 August 2022).

REFERENCES

Chichava, S. (2014b) *Chinese Agricultural Investment in Mozambique: the Case of Wanbao Rice Farm*. SAIS China Africa Research Initiative. Available at: https://www.future-agricultures.org/publications/policy-briefs-document/chinese-agricultural-investment-in-mozambique-the-case-of-wanbao-rice-farm/ (Accessed: 26 August 2022).

Chichava, S. (2015) *Mozambican Elite in a Chinese Rice 'Friendship': An Ethnographic Study of the Xai-Xai Irrigation Scheme*. Future Agricultures. Available at: https://www.future-agricultures.org/publications/working-papers-document/mozambican-elite-in-a-chinese-rice-friendship-an-ethnographic-study-of-the-xai-xai-irrigation-scheme/ (Accessed: 26 August 2022).

Chichava, S. and Alden, C. (2017) 'Civil Society and the Opposition to ProSavana in Mozambique: End of the Line?', in C. Alden, Sérgio Chichava, and A.C. Alves (eds) *Mozambique and Brazil: Forging New Partnership or Developing Dependency?* Johannesburg: Jacana Media, pp. 130–46.

Chichava, S. and Durán, J. (2016) *Civil Society Organisations' Political Control over Brazil and Japan's Development Cooperation in Mozambique: More than a Mere Whim?* 2/2016. London: LSE. Available at: https://www.lse.ac.uk/international-relations/assets/documents/global-south-unit/WPS3.pdf (Accessed: 26 August 2022).

Chichava, S. et al. (2013) 'Brazil and China in Mozambican Agriculture: Emerging Insights from the Field', *IDS Bulletin*, 44(4), pp. 101–15. Available at: https://doi.org/10.1111/1759-5436.12046.

Chichava, S. et al. (2013) 'Discursos e Narrativas sobre o engajamento brasileiro e chinês na Agricultura Moçambicana', in L. de Brito et al. (eds) *Desafios para Moçambique 2013*. Maputo: Instituto de Estudos Sociais e Económicos, pp. 417–38.

Chin, G.T. and Gallagher, K.P. (2019) 'Coordinated Credit Spaces: The Globalization of Chinese Development Finance', *Development and Change*, 50(1), pp. 245–74. Available at: https://doi.org/10.1111/dech.12470.

China Africa Research Initiative (2021) *Data: Chinese Contracts in Africa*, *China Africa Research Initiative*. Available at: http://www.sais-cari.org/data-chinese-contracts-in-africa (Accessed: 21 August 2022).

China Africa Research Initiative and Boston University Global Development Policy Center (2022) *Chinese Loans to Africa Database Version 2.0*. Available at: https://www.bu.edu/gdp/chinese-loans-to-africa-database/ (Accessed: 31 August 2022).

China Construction Communication Company (2019) '国际在线：

REFERENCES

拉穆港口的筑梦人 guoji zaixian: Lamu gangkou de zhu meng ren [China Radio International Online: Lamu port's dream builders]'.

China Daily (2018) 'Kenyan President Opens Chinese-Built Electricity Station'. Available at: https://www.chinadaily.com.cn/a/201805/31/WS5b0f6518a31001b82571d6b6.html (Accessed: 14 August 2022).

Chinese Foreign Ministry (2006) *Kenya*. Available at: http://www.china.org.cn/english/features/focac/183441.htm (Accessed: 14 August 2022).

Chiyemura, F., Gambino, E. and Zajontz, T. (2022) 'Infrastructure and the Politics of African State Agency: Shaping the Belt and Road Initiative in East Africa', *Chinese Political Science Review*, 8(1), pp. 105–31. Available at: https://doi.org/10.1007/s41111-022-00214-8.

Chome, N. (2020) 'Land, Livelihoods and Belonging: Negotiating Change and Anticipating LAPSSET in Kenya's Lamu county', *Journal of Eastern African Studies*, 14(2), pp. 310–31. Available at: https://doi.org/10.1080/17531055.2020.1743068.

Chome, N. et al. (2020) '"Demonstration Fields", Anticipation, and Contestation: Agrarian Change and the Political Economy of Development Corridors in Eastern Africa', *Journal of Eastern African Studies*, 14(2), pp. 291–309. Available at: https://doi.org/10.1080/17531055.2020.1743067.

Christensen, D. (2019) 'Concession Stands: How Mining Investments Incite Protest in Africa', *International Organization*, 73(1), pp. 65–101. Available at: https://doi.org/10.1017/S0020818318000413.

Classen, S.F. (2019) 'Ascensão e Queda do ProSAVANA: da Cooperação Triangular à Cooperação Bilateral Contra-resistência', *Observador Rural* [Preprint], (82). Available at: https://www.researchgate.net/publication/337717678_Ascensao_e_Queda_do_ProSAVANA_da_Cooperacao_Triangular_a_Cooperacao_Bilateral_Contra-resistencia.

CMOC (2017) *Environmental and Social Governance Report 2017*. China Molybdenum Co., Ltd. Available at: https://www1.hkexnews.hk/listedco/listconews/sehk/2018/0329/ltn201803292135.pdf.

Coalition for Human Rights in Development (2017) *The BRICS New Development Bank Strategy. A Civil Society Perspective for Truly Sustainable Infrastructure and Transformative Development Cooperation*. Coalition for Human Rights in Development. Available at: https://rightsindevelopment.org/wp-content/uploads/2017/04/Folheto-The-BRICS-Sustainable2.pdf.

CODED (2020) *Communiqué de presse: Dégradation meurtrière des rivières dans l'hinterland de la ville de Kolwezi et flagrante violation du droit à un environnement sain*. Centre Congolais pour le Développement Durable. Available at: https://congomines.org/system/attachments/

assets/000/001/870/original/CODED_1_%283_files_ merged%29.pdf?1588255902 (Accessed: 2 June 2022).

Coe, N.M. and Jordhus-Lier, D.C. (2011) 'Constrained Agency? Re-evaluating the Geographies of Labour', *Progress in Human Geography*, 35(2), pp. 211–33. Available at: https://doi.org/10.1177/0309132510366746.

Coletta, R.D. (2021) *Bolsonaro agora diz que caixa-preta do BNDES nunca existiu, Folha de Sao Paulo*. Available at: https://www1.folha.uol.com. br/mercado/2021/06/bolsonaro-agora-diz-que-caixa-preta-do-bndes-nunca-existiu.shtml (Accessed: 28 August 2022).

Comaroff, J. and Comaroff, J.L. (2012) 'Theory from the South: Or, How Euro-America is Evolving Toward Africa', *Anthropological Forum*, 22(2), pp. 113–31. Available at: https://doi.org/10.1080/00664677.2012. 694169.

Conde, M. (2017) 'Resistance to Mining: A Review', *Ecological Economics*, 132, pp. 80–90. Available at: https://doi.org/10.1016/j. ecolecon.2016.08.025.

Conectas Direitos Humanos (2018) *Banco Nacional, Impactos Globais: O apoio do BNDES à exportação de bens e serviços de engenharia e seus efeitos sobre o meio ambiente e os direitos humanos*. Sao Paulo: Conectas Direitos Humanos. Available at: https://www.conectas.org/publicacao/ banco-nacional-impactos-globais-o-apoio-bndes-exportacao-de-bens-e-servicos-de-engenharia-e-seus-efeitos-sobre-o-meio-ambiente-e-os-direitos-humanos/ (Accessed: 20 August 2022).

Confederation of Indian Industries (2018) *Project Implementation by Indian Companies in Africa*. Delhi: Confederation of Indian Industries. Available at: https://www.cii.in/ (Accessed: 28 August 2022).

Connolly, P. (2007) *Recent Trends in the Mexican Construction Industry and Outlook for the 21st. Century: Its Image, Employment Prospects and Skill Requirements*. International Labour Organization, pp. 53–76.

Cooke, F.L., Wang, D. and Wang, J. (2018) 'State Capitalism in Construction: Staffing Practices and Labour Relations of Chinese Construction Firms in Africa', *Journal of Industrial Relations*, 60(1), pp. 77–100. Available at: https://doi.org/10.1177/0022185617724836.

Cooke, F.L., Xie, Y. and Duan, H. (2016) 'Workers' Grievances and Resolution Mechanisms in Chinese Manufacturing Firms: Key Characteristics and the Influence of Contextual Factors', *The International Journal of Human Resource Management*, 27(18), pp. 2119–41. Available at: https://doi.org/10.1080/09585192.2016.1164224.

Cooke, P. (1986) 'The Changing Urban and Regional System in the United

Kingdom', *Regional Studies*, 20(3), pp. 243–51. Available at: https://doi.org/10.1080/09595238600185221.

Cooper, F. (1987) *On the African Waterfront: Urban Disorder and the Transformation of Work in Colonial Mombasa*. New Haven: Yale University Press.

Cooper, F. (2002) *Africa since 1940: The Past of the Present*. Cambridge: Cambridge University Press.

Cooper, F. (2014) *Africa in the World*. Cambridge, Massachusetts: Harvard University Press.

Coordination des Actions de Plaidoyer de la Société Civile (2020) *Déclaration de la société civile relative au processus de signature du Cahier des charges entre la Société Minière Tenke Fungurume Mining SA, et les communautés locales dans la Province du Lualaba*. Available at: https://congomines.org/system/attachments/assets/000/001/949/original/De%CC%81claration_Socie%CC%81te%CC%81_Civile_TFM_Cahier_des_charges_26_Juillet_2020_OK.pdf?1595929655 (Accessed: 23 August 2022).

Corkin, L. (2012) 'Chinese Construction Companies in Angola: A Local Linkages Perspective', *Resources Policy*, 37(4), pp. 475–83. Available at: https://doi.org/10.1016/j.resourpol.2012.06.002.

Cornelissen, Scarlett, Fantu Cheru, and Timothy M. Shaw. (2012) 'Introduction: Africa and International Relations in the 21st Century: Still Challenging Theory?', in S. Cornelissen, F. Cheru, and T.M. Shaw (eds) *Africa and International Relations in the 21st Century*, London: Palgrave Macmillan, pp. 1–17.

County Government of Lamu County (2016) 'Revised First Lamu County Integrated Development Plan'. Available at: https://www.devolution.go.ke/wp-content/uploads/2020/02/Lamu-CIDP- 2013-2017.pdf.

Cowen, D. (2014) *The Deadly Life of Logistics: Mapping Violence in Global Trade*. Minneapolis: University of Minnesota Press.

Cox, R.W. (1999) 'Civil Society at the Turn of the Millennium: Prospects for an Alternative World Order', *Review of International Studies*, 25(1), pp. 3–28. Available at: https://doi.org/10.1017/S0260210599000042.

CRBC (2020a) *Construction of Nairobi Expressway Project is in Full-swing*. Available at: https://www.crbc.com/site/crbcEN/381/info/2020/46883499.html (Accessed: 20 August 2022).

CRBC (2020b) *Erection of Box Girder for Nairobi Expressway Project in Kenya Launched*. Available at: https://www.crbc.com/site/crbcEN/381/info/2020/46883833.html (Accessed: 20 August 2022).

Croese, S. (2017) 'State-Led Housing Delivery as an Instrument of Developmental Patrimonialism: The Case of Post-War Angola', *African*

Affairs, 116(462), pp. 80–100. Available at: https://doi.org/10.1093/afraf/adw070.

Da Silva, R. (2020) *Fim do ProSavana: Uma oportunidade para o desenvolvimento agrícola em Moçambique?*, *DW.COM*. Available at: https://www.dw.com/pt-002/fim-do-prosavana-uma-oportunidade-para-o-desenvolvimento-agr%C3%ADcola-em-mo%C3%A7ambique/a-54339235 (Accessed: 27 August 2022).

Dahir, A.L. (2018) *Twice as Many African Presidents Made it to China's Africa Summit than to the UN General Assembly*, *Quartz Africa*. Available at: https://qz.com/africa/1414004/more-african-presidents-went-to-chinas-africa-forum-than-un-general-assembly/ (Accessed: 31 August 2022).

Dávila, J. (2010) *Hotel Trópico: Brazil and the Challenge of African Decolonization, 1950–1980*, *Hotel Trópico*. Durham, NC: Duke University Press.

Death, Carl. 'Introduction: Africa's International Relations'. *African Affairs*, 2015. https://doi.org/10.1093/afraf/adv041.

De Goede, M., Bosma, E. and Pallister-Wilkins, P. (2019) *Secrecy and Methods in Security Research: A Guide to Qualitative Fieldwork*. London; New York: Routledge.

De Guevara, B.B. and Bøås, M. (2020) *Doing Fieldwork in Areas of International Intervention. A Guide to Research in Violent and Closed Contexts*. Bristol: Bristol University Press.

de Renzio, P. and Seifert, J. (2014) 'South-South Cooperation and the Future of Development Assistance: Mapping Actors and Options', *Third World Quarterly*, 35(10), pp. 1860–75. Available at: https://doi.org/10.1080/01436597.2014.971603.

De Waal, A. (ed.) (2015) *Advocacy in Conflict: Critical Perspectives on Transnational Activism*. London: Zed Books.

Debrah, Y.A. and Ofori, G. (1997) 'Flexibility, Labour Subcontracting and HRM in the Construction Industry in Singapore: Can the System Be Refined?', *The International Journal of Human Resource Management*, 8(5), pp. 690–709. Available at: https://doi.org/10.1080/095851997341469.

Deutsche Welle, D. (2020) *Building Africa: Can Europe's construction firms compete with China's? | DW | 21.02.2020*, *DW.COM*. Available at: https://www.dw.com/en/building-africa-can-europes-construction-firms-compete-with-chinas/a-52435595 (Accessed: 14 August 2022).

Development Impact Group (2016) 'Monitoring and Evaluation Mechanism for South-South and Triangular Development Cooperation: Lessons from Brazil for the 2030 Agenda'. United Nations Development Programme Human Development Report Office. Available at: https://www.undp.org/sites/g/files/zskgke326/files/

publications/11875%20-%20Monitoring%20and%20evaluation%20 mechanisms%20for%20South%20-%2006_Web%20Version(2).pdf.

DFID and China Centre for Chinese Studies Stellenbosch (2006) *China's Interest and Activity in Africa's Construction and Infrastructure Sectors*. The Infrastructure Consortium for Africa. Available at: https://www. icafrica.org/en/knowledge-hub/article/chinas-interest-and-activity-in-africas-construction-and-infrastructure-sectors-169/ (Accessed: 21 August 2022).

Driessen, M. (2015) 'Migrating for the Bank: Housing and Chinese Labour Migration to Ethiopia', *The China Quarterly*, 221, pp. 143–60. Available at: https://doi.org/10.1017/S030574101400157X.

Driessen, M. (2016) 'Pushed to Africa: Emigration and Social Change in China', *Journal of Ethnic and Migration Studies*, 42(15), pp. 2491–507. Available at: https://doi.org/10.1080/1369183X.2016.1174569.

Driessen, M. (2019) *Tales of Hope, Tastes of Bitterness: Chinese Road Builders in Ethiopia*. Hong Kong: Hong Kong University Press.

Driessen, M. (2020) 'Pidgin Play: Linguistic Subversion on Chinese-Run Construction Sites in Ethiopia', *African Affairs*, 119(476), pp. 432–51. Available at: https://doi.org/10.1093/afraf/adaa016.

Drogendijk, R. and Blomkvist, K. (2013) 'Drivers and Motives for Chinese Outward Foreign Direct Investments in Africa', *Journal of African Business*, 14(2), pp. 75–84. Available at: https://doi.org/10.1080/15 228916.2013.804320.

du Plessis, R. (2016) *China's African Infrastructure Projects: A Tool in Reshaping Global Norms*. South African Institute of International Affairs. Available at: https://www.jstor.org/stable/resrep25976 (Accessed: 15 August 2022).

Dubey, A.K. (2016) 'India–Africa Relations: Historical Goodwill and a Vision for the Future', in A.K. Dubey and A. Biswas (eds) *India and Africa's Partnership: A Vision for a New Future*. New Delhi: Springer India (India Studies in Business and Economics), pp. 11–39.

Dubey, A.K. and Biswas, A. (eds) (2016) *India and Africa's Partnership: A Vision for a New Future*. New Dehli: Springer.

Dunlap, A. and Jakobsen, J. (2020) *The Violent Technologies of Extraction: Political Ecology, Critical Agrarian Studies and the Capitalist Worldeater*. Cham: Springer International Publishing.

Durán, J. and Chichava, S. (2017) 'Resisting South-South Cooperation? Mozambican Civil Society and Brazilian Agricultural Technical Cooperation', in I. Bergamaschi, P. Moore, and A.B. Tickner (eds) *South-South Cooperation Beyond the Myths: Rising Donors, New Aid Practices?*

London: Palgrave Macmillan (International Political Economy Series), pp. 271–99.

Dye, B.J. (2017) 'The Stiegler's Gorge Dam Hydropower Project: A Briefing Report for WWF', in *The True Cost of Power: The Facts and Risks of Building the Stiegler's Gorge Hydropower Dam in the Selous Game Reserve, Tanzania*. Gland: World Wildlife Fund, pp. 10–35. Available at: https://wwfeu.awsassets.panda.org/downloads/int_stieglergorge_final_1.pdf (Accessed: 28 August 2022).

Dye, B.J. (2021a) 'Brazil's Boom and Bust in Tanzania: A Case Study of Naivety?', in M. Alencastro and P. Seabra (eds) *Brazil–Africa Relations in the 21st Century: From Surge to Downturn and Beyond*. Cham: Springer International Publishing, pp. 73–93.

Dye, B.J. (2021b) *Meeting Africa's Latest Dam Builders: The Indian ExIm Bank, 'Entrepreneurial' Companies and the Outcomes of South-South Cooperation*. Manchester: The University of Manchester.

Dye, B.J. (2022a) 'India's Infrastructure Building In Africa: South-South Cooperation And The Abstraction Of Responsibility', *African Affairs*, 121(483), pp. 221–49. Available at: https://doi.org/10.1093/afraf/adac013.

Dye, B.J. (2022b) 'Uneven convergence in India's development cooperation: the case of concessional finance to Africa', *Third World Quarterly*, 43(1), pp. 166–86. Available at: https://doi.org/10.1080/01436597.2021.1997583.

Dye, B.J. and Alencastro, M. (2020) 'Debunking Brazilian Exceptionalism in its Africa Relations: Evidence from Angola and Tanzania', *Global Society*, 34(4), pp. 425–46. Available at: https://doi.org/10.1080/13600826.2020.1722617.

Dye, B.J. and Soares de Oliveira, R. (2022) 'India–Africa Relations under the UPA Government', in R.K. Laskar (ed.) *Forging New Partnerships, Breaching New Frontiers: India's Diplomacy during the UPA Rule 2004–2014*. Oxford: Oxford University Press.

Easterling, K. (2014) *Extrastatecraft: The Power of Infrastructure Space*. London; New York: Verso.

Edwards, M. (2019) *Civil Society*. 4th edition. Cambridge, Medford: Polity.

Elliott, H. (2016) 'Planning, property and plots at the gateway to Kenya's "new frontier"', *Journal of Eastern African Studies*, 10(3), pp. 511–29. Available at: https://doi.org/10.1080/17531055.2016.1266196.

Emirbayer, M. (1997) 'Manifesto for a Relational Sociology', *American Journal of Sociology*, 103(2), pp. 281–317. Available at: https://doi.org/10.1086/231209.

Enlai, Z. (1964) 'The Chinese Government's Eight Principles for Economic

Aid and Technical Assistance to Other Countries'. Available at: https://digitalarchive.wilsoncenter.org/document/121560.

Eom, J. et al. (2017) *The United States and China in Africa: What Does the Data Say?* Research Report 18/2017. Washington, DC: China Africa Research Initiative (CARI), School of Advanced International Studies (SAIS), Johns Hopkins University. Available at: https://www.econstor.eu/handle/10419/248197 (Accessed: 14 August 2022).

Ericsson, M., Löf, O. and Löf, A. (2020) 'Chinese Control over African and Global Mining: Past, Present and Future', *Mineral Economics*, 33(1), pp. 153–81. Available at: https://doi.org/10.1007/s13563-020-00233-4.

Eyben, R. and Ferguson, C. (2004) 'How Can Donors Become More Accountable to Poor People?', in L. Groves and R. Hinton (eds) *Inclusive Aid*. London: Routledge.

Fadaee, S. (ed.) (2016) *Understanding Southern Social Movements*. London; New York: Routledge.

FASE (2015) *Fundo Nacala—Estrutura original e desdobramentos*. FASE. Available at: https://fase.org.br/pt/biblioteca/fundo-nacala-estrutura-original-e-desdobramentos/ (Accessed: 27 August 2022).

Fearnside, P.M. (2014) 'Impacts of Brazil's Madeira River Dams: Unlearned Lessons for Hydroelectric Development in Amazonia', *Environmental Science & Policy*, 38, pp. 164–72. Available at: https://doi.org/10.1016/j.envsci.2013.11.004.

Fei, D. (2020) 'The Compound Labor Regime of Chinese Construction Projects in Ethiopia', *Geoforum*, 117, pp. 13–23. Available at: https://doi.org/10.1016/j.geoforum.2020.08.013.

Ferguson, J. (2005) 'Seeing Like an Oil Company: Space, Security, and Global Capital in Neoliberal Africa', *American Anthropologist*, 107(3), pp. 377–82. Available at: https://doi.org /10.1525/aa.2005.107.3.377.

Ferguson, J. (2006) *Global Shadows: Africa in the Neoliberal World Order*. Durham, NC: Duke University Press.

Fiddian-Qasmiyeh, E. and Daley, P. (2018) *Routledge Handbook of South-South Relations*. Abingdon; New York: Routledge. Available at: https://www.routledge.com/Routledge-Handbook-of-South-South-Relations/Fiddian-Qasmiyeh-Daley/p/book/9780367659646 (Accessed: 22 February 2022).

Foster, V., Butterfield, W. and Chen, C. (2009) *Building Bridges: China's Growing Role as Infrastructure Financier for Africa*. Washington, DC: The World Bank. Available at: https://doi.org/10.1596/978-0-8213-7554-9.

Fox, J. and Brown, L.D. (eds) (1998) *The Struggle for Accountability: The World*

Bank, NGOs, and Grassroots Movements. Cambridge, Massachusetts: MIT Press.

Frankema, E. and van Waijenburg, M. (2018) 'Africa Rising? A Historical Perspective', *African Affairs*, 117(469), pp. 543–68. Available at: https://doi.org/10.1093/afraf/ady022.

French, H.W. (2014) *China's Second Continent: How a Million Migrants Are Building a New Empire in Africa*. New York: Knopf.

Funada-Classen, S. (2019) *The Rise and Fall of ProSAVANA: From Triangular Cooperation to Bilateral Cooperation in Counter-Resistance*. Observatório do Meio Rural.

Gadzala, A.W. (ed.) (2015) *Africa and China: How Africans and Their Governments are Shaping Relations with China*. Lanham: Rowman & Littlefield.

Gagliardone, I. (2015) 'China and the Shaping of African Information Societies', in A.W. Gadzala (ed.) *Africa and China: How Africans and Their Governments are Shaping Relations with China*. Maryland: Rowman & Littlefield, pp. 45–60.

Gala, I.V. (2019) *Política externa como ação afirmativa: projeto e ação do Governo Lula na África 2003–2006*. Santo André: Editora UFABC.

Gambino, E. (2020) 'La participation chinoise dans le développement des infrastructures de transport au Kenya: une transformation des géométries du pouvoir?', *Critique internationale*. Translated by M. Périer, 89(4), pp. 95–114. Available at: https://doi.org/10.3917/crii.089.0098.

Garcia, A. and Bond, P. (eds) (2015) *BRICS: An Anticapitalist Critique*. Reprint Edition. Chicago, Illinois: Haymarket Books.

Gaventa, J. (2006) 'Finding the Spaces for Change: A Power Analysis', *IDS Bulletin*, 37(6), pp. 23–33. Available at: https://doi.org/10.1111/j.1759-5436.2006.tb00320.x.

Ge, Z. (2018) *What Is China?: Territory, Ethnicity, Culture, and History*. Translated by M.G. Hill. Cambridge, Massachusetts: Harvard University Press.

Gelpern, A. et al. (2021) *AidData | How China Lends: A Rare Look into 100 Debt Contracts with Foreign Governments*. Kiel Institute for the World Economy, Center for Global Development and Aid. Available at: https://www.aiddata.org/publications/how-china-lends (Accessed: 31 August 2022).

Giese, K. and Thiel, A. (2014) 'The Vulnerable Other—Distorted Equity in Chinese–Ghanaian Employment Relations', *Ethnic and Racial Studies*, 37(6), pp. 1101–20. Available at: https://doi.org/10.1080/01419870.2012.681676.

Giese, K. and Thiel, A. (2015) 'The Psychological Contract in Chinese-African Informal Labor Relations', *The International Journal of Human*

REFERENCES

Resource Management, 26(14), pp. 1807–26. Available at: https://doi.or g/10.1080/09585192.2014.971844.

Gill, B. and Reilly, J. (2007) 'The Tenuous Hold of China Inc. in Africa', *Washington Quarterly*, 30(3), pp. 37–52. Available at: https://doi. org/10.1162/wash.2007.30.3.37.

Githaiga, N.M. and Bing, W. (2019) 'Belt and Road Initiative in Africa: The Impact of Standard Gauge Railway in Kenya', *China Report*, 55(3), pp. 219–40. Available at: https://doi.org/10.1177/0009445519853697.

Glasius, M. et al. (2017) *Research, Ethics and Risk in the Authoritarian Field.* Cham: Palgrave Macmillan.

Global Environmental Institute (2016) *Chinese NGOs 'Going Global': Current Situation, Challenges and Policy Recommendations.* Beijing. Available at: http://www.geichina.org/_upload/file/report/NGO_Going_Out_ EN.pdf (Accessed: 20 May 2022).

Global Witness (2017) *Regime Cash Machine: How the Democratic Republic of Congo's Booming Mining Exports are Failing to Benefit Its People.* London. Available at: https://www.globalwitness.org/documents/19146/ Regime_Cash_Machine_Report_Final_Single_pages_BXObnIm.pdf.

Global Witness (2020) *The Deal for DEZIWA: CNMC, Gécamines and the Future of DRC's Copper Trade.* Available at: https://www.globalwitness.org/ documents/19948/The_Deal_for_Deziwa_EN_-_August_2020.pdf.

Gloppen, S. (2008) 'Public Interest Litigation, Social Rights, and Social Policy', in A.A. Dani and A. de Haan (eds) *Inclusive States. Social Policy and Structural Inequalities.* Washington, DC: World Bank, pp. 343–67. Available at: https://www.cmi.no/publications/3054-public-interest-litigation-social-rights.

Göbel, C. (2019) 'Social Unrest in China: A Bird's-Eye View', in T. Wright (ed.) *Handbook of Protest and Resistance in China.* Cheltenham & Northampton: Edward Elgar Publishing, pp. 27–45.

Goetze, C. (2017) *The Distinction of Peace: A Social Analysis of Peacebuilding.* Ann Arbor: University of Michigan Press.

Gomes, G.Z. and Esteves, P. (2018) 'The BRICS Effect: Impacts of South-South Cooperation in the Social Field of International Development Cooperation', *IDS Bulletin*, 49(3). Available at: https://doi. org/10.19088/1968-2018.152.

Gonzalez-Vicente, R. (2011) 'China's Engagement in South America and Africa's Extractive Sectors: New Perspectives for Resource Curse Theories', *The Pacific Review*, 24(1), pp. 65–87. Available at: https:// doi.org/10.1080/09512748.2010.546874.

Goodfellow, T. (2020) 'Finance, Infrastructure and Urban Capital: The Political Economy of African "Gap-Filling"', *Review of African Political*

Economy, 47(164), pp. 256–74. Available at: https://doi.org/10.1080/03056244.2020.1722088.

Gosovic, B. (2016) 'The Resurgence of South-South Cooperation', *Third World Quarterly*, 37(4), pp. 733–43. Available at: https://doi.org/10.1080/01436597.2015.1127155.

GRAIN (2018) *Administrative Court Condemns Mozambican Government to Release Information on Agrarian Program*. Available at: https://farmlandgrab.org/post/view/28460 (Accessed: 27 August 2022).

GRAIN and UNAC (2015) *The Land Grabbers of the Nacala Corridor*. Available at: https://grain.org/entries/5137-the-land-grabbers-of-the-nacala-corridor (Accessed: 27 August 2022).

Grant, R.W. and Keohane, R.O. (2005) 'Accountability and Abuses of Power in World Politics', *American Political Science Review*, 99(1), pp. 29–43. Available at: https://doi.org/10.1017/S0003055405051476.

Gray, K. and Gills, B.K. (2016) 'South-South Cooperation and the Rise of the Global South', *Third World Quarterly*, 37(4), pp. 557–74. Available at: https://doi.org/10.1080/01436597.2015.1128817.

Greenovation:Hub (2014) *China's Mining Industry at Home and Overseas: Development, Impacts and Regulation, Case Studies*. Beijing. Available at: https://www.ghub.org/cfc_en/wp-content/uploads/sites/2/2014/11/China-Mining-at-Home-and-Overseas_Case-study2_EN.pdf (Accessed: 20 May 2022).

Grisa, C. (2018) 'Mudanças nas políticas públicas para a agricultura familiar no Brasil:: novos mediadores para velhos referenciais', *Raízes: Revista de Ciências Sociais e Econômicas*, 38(1), pp. 36–50. Available at: https://doi.org/10.37370/raizes.2018.v38.37.

Gu, J. et al. (2016) 'Chinese State Capitalism? Rethinking the Role of the State and Business in Chinese Development Cooperation in Africa', *World Development*, 81, pp. 24–34. Available at: https://doi.org/10.1016/j.worlddev.2016.01.001.

Gu, J., Shankland, A. and Chenoy, A.M. (eds) (2016) *The BRICS in International Development*. London: Palgrave Macmillan.

Guguyu, O. (2022) 'Handful Chinese firms snap Sh1trn contracts', *Business Daily*. Available at: https://www.businessdailyafrica.com/bd/corporate/companies/handful-chinese-firms-snap-sh1trn-contracts-3672466 (Accessed: 14 August 2022).

Habermas, J. (1996) *Between Facts and Norms: Contributions to a Discourse Theory of Law and Democracy*. Cambridge: Polity.

Hameiri, S. and Jones, L. (2018) 'China Challenges Global Governance? Chinese International Development Finance and the AIIB', *International*

Affairs, 94(3), pp. 573–93. Available at: https://doi.org/10.1093/ia/iiy026.

Harris, D. and Vittorini, S. (2015) 'What Does "Development Cooperation" Mean? Perceptions from India and Africa', in K. Sullivan (ed.) *Competing Visions of India in World Politics: India's Rise Beyond the West*. London: Palgrave Macmillan UK, pp. 94–110.

Harman, S. and Brown W. (2013) 'In from the Margins? The Changing Place of Africa in International Relations'. *International Affairs* 89: pp. 69–87. Available at https://doi.org/10.2307/23479334.

Hatte, S. and Koenig, P. (2020) 'The Geography of NGO Activism against Multinational Corporations', *The World Bank Economic Review*, 34(1), pp. 143–63. Available at: https://doi.org/10.1093/wber/lhy007.

Hecht, G. (2002) 'Rupture-Talk in the Nuclear Age: Conjugating Colonial Power in Africa', *Social Studies of Science*, 32(5–6), pp. 691–727. Available at: https://doi.org/10.1177/030631270203200504.

Heilmann, S. and Perry, E.J. (eds) (2011) *Mao's Invisible Hand: The Political Foundations of Adaptive Governance in China*. Cambridge, Massachusetts; London: Harvard University Press.

Henley, J.S. (1976) 'On the Lack of Trade Union Power in Kenya', *Relations Industrielles / Industrial Relations*, 31(4), pp. 655–67. Available at: https://doi.org/10.7202/028748ar.

Hensengerth, O. (2013) 'Chinese Hydropower Companies and Environmental Norms in Countries of the Global South: The Involvement of Sinohydro in Ghana's Bui Dam', *Environment, Development and Sustainability*, 15(2), pp. 285–300. Available at: https://doi.org/10.1007/s10668-012-9410-4.

Hensengerth, O. (2018) 'China's Investment in African Hydropower: How to Govern the Water–Energy Nexus? Evidence from the Bui Dam in Ghana', in G. Siciliano and F. Urban (eds) *Chinese Hydropower Development in Africa and Asia: Challenges and Opportunities for Sustainable Global Dam Building*. London: Routledge, pp. 35–52.

Hetherington, K. (2016) 'Surveying the Future Perfect: Anthropology, Development and the Promise of Infrastructure', in P. Harvey, C. Jensen, and A. Morita (eds) *Infrastructures and Social Complexity*. London, New York: Routledge, pp. 58–68.

Hibou, B. (1999) 'La "décharge", nouvel interventionnisme', *Politique africaine*, (1), pp. 6–15. Available at: https://doi.org/10.3917/polaf.073.0006.

Hickey, S. and King, S. (2016) 'Understanding Social Accountability: Politics, Power and Building New Social Contracts', *The Journal of Development Studies*, 52(8), pp. 1225–40. Available at: https://doi.org/10.1080/00220388.2015.1134778.

High Court of Kenya (2018) 'Petition 22 of 2012 Mohamed Ali Baadi and Others vs. the AG and others'. Available at: https://naturaljustice. org/wp-content/uploads/2018/05/Final-Judgment.pdf.

Hill, C. (2003) *The Changing Politics of Foreign Policy*. Houndmills, Basingstoke, Hampshire; New York: Palgrave Macmillan.

Hirono, M. (2013) 'Three Legacies of Humanitarianism in China', *Disasters*, 37, pp. S202–S220. Available at: https://doi.org/10.1111/ disa.12022.

Ho, P. (2007) 'Embedded Activism and Political Change in a Semiauthoritarian Context', *China Information*, 21(2), pp. 187–209. Available at: https://doi.org/10.1177/0920203X07079643.

Hodzi, O. (2018) 'China and Africa: Economic Growth and a Non-Transformative Political Elite', *Journal of Contemporary African Studies*, 36(2), pp. 191–206. Available at: https://doi.org/10.1080/0258900 1.2017.1406191.

Hodzi, O. (2020) 'African Political Elites and the Making(s) of the China Model in Africa', *Politics & Policy*, 48(5), pp. 887–907. Available at: https://doi.org/10.1111/polp.12380.

Hofmann, K. et al. (2007) 'Contrasting Perceptions: Chinese, African, and European Perspectives on the China–Africa Summit', *Internationale Politik und Gesellschaft*, (2), pp. 57–90.

Hönke, J. (2010) 'New Political Topographies. Mining Companies and Indirect Discharge in Southern Katanga (DRC)', *Politique Africaine*, (4), pp. 105–27. Available at: https://doi.org/10.3917/polaf.120.0105.

Hönke, J. (2013) *Transnational Companies and Security Governance: Hybrid Practices in a Postcolonial World*. London and New York: Routledge (PRIO New Security Studies).

Hönke, J. (2018a) 'Beyond the Gatekeeper State: African Infrastructure Hubs as Sites of Experimentation', *Third World Thematics: A TWQ Journal*, 3(3), pp. 347–63. Available at: https://doi.org/10.1080/23802014. 2018.1456954.

Hönke, J. (2018b) 'Port Geographies: Africa's Infrastructure Boom and the Reconfiguration of Power and Authority', in J. Schubert, U. Engel, and E. Macamo (eds) *Extractive Industries and Changing State Dynamics in Africa*. London; New York: Routledge, pp. 41–56.

Hönke, J. (2018c) 'Transnational Clientelism, Global (Resource) Governance, and the Disciplining of Dissent', *International Political Sociology*, 12(2), pp. 109–24. Available at: https://doi.org/10.1093/ ips/oly007.

Hönke, J., Cezne, E. and Yang, Y. (2023) 'Liminally Positioned in the

South: Reinterpreting Brazilian and Chinese Relations with Africa', *Global Society*, 37(2), pp. 197–224. Available at: https://doi.org/10.1080/13600826.2022.2094222.

Hönke, J. and Cuesta-Fernandez, I. (2017) 'A Topolographical Approach to Infrastructure: Political Topography, Topology and the Port of Dar es Salaam', *Environment and Planning D: Society and Space*, 35(6), pp. 1076–95. Available at: https://doi.org/10.1177/0263775817707762.

Hönke, J. and Cuesta-Fernandez, I. (2018) 'Mobilising Security and Logistics through an African Port: A Controversies Approach to Infrastructure', *Mobilities*, 13(2), pp. 246–60. Available at: https://doi.org/10.1080/17450101.2017.1417774.

Hopewell, K. (2016) *Breaking the WTO: How Emerging Powers Disrupted the Neoliberal Project*. Stanford, California: Stanford University Press.

Horner, R. (2016) 'A New Economic Geography of Trade and Development? Governing South-South Trade, Value Chains and Production Networks', *Territory, Politics, Governance*, 4(4). Available at: https://doi.org/10.1080/21622671.2015.1073614.

Hossain, N. et al. (2014) *Them Belly Full (But We Hungry): Food Rights Struggles in Bangladesh, India, Kenya*. Brighton: Institute of Development Studies. Available at: https://opendocs.ids.ac.uk/opendocs/handle/20.500.12413/6431 (Accessed: 27 August 2022).

Hsu, J.Y.J. (2015) 'China's Development: A New Development Paradigm?', *Third World Quarterly*, 36(9), pp. 1754–69. Available at: https://doi.org/10.1080/01436597.2015.1046985.

Hsu, J.Y.J., Hildebrandt, T. and Hasmath, R. (2016) '"Going Out" or Staying In? The Expansion of Chinese NGOs in Africa', *Development Policy Review*, 34(3), pp. 423–39. Available at: https://doi.org/10.1111/dpr.12157.

Huang, Z. and Chen, X. (2016) 'Is China Building Africa?', *The European Financial Review*, 22 June. Available at: https://www.europeanfinancialreview.com/is-china-building-africa/ (Accessed: 19 September 2022).

Human Rights Watch and National Coalition of Human Rights Defenders Kenya (2018) *'They Just Want to Silence Us': Abuses Against Environmental Activists at Kenya's Coast Region*. Human Rights Watch. Available at: https://www.hrw.org/report/2018/12/17/they-just-want-silence-us/abuses-against-environmental-activists-kenyas-coast (Accessed: 14 August 2022).

Hunter, W. and Power, T.J. (2019) 'Bolsonaro and Brazil's Illiberal Backlash', *Journal of Democracy*, 30(1), pp. 68–82. Available at: https://doi.org/10.1353/jod.2019.0005.

REFERENCES

IDI (2019) *Safeguarding People and the Environment in Chinese Investments: A Reference Guide for Advocates*. 2nd edition. Asheville: Inclusive Development International. Available at: https://www.inclusive development.net/wp-content/uploads/2020/01/2019_idi_china-safeguards-guide-final.pdf (Accessed: 7 June 2022).

Ilal, A., Kleibl, T. and Munck, R. (2018) 'Postcolonial perspectives on Civil Society in Mozambique: Towards an Alternative Approach for Research and Action', in P. Kamruzzaman (ed.) *Civil Society in the Global South*. London; New York: Routledge, pp. 215–34.

Independent Commission of the South on Development Issues (ed.) (1990) *The Challenge to the South*. Oxford; New York: Oxford University Press.

Inoue, C.Y.A. and Vaz, A.C. (2012) 'Brazil as "Southern Donor": Beyond Hierarchy and National Interests in Development Cooperation?', *Cambridge Review of International Affairs*, 25(4), pp. 507–34. Available at: https://doi.org/10.1080/09557571.2012.734779.

International Articulation of those Affected by Vale (AIAAV) (2021) *Vale Unsustainability Report 2021*. AIAAV. Available at: https://atingidosvale.com/relatorios/vale-unsustainability-report-2021/ (Accessed: 27 August 2022).

International Rights Advocates (2019) *Class Complaint for Injunctive Relief and Damages*. Washington, DC. Available at: https://regmedia.co.uk/2019/12/16/cobalt_lawsuit.pdf (Accessed: 3 June 2022).

Irwin, A. and Gallagher, K.P. (2013) 'Chinese Mining in Latin America: A Comparative Perspective', *The Journal of Environment & Development*, 22(2), pp. 207–34. Available at: https://doi.org/10.1177/1070496513489983.

Issufo, N. (2012) *Governo moçambicano desaloja milhares de camponeses*, *DW.COM*. Available at: https://www.dw.com/pt-002/governo-mo%C3%A7ambicano-desaloja-milhares-de-camponeses/a-16358534 (Accessed: 27 August 2022).

ITIE RDC (2021) *Rapport assoupli: Exercices 2018, 2019, 2020 (1er semestre)*. Initiative pour la Transparence des Industries Extractives. Available at: https://eiti.org/sites/default/files/attachments/rapport_assoupli_itie_rdc_2018_2019_1er_semestre_2020_adopte.pdf (Accessed: 18 May 2022).

James, D. (2011) 'The Return of the Broker: Consensus, Hierarchy, and Choice in South African Land Reform', *Journal of the Royal Anthropological Institute*, 17(2), pp. 318–38. Available at: https://doi.org/10.1111/j.1467-9655.2011.01682.x.

Jauch, H. and Sakaria, I. (2009) *Chinese Investments in Namibia: A Labour Perspective*. Windhoek: Labour Resource and Research Institute (LaRRI).

REFERENCES

Jensen, C.B. and Winthereik, B.R. (2013) *Monitoring Movements in Development Aid: Recursive Partnerships and Infrastructures*. Cambridge, Massachusetts: The MIT Press.

Jerez, B., Garcés, I. and Torres, R. (2021) 'Lithium Extractivism and Water Injustices in the Salar de Atacama, Chile: The Colonial Shadow of Green Electromobility', *Political Geography*, 87, 102382. Available at: https://doi.org/10.1016/j.polgeo.2021.102382.

Jha, K.K. (2002) *Informal Labour in the Construction Industry in Nepal. Sectoral Activities Programme*. 187. Geneva: International Labour Organisation. Available at: https://un.info.np/Net/NeoDocs/View/4991 (Accessed: 23 August 2022).

Jiang, F. (2020) 'Chinese Contractor Involvement in Wildlife Protection in Africa: Case Study of Mombasa–Nairobi Standard Gauge Railway Project, Kenya', *Land Use Policy*, 95, 104650. Available at: https://doi.org/10.1016/j.landusepol.2020.104650.

Jiang, S. and Wu, Y. (2015) 'Chinese People's Intended and Actual Use of the Court to Resolve Grievance/Dispute', *Social Science Research*, 49, pp. 42–52. Available at: https://doi.org/10.1016/j.ssresearch.2014.07.009.

Johansson, K. and Sambo, M. (2014) *As revoltas do pão: um exercício de cidadania?* Maputo: IESE.

Jones, L. and Hameiri S. (2021) *Fractured China*. Cambridge: Cambridge University Press.

Jones, L. and Zeng, J. (2019) 'Understanding China's "Belt and Road Initiative": Beyond "Grand Strategy" to a State Transformation Analysis', *Third World Quarterly*, 40(8), pp. 1415–39. Available at: https://doi.org/10.1080/01436597.2018.1559046.

Joniak-Lüthi, A. (2019) 'Introduction: Infrastructure as an Asynchronic Timescape', *Roadsides*, 1, pp. 3–10. Available at: https://doi.org/10.26034/roadsides-20190012.

Journal@Verdade (2013) *"Wambao Agriculture" os recentes e reais impactos de mais uma bolada dos dragões em nome do desenvolvimento, Moçambique para todos*. Available at: https://macua.blogs.com/moambique_para_todos/2013/08/wambao-agriculture-os-recentes-e-reais-impactos-de-mais-uma-bolada-dos-drag%C3%B5es-em-nome-do-desenvolvimento.html (Accessed: 27 August 2022).

Júnior, F. (2013) *Moçambique: Cheias causam prejuízos de 13 milhões no Baixo Limpopo*, *VOA*. Available at: https://www.voaportugues.com/a/mocambique-cheias-limpopo/1657040.html (Accessed: 29 September 2022).

Kamoche, K. and Siebers, L.Q. (2015) 'Chinese Management Practices in Kenya: Toward a Post-Colonial Critique', *The International Journal of Human Resource Management*, 26(21), pp. 2718–43. Available at: https://doi.org/10.1080/09585192.2014.968185.

Kamruzzaman, P. (2018) 'Introduction—Civil Society in the Global South', in P. Kamruzzaman (ed.) *Civil Society in the Global South.* Abingdon: Routledge, pp. 1–24.

Katz-Lavigne, S. (2019) 'Artisanal Copper Mining and Conflict at the Intersection of Property Rights and Corporate Strategies in the Democratic Republic of Congo', *The Extractive Industries and Society*, 6(2), pp. 399–406. Available at: https://doi.org/10.1016/j.exis.2018.12.001.

Katz-Lavigne, S. (2020) *'Qui ne risque rien, n'a rien': Conflict, distributional outcomes, and property rights in the copper- and cobalt-mining sector of the DRC.* Doctoral thesis. University of Groningen. Available at: https://doi.org/10.33612/diss.112662976.

Katz-Lavigne, S. and Hönke, J. (2018) *Cobalt Isn't a Conflict Mineral.* Available at: https://africasacountry.com/2018/09/cobalt-isnt-a-conflict-mineral (Accessed: 2 June 2022).

Kaul, I. (2013) 'The Rise of the Global South: Implications for the Provisioning of Global Public Goods'. United Nations Development Programme Human Development Report Office. Available at: https://hdr.undp.org/sites/default/files/hdro_1308_kaul.pdf.

Kaushik, S. (2018) *Policy Way Forward for the New Development Bank | Oxfam India.* New Delhi: Oxfam India, Vasudha Foundation. Available at: https://www.oxfamindia.org/workingpaper/6088 (Accessed: 20 August 2022).

Kazungu, K. (2019) 'Take Up Available Jobs without Being Choosy, Lamu Youth Told | Nation', *Nation*, 14 January. Available at: https://nation.africa/kenya/counties/lamu/take-up-available-jobs-without-being-choosy-lamu-youth-told-127678 (Accessed: 14 August 2022).

Keck, M.E. and Sikkink, K. (1998) *Activists beyond Borders: Advocacy Networks in International Politics*, *Activists beyond Borders.* Ithaca, NY: Cornell University Press.

Kelsall, T. (2013) *Business, Politics, and the State in Africa: Challenging the Orthodoxies on Growth and Transformation.* London; New York: Zed Books.

Kennedy, S. (2010) 'The Myth of the Beijing Consensus', *Journal of Contemporary China*, 19(65), pp. 461–77. Available at: https://doi.org/10.1080/10670561003666087.

Kennedy, S. (2017) *Global Governance and China: The Dragon's Learning Curve.* London: Routledge.

REFERENCES

Kenya Human Rights Commission (2015) *Insult to Injury: The 2014 Lamu and Tana River Attacks and Kenya's Abusive Response.* Human Rights Watch. Available at: https://www.hrw.org/report/2015/06/15/insult-injury/2014-lamu-and-tana-river-attacks-and-kenyas-abusive-response (Accessed: 14 August 2022).

Kernen, A. and Lam, K.N. (2014) 'Workforce Localization among Chinese State-Owned Enterprises (SOEs) in Ghana', *Journal of Contemporary China*, 23(90), pp. 1053–72. Available at: https://doi.org/10.1080/10670564.2014.898894.

Kimari, W. and Ernstson, H. (2020) 'Imperial Remains and Imperial Invitations: Centering Race within the Contemporary Large-Scale Infrastructures of East Africa', *Antipode*, 52(3), pp. 825–46. Available at: https://doi.org/10.1111/anti.12623.

Kituo Cha Sheria (2014) *Baseline Survey Report Popular Version—Baseline Survey on Human Rights Violations along the LAPSSET Corridor: A Case Study of Lamu.* Kituao Cha Sheria. Available at: http://www.kituochasheria.or.ke/wp-content/uploads/2016/04/Baseline-survey-final-version.pdf.

Kleibl, T. (2021) *Decolonizing Civil Society in Mozambique: Governance, Politics and Spiritual Systems.* London: Zed Books.

Knutsen, H.M. and Hansson, E. (2010) 'Theoretical Approaches to Changing Labour Regimes in Transition Economies', in A.C. Bergene and S.B. Endresen (eds) *Missing Links in Labour Geography.* Farnham: Ashgate, pp. 155–69.

Koech, G. (2021) 'How the Expressway has Changed Nairobi's Skyline', *The Star.* Available at: https://www.the-star.co.ke/counties/nairobi/2021-12-29-how-the-expressway-has-changed-nairobis-skyline/ (Accessed: 1 September 2022).

Koplatadze, T. (2019) 'Theorising Russian Postcolonial Studies', *Postcolonial Studies*, 22(4), pp. 469–89. Available at: https://doi.org/10.1080/13688790.2019.1690762.

Koster, M. and van Leynseele, Y. (2018) 'Brokers as Assemblers: Studying Development through the Lens of Brokerage', *Ethnos*, 83(5), pp. 803–13. Available at: https://doi.org/10.1080/00141844.2017.1362451.

Kraemer, R., Whiteman, G. and Banerjee, B. (2013) 'Conflict and Astroturfing in Niyamgiri: The Importance of National Advocacy Networks in Anti-Corporate Social Movements', *Organization Studies*, 34(5–6), pp. 823–52. Available at: https://doi.org/10.1177/0170840613479240.

Kragelund, P. (2009) 'Knocking on a Wide-open Door: Chinese Investments in Africa', *Review of African Political Economy*, 36(122), pp. 479–97. Available at: https://doi.org/10.1080/03056240903346111.

Kragelund, P. (2019) *South-South Development.* London: Routledge.

REFERENCES

Kuhn, B. (2018) 'Changing Spaces for Civil Society Organisations in China', *Open Journal of Political Science*, 8(4), pp. 467–94. Available at: https://doi.org/10.4236/ojps.2018.84030.

Kwan, A.S.C. (2016) 'Hierarchy, Status and International Society: China and the Steppe Nomads', *European Journal of International Relations*, 22(2), pp. 362–83. Available at: https://doi.org/10.1177/1354066115598385.

Laher, R. (2011) *Resisting Development in Kenya's Lamu District: A Postcolonial Reading*. 48. Africa Institute of South Africa. Available at: https://www.africaportal.org/publications/resisting-development-in-kenyas-lamu-district-a-postcolonial-reading/.

Lam, K.N.T. (2017) *Chinese State-Owned Enterprises in West Africa: Triple-embedded Globalization*. London: Routledge.

Lancaster, C. (2006) *Foreign Aid: Diplomacy, Development, Domestic Politics*. Chicago, IL: University of Chicago Press.

LAPSSET Corridor Development Authority (2020) *Lamu Port*. Available at: https://bit.ly/3u1sVWE (Accessed: 20 March 2021).

Lardy, N.R. (1975) 'Centralization and Decentralization in China's Fiscal Management', *The China Quarterly*, 61, pp. 25–60. Available at: https://doi.org/10.1017/S0305741000006779.

Large, D. (2021) *China and Africa: The New Era*. Oxford: Polity.

Larkin, B.D. (1973) *China and Africa 1949–1970: The Foreign Policy of the People's Republic of China*. Berkeley, Los Angeles: University of California Press.

Latour, B. (1987) *Science in Action: How to Follow Scientists and Engineers through Society*. Cambridge, Mass: Harvard University Press.

Law, J. (1992) 'Notes on the Theory of the Actor-Network: Ordering, Strategy, and Heterogeneity', *Systems Practice*, 5(4), pp. 379–93. Available at: https://doi.org/10.1007/BF01059830.

Law, J. (2004) 'And if the Global Were Small and Noncoherent? Method, Complexity, and the Baroque', *Environment and Planning D: Society and Space*, 22(1), pp. 13–26. Available at: https://doi.org/10.1068/d316t.

LCDA (2017) *LAPSSET Quarterly Newsletter: November 2016–January 2017*. Available at: https://drive.google.com/file/d/0B7w3900K6lYnbC02SVVBVVBOM0E/view?usp=embed_facebook.

Lee, C.K. (1999) 'From Organized Dependence to Disorganized Despotism: Changing Labour Regimes in Chinese Factories', *The China Quarterly*, 157, pp. 44–71. Available at: https://doi.org/10.1017/S0305741000040200.

Lee, C.K. (2009) 'Raw Encounters: Chinese Managers, African Workers and the Politics of Casualization in Africa's Chinese Enclaves', *The China Quarterly*, 199, pp. 647–66. Available at: https://doi.org/10.1017/S0305741009990142.

Lee, C.K. (2017) *The Specter of Global China: Politics, Labor, and Foreign Investment in Africa*. Chicago, IL: University of Chicago Press.

Lesutis, G. (2020) 'How to Understand a Development Corridor? The Case of Lamu Port–South Sudan–Ethiopia-Transport Corridor in Kenya', *Area*, 52(3), pp. 600–8. Available at: https://doi.org/10.1111/area.12601.

Liang, Z. and Ma, Z. (2004) 'China's Floating Population: New Evidence from the 2000 Census', *Population and Development Review*, 30(3), pp. 467–88.

Lin, J.Y., Liu, M. and Tao, R. (2013) 'Deregulation, Decentralization, and China's Growth in Transition', in D. Kennedy and J.E. Stiglitz (eds) *Law and Economics with Chinese Characteristics*. Oxford: Oxford University Press, pp. 466–90.

Links, S. (2021) 'Ascertaining Agency Africa and the Belt and Road Initiative', in F. Schneider (ed.) *Global Perspectives on China's Belt and Road Initiative*. Amsterdam: Amsterdam University Press, pp. 113–39.

Liu, B. (2021) 'China's State-Centric Approach to Corporate Social Responsibility Overseas: A Case Study in Africa', *Transnational Environmental Law*, 10(1), pp. 57–84. Available at: https://doi.org/10.1017/S2047102520000229.

Liu, J.C.Y. (2013) 'Sino-African Cultural Relations: Soft Power, Cultural Statecraft and International Cultural Governance', in S. Chan (ed.) *The Morality of China in Africa: The Middle Kingdom and the Dark Continent*. London: Zed Books, pp. 47–59.

Lopes, D.B. (2020) 'De-Westernization, Democratization, Disconnection: The Emergence of Brazil's Post-Diplomatic Foreign Policy', *Global Affairs*, 6(2), pp. 167–84. Available at: https://doi.org/10.1080/23340460.2020.1769494.

Lopes, L. and Costa, J. (2018) *Measuring Brazilian South-South Cooperation through a Participatory Approach*. Reality of Aid. Available at: http://www.realityofaid.org/wp-content/uploads/2018/12/2-Measuring-Brazilian-South-South-cooperation-through-a-participatory-approach.pdf.

Lorenz, A. and Thielke, T. (2007) 'The Age of the Dragon: China's Conquest of Africa', *Der Spiegel*. Available at: https://www.spiegel.de/international/world/the-age-of-the-dragon-china-s-conquest-of-africa-a-484603.html (Accessed: 14 August 2022).

Lu, X. and Perry, E.J. (1997) *Danwei: The Changing Chinese Workplace in Historical and Comparative Perspective*. New York: Routledge.

REFERENCES

Lu, Y.-J. and Fox, P.W. (2001) *The Construction Industry in China: Its Image, Employment Prospects and Skill Requirements. Sectoral Activities Programme.* 180. Geneva: International Labour Organisation.

Lumumba-Kasongo, T. (2011) 'China–Africa Relations: A Neo-Imperialism or a Neo-Colonialism? A Reflection', *African and Asian Studies*, 10(2–3), pp. 234–66. Available at: https://doi.org/10.1163/156921011X587040.

Ma, T. (2019) *Anxieties of Development. Emerging Voices in Chinese Social Media.* Available at: https://chublicopinion.com/2019/02/09/anxieties-of-development-emerging-voices-in-chinese-social-media/ (Accessed: 11 November 2019).

Madureira, M. (2014) *Mega-Projectos e Transição Agrária: o caso do projecto Wanbao (Moçambique), CEsA Working Papers.* 126. CEsA—Centre for African and Development Studies. Available at: https://ideas.repec.org/p/cav/cavwpp/wp126.html (Accessed: 27 August 2022).

Maiza-Larrarte, A. and Claudio-Quiroga, G. (2019) 'The Impact of Sicomines on Development in the Democratic Republic of Congo', *International Affairs*, 95(2), pp. 423–46. Available at: https://doi.org/10.1093/ia/iiz001.

Mao, Z. (1965) 'On the Ten Major Relationships', in *Selected Works of Mao Tse-tung Vol. V.* Beijing: Foreign Languages Press.

Marcondes, D. and Mawdsley, E. (2017) 'South-South in Retreat? The Transitions from Lula to Rousseff to Temer and Brazilian Development Cooperation', *International Affairs*, 93(3), pp. 681–99. Available at: https://doi.org/10.1093/ia/iix076.

Martorano, B. et al. (2021) 'Areas in Africa with More Chinese-Backed Projects were More Likely to Experience Protests', *The Conversation.* Available at: http://theconversation.com/areas-in-africa-with-more-chinese-backed-projects-were-more-likely-to-experience-protests-162137 (Accessed: 14 August 2022).

Massey, D. (1995) 'Places and Their Pasts', *History Workshop Journal*, (39), pp. 182–92. Available at: https://doi.org/10.1093/hwj/39.1.182.

Massey, D.B. (1994a) 'A Global Sense of Place', in D. Massey (ed.) *Space, Place and Gender.* Repr. Cambridge: Polity Press, pp. 146–56.

Massey, D.B. (1994b) 'A Place Called Home?', in D. Massey (ed.) *Space, Place and Gender.* Repr. Cambridge: Polity Press, pp. 157–73.

Massey, D.B. (1994c) 'General Introduction', in D. Massey (ed.) *Space, Place and Gender.* Repr. Cambridge: Polity Press, pp. 1–16.

Massey, D.B. (2005) *For Space.* London; Thousand Oaks, California: SAGE.

REFERENCES

Matthews, D. (2020) *Global Value Chains: Cobalt in Lithium-ion Batteries for Electric Vehicles*. Washington , DC: U.S. International Trade Commission. Available at: https://www.usitc.gov/publications/332/working_ papers/id_wp_cobalt_final_052120-compliant.pdf (Accessed: 31 May 2022).

Matti, S.A. (2010) 'The Democratic Republic of the Congo? Corruption, Patronage, and Competitive Authoritarianism in the DRC', *Africa Today*, 56(4), pp. 42–61. Available at: https://doi.org/10.2979/ aft.2010.56.4.42.

Mawdsley, E. (2011) 'The Rhetorics and Rituals of South-South Development Cooperation; Notes on India in Africa', in E. Mawdsley and G. McCann (eds) *India in Africa: Changing Geographies of Power*. Cape Town: Pambazuka Press, pp. 166–86.

Mawdsley, E. (2012a) *From Recipients to Donors: Emerging Powers and the Changing Development Landscape*. London: Zed Books.

Mawdsley, E. (2012b) 'The Changing Geographies of Foreign Aid and Development Cooperation: Contributions from Gift Theory', *Transactions of the Institute of British Geographers*, 37(2), pp. 256–72. Available at: https://doi.org/10.1111/j.1475-5661.2011.00467.x.

Mawdsley, E. (2014a) 'Human Rights and South-South Development Cooperation: Reflections on the "Rising Powers" as International Development Actors', *Human Rights Quarterly*, 36(3), pp. 630–52. Available at: https://doi.org/10.1353/hrq.2014.0044.

Mawdsley, E. (2014b) 'Public Perceptions of India's Role as an International Development Cooperation Partner: Domestic Responses to Rising "Donor" Visibility', *Third World Quarterly*, 35(6), pp. 958–79. Available at: https://doi.org/10.1080/01436597.2014.907721.

Mawdsley, E. (2018) 'Southern Leaders, Northern Followers? Who Has "Socialised" Whom in International Development?', in E. Fiddian-Qasmiyeh and P. Daley (eds) *Routledge Handbook of South-South Relations*. Abingdon; New York: Routledge, pp. 191–204.

Mawdsley, E. (2019) 'South-South Cooperation 3.0? Managing the Consequences of Success in the Decade Ahead', *Oxford Development Studies*, 47(3), pp. 259–74. Available at: https://doi.org/10.1080/13 600818.2019.1585792.

Mawdsley, E., Fourie, E. and Nauta, W. (2019) *Researching South-South Development Cooperation: The Politics of Knowledge Production*. London; New York: Routledge.

Mawdsley, E. and McCann, G. (2011) *India in Africa: Changing Geographies of Power*. Cape Town: Pambazuka Press.

Mawdsley, E. and Roychoudhury, S. (2016) 'Civil Society Organisations and

REFERENCES

Indian Development Assistance: Emerging Roles for Commentators, Collaborators, and Critics', in S. Chaturvedi and A. Mulakala (eds) *India's Approach to Development Cooperation*. Routledge, pp. 115–29.

Mazimhaka, P. (2013) 'China and Africa: An African View', in S. Chan (ed.) *The Morality of China in Africa: The Middle Kingdom and the Dark Continent*. London: Zed Books, pp. 89–121.

Mbembe, J.-A. and Nuttall, S. (2004) 'Writing the World from an African Metropolis', *Public Culture*, 16(3), pp. 347–72. Available at: https://doi.org/10.1215/08992363-16-3-347.

McAdam, D. and Tarrow, S.G. (2019) 'The Political Context of Social Movements', in D.A. Snow et al. (eds) *The Wiley Blackwell Companion to Social Movements*. 2nd edition. Hoboken, NJ: Wiley-Blackwell, pp. 19–42.

McAdam, D., Tarrow, S.G. and Tilly, C. (2001) *Dynamics of Contention*. Cambridge; New York: Cambridge University Press.

McAteer, E. and Pulver, S. (2009) 'The Corporate Boomerang: Shareholder Transnational Advocacy Networks Targeting Oil Companies in the Ecuadorian Amazon', *Global Environmental Politics*, 9(1), pp. 1–30. Available at: https://doi.org/10.1162/glep.2009.9.1.1.

McEwan, C. and Mawdsley, E. (2012) 'Trilateral Development Cooperation: Power and Politics in Emerging Aid Relationships', *Development and Change*, 43(6), pp. 1185–209. Available at: https://doi.org/10.1111/j.1467-7660.2012.01805.x.

McGee, R. (2013) 'Aid Transparency and Accountability: "Build It and They'll Come"?', *Development Policy Review*, 31(s1), pp. 107–24. Available at: https://doi.org/10.1111/dpr.12022.

Mdlalose, B, and Thompson, L. 2018. 'Academic and Civil BRICS 2018: Is There Any Jam to Be Made?' *Mail & Guardian*, 22 June 2018.

Mead, N.V. (2018) 'China in Africa: Win-Win Development, or a New Colonialism?', *Guardian*. Available at: https://www.theguardian.com/cities/2018/jul/31/china-in-africa-win-win-development-or-a-new-colonialism (Accessed: 14 August 2022).

Meng, Q. and Bempong Nyantakyi, E. (2019) *Local Skill Development from China's Engagement in Africa: Comparative Evidence from the Construction Sector in Ghana*. 20/2019. Washington, DC: China Africa Research Initiative (CARI), Johns Hopkins University, pp. 68–85. Available at: https://link.springer.com/10.1057/s41294-021-00154-3.

Mignolo, W. (2012) *The Role of BRICS Countries in the Becoming World Order: 'Humanity', Colonial/Imperial Differences, and the Racial Distribution of Capital and Knowledge*. Brazil: UNESCO and Universidad Candido Mendes, pp. 41–89.

Milani, C.R.S. and Klein, M. (2021) 'South-South Cooperation and

Foreign Policy: Challenges and Dilemmas in the Perception of Brazilian Diplomats', *International Relations*, 35(2), pp. 277–98. Available at: https://doi.org/10.1177/0047117820920906.

Milhorance, C. (2015) 'Economias emergentes e instituições nacionais: debate sobre a presença brasileira no Malawi e em Moçambique', in L. de Brito et al. (eds) *Desafios para Moçambique 2015*. Maputo: Instituto de Estudos Sociais e Económicos, pp. 445–65. Available at: https://agritrop.cirad.fr/597862/ (Accessed: 27 August 2022).

Milhorance, C. and Bursztyn, M. (2017) 'South-South Civil Society Partnerships: Renewed Ties of Political Contention and Policy Building', *Development Policy Review*, 35(S2), pp. O80–O95. Available at: https://doi.org/10.1111/dpr.12218.

Ministério de Economia e Finanças (2022) *Conta Geral do Estado Ano 2021*.

Ministério de Economia e Finanças (2008) 'Plano de Acção para a Produção de Alimentos, 2008–2011'. República de Moçambique.

Ministry of Transport Republic of Kenya (2013) *Environmental and Social Impact Assessment Study Report for Construction of the First Three Berths of the Proposed Lamu Port and Associated Infrastructure*.

Mitra, S. (2018) *Methodology for Tracking Development Assistance from India*. Discussion Paper. New Delhi: Centre for Budget and Governance Accountability, Oxfam India. Available at: https://www.oxfamindia.org/Development-Assistance-Methodology (Accessed: 20 August 2022).

Mitullah, W. V. and Njeri Wachira, I. (2003) *Informal Labour in the Construction Industry in Kenya: A Case Study of Nairobi*. 204. Geneva: International Labour Organisation. Available at: https://ilo.primo.exlibrisgroup.com/discovery/fulldisplay/alma994869303402676/41ILO_INST:41ILO_V2 (Accessed: 23 August 2022).

Modi, R. (2010) 'The Role of India's Private Sector in the Health and Agricultural Sectors of Africa', in F. Cheru and C. Obi (eds) *The Rise of China and India in Africa: Challenges, Opportunities and Critical Interventions*. London, New York: Zed Books Ltd., pp. 120–31.

MOFCOM (2005) 'Companies Law of the People's Republic of China'. Ministry of Commerce of the People's Republic of China. Available at: https://www.ilo.org/dyn/natlex/docs/ELECTRONIC/92643/108008/F-186401967/CHN92643%20Eng.pdf. (Accessed: 26 September 2022).

MOFCOM (2022) *Statistics on China–Africa Economic and Trade Cooperation in 2021*. Available at: http://xyf.mofcom.gov.cn/article/tj/zh/202204/20220403308229.shtml (Accessed: 30 May 2022).

Mohamed, A. (2018) 'Lamu Leaders Plan Protest Over Exclusion of Locals from Lapsset', *Business Daily*. Available at: https://www.

REFERENCES

businessdailyafrica.com/bd/news/counties/lamu-leaders-plan-protest-over-exclusion-of-locals-from-lapsset-2189892 (Accessed: 14 August 2022).

Mohan, G. (2013) 'Beyond the Enclave: Towards a Critical Political Economy of China and Africa', *Development and Change*, 44(6), pp. 1255–72. Available at: https://doi.org/10.1111/dech.12061.

Mohan, G. (2014) 'China in Africa: Impacts and Prospects for Accountable Development', in S. Hickey, K. Sen, and B. Bukenya (eds) *The Politics of Inclusive Development*. Oxford: Oxford University Press, pp. 279–304.

Mohan, G. (2015) 'Queuing up for Africa: The Geoeconomics of Africa's Growth and the Politics of African Agency', *International Development Planning Review*, 37(1), pp. 45–52. Available at: https://doi.org/10.3828/idpr.2015.5.

Mohan, G. and Lampert, B. (2013) 'Negotiating China: Reinserting African agency into China–Africa relations', *African Affairs*, 112(446), pp. 92–110. Available at: https://doi.org/10.1093/afraf/ads065.

Mohan, G. and Power, M. (2008) 'New African Choices? The Politics of Chinese Engagement', *Review of African Political Economy*, 35(115), pp. 23–42. Available at: https://doi.org/10.1080/03056240802011394.

Monjane, B. and Bruna, N. (2020) 'Confronting Agrarian Authoritarianism: Dynamics of Resistance to PROSAVANA in Mozambique', *The Journal of Peasant Studies*, 47(1), pp. 69–94. Available at: https://doi.org/10.1080/03066150.2019.1671357.

Mosley, J. and Watson, E.E. (2016) 'Frontier Transformations: Development Visions, Spaces and Processes in Northern Kenya and Southern Ethiopia', *Journal of Eastern African Studies*, 10(3), pp. 452–75. Available at: https://doi.org/10.1080/17531055.2016.1266199.

Mosse, D. and Lewis, D. (2006) 'Theoretical Approaches to Brokerage and Translation in Development', in D. Lewis and D. Mosse (eds) *Development Brokers and Translators: The Ethnography of Aid and Agencies*. Bloomfield, CT: Kumarian Press, pp. 1–26.

Moyo, J.N. (1993) 'Civil Society in Zimbabwe', *Zambezia*, 20(1), pp. 1–13.

Moyo, S., Yeros, P. and Jha, P. (eds) (2019) *Reclaiming Africa: Scramble and Resistance in the 21st Century*. Singapore: Springer.

Mudimbe, V.Y. (1988) *The Invention of Africa: Gnosis, Philosophy, and the Order of Knowledge*. Bloomington: Indiana University Press.

Mukerji, C. (2010) 'The Territorial State as a Figured World of Power: Strategics, Logistics, and Impersonal Rule', *Sociological Theory*, 28(4), pp. 402–24. Available at: https://doi.org/10.1111/j.1467-9558.2010.01381.x.

Mutua, J. (2022) 'Weakening Shilling Drives up Nairobi Expressway

REFERENCES

Toll Fee Ahead of Launch', *Business Daily*. Available at: https://www.businessdailyafrica.com/bd/economy/weakening-shilling-drives-up-nairobi-expressway-toll-fee-3793036 (Accessed: 20 August 2022).

Mwende, J. (2013) 'Chinese Firm Wins Sh38bn Tender for Lamu Port Berths', *CK*. Available at: https://www.constructionkenya.com/2899/china-communications-wins-lamu-port-tender/ (Accessed: 14 August 2022).

n.a. (1983) 'Zhao on Co-operation with African Countries', *Beijing Review*, 26(4), 24 January.

Natural Justice (2021) *The Natural Justice Annual Report 20192–020*. Natural Justice. Available at: https://naturaljustice.org/wp-content/uploads/2021/12/NJ_ANNUAL-REPORT-2021_WEB-96ppi.pdf.

Nayyar, D. (2016) 'BRICS, Developing Countries and Global Governance', *Third World Quarterly*, 37(4), pp. 575–91. Available at: https://doi.org/10.1080/01436597.2015.1116365.

Ndzovu, H.J. (2014) 'Historical Evolution of Muslim Politics in Kenya from the 1840s to 1963', in *Muslims in Kenyan Politics*. Evanston, IL: Northwestern University Press, pp. 17–50.

Newell, P. and Wheeler, J. (2006) 'Introduction: Rights, Resources and the Politics of Accountability', in P. Newell and J. Wheeler (eds) *Rights, Resources and the Politics of Accountability*. London: Zed Books, 1–36.

NGO Forum on ADB (2015) *NGO Forum on ADB Comprehensive Critique on AIIB's Draft Environmental and Social Framework (ESF)*. Business & Human Rights Resource Centre. Available at: https://www.business-humanrights.org/en/latest-news/ngo-forum-on-adb-comprehensive-critique-on-aiibs-draft-environmental-and-social-framework-esf/ (Accessed: 20 August 2022).

Nicolini, D. (2009) 'Zooming In and Out: Studying Practices by Switching Theoretical Lenses and Trailing Connections', *Organization Studies*, 30(12), pp. 1391–418. Available at: https://doi.org/10.1177/0170840609349875.

Nicolini, D. (2016) 'Is Small the Only Beautiful? Making Sense of "Large Phenomena" from a Practice-Based Perspective', in A. Hui, T. Schatzki, and E. Shove (eds) *The Nexus of Practices*. London: Routledge, pp. 110–25.

Njiraini, J. (2010) 'China's Dominance in Kenya Worries Washington', *The Standard*. Available at: https://www.standardmedia.co.ke/financial-standard/article/2000024581/chinas-dominance-in-kenya-worries-washington.

Njunge (2019) 'Kenyan Fishermen Fight for Livelihoods as Lamu Port Nears Completion', *China Dialogue Ocean*. Available at: https://

REFERENCES

chinadialogueocean.net/en/fisheries/9902-kenyan-fishermen-chinese-lamu-port/ (Accessed: 20 August 2022).

Nkumba, E.U. (2020) 'How to Reduce Conflicts Between Mining Companies and Artisanal Miners in the Province of Lualaba: Overcoming the Policy and Systemic Barriers to a Model that Respects Human Rights', *Business and Human Rights Journal*, 5(2), pp. 296–302. Available at: https://doi.org/10.1017/bhj.2020.15.

Nordin, A.H.M. (2016) *China's International Relations and Harmonious World: Time, Space and Multiplicity in World Politics*. London: Routledge.

Nordin, A.H.M. et al. (2019) 'Towards Global Relational Theorizing: A Dialogue between Sinophone and Anglophone Scholarship on Relationalism', *Cambridge Review of International Affairs*, 32(5), pp. 570–81. Available at: https://doi.org/10.1080/09557571.2019.1643978.

Nugent, P. (2018) 'Africa's Re-Enchantment with Big Infrastructure: White Elephants Dancing in Virtuous Circles?', in J. Schubert, U. Engel, and E. Macamo (eds) *Extractive Industries and Changing State Dynamics in Africa*. London; New York: Routledge, pp. 22–40.

Odhiambo, M.O. (2014) *The Unrelenting Persistence of Certain Narratives: An Analysis of Changing Policy Narratives about the ASALs in Kenya*. Available at: https://pubs.iied.org/10081iied (Accessed: 15 August 2022).

Office of Policy Planning (2020) *The Elements of the China Challenge*. U.S. Department of State: Office of the Secretary of State. Available at: https://www.state.gov/wp-content/uploads/2020/11/20-02832-Elements-of-China-Challenge-508.pdf.

Olander, E. (2021) 'Podcast: The Future of Chinese-Financed Infrastructure in Kenya'. Available at: https://chinaafricaproject.com/podcasts/the-future-of-chinese-financed-infrastructure-in-kenya/.

Olorunfemi, F. et al. (2017) 'Hope, Politics and Risk: The Case of Chinese Dam in Nigeria', *Energy and Environment Research*, 7(2), pp. 1–13. Available at: https://doi.org/10.5539/eer.v7n2p1.

Ong, A. (2006) *Neoliberalism as Exception: Mutations in Citizenship and Sovereignty*. Durham, NC: Duke University Press.

Onjala, J. (2018) 'China's Development Loans and the Threat of Debt Crisis in Kenya', *Development Policy Review*, 36, pp. O710–O728. Available at: https://doi.org/10.1111/dpr.12328.

Opitz, S. and Tellmann, U. (2012) 'Global Territories: Zones of Economic And Legal Dis/connectivity', *Distinktion: Scandinavian Journal of Social Theory*, 13(3), pp. 261–82. Available at: https://doi.org/10.1080/1600910X.2012.724432.

Opondo, M. (2009) *The Impact of Chinese Firms on CSR in Kenya s Garment Sector*. The International Research Network on Business, Development and Society. Available at: https://docplayer.net/151286823-The-impact-of-chinese-firms-on-csr-in-kenya-s-garment-sector.html (Accessed: 15 August 2022).

Otele, O.M. (2016) 'Rethinking African Agency within China–Africa Relations through the Lens of Policy Transfer: A Framework for Analysis', *The African Review: A Journal of African Politics, Development and International Affairs*, 43(1), pp. 75–102.

Owusu, K. et al. (2017) 'Resource Utilization Conflict in Downstream Non-Resettled Communities of the Bui Dam in Ghana', *Natural Resources Forum*, 41(4), pp. 234–43. Available at: https://doi.org/10.1111/1477-8947.12139.

Oya, C. (2019) 'Labour Regimes and Workplace Encounters between China and Africa', in A. Oqubay and J. Yifu (eds) *China–Africa and an Economic Transformation*. Oxford: Oxford University Press, pp. 239–62.

Pain pour le prochain and Action de Carême (2018) *Glencore en RD Congo: une diligence raisonnable incomplète*. Lausanne. Available at: https://sehen-und-handeln.ch/content/uploads/2018/04/Rapport_Glencore_Congo_2018_F.pdf (Accessed: 9 June 2022).

Pallas, C.L. and Bloodgood, E.A. (2022) *Beyond the Boomerang: From Transnational Advocacy Networks to Transcalar Advocacy in International Politics*. Tuscaloosa: University of Alabama Press.

Pan, C. (2012) *Knowledge, Desire and Power in Global Politics: Western Representations of China's Rise*. Cheltenham: Edward Elgar.

Park, S. (2019) 'Changing the International Rule of Development to Include Citizen Driven Accountability—A Successful Case of Contestation', in F. Anderl et al. (eds) *In Rule and Resistance beyond the Nation State: Contestation, Escalation, Exit*. London: Rowman & Littlefield, pp. 27–48.

Patey, L.A. (2011) 'Fragile Fortunes: India's Oil Venture into War-Torn Sudan', in E. Mawdsley and G. McCann (eds) *India in Africa: Changing Geographies of Power*. Cape Town: Pambazuka Press, pp. 153–64.

Phillips, J. (2019) 'Who's in Charge of Sino-African Resource Politics? Situating African State Agency in Ghana', *African Affairs*, 118(470), pp. 101–24. Available at: https://doi.org/10.1093/afraf/ady041.

Plesch, D. (2016) 'The South and Disarmament at the UN', *Third World Quarterly*, 37(7), pp. 1203–18. Available at: https://doi.org/10.1080/01436597.2016.1154435.

Plummer, A. (2019) 'Kenya and China's Labour Relations: Infrastructural Development for Whom, by Whom?', *Africa*, 89(4), pp. 680–95. Available at: https://doi.org/10.1017/S0001972019000858.

Pomeroy, M. et al. (2016) 'Civil Society, BRICS and International Development Cooperation: Perspectives from India, South Africa

REFERENCES

and Brazil', in J. Gu, A. Shankland, and A. Chenoy (eds) *The BRICS in International Development*. London: Palgrave Macmillan (International Political Economy Series), pp. 169–206.

Ponguane, S.J.A., Mussumbuluco, B. and Mucavele, N. (2021) 'Land Grabbing or Rice Sector Development Opportunity? The Case of WANBAO Project in Gaza', *Journal of Asian Rural Studies*, 5(2), pp. 135–142. Available at: https://doi.org/10.20956/jars.v5i2.2782.

Pouliot, V. (2016) *International Pecking Orders: The Politics and Practice of Multilateral Diplomacy*. Cambridge: Cambridge University Press.

Prashad, V. (2014) *The Poorer Nations: A Possible History of the Global South*. London, New York: Verso Books.

Pratt, M.L. (1992) *Imperial Eyes: Travel Writing and Transculturation*. London: Routledge.

Prause, L. (2020) 'Conflicts Related to Resources: The Case of Cobalt Mining in the Democratic Republic of Congo', in A. Bleicher and A. Pehlken (eds) *The Material Basis of Energy Transitions*. London; San Diego, California: Academic Press, pp. 153–67.

Prause, L. and Le Billon, P. (2020) 'Struggles for Land: Comparing Resistance Movements Against Agro-Industrial and Mining Investment Projects', *The Journal of Peasant Studies*, 48(5), pp. 1100–23. Available at: https://doi.org/10.1080/03066150.2020.1762181.

PremiCongo (2018) *Human Rights Violations by Chinese Mining Companies in the Democratic Republic of Congo: The Case of China Nonferrous Metal Mining Co. in Mabende*. Lubumbashi. Available at: https://docs.wixstatic.com/ugd/81d92e_c1cc8faa519a4a2f827e083534249e07.pdf (Accessed: 3 June 2022).

Procopio, M. (2018) 'Kenyan Agency in Kenya–China Relations: Contestation, Cooperation and Passivity', in C. Alden and D. Large (eds) *New Directions in Africa–China Studies*. Abingdon: Routledge, pp. 173–86.

Pun, N. and Smith, C. (2007) 'Putting Transnational Labour Process in Its Place: The Dormitory Labour Regime in Post-Socialist China', *Work, Employment and Society*, 21(1), pp. 27–45. Available at: https://doi.org/10.1177/0950017007073611.

Qiang, D. (2019) *Chinese NGOs Working Abroad: The Top Ten Stories of 2018—China Development Brief*. China Development Brief. Available at: https://chinadevelopmentbrief.org/reports/chinese-ngos-working-abroad-the-top-ten-stories-of-2018/ (Accessed: 20 August 2022).

Quijano, A. (2007) 'Coloniality and Modernity/Rationality', *Cultural Studies*, 21(2–3), pp. 168–78. Available at: https://doi.org/10.1080/09502380601164353.

REFERENCES

Raeymaekers, T. (2014) *Violent Capitalism and Hybrid Identity in the Eastern Congo: Power to the Margins.* Cambridge: Cambridge University Press.

RAID and CAJJ (2021) *The Road to Ruin: Electric Vehicles and Workers' Rights Abuses at Dr Congo's Industrial Cobalt Mines.* Available at: https://www.raid-uk.org/sites/default/files/report_road_to_ruin_evs_cobalt_workers_nov_2021.pdf (Accessed: 5 April 2022).

Reilly, James, and Wu Na (2007) 'China's Corporate Engagement in Africa', in Kitissou, Marcel (2007). *Africa in China's Global Strategy.* London: Adonis & Abbey Publishers Ltd.

Republic of Kenya (1965) *African Socialism and Its Application to Planning in Kenya.* Republic of Kenya. Available at: https://www.knls.ac.ke/images/AFRICAN-SOCIALISM-AND-ITS-APPLICATION-TO-PLANNING-IN-KENYA.pdf.

República de Moçambique (2008) 'PLANO DE ACÇÃO PARA A PRODUÇÃO DE ALIMENTOS 2008 - 2011'. Available at: https://www.iese.ac.mz/lib/saber/alimentos.pdf.

Reuters (2019) 'Tanzania's China-backed $10 Billion Port Plan Stalls Over Terms: Official', *Reuters*, 23 May. Available at: https://www.reuters.com/article/us-tanzania-port-idUSKCN1ST084 (Accessed: 25 May 2023).

Reyna, S.P. (2007) 'The Traveling Model That Would Not Travel: Oil, Empire, and Patrimonialism in Contemporary Chad', *Social Analysis*, 51(3). Available at: https://doi.org/10.3167/sa.2007.510304.

Ribeiro, C.O. (2008) 'Crise e castigo: as relações Brasil-África no governo Sarney', *Revista Brasileira de Política Internacional*, 51(2), pp. 39–59. Available at: https://doi.org/10.1590/S0034-73292008000200004.

Riisgaard, L. and Okinda, O. (2018). 'Changing Labour Power on Smallholder Tea Farms in Kenya', *Competition & Change*, 22(1), pp. 41–62.

Robinson, W.I. (2015) 'The Transnational State and the BRICS: A Global Capitalism Perspective', *Third World Quarterly*, 36(1), pp. 1–21. Available at: https://doi.org/10.1080/01436597.2015.976012.

Rodgers, D. and O'Neill, B. (2012) 'Infrastructural Violence: Introduction to the Special Issue', *Ethnography*, 13(4), pp. 401–12. Available at: https://doi.org/10.1177/1466138111435738.

Roesch, O. (2014) 'Renamo and the Peasantry in Southern Mozambique: A View from Gaza Province', *Canadian Journal of African Studies / Revue canadienne des études africaines*, 26(3), pp. 462–84. Available at: https://doi.org/10.1080/00083968.1992.10804299.

Rolland, N. (2020) *China's Vision for a New World Order: Implications for the United States.* 83. Washington, DC: National Bureau of Asian Research.

Available at: https://www.nbr.org/publication/chinas-vision-for-a-new-world-order-implications-for-the-united-states/ (Accessed: 1 September 2022).

Rosemont, H. and Ames, R.T. (2016) *Confucian Role Ethics: A Moral Vision for the 21st Century?* Göttingen, Germany; Taipei, Taiwan: V&R Unipress; National Taiwan University Press.

Rosenstein-Rodan, P.N. (1943) 'Problems of Industrialisation of Eastern and South-Eastern Europe', *The Economic Journal*, 53(210–11), pp. 202–11. Available at: https://doi.org/10.2307/2226317.

Rossi, A. (2017) *O aeroporto fantasma feito pela Odebrecht em Moçambique, que o BNDES financiou e tomou calote*, BBC News Brasil. Available at: https://www.bbc.com/portuguese/brasil-42074053 (Accessed: 28 August 2022).

Rottenburg, R. (2009) *Far-Fetched Facts: A Parable of Development Aid.* Cambridge, Mass: The MIT Press.

Rounds, Z. and Huang, H. (2017) *We Are Not So Different: A Comparative Study of Employment Relations at Chinese and American Firms in Kenya.* Working Paper 2017/10. China Africa Research Initiative (CARI), Johns Hopkins University, Washington, DC. Available at: https://www.econstor.eu/handle/10419/248138 (Accessed: 23 August 2022).

Routledge, P., Nativel, C. and Cumbers, A. (2006) 'Entangled Logics and Grassroots Imaginaries of Global Justice Networks', *Environmental Politics*, 15(5), pp. 839–59. Available at: https://doi.org/10.1080/09644010600937272.

Rowden, R. (2011) 'India's Role in the New Global Farmland Grab—An Examination of the Role of the Indian Government and Indian Companies Engaged in Overseas Agricultural Land Acquisitions in Developing Countries'. Available at: https://www.macroscan.org/anl/aug11/pdf/Rick_Rowden.pdf (Accessed: 22 February 2022).

Roy, A. and Crane, E.S. (eds) (2015) *Territories of Poverty: Rethinking North and South.* Athens, Georgia: University of Georgia Press.

Rubbers, B. (2020) 'Governing New Mining Projects in D.R. Congo. A View from the HR Department of a Chinese Company', *The Extractive Industries and Society*, 7(1), pp. 191–8. Available at: https://doi.org/10.1016/j.exis.2019.12.006.

Rubbers, B. (ed.) (2021) *Inside Mining Capitalism: The Micropolitics of Work on the Congolese and Zambian Copperbelts.* Woodbridge: James Currey.

Ryan, H.E. (2019) 'Protests in the Gambia Highlight Tensions over Chinese Investment in Africa', *The Conversation*. Available at: http://

theconversation.com/protests-in-the-gambia-highlight-tensions-over-chinese-investment-in-africa-119221 (Accessed: 8 September 2022).

SAIS-CARI (2022) 'Data: Chinese Investment in Africa', *China Africa Research Initiative*. Available at: http://www.sais-cari.org/chinese-investment-in-africa (Accessed: 30 May 2022).

Sambo, M.G. (2020) 'Investimento directo estrangeiro e o desenvolvimento socioeconomico em Moçambique', in S. Forquilha (ed.) *Desafios para Moçambique 2020*. Maputo: Instituto de Estudos Sociais e Económicos, pp. 281–309.

Sampaio, A.A. (2019) *Closed, Unapproachable and Opaque—How the New Development Bank Drafted its Access to Information Policy*, Medium-International Accountability Project. Available at: https://accountability.medium.com/closed-unapproachable-and-opaque-how-the-new-development-bank-drafted-its-access-to-1561343a20bd (Accessed: 20 August 2022).

Sandbrook, R. (1972) 'Patrons, Clients, and Unions: The Labour Movement and Political Conflict in Kenya', *Journal of Commonwealth Political Studies*, 10(1), pp. 3–27. Available at: https://doi.org/10.1080/14662047708447155.

Sändig, J. (2021) 'Contesting Large-Scale Land Acquisitions in the Global South', *World Development*, 146, 105581. Available at: https://doi.org/10.1016/j.worlddev.2021.105581.

Sändig, J., Bernstorff, J. von and Hasenclever, A. (2020) *Affectedness and Participation in International Institutions*. Abingdon: Routledge.

SASAC (2011) *Guidelines to the State-Owned Enterprises Directly under the Central Government*. Available at: http://en.sasac.gov.cn/2011/12/06/c_313.htm (Accessed: 5 June 2020).

Sassen, S. (2006) *Territory, Authority, Rights: From Medieval to Global Assemblages*. Princeton, Oxford: Princeton University Press.

Saxena, P. (2016) 'Lines of Credit: Policy Matrix Revisited', *International Studies*, 53(1), pp. 44–58. Available at: https://doi.org/10.1177/0020881717708081.

Schatzki, T.R., Knorr-Cetina, K. and Savigny, E. von (eds) (2001) *The Practice Turn in Contemporary Theory*. New York; London: Routledge.

Schlesinger, S. (2014) *Brazilian Cooperation and Investment in Africa*, 31. Available at: https://www.oxfam.org.hk/en/what-we-do-category/advocacy-and-campaign/china-and-the-developing-world/publications/brazilian-cooperation-and-investments-in-africa (Accessed: 27 August 2022).

Schlichte, K. (2005) *Der Staat in der Weltgesellschaft: Politische Herrschaft in Asien, Afrika und Lateinamerika*. Frankfurt am Main: Campus Verlag.

Schmitz, C.M. (2020) 'Doing Time, Making Money at a Chinese State Firm

REFERENCES

in Angola', *Made in China Journal*, 5(3), pp. 52–7. Available at: https://doi.org/10.22459/MIC.05.03.2020.06.

Schramm, A. (2020) *Legal Mobilization in Large-Scale Land Deals: Evidence from Sierra Leone and the Philippines*. Baden-Baden: Nomos.

Schramm, A. and Sändig, J. (2018) 'Affectedness Alliances: Affected People at the Centre of Transnational Advocacy', *Third World Thematics: A TWQ Journal*, 3(5–6), pp. 664–83. Available at: https://doi.org/10.1080/23802014.2018.1575767.

Schubert, J., Engel, U. and Macamo, E. (2018) *Extractive Industries and Changing State Dynamics in Africa*. London; New York: Routledge.

Scoones, I. et al. (2016) 'A New Politics of Development Cooperation? Chinese and Brazilian Engagements in African Agriculture', *World Development*, 81, pp. 1–12. Available at: https://doi.org/10.1016/j.worlddev.2015.11.020.

Scoones, I., Cabral, L. and Tugendhat, H. (2013) 'New Development Encounters: China and Brazil in African Agriculture', *IDS Bulletin*, 44(4), pp. 1–19. Available at: https://doi.org/10.1111/1759-5436.12038.

Seibert, G. (2019a) 'Brazil–Africa Relations from the Sixteenth to Twentieth Century', in G. Seibert and P.F. Visentini (eds) *Brazil–Africa Relations*. Woodbridge, Suffolk; Rochester, NY: James Currey, pp. 11–46.

Seibert, G. (2019b) 'Brazil's Development and Financial Cooperation with African Countries', in G. Seibert and P.F. Visentini (eds) *Brazil–Africa Relations*, pp. 99–130.

Seibert, G. and Visentini, P.F. (eds) (2019) *Brazil–Africa Relations: Historical Dimensions and Contemporary Engagements, from the 1960s to the Present*. Woodbridge, Suffolk; Rochester, NY: James Currey.

Sena, K. (2012) 'Lamu Port—South Sudan–Ethiopia Transport Corridor (LAPSSET) and Indigenous People in Kenya'. International Work Group for Indigenous Affairs. Available at: https://doi.org/10.1163/2210-7975_HRD-1031-0185.

Sending, O. (2015) *The Politics of Expertise: Competing for Authority in Global Governance*. Ann Arbor, MI: University of Michigan Press.

Sergot, B. and Saives, A.-L. (2016) 'Unplugged—Relating Place to Organization: A Situated Tribute to Doreen Massey', *M@n@gement*, 19(4), pp. 335–52. Available at: https://doi.org/10.3917/mana.194.0335.

Sha, K. and Jiang, Z. (2003) 'Improving Rural Labourers' Status in China's Construction Industry', *Building Research & Information*, 31(6), pp. 464–73. Available at: https://doi.org/10.1080/0961321032000166406.

Shani, G. (2015) *Religion, Identity and Human Security*. London: Routledge.

REFERENCES

Shankar, S. (2021) *An Uneasy Embrace. India, Africa and the Spectre of Race.* London: Hurst Publishers.

Shankland, A. and Gonçalves, E. (2016) 'Imagining Agricultural Development in South-South Cooperation: The Contestation and Transformation of ProSAVANA', *World Development*, 81, pp. 35–46. Available at: https://doi.org/10.1016/j.worlddev.2016.01.002.

Shankland, A., Gonçalves, E. and Favareto, A. (2016) *Social Movements, Agrarian Change and the Contestation of ProSAVANA in Mozambique and Brazil.* 137. Future Agricultures Consortium. Available at: https://opendocs.ids.ac.uk/opendocs/handle/20.500.12413/12687 (Accessed: 27 August 2022).

Shaohua, Z. (2005) *Rural Labour Migration in China: Challenges for Policies.* 10. UNESCO. Available at: https://unesdoc.unesco.org/ark:/48223/pf0000140242 (Accessed: 23 August 2022).

Shaw, T.M. (2010) 'China, India and (South) Africa: What International Relations in the Second Decade of the Twenty-First Century?', in F. Cheru and C. Obi (eds) *The Rise of China and India in Africa: Challenges, Opportunities and Critical Interventions.* London: Zed Books Ltd., pp. 13–20.

Sheehy, T.P. (2022) '10 Things to Know about the U.S.–China Rivalry in Africa', United States Institute of Peace. Available at: https://www.usip.org/publications/2022/12/10-things-know-about-us-china-rivalry-africa (Accessed: 3 May 2023).

Shelton, G. and Paruk, F. (2008) 'The Forum on China–Africa Cooperation: A Strategic Opportunity', *Institute for Security Studies Monographs* [Preprint], (156).

Shieh, S. (2022) 'Civil Society's Multifaceted Response to China's Belt and Road Initiative', *Global China Pulse*, 1(1), pp. 99–109.

Shih, C. et al. (2019) *China and International Theory: The Balance of Relationships.* Abingdon; New York: Routledge.

Shinn, D.H. and Eisenman, J. (2012) *China and Africa: A Century of Engagement.* Philadelphia: University of Pennsylvania Press.

Shipton, L. and Dauvergne, P. (2021) 'The Politics of Transnational Advocacy Against Chinese, Indian, and Brazilian Extractive Projects in the Global South', *The Journal of Environment & Development*, 30(3), pp. 240–64. Available at: https://doi.org/10.1177/10704965211019083.

Sierra, J. and Hochstetler, K. (2017) 'Transnational Activist Networks and Rising Powers: Transparency and Environmental Concerns in the Brazilian National Development Bank', *International Studies Quarterly*, 61(4), pp. 760–73. Available at: https://doi.org/10.1093/isq/sqx069.

REFERENCES

Sikkink, K. (2005) 'Patterns of Dynamic Multilevel Governance and the Insider-Outsider Coalition', in D. Della Porta and S.G. Tarrow (eds) *Transnational Protest and Global Activism*. Lanham: Rowman and Littlefield, pp. 151–74.

Sinha, S. (2021) '"Strong Leaders", Authoritarian Populism and Indian Developmentalism: The Modi Moment in Historical Context', *Geoforum*, 124, pp. 320–33. Available at: https://doi.org/10.1016/j. geoforum.2021.02.019.

Soares de Oliveira, R. (2015) *Magnificent and Beggar Land: Angola since the CivilWar*. London: Hurst Publishers.

Sohn, I. (2011) 'After Renaissance: China's Multilateral Offensive In The DevelopingWorld', *European Journal of International Relations*, 18(1), pp. 77–101. Available at: https://doi.org/10.1177/1354066110392083.

Solinger, D.J. (1999) 'China's Floating Population: Implications for State and Society', in Goldman, M. and MacFarquhar, R. eds., 1999. *The Paradox of China's Post-Mao Reforms*. Cambridge, MA: Harvard University Press.

SOMO (2021) *China's Global Mineral Rush: Learning from Experiences Around Controversial Chinese Mining Investments*. Available at: https://www. somo.nl/wp-content/uploads/2021/06/Chinas-global-mineral-rush. pdf (Accessed: 7 April 2022).

Sondarjee, M. (2020) 'Collective Learning at the Boundaries of Communities of Practice: Inclusive Policymaking at the World Bank', *Global Society*, 35(3), pp. 1–20. Available at: https://doi.org/10.1080 /13600826.2020.1835833.

Sørensen, N.N. (2018) 'Diffusing Gender Equality Norms in the Midst of a Feminicide Pandemic: The Case of AMEXCID and Decentralized Mexican South-South Cooperation', *Progress in Development Studies*, 18(2), pp. 95–109. Available at: https://doi.org/10.1177/ 1464993417750293.

Soulé, F. (2020) '"Africa+1" Summit Diplomacy and the "New Scramble" Narrative: Recentering African Agency', *African Affairs*, 119(477), pp. 633–46. Available at: https://doi.org/10.1093/afraf/adaa015.

Soulé, F. (2022) *Negotiating Local Business Practices With China in Benin*. Carnegie Endowment for International Peace.

Sousa, O.L. de (2011) *Representação e participação política em Moçambique a crise da representação política nas assembleias representativas: o caso da Assembleia Municipal de Xai-Xai*. Universidade Eduardo Mondlane. Available at: http://monografias.uem.mz/jspui/handle/123456789/122 (Accessed: 27 August 2022).

Soy, A. (2023) 'Why Russia's Invasion of Ukraine Still Divides Africa', *BBC*

REFERENCES

News, 25 February. Available at: https://www.bbc.com/news/world-africa-64759845 (Accessed: 3 May 2023).

Steinhardt, H.C. and Wu, F. (2016) 'In the Name of the Public: Environmental Protest and the Changing Landscape of Popular Contention in China', *The China Journal*, 75, pp. 61–82. Available at: https://doi.org/10.1086/684010.

Stiglitz, J. (2003) 'Challenging the Washington Consensus', *The Brown Journal of World Affairs*, 9(2), pp. 33–40.

Stolte, C. (2015a) *Brazil's Africa Strategy: Role Conception and the Drive for International Status*. New York: Palgrave Macmillan.

Stremlau, J.J. (2023) 'US–China Tensions: How Africa Can Avoid Being Caught in a New Cold War', *The Conversation*. Available at: http://theconversation.com/us-china-tensions-how-africa-can-avoid-being-caught-in-a-new-cold-war-201679 (Accessed: 3 May 2023).

Stuenkel, O. (2017) *Post-Western World: How Emerging Powers Are Remaking Global Order*. Cambridge; Malden, Massachusetts: Polity Press.

Stuenkel, O. (2020) *The BRICS and the Future of Global Order*. Lanham: Rowman & Littlefield.

Sum, N.-L. (2019) 'The Intertwined Geopolitics and Geoeconomics of Hopes/Gears: China's Triple Economic Bubbles and the "One Belt One Road" Imaginary', *Territory, Politics, Governance*, 7(4), pp. 528–52. Available at: https://doi.org/10.1080/21622671.2018.1523746.

Sumich, J. (2010) 'The Party and the State: Frelimo and Social Stratification in Post-socialist Mozambique: The Party and the State in Post-socialist Mozambique', *Development and Change*, 41(4), pp. 679–98. Available at: https://doi.org/10.1111/j.1467-7660.2010.01653.x.

Summers, G.F. (1986) 'Rural Community Development', *Annual Review of Sociology*, 12(1), pp. 347–71. Available at: https://doi.org/10.1146/annurev.so.12.080186.002023.

Sun, Y. (1924) 'Sanminzhuyi, Minquanzhuyi, Di er jiang (Three Principles of the People, the Rights of the People, Second Lecture)'. The Museum of Dr. Sun Yat-sen. Available at: http://www.sunyat-sen.org/index.php?m=content&c=index&a=show&catid=46&id=6631.

Swider, S. (2011) 'Permanent Temporariness in the Chinese Construction Industry', in S. Kuruvilla, C.K. Lee, and M.E. Gallagher (eds) *From Iron Rice Bowl to Informalization*. Ithaca, NY: Cornell University Press, pp. 138–54.

Swider, S. (2015) 'Building China: Precarious Employment among Migrant Construction Workers', *Work, Employment and Society*, 29(1), pp. 41–59. Available at: https://doi.org/10.1177/0950017014526631.

REFERENCES

Tang, X. (2020) *Coevolutionary Pragmatism: Approaches and Impacts.* Cambridge: Cambridge University Press.

Tan-Mullins, M. (2014) 'Successes and Failures of Corporate Social Responsibility Mechanisms in Chinese Extractive Industries', *Journal of Current Chinese Affairs*, 43(4), pp. 19–39. Available at: https://doi.org/10.1177/186810261404300402.

Tan-Mullins, M., Mohan, G. and Power, M. (2010) 'Redefining "Aid" in the China–Africa Context', *Development and Change*, 41(5), pp. 857–81. Available at: https://doi.org/10.1111/j.1467-7660.2010.01662.x.

Tarrow, S.G. (2005) *The New Transnational Activism.* Cambridge: Cambridge University Press.

Taylor, I. (2014) *Africa Rising? BRICS—Diversifying Dependency.* Oxford: James Currey.

Taylor, I. (2016) 'India's Economic Diplomacy in Africa', in A.K. Dubey and A. Biswas (eds) *India and Africa's Partnership: A Vision for a New Future.* New Delhi: Springer India, pp. 99–113.

Taylor, I., van der Merwe, J. and Dodd, N. (2016) 'Nehru's Neoliberals: Draining or Aiding Africa?', in J. van der Merwe, I. Taylor, and A. Arkhangelskaya (eds) *Emerging Powers in Africa: A New Wave in the Relationship?* Cham: Springer International Publishing, pp. 107–28.

Taylor, I. and Xiao, Y. (2009) 'A Case of Mistaken Identity: "China Inc." and Its "Imperialism" in Sub-Saharan Africa', *Asian Politics & Policy*, 1(4), pp. 709–25. Available at: https://doi.org/10.1111/j.1943-0787.2009.01149.x.

Taylor, M. and Rioux, S. (2018) *Global Labour Studies.* Malden, MA: Polity.

Tickner, Arlene B., and Karen Smith, eds. 2020. *International Relations from the Global South: Worlds of Difference.* Abingdon and New York: Routledge.

Thakur, R. (2014) 'How Representative are BRICS?', *Third World Quarterly*, 35(10), pp. 1791–808. Available at: https://doi.org/10.1080/01436597.2014.971594.

The Carter Center (2017) *A State Affair: Privatizing Congo's Copper Sector.* Atlanta. Available at: https://www.cartercenter.org/resources/pdfs/news/peace_publications/democracy/congo-report-carter-center-nov-2017.pdf.

The Economic Times (2018) 'Several Indian Companies Debarred by World Bank in 2018', *Economic Times*, 4 October. Available at: https://economictimes.indiatimes.com/news/company/corporate-trends/several-indian-companies-debarred-by-world-bank-in-2018/articleshow/66067061.cms (Accessed: 28 August 2022).

The Economist (2011) 'Africa Rising', *The Economist*, 3 December. Available at: https://www.economist.com/leaders/2011/12/03/africa-rising (Accessed: 22 February 2022).

Thompson, P. (1990) 'Crawling from the Wreckage: The Labour Process and the Politics of Production', in D. Knights and H. Willmott (eds) *Labour Process Theory*. London: Palgrave Macmillan, pp. 95–124.

Topsøe-Jensen, B. (2015) *Mapping Study of Civil Society Organizations in Mozambique*. ALTAIR Asesores and Agriconsulting. S.L. Available at: https://eeas.europa.eu/archives/delegations/mozambique/documents/news/mappingsco/20151020_mappingstudy_onlineversion.pdf.

Tsai, W.-H. and Dean, N. (2014) 'Experimentation under Hierarchy in Local Conditions: Cases of Political Reform in Guangdong and Sichuan, China', *The China Quarterly*, 218, pp. 339–58. Available at: https://doi.org/10.1017/S0305741014000630.

Tsai, W.-H. and Tian, G. (2021) 'The Role of China's County-level Research Offices in Policy Adaptation', *Journal of Chinese Political Science* [Preprint]. Available at: https://doi.org/10.1007/s11366-021-09770-3.

Tsing, A.L. (2004) *Friction: An Ethnography of Global Connection*. Princeton: Princeton University Press.

UN General Assembly (2018) 'United Nations Declaration on the Rights of Peasants and Other People Working in Rural Areas'. United Nations General Assembly. Available at: https://www.fao.org/family-farming/detail/en/c/1197482/.

UNDP China (2019) *Report on the Sustainable Development of Chinese Private-Owned Enterprises along the Belt and Road*. United Nations Development Programme. Available at: https://www.undp.org/china/publications/report-sustainable-development-chinese-private-owned-enterprises-along-belt-and-road (Accessed: 26 September 2022).

UNHCR (2012) 'Mandate of the Special Rapporteur on the rights of indigenous peoples—Office of the United Nations High Commissioner for Human Rights'. Available at: https://doi.org/10.1163/9789004502758_044.

United Nations Development Programme China (2017) *Communicating Development Cooperation to Domestic Audiences—Approaches and Implications for South-South Cooperation Providers*. Beijing: United Nations Development Programme China. Available at: https://www.undp.org/china/publications/communicating-development-cooperation-domestic-audiences (Accessed: 20 August 2022).

Vaes, S. and Huyse, H. (2013) 'New Voices on South-South Cooperation between Emerging Powers and Africa. African Civil Society Perspectives'. HIVA-KU Leuven. Available at: https://lirias.kuleuven.be/1899363&lang=en.

REFERENCES

Vaid, K.N. (1999) 'Contract labour in the construction industry in India', in D.P.A. Naidu (ed.) *Contract labour in South Asia Asia-Pacific*. Geneva: International Labour Organisation, pp. 4–65.

Vale (no date) *Vale Announces the Sale of Its Coal Assets*. Available at: http://www.vale.com/EN/aboutvale/news/Pages/vale-announces-the-sale-of-its-coal-assets.aspx (Accessed: 27 August 2022).

van der Loop, T. (1992) 'Industrial Dynamics and Fragmented Labour Markets: Construction Firms and Labourers in India', *Netherlands Geographical Studies* [Preprint], (139).

van der Westhuizen, J. and Milani, C.R.S. (2019) 'Development Cooperation, the International–Domestic Nexus and the Graduation Dilemma: Comparing South Africa and Brazil', *Cambridge Review of International Affairs*, 32(1), pp. 22–42. Available at: https://doi.org/10.1080/09557571.2018.1554622.

van Noort, C. (2019) 'The Construction of Power in the Strategic Narratives of the BRICS', *Global Society*, 33(4), pp. 462–78. Available at: https://doi.org/10.1080/13600826.2019.1581733.

Viana, N. (2016) 'A equação brasileira', *Agência Pública*. Available at: https://apublica.org/2016/02/a-equacao-brasileira/ (Accessed: 28 August 2022).

Viana, N. and Capai, E. (2016) 'Em Angola, a Odebrecht no espelho', *Agência Pública*. Available at: https://apublica.org/2016/02/em-angola-a-odebrecht-no-espelho/ (Accessed: 28 August 2022).

Visser, R. and Cezne, E. (2023) 'Racializing China–Africa Relations: A Test to the Sino-African Friendship', *Journal of Asian and African Studies*, 002190962311680. Available at: https://doi.org/10.1177/00219096231168062.

Viswanathan, H.H.S.V. and A.M. and H.H.S. and Mishra, A. (2019) 'The Ten Guiding Principles for India-Africa Engagement: Finding Coherence in India's Africa Policy', *ORF Occasional Paper*. Available at: https://www.orfonline.org/research/the-ten-guiding-principles-for-india-africa-engagement-finding-coherence-in-indias-africa-policy/ (Accessed: 29 August 2022).

Vogel, C.N. (2022) *Conflict Minerals, Inc.: War, Profit and White Saviourism in Eastern Congo*. London: Hurst Publishers.

wa Thiong'o, N. (2012) *Globalectics: Theory and the Politics of Knowing*. New York: Columbia University Press.

Wahlström, M. and Peterson, A. (2006) 'Between the State and the Market: Expanding the Concept of "Political Opportunity Structure"',

Acta Sociologica, 49(4), pp. 363–77. Available at: https://doi. org/10.1177/0001699306071677.

Wai, Z. (2020) 'Resurrecting Mudimbe', *International Politics Reviews*, 8(1). Available at: https://doi.org/10.1057/s41312-020-00075-w.

Waisbich, L.T. (2021a) 'Negotiating Foreign Policy from Below: Voice, Participation and Protest', in F. Anciano and J. Wheeler (eds) *Political Values and Narratives of Resistance*. London: Routledge.

Waisbich, L.T. (2021b) 'Participation, Critical Support and Disagreement: Brazil–Africa Relations from the Prism of Civil Society', in M. Alencastro and P. Seabra (eds) *Brazil–Africa Relations in the 21st Century: From Surge to Downturn and Beyond*. Cham: Springer International Publishing, pp. 113–32.

Waisbich, L.T. (2021c) *Re-Politicising South-South Development Cooperation: Negotiating Accountability at Home and Abroad*. PhD Dissertation. University of Cambridge.

Waisbich, L.T. (2022) '"The Bank We Want": Chinese and Brazilian Activism around and within the BRICS New Development Bank (NBD)', in P. Amar et al. (eds) *The Tropical Silk Road: The Future of China in South America*. Stanford, California: Stanford University Press, pp. 190–203.

Waisbich, L.T., Pomeroy, M. and Leite, I.C. (2021) 'Travelling Across Developing Countries: Unpacking The Role of South-South Cooperation and Civil Society in Policy Transfer', in O. Porto de Oliveira (ed.) *Handbook of Policy Transfer, Diffusion and Circulation*. Cheltenham; Northampton, Massachusetts: Edward Elgar Publishing, pp. 214–36.

Waisbich, L.T., Silva, D.M. and Suyama, B. (2017) 'Monitoring and Measuring of South-South Cooperation Flows In Brazil'. Articulação SUL. Available at: https://articulacaosul.org/wp-content/uploads/2017/04/Briefing-1.pdf (Accessed: 22 February 2022).

Waites, M. (2019) 'Decolonizing the Boomerang Effect in Global Queer Politics: A New Critical Framework for Sociological Analysis of Human Rights Contestation', *International Sociology*, 34(4), pp. 382–401. Available at: https://doi.org/10.1177/0268580919851425.

Wakenge, C.I. (2018) *Mining Minerals or Mining The State? The Practical Norms Governing Mineral Extraction in Former Katanga, Democratic Republic of Congo*. London: Secure Livelihoods Research Consortium, Overseas Development Institute (ODI).

Wang, G. (1968) 'Early Ming Relations with Southeast Asia: A Background Essay', in J.K. Fairbank (ed.) *The Chinese World Order*. Cambridge, Massachusetts: Harvard University Press, pp. 34–62.

REFERENCES

Wang, G. (2013) *The Chinese State and the New Global History*. Hong Kong: The Chinese University Press.

Wang, G. (2014) *Another China Cycle: Committing to Reform*. Hackensack, NJ: World Scientific.

Wang, H. and Hu, X. (2017) 'China's "Going-Out" Strategy and Corporate Social Responsibility: Preliminary Evidence of a "Boomerang Effect"', *Journal of Contemporary China*, 26(108), pp. 820–33. Available at: https://doi.org/10.1080/10670564.2017.1337301.

Wang, Y. and Wissenbach, U. (2019) 'Clientelism at Work? A Case Study of Kenyan Standard Gauge Railway project', *Economic History of Developing Regions*, 34(3), pp. 280–99. Available at: https://doi.org/10.1080/20780389.2019.1678026.

Wegenast, T. et al. (2019) 'At Africa's Expense? Disaggregating the Employment Effects of Chinese Mining Operations in sub-Saharan Africa', *World Development*, 118, pp. 39–51. Available at: https://doi.org/10.1016/j.worlddev.2019.02.007.

Wells, J. (2009) 'Labour Mobilisation in the Construction Industry', *CIB Construction in Developing Countries International Symposium 'Construction in Developing Economies: New Issues and Challenges'*, Santiago, Chile, pp. 1–9. Available at: https://www.irbnet.de/daten/iconda/CIB1941.pdf.

Wells, J. and Jason, A. (2010) 'Employment Relationships and Organizing Strategies in the Informal Construction Sector', *African Studies Quarterly*, 11(2–3), pp. 107–24. Available at: http://erepository.uonbi.ac.ke/handle/11295/162098.

Weng, L. et al. (2013) 'Mineral Industries, Growth Corridors and Agricultural Development in Africa', *Global Food Security*, 2(3), pp. 195–202. Available at: https://doi.org/10.1016/j.gfs.2013.07.003.

Wethal, U. (2017) 'Workplace Regimes in Sino-Mozambican Construction Projects: Resentment and Tension in a Divided Workplace', *Journal of Contemporary African Studies*, 35(3), pp. 383–403. Available at: https://doi.org/10.1080/02589001.2017.1323379.

Whitfield, L. (2018) *Economies after Colonialism: Ghana and the Struggle for Power*. Cambridge: Cambridge University Press.

Whittaker, H. (2012) 'Forced Villagization during the Shifta Conflict in Kenya, ca. 1963–1968', *The International Journal of African Historical Studies*, 45(3), pp. 343–64. Available at: https://www.jstor.org/stable/24393053.

Wilhelm, C. and Maconachie, R. (2021) 'Exploring Local Content in Guinea's Bauxite Sector: Obstacles, Opportunities and Future trajectories', *Resources Policy*, 71, 101935. Available at: https://doi. org/10.1016/j.resourpol.2020.101935.

Wise, T.A. (2019) 'Sementes da Resistência, Colheitas de Esperança:Camponeses impedem uma usurpação de terra em Moçambique', *Ja4Change*. Available at: https://justica-ambiental. org/2019/07/18/sementes-da-resistencia-colheitas-de-esperanca camponeses-impedem-uma-usurpacao-de-terra-em-mocambique/ (Accessed: 27 August 2022).

Wissenbach, U. and Wang,Y. (2017) *African Politics Meets Chinese Engineers: The Chinese-Built Standard Gauge Railway Project in Kenya and East Africa.* No 2017/13. China Africa Research Initiative (CARI), Johns Hopkins University, Washington, DC. Available at: http://hdl.handle. net/10419/248141.

Wolford, W. and Nehring, R. (2015) 'Constructing Parallels: Brazilian Expertise and the Commodification of Land, Labour and Money in Mozambique', *Canadian Journal of Development Studies / Revue canadienne d'études du développement*, 36(2), pp. 208–23. Available at: https://doi. org/10.1080/02255189.2015.1036010.

Wu, D. (2021) *Affective Encounters: Everyday Life among Chinese Migrants in Zambia.* New York: Routledge.

Xinhua (2015) 'East Africa: Chinese-Built Lamu Port on Course to Transform Kenya, E. Africa', *Forum on China–Africa Cooperation.* Available at: https://allafrica.com/stories/201507151694.html (Accessed: 15 August 2022).

Xu,Y.XC. (2014) 'Chinese State-Owned Enterprises in Africa: Ambassadors or Freebooters?' *Journal of Contemporary China,* 23(89), pp. 822–40. https://doi.org/10.1080/10670564.2014.882542.

Yalom, I.D. (1980) *Existential Psychotherapy.* New York: Basic Books.

Yan,Y. (1996) *The Flow of Gifts: Reciprocity and Social Networks in a Chinese Village.* Stanford, CA: Stanford University Press.

Yang,Y. (2019) '拉穆港口的筑梦人 Lamu gangkou de zhu meng ren [Lamu port's dream builders]', *Central Radio and Television Station International.* Available at: http://news.cri.cn/20190327/6a5914bf-32aa-d6c3-dc98-e0d0ffc5efff.html (Accessed: 23 August 2022).

Yankson, P.W.K. et al. (2018) 'The Livelihood Challenges of Resettled Communities of the Bui Dam Project in Ghana and the Role of Chinese Dam-Builders', *Development Policy Review*, 36, pp. O476–O494. Available at: https://doi.org/10.1111/dpr.12259.

Yeophantong, P. (2020) 'China and the Accountability Politics of Hydropower Development: How Effective are Transnational Advocacy

REFERENCES

Networks in the Mekong Region?', *Contemporary Southeast Asia*, 42(1), pp. 85–117. Available at: https://doi.org/10.1355/cs42-1d.

Yutong, Y. (2018) *China–Africa Ties: 'Five Nos' and Eight Initiatives for the New Era*, *CGTN*. Available at: https://news.cgtn.com/news/3d3d67 4d344d444d7a457a6333566d54/share_p.html (Accessed: 29 August 2022).

Zarakol, A. (2019) '"Rise of the Rest": As Hype and Reality', *International Relations*, 33(2). Available at: https://doi.org/10.1177/ 0047117819840793.

Zhang, C. (2019) '"Aid + Investment": The Sustainable Development Approach of China's Agricultural Aid Project in Mozambique', in M. Huang, X. Xu, and X. Mao (eds) *South-South Cooperation and Chinese Foreign Aid*. Singapore: Springer Singapore, pp. 211–31.

Zhang, C. et al. (2019) 'Role Tension and Adaptation in a Chinese Agricultural Aid Project in Mozambique', *Journal of International Development*, 31(3), pp. 231–46. Available at: https://doi.org/10.1002/jid.3402.

Zhang, F. (2013) 'The Rise of Chinese Exceptionalism in International Relations', *European Journal of International Relations*, 19(2), pp. 305–28. Available at: https://doi.org/10.1177/1354066111421038.

Zhao, Q. (2020) 'How to Establish Labor Protection Standards for Kenyan Local Workers in Chinese Multinational Corporations', *Washington International Law Journal*, 29(2), pp. 455–83. Available at: https:// digitalcommons.law.uw.edu/wilj/vol29/iss2/8.

Zhao, S. (2014) 'A Neo-Colonialist Predator or Development Partner? China's engagement and rebalance in Africa', *Journal of Contemporary China*, 23(90), pp. 1033–52. Available at: https://doi.org/10.1080/1 0670564.2014.898893.

Zhu, K., Mwangi, B., & Hu, L. (2023). Socio-economic Impact of China's infrastructure-led growth model in Africa: A case study of the Kenyan Standard Gauge Railway. *Journal of International Development*, 35(4), 614–638. https://doi.org/10.1002/jid.3684

Zou, L. (2014) *China's Rise: Development-Oriented Finance and Sustainable Development*. Singapore: World Scientific Publishing Co. Pte Ltd.

INDEX

Note: Page numbers followed by '*n*' refer to notes, '*t*' refer to tables, '*f*' refer to figures.